# EXPLORING
# MICROSOFT WORKS
# FOR THE
# MACINTOSH

# EXPLORING
# MICROSOFT WORKS
# FOR THE
# MACINTOSH

VERSION 2.0

## Ray Nanney / Hayden Porter / Ken Abernethy

Furman University

**JOHN WILEY & SONS, INC**
New York   Chichester   Brisbane   Toronto   Singapore

# ACKNOWLEDGEMENTS

The authors have had support from a number of persons and organizations in the course of preparing this manuscript. While it is not possible to mention all of them in the short space provided here, we will mention some without whose help we could not have been successful. We express our appreciation to our editor, Joe Dougherty, for his assistance, encouragement, and help on meeting a tight time schedule. To the staff at Wiley, including Deborah Herbert, Madelyn Lesure, Genevieve Scandone, and Joe Ford, we express our gratitude for a job well done in designing the book, the cover, and the high quality copyediting, as well as working closely with us during our laying out of the book.

We also wish to express our appreciation to the administration of Furman University, in particular, President John E. Johns and Vice President for Academic Affairs and Dean, John Crabtree, Jr., who have provided generous support for this project by providing funds to remodel a Macintosh laboratory, properly equip it, as well as provide staff support and underwrite our duplication expenses. Grant support from Apple Computer, Inc. and the National Science Foundation also helped to initially equip our laboratory and is gratefully acknowledged.

Our special thanks go to David Hutchens for carefully reading and for providing many helpful comments while he class tested the manuscript. In addition, we thank students Mitch Byers, Tiffany Earle, Bruce Johnson, Sharon Kay, Marsha Lightsey, and Norman Tillotson for carefully working through each lesson in the final draft of the manuscript and providing helpful feedback on the book materials. Our devoted departmental secretary, Rhonda Childress, also receives our special thanks for all her efforts in support of the project.

Finally, we greatfully acknowledge the support of our families, especially our wives, Lib, Pat and Sherry, who spent many hours without husbands and who often willingly proofread the many revisions of each chapter.

# PREFACE

This book is a self-contained introduction to the use of Microsoft Works and the Macintosh. It is organized in the form of tutorials that teach you how to use the Macintosh desktop, and the four integrated software tools provided by Microsoft Works — word processing, database, spreadsheet, and communications. In addition to the tutorials, background sections are provided to help you gain an overview of the concepts you are learning so that you will be better able to apply Microsoft Works creatively and confidently to assist you in your own work.

The book is designed to let you become competent with, rather than merely exposed to, the use of this powerful productivity enhancing computer environment. Conseqently, you will quickly be able to use your Macintosh and Microsoft Works in a wide variety of helpful ways. The approach taken in the text is more in depth than that found in many books of this kind. Once gained such competence will allow you to control the computer to carry out efficiently and easily the things you wish the computer to do for you. Because of the user friendly nature of the Macintosh and the consistent interface presented by each of the Microsoft Works modules, you will find that this greater depth of understanding is relatively easy to attain.

The tutorials in the text are very practically oriented. For example, you will learn to create a resume, a database of your record collections, and how to analyze home mortgages and produce charts of the results. As a special component of the text, we have an developed an integrated project that illustrates how you can combine modules in Microsoft Works to create a database of names for a health study, to design and send a form letter to the participants in the study, to store the survey results in a second database, and to analyze and graph the results of the study using a spreadsheet.

For instructors, we provide a disk containing solutions of all the lesson activities and projects presented in the book. Also, a test bank, and set of transparency masters are available.

It is our hope that our book will guide you to becoming a competent and creative user of Microsoft Works on the Macintosh so that you can join the group of individuals who use computers productively.

Ray Nanney
Hayden Porter
Ken Abernethy

# CONTENTS

## CHAPTER 2.  INTRODUCING WORKS

## CHAPTER 3.  USING WORKS WP

# CONTENTS

# CHAPTER 6.  A PROJECT INTEGRATING THE WORKS MODULES

# CHAPTER 7.  USING WORKS CM

# CONTENTS

# 1

# USING THE MACINTOSH DESKTOP

When you have completed the Macintosh desktop tutorial you will be able to:

- ❏ Turn on your computer and boot your system.
- ❏ Shut down your computer.
- ❏ Use the mouse.
- ❏ Explore the Macintosh desktop interface.
- ❏ Initialize a floppy disk.
- ❏ Open and close disks and folders.
- ❏ Arrange items on your desktop.
- ❏ Copy files and disks.
- ❏ Rename files and disks.
- ❏ Delete files and erase disks.
- ❏ Create and manage folders.
- ❏ Locate a folder or a file on a disk.
- ❏ Navigate through the file system from the desktop.
- ❏ Print a disk directory.
- ❏ Access network resources.

## TUTORIAL OUTLINE

1

# CHAPTER 1. USING THE MACINTOSH DESKTOP

# TUTORIAL INTRODUCTION

In this first tutorial you will begin using a Macintosh computer and will learn about its operating system. The operating system is composed of special-purpose programs. Unlike application software programs, such as Works, whose purpose is to help you create documents, draw charts, and the like, the purpose of the operating system programs is to allow you to interact with the computer and to manage the resources of your computing environment. As you work your way through these lessons, you will learn about the wide variety of resources that are available to you in the Macintosh computing environment. On the Macintosh, the interaction between the human and the computer is visually oriented and is highly intuitive. Before you are ready to start using your computer, there are several concepts and terms that you will need to understand. The purpose of the first section of this tutorial is to provide a basic understanding of these concepts and terms.

## OVERVIEW OF THE MACINTOSH INTERFACE

The Macintosh human-computer interface is a visually oriented interface that is based on the model of information organization in a noncomputerized office. The starting point for this organization is the **Macintosh desktop**. The desktop is the display screen with which you work when you are interacting with the Macintosh. On this electronic analog of a real desktop you will open **disks** (which you might think of as filing cabinet drawers), into which can be placed numbers of electronic **files** and **folders** that contain various information.

A great variety of entities exist as files, including such things as word processing documents, charts, and pictures. Folders are used to organize your files into related groups—just as you would do with a filing cabinet in a noncomputerized office. Folders can contain files and other folders. Any item that can appear on the desktop, such as a file, folder, or disk, is called an object. To view the contents of an object, you open a window to that object. You can have many windows open on your desktop at one time, but only one window can be active. Only the objects in the active window can be manipulated. There is also a Trash Can object on the desktop which is for the disposing of unwanted files and/or folders.

Disks, files, folders, and the trash can are all represented on the electronic desktop by **icons**, or symbolic pictures, whose shapes suggest to us the kinds of objects they represent. The manipulation of files, folders, and the windows associated with them is accomplished primarily through the use of a **mouse** (see Figure 1.1). As the mouse moves, the **mouse pointer** is moved on the computer desktop screen. You may position this pointer to "touch" objects or areas of the screen—that is, to point them out to the computer.

Actions on the objects touched by the pointer are accomplished through a **click button** on top of the mouse. By manipulating this button you can open and close windows, resize and reposition windows, move files to the trash can or into different folders, and do many other useful tasks that help you to manage your desktop resources.

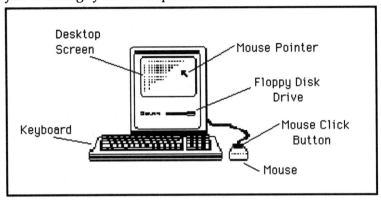

**Figure 1.1.** A Macintosh Computer.

**Some Example Desktops.** Figure 1.2 shows a Macintosh desktop with two disk icons present, a disk named *Hard Disk* and a disk named *Letters*; also shown is the *Trash* icon. Note carefully the shape of each of the icons. In the upper left part of the desktop you see the mouse pointer (just under the name **File**). The five items (of which **File** is one) in the row across the top of the desktop are the names of menus. Inside these menus are lists of commands that you may issue to be carried out by the computer.

Opening an object is accomplished by moving the mouse pointer over the object's icon and then clicking the mouse twice in rapid succession (called "double clicking"). Alternatively, the object may be highlighted by moving the mouse pointer over it and clicking and then opened by selecting *Open* from the **File** menu. In Figure 1.3, the desktop of Figure 1.2 is shown after a window has been opened for the *Hard Disk* icon. Note that the *Hard Disk* contains various folders, which are displayed in its window. Again, observe that the shape of the folder icon reminds you of the *kind* of object it represents. We expect each of the folders displayed in this window to contain additional files and/or other folders.

If the *Works* folder (shown in Figure 1.3) is opened, the desktop shown in Figure 1.4 appears. Notice that on this desktop two windows appear: one showing the contents of *Hard Disk* and the other showing the contents of the folder *Works*. Because we most recently opened the *Works* folder, its window is the active window. When a window is active, the objects inside it may be manipulated. The active window always has the horizontal bars along its top border. Note the icons appearing in the *Works* folder.

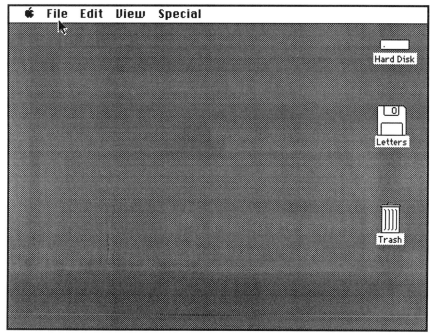

**Figure 1.2.** Macintosh Desktop with Two Disk Icons and the *Trash* Icon.

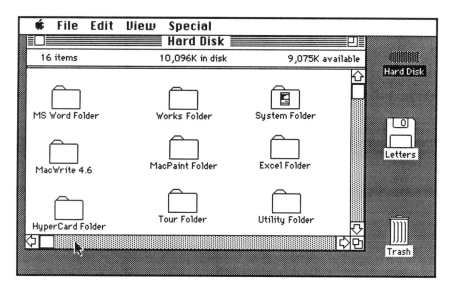

**Figure 1.3.** Desktop of Figure 1.2 with Hard Disk Window Opened.

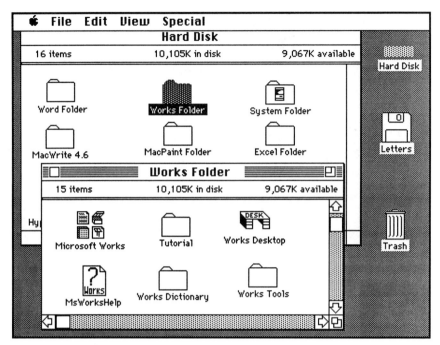

**Figure 1.4.** The Desktop of Figure 1.3 with the *Works* Folder Opened.

The Macintosh interface is remarkably uniform, that is, the desktop and all the applications use essentially the same mode of communication with the computer. Because of this uniformity, you will quickly learn to be a productive user of the Macintosh.

## OPERATIONS WITH THE MOUSE

The mouse is the primary means through which you interact with the objects on the desktop. In this section we consider several of the most important **mouse operations**. These operations are highly intuitive and can be easily mastered. They form the basis of most communications when one uses a Macintosh.

**Pointing.** The position of the pointer on the Macintosh desktop (i.e., the screen of the computer) can be controlled by moving the mouse on the *actual* desktop. The mouse operation *point* is defined as the action of positioning the *tip* of the pointer over a object on the screen.

**Clicking.** The operation *clicking* is defined as a rapid press and release of the button found at the top of the mouse.

**Selecting.** The operation *selecting* is defined as pointing to a object and clicking; when an object is selected it will become highlighted (displayed in reverse video — as the *Hard Disk* icon is in Figure 1.3). If the mouse pointer is moved to a second object and the button is clicked, the second object is selected and the previously selected object is no longer selected.

**Dragging.** The operation *dragging* is defined as follows.

An object is pointed to.

The button on the mouse is pressed and held.

While holding down the button on the mouse, the mouse is moved to a new position.

When the desired position is attained, the mouse button is released.

This operation is often used to reposition an object such as a folder or window on the desktop or to select a sequence of characters or words for editing.

**Double Clicking.** Double clicking is performed by clicking the mouse button twice in rapid succession. This operation is useful when you want to open an object such as a folder to see what's inside.

**Shift Clicking.** Shift clicking consists of holding down the *Shift* key while the mouse is repeatedly pointed to objects and clicked. In this way, each new object selected becomes highlighted and remains highlighted even as additional objects are selected. If the *Shift* key is released and the mouse is clicked, the previously selected objects are deselected and hence are no longer highlighted. The operation of shift clicking is useful in selecting multiple objects to be treated as a unit, as, for example, when you want to move a group of icons at one time.

## OVERVIEW OF COMPUTER COMPONENTS

From a functional perspective all computers can be viewed as consisting of input devices, a central processing unit, memory, and output devices, as shown in Figure 1.5. The central processing unit receives information from the outside world by means of the input devices, manipulates the information based on the instructions stored in memory, and sends the results to one or more of the output devices.

**Central Processing Unit.** Inside the **central processing unit** of the computer are two subunits: the **control unit** and the **arithmetic logic unit.** The control unit manages the activities of all the components that make up the computer. When manipulations of information are required, such as adding or subtracting numbers, the control unit routes the information to the arithmetic logic unit, where the actual operations on the information take place. In your Macintosh, all the electronic circuitry necessary for the control unit and arithmetic logic unit functions are located on a single-chip central processing unit called a *microprocessor*.

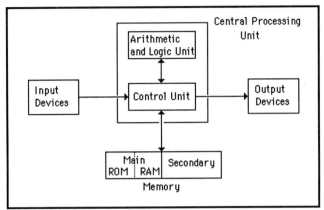

**Figure 1.5.** Functional Organization of a Computer.

**Main Memory.** Normally, as a program is being executed, data being used by the program itself, as well as other information are all stored in the computer's **main memory**. Main memory is composed of two different kinds of chips that reside inside the computer's housing.

Computer memory that is used by application programs is called random access memory, or **RAM,** because the memory cells can be accessed efficiently in any desired order. Information may be transferred to and from RAM as dictated by the control unit. An essential feature of RAM is that it is **volatile.** This means that if the power to a computer is turned off for any reason, its RAM contents will be forgotten. Lost forever! Because your working results are usually held in RAM, it is important to save your work every 10 to 15 minutes during a work session to a more permanent and secure medium. This medium is called secondary memory and will be discussed in the next section. Additional chips can often be purchased to expand the amount of RAM in a computer.

Read only memory, or **ROM,** is computer memory in which cell contents can be read *but not changed.* ROM is **nonvolatile;** its contents are not lost when the power is turned off. Part of the operating system is stored in ROM. When the computer is first turned on, the control unit causes the part of the operating system program in ROM to be accessed automatically. This part of the operating system reads the remainder of the operating system from secondary storage. The process of allowing the operating system to take control of your communication with the computer is called **booting** the computer. You will learn to boot your computer in the first lesson of this tutorial.

**Secondary Memory.** Computer RAM is expensive as well as volatile. For these reasons, **secondary memory** is used for inexpensive and more permanent storage of programs and data. The most common secondary memory device is the magnetic **disk drive.** These devices store information on small circular metal or plastic **disks** that are coated with a magnetic material. **Cartridge tape drives** are another type of secondary memory device commonly available for a computer system. Information on a disk or tape is grouped into larger units called **files.** The computer user gives a file a name. Once the file is named, the information in the file can be accessed by using this name.

There are two kinds of magnetic disk drives, **hard disk drives** and **floppy disk drives**. Hard disk drives have their disks sealed inside the drive case. Floppy disk drives use a small cartridge that contains the actual disk. The cartridges are called **floppy disks** or **disks,** and they can be inserted and removed from the disk drive.

Hard disk and floppy disk drives may be internally or externally installed. The computer shown in Figure 1.6 has two internal floppy disk drives and an external hard disk located under the computer case. A disk can be inserted into either of the internal floppy disk drives. An external floppy disk drive, if connected, normally would be positioned beside the computer.

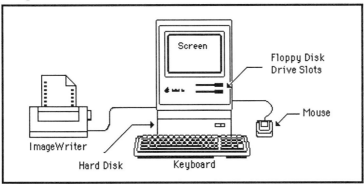

**Figure 1.6.** A Macintosh SE Computer with Printer.

The size of computer memory, whether it be main or secondary memory, is measured in the number of **bytes** it contains. A byte is the amount of memory required to store one character (one symbol on the keyboard). Because computer memories consist of hundreds of thousands to tens of millions of bytes, memory sizes are usually specified by using the units of *K* or *M*, which are defined as follows:

$$1K = 1024 = 2^{10} \text{ (approximately 1000)}$$

$$1M = 1024 \times 1024 = 1,048,576 = 2^{20} \text{ (approximately 1 million)}$$

For example, 512Kbytes of RAM is actually 524,288 bytes (or characters). The unit K defined above is usually called *kilo,* and the unit M above is usually called *mega.*

A floppy disk for the Macintosh floppy disk drive is a 3.5-in. disk enclosed in a plastic case for protection. These disks are portable and hold either 400K, 800K, or 1.4Mbytes of information, depending on the kind of disk and drive being used. Disks are classified according to whether a single side (SS) or both sides (DS) of the disk are used and whether double-density (DD) or high-density (HD) packing of the information is employed.

The Mac 128 and Mac 512 computers can read and write disks containing 400Kbytes. These are termed SS/DD disks because only one side is used with double-density packing of the information. All other Macintoshes can use these disks. An 800K disk is termed DS/DD because both sides of the disk are used with double-density packing of the information. Many of the newer Macintosh SEs and Mac IIs (such as the IIx, IIcx, IIsi, IIci, and IIxf) can also use 1.4M disks. These latter disks are termed DS/HD because both sides of the disk are used with high-density packing of the information. Assuming that a page of text has 43 lines, each containing 65 characters, a 400Kbyte disk can hold about 143 pages of text, an 800Kbyte disk can hold about 286 pages of text, and a 1.4Mbyte disk can hold about 500 pages of text.

A hard disk can store much more information than a floppy disk. Today, 20Mbyte to 80Mbyte hard disks are commonly used on the Macintosh. Also, the operating speed of hard disk drives is much greater than that of floppy disk drives. If a hard disk drive is mounted internally in a Macintosh SE or Macintosh II computer, it usually takes up one of the slots normally occupied by a floppy disk drive. Hard disk drives are actually required to run some of the larger software packages on a Macintosh.

**Input Devices.** An example of an **input device** for the Macintosh is the *mouse* (see Figure 1.6), which is used to control the pointer on the screen. Another common input device is the *keyboard*, which is used for typing information to be used by the computer. This information may consist of commands you wish the computer to perform, the text for documents, or the data for calculations.

**Output Devices.** The *screen*, or *CRT* (Cathode Ray Tube), is the primary **output device** of the Macintosh. Computer screens that are a direct image of the contents of memory are called **memory-mapped graphics** screens. If you were to examine the screen of a Macintosh under a magnifying glass you would see that it is composed of a matrix of dots. Each dot is one elemental unit of information and is termed a **pixel** (picture element). All text and graphics displayed on Macintosh computers are drawn as memory-mapped graphics objects. This underlying unifying aspect of the Macintosh design means that text, graphics, pictures, and so on, can all be naturally and conveniently integrated in a single document. Most personal computers do not use memory-mapped displays for both text and graphics. Instead they employ one kind of display for text and another for graphics. As a consequence, it is more difficult for software applications on these computers to integrate text and graphics within single documents.

The Apple *ImageWriter*®*II* and *ImageWriter*® *LQ* printers are output devices that can print a dot on a page for each dot displayed on the screen. Text, graphics, and even pictures displayed on the screen can, therefore, be easily output on the ImageWriter.

The Apple *LaserWriter*®printer, based on photocopy technology, is another popular output device for Macintosh computers. This printer, which can print with a resolution of 300 dots per inch, is often used for important correspondence and for desktop publishing. Like the Image-Writer, it can integrate text, graphics, and pictures. Some LaserWriter printers use **Postscript,** a special language that describes how pages of documents should appear no matter what the resolution of the printing device. Access to this language allows very impressive desktop publishing output.

**Networks of Computers and Devices.** In most Macintosh computer laboratory areas or office environments, printers will be shared over a network. **Network** is the term used to describe interconnections of groups of computers and devices. A graphical representation of an example network is shown in Figure 1.7. In this example network, there are eight computers and four shared printers plus a special dedicated computer called a **file server**. All of these are connected by cables over which information can be exchanged.

When we say that a device is shared on a network we mean that any user connected to the network is able to **allocate** that device; that is, the device can be temporarily controlled by that particular user's computer. Thus, if a printer on the network is not currently being used for printing by someone else, it can be allocated for your use in printing.

In addition to printer services, a network may provide a file server computer. Computer software can be very expensive. Many application packages cost $500.00 or more per copy. It is not possible for most organizations to provide large numbers of copies of such software. If a network contains a file server computer, then users anywhere on the network can use applications stored on that computer's hard disk just as if they were stored on their own disks.

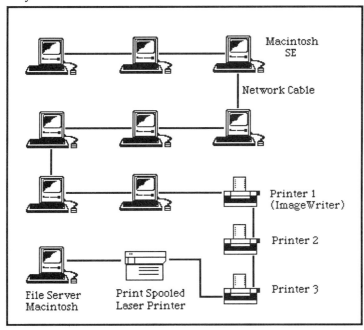

**Figure 1.7.** A Typical Macintosh Network.

# BOOTING AND SHUTTING DOWN THE COMPUTER

After completing this lesson, you will be able to:

❏ Start up your computer.

❏ Perform basic mouse operations.

❏ Shut down your computer.

## LESSON BACKGROUND

In this lesson you will learn to boot your computer so that you may communicate with it. You will also experience the feel of using the Macintosh computer by working through a guided tour that has been created by Apple Computer, Inc. You will then learn how to shut down your computer safely.

Recall from the discussion above that only a part of the operating system is stored in the internal ROM of your computer. The remainder of the operating system is stored on disk files. To obtain the entire operating system on the Macintosh, you must provide your computer with access to the files named *System* and *Finder*. These two files contain the parts of the operating system that are necessary to allow you to communicate with your computer. They are normally located on a disk inside a special folder named the *System Folder*. The details of how you provide your computer with access to the *System Folder* will depend on the kind of disk drives that your computer has.

To prepare for Lesson 1 you will need to obtain a floppy disk that contains the Apple Computer, Inc. developed tour of the Macintosh for your specific type of Macintosh computer. Thus, you will need to identify the kind of Macintosh computer you have and how it is configured.

The Macintosh family of computers can be broken into two main groups: the classic group and the Mac II group. The classic group is composed of the Mac 512K, Mac 512KE, Mac Plus, and Mac SE; the Mac II group is composed of the Mac II, Mac IIcx, Mac IIci, Mac IIx, and Mac IIfx. New members in each of the groups will continue to be added. Macintosh computers belonging to the classic group have their display screen and one or two internal floppy disk drives contained in a single molded case with a groove on the top of the case that can be used as a handle to carry the combined computer and screen unit. The appearance of a member of the classic group is similar to that of Figure 1.6. In contrast, the Mac II group is modular in construction, with the computer case (rectangular box) separate from the display screen.

Determine to which group your computer belongs and place a circle around it in the space provided for later reference.

The computer I'm using is in:  **Mac Classic Group   Mac II Group**

**Mac Classic Group Power Switch Location.**  The power switch for the classic group is located on the left side of the back of the case about halfway down from the top of the computer. This switch is used to turn on power to a classic group computer.

**Mac II Group Power Switch Location.**  The power switch for the Mac II group is located on the back of the case in the lower right-hand corner. However, you will normally need to use this switch only in the rare occurrence that your system locks up and fails to respond to the commands you issue. Instead, located on the keyboard either near the top center or at the top right corner, depending on your model of keyboard, is a key that has a triangle imprinted on it. Pressing this key will turn the power on to your computer. (Note: Some classic group computers may also have this key on their keyboards; however, pressing it will not turn the power on to the computer.)

## RUNNING THE APPLE-PROVIDED MACINTOSH TOUR

To gain your first experience with turning on and using your Macintosh, perform the following. Note that your computer should not be turned on as you begin this exercise. If your computer is turned on and you do not know how to turn it off, contact your laboratory manager. You should plan to spend approximately one hour to work through this tour.

- Pick up the disk that contains the Macintosh tour. Hold the back edge of this disk between your thumb and forefinger. The metal shutter should face toward the Macintosh and the notched corner of the disk should be in the right front corner.

- Gently slide the disk into an internal disk drive slot of your computer. (If your computer has more than one internal floppy disk drive, it will not matter into which drive you insert the disk.)

- When the disk is almost completely inserted, release your hold on it and use your thumb to gently press the disk further into the slot until the computer snaps the disk into place. Note that this is a very gentle process — you should not require force to insert the disk.

- If your computer has an external hard disk drive, turn the power on to that drive at this time. An external hard disk drive will normally be a rectangular box located under the computer or placed on either side of the computer case. This box will have a power switch on it (usually at the back of its case) and will contain no slots for floppy disks.

- Now, turn on the computer by using the power switch on the back of the case for a classic group computer or the triangle imprinted key on the keyboard for a Mac II group computer.

- You will probably hear sounds from the disk drive as it reads in the operating system from the tour disk. Soon a street scene will be displayed on the right half of your computer screen. On the left half will be displayed the title of the Macintosh tour you will be using.

- Watch this display for a few moments without typing on the keyboard or manipulating the mouse. The computer will automatically begin a tutorial that will teach you the mouse operations of pointing, clicking, and dragging. Follow the instructions presented.

- When this initial tutorial sequence has ended, a screen will appear showing a menu of tutorials that describe additional features of the Macintosh interface. Work through each of these in succession. Repeat any as necessary until you are comfortable with the ideas being presented.

- After completing the tour, click on the box labeled *Quit the Tour*. A new dialog box will be presented that asks if you are sure that you wish to quit the tour. Point to the button labeled *Yes* and click.

- At this point one of several things will happen, depending on how your computer is configured. If your computer is configured with no hard disks (either internal or external), then the screen will go dark, the Macintosh Tour Disk will be ejected, and a flashing question mark will be displayed. If this happens on your computer, circle the statement below, indicating your computer has only floppy disk drives, turn off the computer, and proceed with the section of this lesson entitled *Booting a Macintosh Having only Floppy Disk Drives*.

**My Computer Has Only Floppy Disk Drives**

- Alternatively, if your computer has internal and/or external hard drives then when you click *Yes*, the screen will go dark, the Macintosh Tour Disk will be ejected and the computer will boot from the *System Folder* contained on one of these hard disks. Circle the statement below indicating that your computer has at least one internal or external hard disk drive.

**My Computer Has Hard Disk Drives**

- Select *Shut Down* from the **Special** menu. This will cause your computer screen to go dark again.

- Turn off the computer and any external disk drives.

- Proceed to the section of this lesson entitled *Booting a Macintosh with Hard Disk Drives.*

## BOOTING A MACINTOSH WITH HARD DISK DRIVES

It is assumed that your computer is turned off as you start this part of Lesson 1. If it is not, then first perform the actions in the section of this lesson entitled *Shutting Down Your Computer,* or ask your laboratory manager for help. If your computer contains a hard disk drive, the *System Folder* will normally reside on that drive. To boot a Macintosh computer that contains a *System Folder* on a hard disk drive perform the following.

- If your computer has one or more *external* hard disk drives, then turn them on at this time. Next, turn on your Macintosh. For the Mac classic group, this requires turning on the power switch on the back left side of the case. For the Mac II group, this requires pressing the triangle-marked key on the keyboard. The computer will automatically read in the *System* and *Finder* files from the hard disk.

- As the system boots you will see the *System Disk* icon of Figure 1.8(C) displayed on the screen. A message will appear welcoming you to the Macintosh.

- After the system boots, you will see a desktop similar to the example shown in Figure 1.9. If this occurs, go to the section entitled *Shutting Down Your Computer.*

- If the icon of Figure 1.8(A) appears, then either your hard disk does not contain a *System Folder* or you forgot to turn on your external drive (if present). Consult your laboratory manager in the former case.

- If you forgot to turn on the external drive, first turn off your computer.

- Next, turn on the external drive.

- Then, turn on your computer. If the *System Disk* icon of Figure 1.8(C) is still not displayed on the screen, contact your laboratory manager.

- Go to the section entitled *Shutting Down Your Computer.*

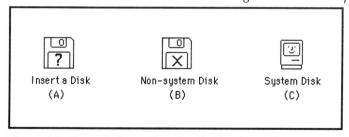

**Figure 1.8.** Example Icons That Can Be Displayed During the Boot Process.

## BOOTING A MACINTOSH HAVING ONLY FLOPPY DISK DRIVES

To perform the activities of this section you require a *System Disk*. Recall that this disk contains both the *System* and *Finder* files. To boot a Macintosh computer that has only floppy disk drives (or one that contains hard disk drives with no *System Folder*), perform the following.

- Turn the power on to your computer. For the Mac classic group this requires turning on the power switch on the back left side of the case. For the Mac II group this requires pressing the triangle-marked key on the keyboard. You should see displayed the icon in Figure 1.8(A) as the computer warms up. This indicates that the computer is waiting for a disk that contains the *System Folder*. [If the icon of Figure 1.8(C) appears, then your computer contains an internal hard disk and you will not need to use the floppy *System Disk*.]

- Pick up the floppy *System Disk* that contains the *System Folder*. Hold the back edge of this disk between your thumb and forefinger. The metal shutter should face toward the Macintosh and the notched corner of the disk should be in the right front corner.

- Gently slide the disk into the internal disk drive slot of your computer. (If your computer has more than one internal floppy disk drive, it will not matter into which drive you insert the disk.)

- When the disk is almost completely inserted, release your hold on it and use your thumb to gently press the disk further into the slot until the computer snaps the disk into place. Note that this is a very gentle process — you should not require force to insert the disk.

- The *System Disk* icon shown in Figure 1.8(C) should now be displayed, indicating that the operating system is loading from your disk. After the boot process is completed, you will see a sample desktop displayed such as that in Figure 1.9. When you have successfully completed these steps go to the section entitled *Shutting Down Your Computer*.

- If the icon of Figure 1.8(B) is displayed and the computer ejects the disk, then that disk does not contain the *System* and/or *Finder* files. Remove it from the slot. Check to see if you have inserted the correct disk. If not, insert the correct disk and the system should boot. If you have inserted the correct disk, then the disk is faulty and you must obtain another one from your laboratory manager.

## SHUTTING DOWN YOUR COMPUTER

Once the computer has been successfully booted, you will be able to communicate with it. You will see how to issue several commands to the computer in Lesson 2. However, as the next step in this lesson you will learn how properly to turn off the power for your computer. We term this process **shutting down your computer**. You should always follow these steps, if possible, because they ensure that your data will be safely saved to your disk. Failure to follow these steps can result in a loss of *all* the data as well as a loss of the ability to reboot the computer using this *System Disk*.

To shut down the computer you must see the desktop displayed on the screen. The desktop can be recognized by the appearance of the menu bar shown in Figure 1.9 containing the names **File**, **Edit**, **View**, and **Special**. (On a Mac II group computer that is operating in the color mode, the name **Color** will also appear on the menu located to the right of the name **Special**.) The desktop is also characterized by a uniform background pattern or color (in this case gray). Note the disk icon named *System Disk*. Your boot disk may have some other name. At the bottom of the screen is the trash can icon named *Trash* that can be used to remove files from your disk.

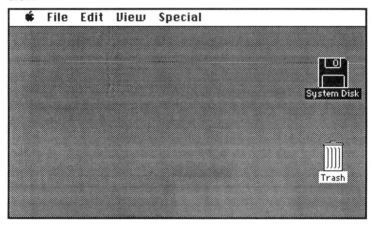

**Figure 1.9.** Example Desktop Displayed after Successfully Booting the Computer.

Perform the following to shut down your computer.

- As you look at your Macintosh desktop you will see a dark arrow called the *mouse pointer*. Move the mouse on the real desktop and note this causes the pointer on the Macintosh screen to move correspondingly.

- Move the mouse as necessary to cause the pointer to touch the *Trash* icon.

- Next place the pointer over the V in the name **View**.

- Continue practicing moving the mouse until you have some confidence in using it to position the pointer where you would like.

- Position the pointer over the name **Special**. Note that the mouse has a button located on it.

- With the pointer positioned over the word **Special** in the menu bar, press the mouse button. The menu will be pulled down to reveal a number of choices such as those shown in Figure 1.10. (Do not move the mouse in the process, the pointer should remain over the word **Special.**)

- Release the button. Note that the menu rolls back up.
- Now cause the menu to pull down again. Drag the pointer down so that different elements in the menu appear highlighted. Do not release the mouse button yet.

**Figure 1.10.** Selecting the *Shut Down* Command.

- Drag the pointer so that the entry *Shut Down* is highlighted, as shown in Figure 1.10.

- While holding the mouse steady, gently release the mouse button. The act of releasing the button causes the command or option that is highlighted in the menu to be performed. When a command is carried out by a computer, we say the command is executed. In this case, the computer will execute the *Shut Down* command.

- If you are using a Mac II group computer, the screen will go blank, as the power is automatically turned off. Turn off any external hard disks at this time.

- If you are using a Mac classic group computer, you should now see the message "**You may now switch off your Macintosh safely**" displayed in a dialog box as shown in Figure 1.11. Turn off the Macintosh by turning off the power switch on the back left-hand side of the case. If you have external hard disks connected to your computer, you should also turn them off as well.

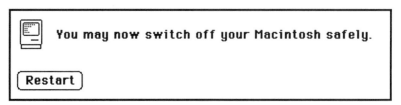

**Figure 1.11.** Dialog Box Resulting from the *Shut Down* Command for a Mac Classic Group Computer.

- You have now successfully shut down the computer. Observe that any floppy disks that may have been inserted in the computer are ejected at this time.

To complete this lesson, practice booting and shutting down your computer several times.

**If Your Computer Does Not Respond**. Note that in certain instances, while you are using the computer, it may hang up. That is, you may find that the commands you issue no longer have any effect on the actions of the computer. In these instances you may be forced to turn the power off to your computer without following the steps listed above. To turn the power off to a Mac classic group computer simply turn off the power switch on the back left-hand side of the case. To turn the power off to a Mac II group computer, hold in the power switch located in the right back corner of the case.

Unfortunately, any work you have not saved will be lost if you are forced to turn off the computer without going through the *Shut Down* command of the **Special** menu. Furthermore, it is even possible that the disk you are using may have all its information damaged in this process. Consequently, you should turn off the computer in this manner only when **absolutely necessary**.

# INITIALIZING A FLOPPY DISK

After completing this lesson you will be able to:

❑ Initialize a floppy disk.

## LESSON BACKGROUND

In this lesson you will initialize a floppy disk. The initialization process (sometimes called *formatting*) creates special areas on a disk that allow storage of data and programs. A disk cannot be used to store information until it has been initialized. The initialization process determines the amount of information that can be stored on the disk; recall that there are two different densities of information storage on Macintosh disks, DD and HD. The initialization process also determines whether one side or two sides of a disk are used.

On many different computers, initialization can be done only by issuing a direct command to the operating system. This may not be possible if you are currently using an application. Fortunately, with a Macintosh, any time an uninitialized disk is inserted into a floppy drive, you will be allowed to initialize the disk. An example dialog box for this process is shown in Figure 1.12.

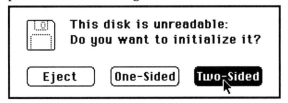

**Figure 1.12.** Example Dialog Box for Initializing a 400K or 800K Disk.

To perform this lesson you must have a new floppy disk. The disk you require depends on the kind of disk drives used in your computer. There are three kinds of Macintosh floppy disk drives. The Mac 512K and earlier Macintoshes have 400Kbyte disk drives that write only on one side of a disk. The disks normally used are SS/DD 3.5-in. disks. (You may, however, also use the 3.5-in. DS/DD, but note that the maximum storage available is 400Kbytes.) The Mac 512KE, Plus, and early SE and Mac II computers have 800K drives that normally use the DS/DD 3.5-in. disks.

(You may, however, use also 3.5-in. SS/DD with the maximum storage available being 400Kbytes. Note that it is often possible to format a SS/DD disk to 800Kbytes by using both sides, but this is not a recommended process.). The Mac IIx, IIcx, IIci, IIfx, and later models of the Mac SE all have 1.4Mbyte drives, and DS/HD 3.5-in. disks are required by these computers to achieve 1.4M of storage. (You may also use either the 3.5-in. SS/DD or DS/DD disks, but they have a maximum storage capacity of 800Kbytes).

You may easily distinguish between high-density and double-density disks. High-density disks have two small square cutouts at opposite corners of the back edge of the disk case. They are usually imprinted with *HD* near the notch on the front of the disk. In contrast, double-density disks have only a single square cutout located on the back edge of the disk. There are no external differences between SS/DD and DS/DD disks, although *single sided* is sometimes stamped on the sliding metal shutter.

Macintosh drives are **upward compatible**. This means that a disk initialized on a 400K disk drive can also be read from and written to using both 800K and 1.4M drives. Similarly, a disk initialized to 800Kbytes using an 800K drive can always be read from and written to using a 1.4M drive.

The drives are not **downward compatible**, however; thus, a disk initialized to 1.4Mbytes cannot be read from or written to using either an 800K or a 400K drive. Similarly, a disk initialized to 800Kbytes cannot be read from or written to using a 400K drive.

Any attempt to insert a disk initialized to a higher density into a lower density drive will produce a dialog box similar to that in Figure 1.12. This is the same message you will receive if an uninitialized disk is inserted. *If you proceed with the initialization process all data on that disk will be destroyed and the disk will be reinitialized to a lower storage capacity.* Consequently, if you see this message, make sure that the disk you are initializing is either new or one whose contents are no longer important to you. If you have access to a variety of Macintosh computers having different kinds of drives, it is very important to keep in mind the nature of disk compatibility from one computer to another.

For optimal transportability of information between different kinds of Macintosh computers, the 400K initialization is the best to use; however, the limited amount of storage on a 400K disk can create difficulties in transferring large files. Most Macintosh computers (any Mac 512KE or later and all Mac II group) have a drive that can store at least 800Kbytes. If you don't need to use a Mac 512 or earlier computer in your environment, then initialization to 800Kbytes provides excellent transportability.

## FLOPPY DISK INITIALIZATION USING MULTIPLE DRIVES

It is assumed that you have a disk that is compatible with the particular floppy disk drives in your computer. Make sure that you have applied the paper label to the disk case and have written your first initial, middle initial, and last name on the label so that the disk can be identified. To initialize your disk, perform the following.

- Boot your computer as described in Lesson 1.
- Once the desktop such as in Figure 1.9 is displayed, insert a new blank disk into an empty floppy drive on your computer.

*Steps for 800K drives or 800K disks in a 1.4M drive.*

- If your computer contains 800K disk drives or you are using an 800K floppy disk in a 1.4M drive, then the dialog box of Figure 1.12 will appear.
- To initialize your disk to 800Kbytes, move the pointer over the *Two-Sided* button and click. (You may also initialize to 400Kbytes by selecting *One-Sided*, but this process is normally used only if you need to use this disk on a computer with 400K disk drives.)
- A second dialog box will warn you that all the information on this disk will be erased by the initialization process. If you are sure that you have the correct disk in the drive, click the *Erase* button. Otherwise click *Cancel*. Your disk will be ejected and you may verify that you have the correct disk. Repeat the above process again when you have the correct disk.
- You will then be presented with a dialog box asking you to name the disk. Type your first and middle initials followed by your last name so the disk can be easily identified.
- The initialization process will begin. It will take about a minute or so to finish. In addition to the *System Disk* icon, your disk's icon also will now appear on the desktop. If this occurs, you may skip to the last paragraph of this lesson.
- If the computer fails to properly initialize your disk, it will print a message stating *Initialization Failed*. Click the *OK* button and your disk will be ejected. Repeat the initialization process one more time. If the process fails again, your disk is faulty and you must obtain a new one. Repeat the process above with your new disk.

*Steps for 400K drive or a 1.4M floppy disk in a 1.4M drive:*

- If your disk drive is a 400K drive or alternatively is a 1.4M drive with a 1.4M floppy disk inserted, the dialog box will have only the buttons *Eject* and *Initialize*. Click the *Initialize* button.
- A second dialog box will appear warning you that all the information on this disk will be erased as a result of the initialization process. Click the *Erase* button when you are sure you wish to proceed. Otherwise click *Cancel*. Your disk will be ejected and you may verify that you have the correct disk. Repeat the above process when you have the correct disk.
- When the next dialog box is presented, name the disk by typing your first initial, middle initial, and last name so that your disk may be easily identified. After the initialization is completed, your disk's icon will appear on the desktop in addition to that of

the *System Disk*. If this occurs, you may skip to the last paragraph of this lesson.

- If the computer fails to properly initialize your disk, it will print out a message stating *Initialization Failed* and eject your disk. Repeat the initialization process one more time. If the process fails again, your disk is faulty and you must obtain a new one and repeat the process above.

## FLOPPY DISK INITIALIZATION USING A SINGLE DRIVE

It is assumed that you have a disk that is compatible with the particular floppy disk drive in your computer. Make sure that you have applied the paper label to the disk case and have written your first initial, middle initial, and last name on the label so that the disk can be identified. To initialize your disk, perform the following.

- Boot your computer as described in Lesson 1.
- If your computer has only one floppy drive and no hard drives, then you must eject the *System Disk* now contained in that drive before you can insert the new disk. Move the mouse pointer to the **File** menu.
- Drag down to the *Eject* operation and release the mouse button. The *System Disk* will be ejected.
- Remove this disk. Now insert your new blank disk. A dialog box similar to that of Figure 1.12 will appear. Follow the steps outlined above for a multiple drive computer. You may be asked to exchange disks during the initialization process. Follow these instructions as presented. Once you have initialized your disk, its icon will appear on the desktop in addition to that of the *System Disk*.

The initialization process is now completed, and your disk is now able to store your information. You will use this disk in later lessons of this tutorial. If you do not wish to proceed directly to the next lesson, you may *Shut Down* the computer as discussed in Lesson 1.

# MANIPULATING OBJECTS ON THE DESKTOP

After completing this lesson you will be able to:

❑ Open a disk window.

❑ Open a folder window.

❑ Close a disk or folder window.

❑ Drag a folder or disk window.

❑ Alter the size of a window.

❑ Scroll a window horizontally or vertically.

❑ Open multiple window folders.

❑ Choose the active window.

❑ Insert one folder into another.

❑ Remove one folder from inside another.

## COMMON FEATURES OF WINDOWS

You must become comfortable with manipulating windows on the desktop because much of your work will require moving, opening and closing, and scrolling inside windows. All Macintosh windows have many common features, regardless of whether they appear on the desktop or in an application. Some of these features are identified in Figure 1.13.

**Close Box.** Closing a window causes it to disappear from the screen. You may close a window by pointing to the *Close Box* and clicking. (While the button is pressed, a "star" appears in the *Close Box*. Releasing the button closes the window. If the pointer is moved from the *Close Box* before the mouse button is released, the window will not be closed.) The active window can also be closed by selecting *Close* in the **File** menu.

**Title Bar.** The *Title Bar* is the top line of the window. It contains the *Close Box*, the name of the open object, and the *Zoom Box*. The active window is always identified by a series of horizontal lines in its *Title Bar*. Inactive windows do not have this striping in their *Title Bars*.

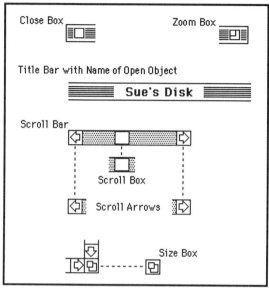

**Figure 1.13.** Common Features of Windows.

**Name of Open Object**. The name of the open object is always displayed in the middle of the *Title Bar*.

**Zoom Box**. The *Zoom Box*, which is located in the right-hand corner of the *Title Bar*, is used to switch between a smaller or a larger version of the window. The *Zoom Box* is often but not always present in a window.

**Scroll Bars**. A Macintosh window allows you to view part of a scene that may be so large that not all of it can be seen at once. A scene may be, for example, a picture produced by a paint program, the folders on the desktop, or the words, lines, and pages of a word processing document. The *Scroll Bars* allow you to position the window so that you can see a different part of the scene. Elements in the *Vertical Scroll Bar* allow you to move through the scene vertically. If the scene is a typed document produced by a word processing program, the *Vertical Scroll Bar* is used to move to different lines and different pages in the document. Using the *Horizontal Scroll Bar* elements, you may look at parts of the scene that are too wide to fit on the screen.

**Scroll Arrows**. A window may have as many as four *Scroll Arrows*: two in the *Vertical Scroll Bar* and two in the *Horizontal Scroll Bar*. These arrows are used to move the window to a new location in the scene. In the vertical scroll bar, the upward pointing *Scroll Arrow* at the top of the bar can be used to move the window backward in the scene. For example, in a word processing document, this would allow you to see previously typed lines.

To use the *Scroll Arrow*, point to the arrow, and click once for each line the window is to be moved. Alternatively, the mouse button can be pressed down and held until the window has been positioned as desired for viewing the scene. The downward pointing *Scroll Arrow* is used in the same way to move the window down through the scene. For wide scenes the *Scroll Arrows* in the horizontal scroll bar move the window in the indicated direction.

**Scroll Box.** A *Scroll Box* shows the relative position of the window in the scene. Thus, if the *Scroll Box* is positioned at about the middle of the *Scroll Bar*, the window is in the middle of the scene. The *Scroll Boxes* can be used to move quickly through the scene by dragging the *Vertical* or *Horizontal Scroll Box* to the desired relative position in the scene. Releasing the button will position the view in the window to that position. Alternatively, you may move the window exactly one window height at a time forward or backward by positioning the cursor in the *Scroll Bar* above or below the *Vertical Scroll Box* and clicking. You may move the window exactly one window width right or left by clicking in the *Scroll Bar* to the right or left of the *Horizontal Scroll Box*. If no *Scroll Box* appears then the extent of the scene is fully displayed in the window in the corresponding direction.

**Size Box.** The *Size Box* is used to change the size of a window in width and/or height as it is displayed on the desktop. To change the size, drag the *Size Box*. A dotted line will show the outline of the changing size of the window. When the desired size is obtained, release the button and the window will assume that size. An example of enlarging a window is shown just before the release of the mouse button in Figure 1.14.

**Moving Windows.** When you have several windows on your desktop at once, it is sometimes hard or impossible to see a window that you might want to use as your new active window, because that window is covered by other windows. Resizing windows will take care of this problem in some cases, but in others you may need to move some windows around on the desktop. A window may be moved by dragging its *Title Bar*.

Note that to perform any of the above operations on a window, the window must be active. To make a window the active window, you need only click anywhere in its display area. If other windows hide a given window, you may close them or drag them out of the way to gain access to the window of interest.

## OPENING AND CLOSING A DISK ICON

In this section of Lesson 3, you will investigate the use of commands to open and close a disk icon on the desktop. You open a disk icon in one of two ways: by double clicking or by choosing *Open* from the **File** menu. You close a disk in one of two ways: by clicking the *Close Box* or by choosing *Close* from the **File** menu. Perform the following.

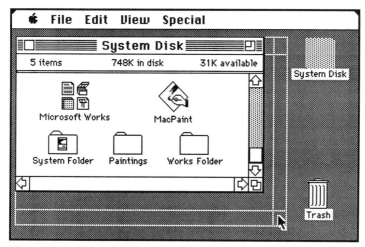

**Figure 1.14.** Using the *Size Box*.

- Boot your Macintosh as described in Lesson 1.
- You should see displayed a desktop similar to that of Figure 1.9. If instead you see one or more windows such as the ones shown in Figure 1.15, point to the **File** menu, drag down to *Close*, and release the mouse button. Repeat selecting *Close* until all you see on the desktop are the icons of the *System Disk* (the one with which you booted the computer) and the *Trash*.
- Double click the *System Disk* icon (i.e., move the pointer over the disk icon and click twice in rapid succession). The disk should open into a window whose appearance is somewhat like that in Figure 1.15. Note that the speed at which you perform the clicking is critical. If you do not press the button twice rapidly, the disk will not open. Also, you must be careful not to move the mouse, even slightly, between clicks. The objects now displayed are those contained by the disk.

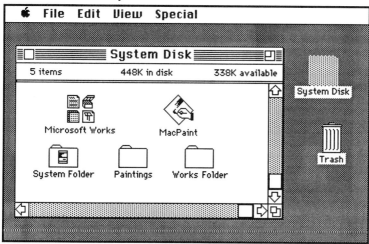

**Figure 1.15.** The *System Disk* Opened.

- Familiarize yourself with the location of the *Close Box* in Figure 1.16 (it is in the upper left-hand corner position in the figure). Locate the *Close Box* for your disk window and click it (i.e., position the tip of the pointer at the center of the *Close Box* on the disk window and click). The window disappears back into the disk.
- Point to the disk icon and click. It should now be highlighted.
- Drag down to *Open* in the **File** menu and release the mouse button. The disk window opens just as if you had double clicked it. Note the horizontal lines in the *Title Bar* indicating that this window is the active window.
- Drag down to *Close* in the **File** menu. The window closes exactly as if you had clicked on the *Close Box*. Choosing *Close* in the **File** menu will always close the active window.

You should now see a desktop on the screen similar to that of Figure 1.9 with no windows open.

## COMMON OPERATIONS ON WINDOWS

In the next part of Lesson 3 we explore some common operations on windows. Consult Figure 1.16 for the location of window elements that will be discussed.

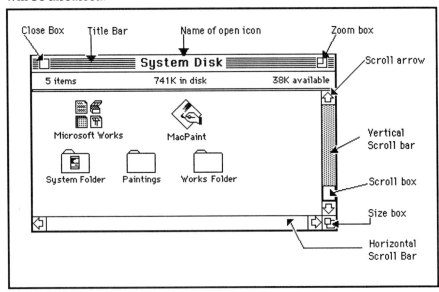

**Figure 1.16.** Common Window Elements.

Perform the following.

- Open your disk window again by double clicking the disk icon.
- Point to the center of the *Size Box* on your window. (Refer to Figure 1.16 to identify the *Size Box* location on a window.) Drag the

pointer upward and to the left. Notice that the outline of the window appears reduced in size. Release the button. The window is reduced to the size of the outline.

- Practice changing the size of the window by dragging the *Size Box* until you feel comfortable with this operation.

- Next, position the mouse pointer into the area of the window called the *Title Bar*. Do not choose the *Close Box* or the *Zoom* Box areas, however. Refer to Figure 1.16 as necessary to locate these areas.

- Drag the mouse around. Notice that the window outline is repositioned following the mouse movement, but it is not altered in size. Release the button and the window is redrawn at the outlined position last shown. If the window did not move, then you did not have the pointer in the *Title Bar* of the window when you pressed the mouse button for the drag operation.

- Use the *Size Box* to reduce the window size so that only two icons are shown.

- Position the mouse pointer so that its tip is in the right-pointing *Scroll Arrow* at the bottom of the window.

- Hold down the mouse button and note how the data in the window scrolls across.

- Point to the right *Scroll Arrow*.

- Hold down the mouse button; observe how the data in the window moves in the opposite direction.

- Drag the *Scroll Box* in the *Horizontal Scroll Bar* and release it. Note that this also repositions the area viewed in the window. When the button is released, the window position jumps to the relative position shown in the *Scroll Bar*.

- Verify that the *Vertical Scroll Arrows* and *Scroll Box* work in the same manner as you found for their horizontal counterparts.

- Change the size of the window to be about one-quarter the size of the screen using the *Size Box*. Without resizing, drag the window to the upper left-hand corner of the screen.

- Click on the *Zoom Box*. The disk window should now fill most of the screen.

- Click on the *Zoom Box* again. The window should return to its earlier size. The *Zoom Box* will allow you to toggle between a full-sized window and a smaller window whose size you set using the *Size Box*.

You have completed the section describing common operations on windows. Close all open windows and return the screen to a form similar to that of Figure 1.9.

## MANIPULATING OBJECTS WITH MULTIPLE WINDOWS OPEN

In this part of Lesson 3, you will work with objects in a window and see that more than one window can be present on the screen at one time. You will also learn how to manipulate objects in a window and move them from one window to another. Perform the following.

- Open the *System Disk* so that you observe a screen display similar to that of Figure 1.15. Use the *Size Box* to alter the size of this window on your screen to the approximate size shown in Figure 1.15. Drag the window into the approximate position shown in Figure 1.15.

- Double click the *System Folder*. You should find that two windows are now open on your screen.

- Resize and reposition the *System Folder* window such that only the right half of the *System Disk* window is obscured by the *System Folder* window.

- Note that the *System Disk* window has no horizontal bars across its *Title Bar*. These bars do, however, appear in the *System Folder's Title Bar* and indicate that the *System Folder* window is the active window.

- Now move the mouse pointer into any area of the *System Disk* window and click. Notice that the *System Disk* window appears immediately on top of the *System Folder* window and that the *System Disk* window now has bars displayed within its title bar area. Thus, clicking in a window makes that window become the active window.

- Practice alternating the active window back and forth between the *System Disk* and the *System Folder* windows by clicking. Note that you can drag or resize a window as necessary to gain access to a window under it. (Alternatively, you may also close a window to gain access to a window under it and later reopen the first window if necessary.)

- Close the *System Folder* by clicking its *Close Box*. If necessary, gain access to the *Close Box* by making the *System Folder* the active window by clicking in any part of its window.

## CREATING AND REPOSITIONING FOLDERS

In this section of Lesson 3, you will create a new folder and learn to position it on the screen where you desire.

- Insert the disk you initialized in Lesson 2 into one of the available floppy disk drives on your computer. (If you have a one floppy drive system that has the *System Disk* already in the drive, eject the *System Disk* by clicking the *System Disk* icon to select it and then dragging to *Eject* under the **File** menu. Then insert your initialized disk.)

- Open your disk by double clicking its icon. An empty window should appear. Check to see that the name of the window is the name of your disk. If not, close the window shown and repeat the above carefully so that *your* disk window is opened.

- Select *New Folder* in the **File** menu. In your disk window will appear an icon of a folder named *Empty Folder*. This folder will be highlighted.

- Type the name *Outer Folder*. The new folder should now be named *Outer Folder*.

- With the mouse pointer over this folder, drag the folder. Note that the outline of the *Outer Folder* moves correspondingly.

- Using this method drag the *Outer Folder* to another area in your disk window.

- Release the mouse button and note that the icon of the *Outer Folder* is repositioned to the outlined position. Any object in a window may be moved in this way, whether it be a file or a folder.

## CREATING A FOLDER HIERARCHY

In this section of Lesson 3, you will create another new folder and place it inside the *Outer Folder* you just created. This process is called building a folder hierarchy. (Note: If your computer is a Mac 512K or earlier model, you will not be able to perform exercises that involve manipulating folders inside other folders.)

- Select *New Folder* again. Another folder named *Empty Folder* will appear. Type the name *Inner Folder*.

- Drag this folder on top of the folder named *Outer Folder*. *Outer Folder* should now also become highlighted. If *Outer Folder* is not highlighted, continue dragging until *Outer Folder* is highlighted.

- Release the mouse button and the icon of *Inner Folder* should disappear. Open *Outer Folder* by double clicking its icon to observe that *Inner Folder* has been positioned inside *Outer Folder* in the file hierarchy.

By dragging an object over a folder and releasing the button, you place it in that folder.

## REMOVING OBJECTS FROM FOLDERS

By dragging an object out of a folder and releasing the button, you remove it from that folder. Perform the following.

- With *Outer Folder* opened to display *Inner Folder*, position and resize the *Outer Folder* window such that approximately one-half of your disk's window is shown on the screen.

- If necessary, scroll the *Outer Folder* window until you see the folder named *Inner Folder*.

- Drag *Inner Folder* into your disk's window area and release the button. The folder will be moved from *Outer Folder* window to your disk's window.

- Close the *Outer Folder* window. Notice that *Inner Folder* remains displayed. You have moved it up one level in folder hierarchy; that is, you no longer have to open *Outer Folder* to view it.

- Drag *Inner Folder* over *Outer Folder* again. As you do so, the *Outer Folder* will become highlighted.

- Release the button. The *Inner Folder* will disappear from the screen again.

- Verify by opening *Outer Folder* that *Inner Folder* has again been placed one level deeper in the hierarchy.


## COPYING A FILE FROM ONE DISK TO ANOTHER

In this part of the lesson, you will learn how to copy a file from one disk to another. This section assumes that your *System Disk* contains an icon named the *Scrapbook File*. This icon is commonly contained in the *System Folder*. If you cannot find this icon on your *System Disk*, you may skip this part of the lesson. Perform the following.

- Close all windows so that only the icons of your disk, the *System Disk*, and the *Trash* appear on the screen.

- Open the *System Disk* by double clicking to display its window. Drag the window to the upper left-hand corner of the screen. Using the *Size Box*, set the size of the window to be about one quarter of the screen.

- Double click on the *System Folder* to open its window. Drag this window to the upper center of the screen. Set its size to be about the same as the *System Disk* window. Leave the lower right-hand area of the screen free.

- Scroll in the *System Folder* window until you find an icon named *Scrapbook File*.

- Open your disk icon by double clicking it.

- Set the size of this window to be about one-quarter of the screen and drag this window to the lower right-hand corner of the screen.

- Open the folder named *Outer Folder*.

- Position the *Outer Folder* window so that it covers most of the lower right-hand corner of the screen.

- Scroll in this window until the *Inner Folder* icon is visible.

- Move the mouse pointer back to the *System Folder* window and click on the *Scrapbook File* icon to highlight it.

- Drag this icon over the *Inner Folder* icon displayed in the lower right-hand area of the screen. The latter should become highlighted.

- Release the button. The *Scrapbook File* icon will now be copied from the *System Disk* to your disk and placed inside the *Inner Folder*.

- Open the *Inner Folder* icon to observe that a copy of the *Scrapbook* has been made on your disk.

- Verify that the *Scrapbook File* icon still resides in the *System Folder* of the *System Disk* by accessing the window of this folder.

The process of copying a folder from one disk to another requires simply that you drag the folder rather than the file to the disk to which it is to be copied. When a folder is copied, *all* the files and folders within that folder are also copied. Also note that as you transfer objects from one disk to another, you are always copying them. The objects are never deleted from the source disk.


## USING THE TRASH

The *Trash* is used to delete files and folders from your disk. To use the *Trash* perform the following.

- Make the *Inner Folder* window the active window and scroll to display the *Scrapbook File* icon.

- Click on this icon and drag it over the *Trash* icon. The *Trash* icon should become highlighted. (Note: You may have to resize and/ or reposition windows to perform this operation.)

- Release the mouse button with the *Trash* icon highlighted. If the file remains on the desktop, then you did not have the *Trash* highlighted when you released the button. Reselect the icon and drag over the *Trash* as described above. You may be given a dialog box asking if you want to throw away the *Scrapbook* file. Click *OK* in this box. The file will disappear into the *Trash*.

- Verify that the file has been placed in the trash by double clicking the *Trash* icon. You should see the *Scrapbook File* icon inside.

- Close the *Trash* window by clicking in its *Close Box*.

- Empty the trash by selecting *Empty Trash* from the **Special** menu.

- Open the *Trash* icon. You will see that its contents have been deleted; that is, the file has been removed from your disk.

- Close the *Trash* window. Close the *Inner Folder* window.

## SHIFT CLICKING TO SELECT MULTIPLE OBJECTS

One final concept will be emphasized before ending this lesson. Shift clicking may be used to highlight more than one object at a time. Perform the following.

- Make the *System Folder* window the active window.
- Highlight the *Scrapbook File* icon by clicking it.
- Simultaneously highlight the *Clipboard File* icon by scrolling in the window until it is found, holding down the *Shift* key, and clicking on the *Clipboard File* icon. Release the *Shift* key.
- Drag one of the highlighted icons over the *Inner Folder* icon so that it becomes highlighted. (Note that when the mouse pointer is over *Inner Folder*, the folder will become highlighted even if the icons cannot be positioned as desired.)
- Release the mouse button. Both the *Scrapbook File* and the *Clipboard File* are copied into the *Inner Folder* in one operation.
- Verify that this process has copied both files into *Inner Folder* by opening this folder.
- Delete the *Clipboard File* from *your* disk by dragging it into the *Trash*. Leave the *Scrapbook File* for a later exercise.
- Empty the *Trash*.

You have now completed Lesson 3. Close all open windows on your desktop. If you do not wish to proceed directly to the next lesson, select *Shut Down* from the **Special** menu and shut down your computer.

# ALLOCATING A PRINTER

After completing this lesson, you will be able to:

❏ Choose a printer for your output.

❏ Print the directory of your disk.

## CHOOSING A PRINTER

Printers may be either **directly connected** to your computer or **connected via a network**. The way you access the printer will depend on how the printer is connected. If you have a printer located next to your computer and there is a single cable that runs from the printer directly into the back of the computer, then your printer is most likely directly connected to the computer. If there are cables that enter and leave a small box that is plugged into the back of your computer and your printer, then you most likely have network access to your printers.

## CHOOSING A NETWORKED PRINTER

Perform the following instructions if your printers are connected to a network.

- Boot your Macintosh if it is not already booted and insert your disk into the disk drive. You should see the desktop displayed along with the icon of your disk.

- Open your disk to display its contents.

- Point to the **Apple** menu icon located in the upper left-hand position of the menu bar.

- Drag to *Chooser* and release the button. You should see one or more icons displayed. These may be titled *AppleTalk I...*, *AppleTalk LQ*, and/or *LaserWriter*.

- Select the *AppleTalk I...* icon if you wish your output to appear on an ImageWriter dot matrix printer. Select *AppleTalk LQ* if you wish your output to appear on an ImageWriter LQ dot matrix printer. Select *LaserWriter* if you wish your output to be printed on a LaserWriter.

- When you select one of these icons by clicking it, the names of all printers of that type that are available on your network are displayed in the box labeled *Select a printer:*. If no names appear, then no printers of that type are currently available.
- Click on the printer name you wish to use. This operation allocates that printer for your use in any subsequent print operation. If your printer is a spooled device, the name of a spooler for that device may appear instead of the device's name. Click on this spooler name instead.
- Close the dialog box. You will be returned to the desktop.
- Under the **File** menu, select *Print Directory*. A picture of your disk's folders and files as they appear in the disk's window will be displayed on the printer.

## CHOOSING A DIRECTLY CONNECTED PRINTER

- Boot your Macintosh if it is not already booted and insert your disk into the disk drive. You should see the desktop displayed along with the icon of your disk.

- Open your disk to display its contents.

- Point to the **Apple** menu icon located in the upper left-hand position of the menu bar.

- Drag to *Chooser* and release the button. You should see one or more icons displayed. These may be titled *ImageWriter, LQ ImageWr..., LaserWriter*, and so forth.

- Click the icon that matches the kind of printer that is attached to your computer.

- Two icons will be displayed indicating the modem and printer ports. Click the appropriate icon. This selection indicates to the computer into which of two possible connections on the back of the computer case your printer cable is plugged. If you don't know, follow the cable from the printer to see where it is plugged into the computer. Over that connection is imprinted into the computer case one of these icons.

- Close the dialog box. You will be returned to the desktop.

- Under the **File** menu, select *Print Directory*. A picture of your disk's folders and files as they appear in the disk's window will be displayed on the printer.

You have completed Lesson 4. If you do not wish to proceed directly to the next lesson, shut down the computer.

# MORE ABOUT THE HIERARCHICAL FILE SYSTEM

After completing this lesson, you will be able to:

- ❏ Design a folder hierarchy.
- ❏ Alter the structure of the folder hierarchy.
- ❏ Insert a file into the folder hierarchy.
- ❏ Alter the location of a folder in the hierarchy.
- ❏ Find a file in the folder hierarchy.
- ❏ Delete a folder or file from the hierarchy.

## UNDERSTANDING HIERARCHICAL FILE SYSTEMS

It is important that you thoroughly understand the nature of the **hierarchical file system** (HFS) that you will be using on the Macintosh computer. (*Note*: Older versions of the Macintosh do not support HFS; your instructor will provide information needed if you are using such a machine.) As we have shown in some of our prior examples, it is possible to have the desktop organized so that folders appear in other folders. By using this feature of file management, you will be able to build a hierarchy of file and folder organization that allows for efficient and productive retrieval of information that you have stored on your disks.

Many computer systems make use of hierarchical file systems, including computers using the UNIX operating system and the popular DOS, Microsoft Windows, OS2, and other operating systems for the IBM PC and its compatibles. Although the Macintosh hierarchical system will be somewhat simpler to understand because of its direct analogy with a filing cabinet and its familiar folder filing system, what you learn here will be immediately applicable to a hierarchical file system of any computer, not just the Macintosh.

At the top of the hierarchy of the Macintosh file system is a disk. As you have already learned, there may be more than one disk drive attached to the computer, and certainly a floppy disk drive may have more than one disk used with it. Within a given disk, you may place files and folders. Each folder may in turn hold files and other folders. An example arrangement is diagrammed in Figure 1.17. Here two disks are shown named *MyDisk* and *Hard Disk.*

If the *Hard Disk* icon were opened from the desktop, then the three folders, *System Folder, Works Folder,* and *MacPaint,* would be seen in the *Hard Disk* window. If the *System Folder* were opened, then the icon for the *Finder* would be displayed given this hierarchy. Alternatively, if the *Works Folder* were opened, then the icons for *Microsoft Works* and *MsWorksDict* would be displayed.

If the *MyDisk* icon were opened from the desktop, then the four folders *Works WP, Works DB, Works SS,* and *MacDeskTop* folders would be displayed in the *MyDisk* window. If the *Works DB* folder were opened, then the four folders *Lesson1, Lesson2, Lesson3,* and *Lesson4* would be displayed, and so on.

The Macintosh uses the **complete path name** in the hierarchy to identify a file or a folder. A complete path name consists of the disk name followed by each subsequent folder that must be opened to reach the desired file or folder. To identify the *Scrapbook File* in Figure 1.17, the complete path name *MyDisk:MacDeskTop/Lesson4/Scrapbook File* is actually used by the computer. Because the complete path name is used, there can be many folders and/or files with the same simple name whose complete path names are quite distinct. For example, in Figure 1.17 there are two folders titled *Lesson4.* The computer is not confused about which of these similarly named folders we are working with because we must always specify the path to the folder before we can use it. We usually do this explicitly by opening the appropriate sequence of folders, hence, setting the context, until the desired folder or file icon is located in the active window.

For example, to get inside folder *Lesson4,* in the *Works DB* folder, you would need to navigate your way through the hierarchical file system by opening *MyDisk,* opening the *Works DB* folder, and finally opening the *Lesson4* folder. Because the computer has been shown the path *MyDisk:Works DB/Lesson4* in this process, there is no ambiguity about which *Lesson4* folder you intend to use.

If you attempt to move two objects with the same name to the same folder within your hierarchy, you would be requesting the placement of two objects with the *same complete path name.* This cannot occur and one of them must replace the other! If the message *Replace file (folder) of the same name?* appears in a dialog box when you move an object from one folder to another, you should understand that your requested operation is attempting to position two files or folders having the same name with identical paths in the hierarchy.

If you proceed with the operation, the file or folder already in place within the folder will be replaced (and hence, destroyed) by the new one. There are many times when you will want exactly this action to be taken (when you are updating a file by moving a more recent copy to the folder, for example). However, it should be obvious that this procedure should be done with caution.

As an example, if you were to drag the *Lesson4* folder currently contained in the *MacDeskTop* to the *Works DB* folder, the above message would appear. Through this process, you would be attempting to creat two folders named *Lesson4* with the same complete path name *MyDisk:Works DB/Lesson4*. If you were to click *OK* when the message appeared warning you of the duplicate names, then the old *Lesson4* folder would be replaced by the new *Lesson4* folder and inside it would be the *Scrapbook File*. Also, if you opened the *MacDeskTop* folder, you would find it empty because whenever you move (copy) a folder, everything in it is moved (copied) as well.

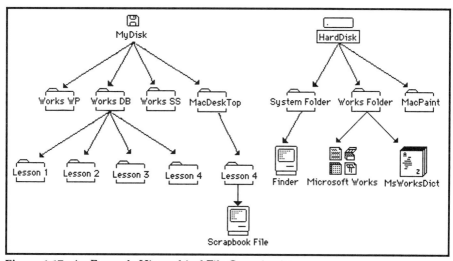

**Figure 1.17.** An Example Hierarchical File Organization.

# BUILDING A HIERARCHY WITH FOLDERS

In this part of Lesson 5, you will build a hierarchy of folders necessary for use in the remaining tutorials of this book. Your hierarchy will resemble some of that shown in Figure 1.17. You will create a folder for each of the three components of Works and a folder for the desktop documents as well. Perform the following.

- Boot your computer if your computer is not already booted.

- Close all open windows on your *System Disk*.

- Insert the disk you initialized in Lesson 3 into an open floppy drive.

- Double click your disk's icon to open your disk. Subsequent references to this disk will be termed *MyDisk*.

- You should see the folder named *Outer Folder* in the open window.

- Select *New Folder* from the **File** menu. A folder named *Empty Folder* will appear in your window.
- Type the name *Works DB* to name this folder.
- Open the *Works DB* folder by double clicking it.
- Select *New Folder* from the **File** menu. Type the name *Lesson1* to name the folder.
- Repeat the immediately preceeding step to create 10 more folders named *Lesson2* through *Lesson11*.
- Note that if you mispelled any of the folder names, you can rename a folder easily. To do this, first select the folder by clicking its icon, then type the new name while the folder is selected.
- Close the *Works DB* folder by clicking its *Close Box*. The *MyDisk* window should be active.
- Create a new folder named *Works WP*.
- Open this folder by double clicking it.
- Create in it 11 new folders named *Lesson1* through *Lesson11*.
- Close the *Works WP* window by clicking its *Close Box*. The *MyDisk* window should again be active.
- Create a new folder named *Works SS*.
- Open this folder by double clicking it.
- Create in it 9 new folders named *Lesson1* through *Lesson9*.
- Close the *Works SS* window by clicking its *Close Box*. The *MyDisk* window should be active.
- Create a new folder named *MacDeskTop*.
- Open this folder by double clicking it.
- Create in it one new folder named *Lesson4*.
- Close the *MacDeskTop* window by clicking its *Close Box*. The *MyDisk* window should be active.

You have now created the folder hierarchy that will be used in the remainder of the tutorial lessons in this book. In the next segment of this lesson, you will move your copy of the *Scrapbook* into the hierarchy at the position shown in Figure 1.17 and delete the folders *Outer* and *Inner*.

- Double click the *MacDeskTop* folder to open it.
- Double click the *Lesson4* folder inside this window to open it.
- Size the *Lesson4* window to be about one-quarter the size of the screen and drag it to the upper right-hand corner of the screen.
- Make the *MyDisk* window the active window by clicking anywhere in it. You may need to move other windows to see it.
- Open the *Outer* folder by double clicking it. Move and size this folder as necessary to keep from obscuring the *Lesson4* folder.
- Open the *Inner* folder by double clicking it. Scroll in this window until you see the *Scrapbook File* icon.

- Make the size of the *Inner* window about one-quarter of the screen. Drag it to the upper left-hand corner of the screen. The *Inner* and *Lesson4* windows should be next to each other and unobstructed.

- Drag the file named *Scrapbook File* from the *Inner* window into the *Lesson4* window and release the button. (Scroll inside the *Inner* folder as necessary to locate the *Scrapbook File* icon so that you may drag it.) The *Scrapbook File* icon should now appear in the *Lesson4* folder.

- Close the *Lesson4* folder.

- Close the *MacDeskTop* folder.

- Close the *Inner* folder.

- Close the *Outer* folder.

- Verify that the *Scrapbook File* file is inside the *Lesson4* folder which is inside the *MacDeskTop* folder by opening these folders. If the *Scrapbook File* is found, then proceed with the next step. Otherwise find the *Scrapbook File* by looking into the various folders. When you locate it, place it in the hierarchy as shown in Figure 1.17. Verify that it is in the correct location by closing all the folders and then opening the *MacDeskTop* and *Lesson4* folders.

- Close the *MacDeskTop* and *Lesson4* folders.

- Drag the *Outer* folder to the *Trash Can* icon.

- Select *Empty Trash* from the **Special** menu. You have removed both the *Outer* and *Inner* folders from your disk. (Recall that when you move a folder from one place to another, all its contents are moved as well.)

- Close all your open windows.


# FINDING LOST OR MISPLACED FOLDERS AND FILES

A hierarchical file system allows you to organize your files so that they are easy to find, even if you have hundreds of them. However, you must develop some conventions in structuring your folders and files. If you use no discipline in structuring them, you will soon become lost in a jumble of folders, and you will be unable to find anything!

If you have developed a reasonable organization method, you will usually have little difficulty finding what you need. However, on occasion, you may lose track of where in the hierarchy you have stored a folder or a file. Rather than hunting through folder after folder to locate it, there is a better way—if you can remember the name or part of the name of the folder or file. Under the **Apple** menu is a command *Find File* that can be used to show you the path that must be followed to locate your folder or file.

For example, Figure 1.18 shows the result of performing *Find File* when the name *Scrap* has been typed in and *MyDisk* is the disk searched. The search is started by clicking the *person running* icon. It may be stopped by selecting the *stop sign* icon if the object appears in the dialog box early during the search.  Because *Find File* will search the entire disk to find all occurrences of a given name, it can take some time to search a large hard disk drive, and thus halting the search can save you waiting.  The *Find File* command will find any file whose name *contains* the string you ask it to search for ("Scrap" in this case).  Once the search is completed or you have halted it, click on the desired name in the large scroll box and the path to that object will be displayed in the small rectangular scroll box in the lower right-hand corner of the dialog box, as shown in Figure 1.18.  The *Find File* command will also find matches of an entire name if you remember it.  However, the full name must be remembered *exactly*; otherwise the computer will find no match.

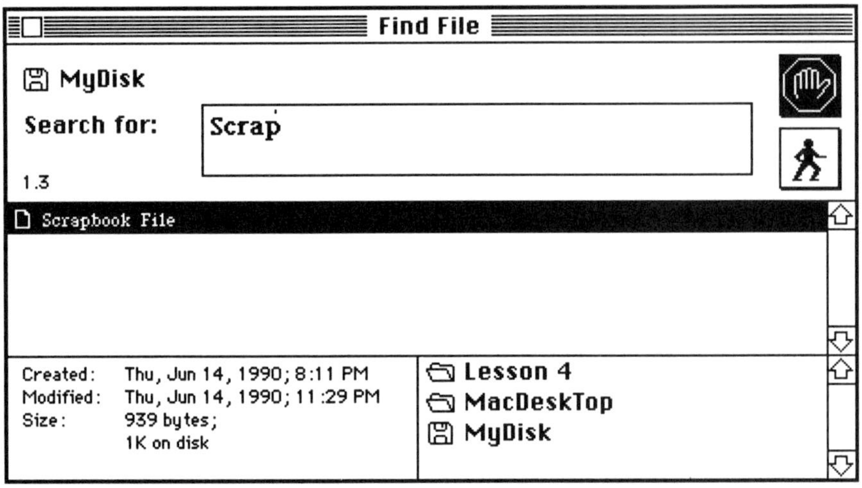

**Figure 1.18.**  Using *Find File* to Locate the Path to a Particular File.

If the name you enter in the *Find File* command dialog box has more than one match with folder or file names on your disk, there will be several lines in the large scroll box.  Figure 1.19 shows the result of typing *Lesson4* into the *Search for:* box.  Note that four names *Lesson4* appear.  Recall that a *Lesson4* folder was created inside each of the four folders *Works WP*, *Works DB*, *Works SS*, and *MacDeskTop* you created earlier.  In this example, clicking on the first of these shows the path *MyDisk:Works WP/Lesson4*.

To experiment with the use of *Find File*, perform the following.

- If your desktop has any open windows close them.
- Drag to *Find File* under the **Apple** menu and release.  If *Find File* does not appear in the list, it has not been installed on your computer and you will not be able to perform this part of the lesson.  Simply drag the pointer back to the **Apple** icon and release the button.  Continue on to Lesson 6.
- A dialog box similar to that of Figure 1.18 should appear.
- In the upper left-hand corner of this dialog box is the icon of a disk.  If your disk name does not appear here, click on this icon

42

until it does. By this process you are selecting the disk on which the search will be carried out.

- Now click in the dialog box named *Search for:*.

- Type in *Scrap*. This is the part of the name for which you wish to search.

- Click on the *man running* icon. You should see appear shortly in the top scroll box the name *Scrapbook File*. The *stop sign* icon will then be highlighted, indicating that the search is completed.

- Click on the name *Scrapbook File* in the large scroll box. The path to this file should now be displayed in the small scroll box. By opening the disk and the folders shown, you will be able to locate this file on your disk.

- Drag from left to right across the dialog box named *Search for:*. All the text should become highlighted. Release the button.

- Type *Lesson4*.

- Click on the *man running* icon. You should now see a display similar to that of Figure 1.19 with four names *Lesson4* appearing in the scroll box.

- Click on each name to verify that you are given paths into each of the four folders you created earlier.

This concludes Lesson 5. Close all windows. If you do not wish to proceed directly to the next lesson, shut down your computer.

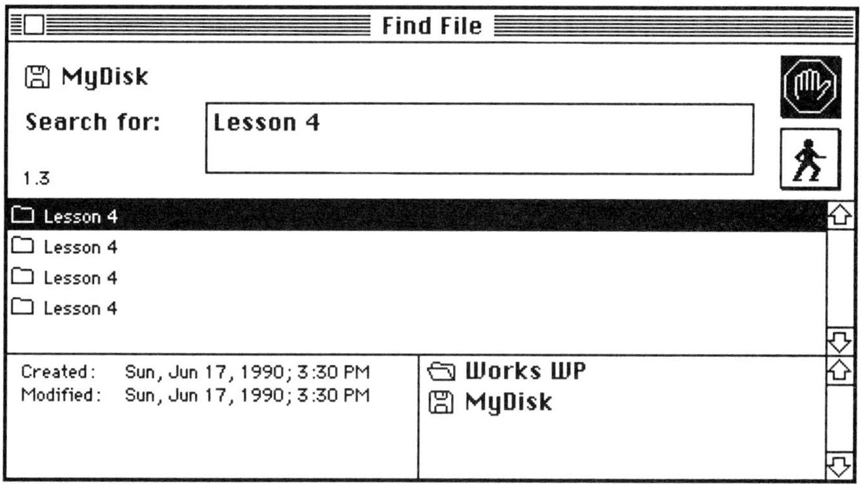

**Figure 1.19.** Illustrating Multiple Objects Matching the Name.

# LESSON 6

# MANAGING ADDITIONAL RESOURCES

Concepts discussed in this lesson may be considered optional and are essential only for more advanced users. After completing this lesson, you will be able to:

❑ Manage the Clipboard and Scrapbook files.

❑ Manage the Control Panel.

❑ Manage printing resources.

❑ Manage fonts and desk accessories.

❑ Manage special disk operations.

## OVERVIEW OF OTHER KINDS OF COMPUTER RESOURCES

This lesson provides a brief overview of some other kinds of computer resources you will need to manage. Thus far you have learned how to work with floppy disks, printers, network printers, and file servers and how to manage your hierarchical file system. There are a number of other resources that you will need to manage if you wish to take full advantage of your computer.

## MANAGING THE CLIPBOARD

The information contained in the Clipboard is determined by the most recent *Cut* or *Copy* command executed from within the **Edit** menu. This information is retained in the Clipboard until some other *Cut* or *Copy* command is carried out. Consequently, information may be transferred from one application to another by using the Clipboard. There is an icon in the *System Folder* named *Clipboard* and this file contains the current Clipboard information. A *Paste* command issued from the **Edit** menu causes a copy of the information in the Clipboard to be entered into an application's context at the current pointer position. The *Paste* command does not empty the Clipboard, and any number of additional *Paste* commands may be performed transferring the same information each time. Note, however, that there is only one storage area associated with the

Clipboard. The information stored there is lost as soon as another *Cut* or *Copy* command is issued. In contrast, the Scrapbook provides a storage area that can contain a large number of individual Clipboard images.

## MANAGING THE SCRAPBOOK

Information from the Clipboard may be retained on a disk for future reference. This is accomplished by first moving the information onto the Clipboard using a *Cut* or a *Copy* command as discussed above. The information may then be pasted into the Scrapbook using the *Paste* command. The Scrapbook is a file that is stored in the *System Folder*. If you change the *System Folder* for some reason, such as rebooting the computer from a new disk, the new disk will become the one used for all Scrapbook operations. Note that you can copy the Scrapbook from one disk to another because it is a file.

To paste information into the Scrapbook, select the *Scrapbook* command from the **Apple** menu. A window into the Scrapbook will appear (Figure 1.20). The scroll bar at the bottom of the window allows you to scroll through the different entries in the Scrapbook. At the left end of the scroll bar are shown two numbers separated by a slash. The number to the left of the slash is the number of the entry in the Scrapbook you currently are viewing. The number to the right of the slash shows the total number of entries currently in the Scrapbook. At the other end of the scroll bar is an indication of the kind of data format that is used to store the current entry. Selecting the *Paste* command from the **Edit** menu allows the current contents of the Clipboard to be inserted into the Scrapbook in a position *before* the currently displayed page.

To copy information from the Scrapbook into an application, it is first necessary to move the information into the Clipboard from the Scrapbook and then to copy the Clipboard into the application's context. You can do this by first opening the Scrapbook by selecting the *Scrapbook* command from the **Edit** menu. The *Scrapbook* window will be displayed as the active window, as shown in Figure 1.20. Next, scroll through the Scrapbook using the scroll arrows until the information you wish to use appears in the window. Now select either the *Cut* or the *Copy* command from the **Edit** menu. Note that *Cut* removes the entry from the Scrapbook when the information is transferred to the Clipboard. *Copy* copies the information to the Clipboard without removing it from the Scrapbook. At this point, the desired information is contained in the Clipboard.

Next, you make the application context the active window by either closing the *Scrapbook* window (by clicking in its *Close Box*) or alternatively by clicking in the application window area. Finally, select the *Paste* command from the **Edit** menu. *Paste* will transfer the information from the Clipboard into the application context, as it is now the active context. Note that if you forget to deselect the Scrapbook, and hence leave its window as the active window, the contents of the Clipboard will simply be inserted into the Scrapbook again!

The Scrapbook can quickly become very large, particularly if you are copying numerous pictures into it. Because the Scrapbook is a file, it can use a very large amount of the space that you have available on a disk. To remove entries from the Scrapbook, it is necessary only to *Cut* them when the *Scrapbook* window is active. Because *Cut* removes an entry from the Scrapbook, each *Cut* operation decreases by one the number of entries in the Scrapbook. If desired, the entire Scrapbook can be emptied in this way—one at a time.

**Figure 1.20.** *Scrapbook* Window Activated.

## MANAGING THE CONTROL PANEL

The human-computer interface can also be managed by changing the sensitivity of the mouse to your hand movements, changing the speed at which letters are repeated as you hold down a key, changing the background pattern on the desktop, and so on. Operations of this kind are accessible under the *Control Panel* in the **Apple** menu.

To experience using the *Control Panel* perform the following.

- Close all open windows so that you are in the desktop context.

- Select *Control Panel* from the **Apple** menu. You will see a dialog box presented similar to that in Figure 1.21.

- Scroll through the dialog box until you see the *Sound Resource* icon shown highlighted in Figure 1.22.

- Click on the *Sound Resource* icon. Your screen should now appear similar to that of Figure 1.22. The *Sound Resource* is used to set the volume of sounds that are emitted from your computer as well as the kinds of sounds that are emitted.

- Drag the sliding bead in the *Speaker Volume* rectangle to its highest position, 7 on the scale, and release the button. A loud sound will be heard.

- Drag the sliding bead to the 2 position on the scale and release. A soft sound will be heard.

- Adjust the level of sound to your liking.

- Click on the *Clink-Klank* setting in the *Alert Sound Setting* scroll window. You will hear the sound of tin can being struck.

- Click the other sounds in this scroll box to sample them.

- Choose the one you like best and close the *Control Panel*. Any time a sound is to be emitted by the operating system, it will use the one you have chosen.

- You may experiment with other resources in the *Control Panel*. Note that you may set the date and time, set the background pattern displayed on the desktop, and so on.

- When finished experimenting, close the *Control Panel* by clicking in its *Close Box*.

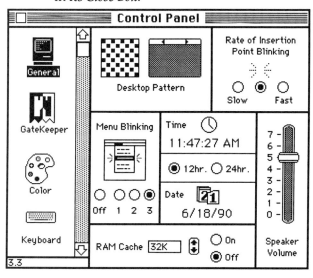

Figure 1.21. Control Panel Dialog Box.

## UNDERSTANDING THE FINDER

The communication between you and the Macintosh computer is accomplished through a special component of the operating system called the *Finder*. Through the *Finder* you will issue many of the commands necessary to perform resource management operations. There are actually three versions of the human-computer interface—*MiniFinder*, *Finder*, and *MultiFinder*—and the nature of the desktop interface is different for the three versions. Our discussions in this text will always assume that you are using the *Finder*, but for the sake of completeness we describe briefly some features of the *MiniFinder* and the *MultiFinder*.

The *MiniFinder* program takes up much less space on a disk and in memory than the *Finder*, but it does not provide as many functions. It was developed so that computers with limited memory and disk storage would be able to execute some large software applications. You will normally need the *MiniFinder* only if you have a small amount of disk space (i.e., a single 400Kbyte disk drive) and 512K or less of RAM.

At the time of writing, the *MultiFinder* is the most recently released human-machine interface program available for the Macintosh. It provides a larger set of operations than does the *Finder*. One of the *MultiFinder's* most important features is the ability to change from one application to another (or even move to the desktop) without quitting an application. It also provides the ability to do some computation in the "background" (perhaps, for example, computing some complex formulas in a spreadsheet) while you continue working on some other activity such as word processing.

In the discussion that follows we assume that you have installed on your computer system version 6.1.4 of the *Finder* and version 6.0.4 of the *System*. Most of the resource management operations that we describe appear almost the same if you are using either the *Finder* or the *MultiFinder*. If you are using a version of the *Finder* that is earlier or later than 6.1.4, your menu options may appear slightly different from those discussed here.

To find out which version of the *Finder* you are using, select the *About the Finder* command from the **Apple** menu from within the desktop, as shown in Figure 1.23. Note that your **Apple** menu choices will almost certainly be different from those shown. The reason is that commands can easily be added to or deleted from this menu, as you will see later.

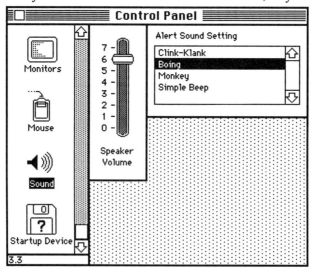

**Figure 1.22.** Dialog Box for the *Sound Resource*.

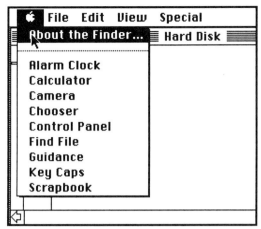

**Figure 1.23.** Getting Information about the *Finder* Version You Are Using.

After selecting the *About the Finder* command, a window like that shown in Figure 1.24 will be displayed. This window shows both the *Finder* version number and the *System* version you are using. It also shows how much RAM is in your computer and how the memory is allocated.

Note that different versions of applications, such as Works, are developed for use with certain *System* and *Finder* versions and may not work with others. Hence, changing the *System* or *Finder* can have important consequences and should be done only after careful consideration.

```
▤▢▦▦▦▦▦▦ The Macintosh™ Finder ▦▦▦▦▦▦▦▦▦
   Finder :   6.1.4            Larry, John, Steve, and Bruce
   System :  6.0.4             ©Apple Computer, Inc. 1983-89

   Total Memory :    1,024K

   ▤ Finder          868K     ▓▓░░░░░░░░░░░░░░░░░░░░░░░░░░
   ▤ System          156K     ▓▓░

                                                  ▶
```

**Figure 1.24.** Determining *Finder* and *System* Versions and RAM Allocations.

To investigate the use of *About the Finder* perform the following.

- Close all windows so that the desktop context is active.
- Choose *About the Finder* under the **Apple** menu.
- You should see a dialog box similar to that in Figure 1.24 displayed. Note the version of the *Finder* and *System* files you are using and the total amount of memory on your computer.
- Close the dialog box by clicking in its *Close Box*.

This completes the hands-on work in this lesson.  The remaining sections are presented for general information.  You will find them useful for reference as you gain more experience using your Macintosh.

## MANAGING PRINTING RESOURCES

In this section we discuss some concepts that allow you to have maximum flexibility using your printing resource.

**Printer Drivers.**  In order to print on a printer, the operating system program makes use of small programs called **printer drivers**.  These programs convert the output from your application, such as Works, into information that the printer needs in order to print the documents that you create.  Your computer can use many different printers, and each one of them requires its own driver program.

Driver programs for each printer must reside in the *System Folder*.  For example, the system folder usually has in it icons named *ImageWriter* and *LaserWriter*.  These files contain the driver programs for the respective printers.  If you do not have a *LaserWriter* icon in your *System Folder*, you will not be able to print on the Apple LaserWriter printer, even if one is attached to your computer or to an AppleTalk network to which you have access.  All peripherals such as plotters, scanners, and so on must have drivers in the system folder to translate input or output into meaningful data for use by the device.

**Defining the Page Setup.**  Printers come in different sizes and are capable of printing on paper of different sizes and in different orientations.  Specification of these available resources is normally done by using the *Page Setup* command under the **File** menu.  Figure 1.25 shows the result of selecting the *Page Setup* command from the desktop context when the ImageWriter has been previously selected using the *Chooser* command.

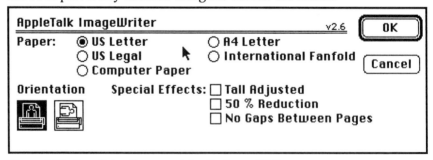

**Figure 1.25.** *Page Setup* Command for the ImageWriter.

As shown in this screen image, a variety of paper size choices can be used.  Some control can be exercised about the size of the output to be printed.  For example, there is an option to use a 50 percent size reduction in the output by clicking on the square button so named.

In addition, the orientation of the text or painting on the page can be selected. In the lower left-hand side of the dialog box are shown the icons of a printer in which an image is printed across the narrow width of the paper, the usual orientation (sometimes called *portrait* orientation). Alternatively, the information may be printed oriented along the length of the page rather than the width (sometimes called *landscape* orientation). Pointing and clicking will choose between the two orientations. Finally, if desired, no spacing need be inserted at the end of a page. Thus, if the *No Gaps Between Pages* box is checked, the printer treats the paper as if it is a long, continuous roll. Very large banners and/or drawings can be produced in this manner.

A similar dialog box is produced if the printer selected is the LaserWriter instead of the ImageWriter. An example of this dialog box is shown in Figure 1.26. You will note that a few added options are available.

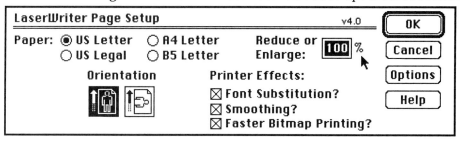

**Figure 1.26** . *Page Setup* Command for LaserWriter.

One of the major differences between the LaserWriter dialog box in Figure 1.26 and the ImageWriter one in Figure 1.25 is that a variable degree of enlargement or reduction of the print size is possible. Font substitution may be used to produce higher quality output than certain fonts selected in your application. Note that the orientation of the output on the page can be selected using either the ImageWriter or the LaserWriter.

Figure 1.27 shows the increased flexibility for controlling the output that is possible using the *Page Setup* **command** within Works. Many of the same options for controlling the printed output within Works context are the same as those available in the desktop context. Additional features specific to the word processing context also are provided, such as the ability to specify the margins within which the text will be printed. In Works, the top, bottom, left, and right margin positions of the page are separately controlled. This allows precise formatting of the printed output. In Figure 1.27 the margins are all set to 1 in. The *Header* and *Footer* boxes provide a means to add running headers and/or footers to your documents. You will investigate these features later in this book.

## MANAGING FONTS AND DESK ACCESSORIES

When you become more experienced using your Macintosh, you will be interested in tailoring it to fit your own needs. Two major interests you will probably have are installing custom fonts into your *System* file and adding desk accessories to the **Apple** menu.  In this section, we describe the process by which both of these activities can be done.

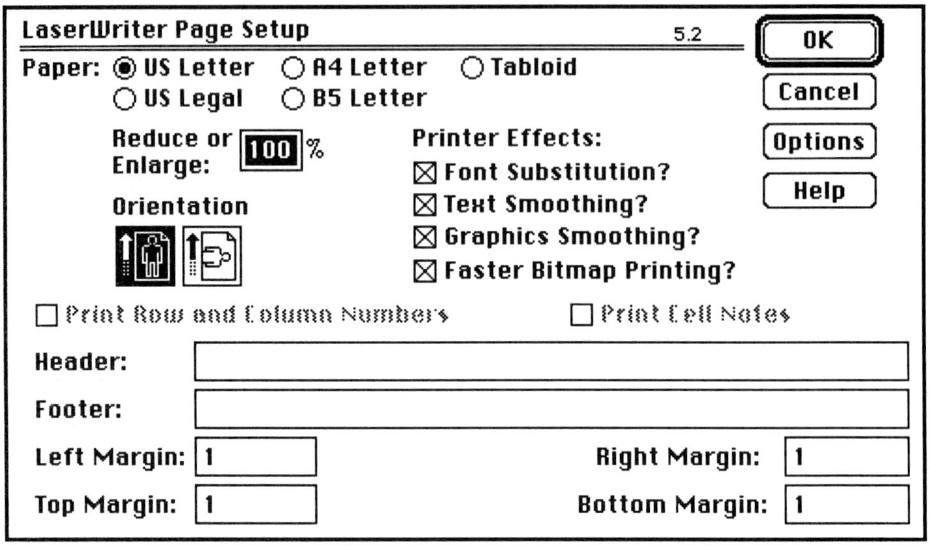

**Figure 1.27.** *Page Setup* Command Selected in Works Context with the LaserWriter Printer Selected in the *Chooser*.

Because the Macintosh uses a memory-mapped screen to produce all its text and graphics, an extremely wide range of font sizes and styles is available to the user.  Fonts may include foreign alphabets, mathematical symbols, chemical symbols, and so on.  Each of the symbols can be selected by typing a key on the keyboard after the appropriate font has been selected from a pulldown menu.  A font size can also be chosen in this same manner.  The desk accessory *Key Caps* listed in Figure 1.23 can be used to show the font selected.

Font sizes are shown in two ways in a pulldown menu.  They appear to be either bold or outlined.  Outlined fonts give the best possible output appearance when using the printers or when displayed on the screen. Exact patterns for these sizes are stored in the *System* file.  Those sizes that are shown in bold type are interpolated from other sizes.  They are *not* available in the *System* file.  That is, the computer must make a guess about how each character should appear because no exact pattern is defined for it to use.  Also, the styles of font that the computer can use are determined by the styles that are available in the *System* file.  The computer cannot display fonts that are not contained in its *System* file.

Managing the fonts that are available in the *System* file is relatively easy. There is a utility program called *Font/DA Mover* (DA stands for Desk Accessory) that normally is stored in the *Utilities* folder of a *System Disk*.  This program is used to transfer font styles and sizes into or out of a *System* file. Each combination of style and size of a font takes up considerable space on a disk.  Thus, you need the option both **to add and to delete** fonts from the *System* file.

Execution of the *Font/DA Mover* utility program is carried out by finding the icon shown in Figure 1.28 and opening it. The *Font/DA Mover* utility program shows the screen of Figure 1.29 when it is executing. The program can be used to move either fonts or programs called desk accessories into the *System* file. You determine which action will be performed by clicking in the appropriate button at the top of the dialog box. For this example, the *Font* button has been selected. The *System* file into which the fonts are to be copied or deleted is shown on the left. It will be automatically opened if you have a system disk in a drive. The rectangle on the right is used to select the fonts to be entered into the *System* file from some other source, provided that you open such a source. Note that in the large rectangle at the bottom of the dialog box the style and size of any font selected are shown.

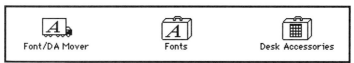

Font/DA Mover        Fonts        Desk Accessories

**Figure 1.28.** *Font/DA Mover* Icon (left), Suitcase of Fonts, (center) and Suitcase of Desk Accessories (right).

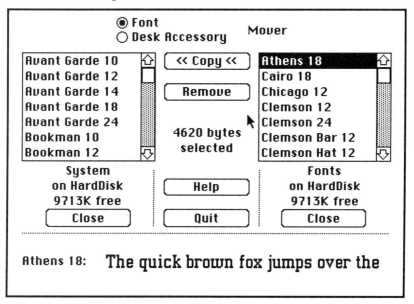

**Figure 1.29.** Dialog Box for *Font/DA Mover* Program.

For example, the standard system disks sent from Apple along with a Macintosh computer contain a selection of fonts in addition to the ones already present in the *System* file. These fonts are contained in the suitcase icon labeled with the script "A" in Figure 1.28 and found in the *Utility* folder. In our example, if this source of fonts is opened, any of the fonts available in this file may be copied into the *System*. Remember, however, that adding fonts increases the size of the *System* file. To copy a font set into the *System* file, click on the font name and size desired. The *Copy* button will become bold. Then click *Copy*, and the font selected will be transferred.

**Desk Accessories.** Desk accessories are programs that can be executed by selecting their names under the **Apple** menu. These include such programs as the *Calculator, Alarm Clock, Note Pad,* and so on. Many public domain desk accessory programs, which can be obtained at no cost, will perform certain functions you might require. For example, there are scientific calculator desk accessory programs that can compute the standard scientific functions in addition to performing arithmetic.

Once you have a source of desk accessories, you may copy them into the *System* file using a method analogous to that used for the fonts mentioned earlier. Here select the *Desk Accessory* button in the *Font/DA Mover* program once you have opened it. Open the file having the source of desk accessories you wish to use; your *System* file will automatically be opened for you if it is available. Select each new desk accessory you wish to add by shift clicking. Then click on *Copy* and your selected desk accessories will be copied to the *System*.

Once a new desk accessory has been copied into the *System*, it may be executed by selecting it from the **Apple** menu. Desk Accessories are usually available in application contexts.


## SPECIAL DISK MANIPULATIONS ON THE DESKTOP

In this section, you will learn some of the basic techniques for managing your disk collection. In particular, you will learn how to create a backup copy of a floppy disk by copying the contents of one entire disk to another disk. In addition, you will learn how to transfer all the information on a floppy disk to a hard disk.

**Copying an Entire Floppy Disk to Another Floppy Disk.** Occasionally, you will want to copy one entire floppy disk to another. For example, you should make a backup copy of each of the disks you receive when you purchase software, and then use the backup disk. In the event the latter disk becomes corrupted and can no longer be read from or written to, you may make another copy of the original disk and begin again.

As with software applications, backup copies of important work you are doing with the computer should always be kept. When a floppy disk drive reads information from a disk, the disk read-write head of the drive is actually touching the disk surface. Eventually this contact will wear away the surface and the disk will become unreadable. Also on rare occasions a mechanical malfunction of the disk drive mechanism can occur that will destroy a floppy disk. Thus, you should never assume that information on a floppy disk is permanently stored or recoverable. Backup copies of anything valuable or important to you should always be made! This takes only a few moments and should become a habit. Consider the hours of time that you will invest in working with your computer and you will see why this is wise advice to follow!

**Copying Disks using a Single Disk Drive.** Suppose you have a *one-disk-drive system* and wish to copy an entire disk. The disk to be copied should be placed in the floppy drive. After its icon appears on the desktop, use the *Eject* command in the **File** menu to remove the disk from the drive. Next place the disk that will receive the copy (the destination disk) into the drive. (Note that completing the copy process will overwrite any information currently on the destination disk). Now you will have icons for two disks on the desktop. Drag the icon of the disk to be copied onto the icon of the disk to receive the copy. Be very careful that you do not confuse the icons for the source and destination disks!

For example, to copy the disk named *Chapter Two* to the disk named *Backup*, drag the *Chapter Two* disk icon onto the *Backup* disk icon as shown in Figure 1.30. Note that the line connecting the icon and its moved outline as shown in Figure 1.31 does not actually appear on the screen as you perform the drag operation; it is shown here only to indicate the direction of the movement of the icon. *Remember that the contents of the disk named* Backup *will be lost and be replaced with the contents of the disk named* Chapter Two.

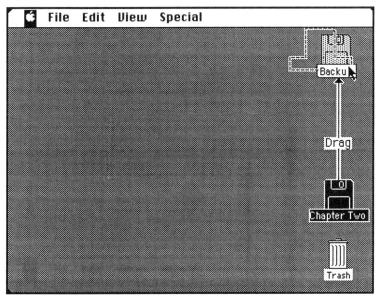

**Figure 1.30.** Copying an Entire Disk to a Similar Disk.

Once your pointer is over the *Backup* disk, its icon will darken. Release the button and the copying will begin. The copy operation will not occur until the *Backup* disk becomes highlighted. If you fail to move the cursor properly over the *Backup* disk, you simply move the *Chapter Two* icon to a different location on the desktop, and no copying will occur.

An *Exchange Disk* message of the type shown in Figure 1.31 may be displayed a number of times during this copy process. You must follow these instructions to completion; otherwise you may lose information on *both* disks.

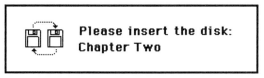

**Figure 1.31.** The *Exchange Disk* Message.

**Copying Disks using Multiple Floppy Disk Drives.** If you have two floppy disk drives available on your system, insert the disk to be copied in one drive and the disk that is to receive the copy in the other drive. Drag the icon of the disk to be copied over the icon of the disk to receive the copy as described earlier. Follow the instructions that appear on the screen. You may need to insert the disk containing the *System Folder* to complete the copy.

**Copying a Floppy Disk to a Hard Disk Drive.** A special situation arises when an entire **floppy disk is copied to a hard disk**. Often the hard disk is the system disk, and its icon, which is shown in Figure 1.32, is in the upper right-hand corner of the desktop. The process for dragging the icon of the disk to be copied is the same as that just described. However, because the hard disk has a much greater storage capacity than a 3.5 in. disk (perhaps 20 to 80 times as much capacity), there may be room for many of these smaller disks to be copied to one hard disk.

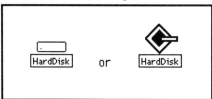

**Figure 1.32.** Forms of the *Hard Disk* Icon.

The *Finder* assumes that you do not intend to replace the *entire* contents of the hard disk with the contents of the floppy disk. Therefore, when a floppy disk is copied to the hard disk, none of the previous information on the hard disk will be removed. To keep the files of the floppy disk together, all the floppy disk's information is copied to the hard disk as the contents of a folder having the same name as the floppy disk. A message of the type shown in Figure 1.33 is displayed to remind you of this action.

Note that if you wish to copy one entire floppy disk to another floppy on a system having available one floppy disk drive and a hard disk, it will normally be faster to copy the floppy first to the hard disk and then copy the disk folder from the hard disk to the second floppy.

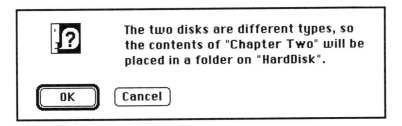

**Figure 1.33.** Copying to Different Disk Types.

**Erasing a Disk.** At times, you may wish to remove all the information stored on a disk, often because you want to use the disk for other purposes and thus reclaim all the storage. This process is called **erasing**, or reinitializing, a disk. The most efficient way to erase a disk is to use the *Erase Disk* command in the **Special** menu, after selecting the disk to be erased. If you are using a Macintosh with an 800K disk drive, the message shown in Figure 1.34 will be displayed. Systems with 400K drives or with a 1.4M disk inserted in a 1.4M drive will not provide the choice between the *One-Sided* and *Two-Sided* buttons. Read this message carefully to be sure that the name of the disk is the one you wish to erase. Once the erase process is started, *all* the information on the disk is lost. *There is no option to undo this command!*

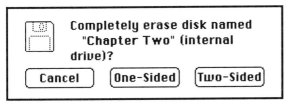

**Figure 1.34.** The *Erase Disk* Message.

This concludes Lesson 6 and this chapter. Clean up the desktop and shut down your computer.

# 2

# INTRODUCING WORKS

When you have completed the Introducing Works tutorial you will be able to:

❏ Explain the essential functions of the Works integrated software package.

❏ Start and quit the Works program.

❏ Open existing Works word processing, spreadsheet, and database documents.

❏ Make some simple modifications to existing Works documents.

❏ Save the modified documents.

❏ Use the Works Help feature.

## TUTORIAL OUTLINE

## WHAT IS INTEGRATED SOFTWARE?

A typical integrated software package includes four basic components or modules: a word processor, a spreadsheet program, a database management system, and a communications module. Additionally, some integrated packages also provide various drawing capabilities. Such packages are called "integrated" because of the ease with which data may be moved between the different modules within the packages.

Integrated software packages provide some very important conveniences and advantages. For example, it is possible for you to have documents from several different kinds of applications software open at the same time, moving from one document to another by simply changing the active window. This ability provides a great advantage over having always to quit one application to access a different application. Additionally, with an integrated package, you are guaranteed a high degree of user interface consistency for all the applications included in the package. This can greatly reduce the learning time over that required to learn separate stand-alone packages for word processing, spreadsheet, database, and communications applications. Finally, the cost of an integrated package is considerably lower than the cost of the stand-alone packages required in its place.

Of course, as you might expect from the above comments concerning package costs, the number of features in each component of an integrated package is fewer than is typically available in a corresponding stand-alone package. Whether the additional features justify the increased costs and learning time of several stand-alone packages over an integrated package depends largely on the use for which the software is being considered. As you will learn, for a great many uses, an integrated package provides ample power and features.

In the next section we quickly preview some of the major features of the Microsoft Works program. These features as well as many others will be treated in detail in subsequent chapters. For now, concentrate on thinking about what you might do with the components of Works to solve information problems of interest to you.

## AN OVERVIEW OF MS WORKS

Microsoft Works (also referred to as MS Works, or just Works) is an integrated package that contains the four basic types of application modules: a word processor, a spreadsheet package, a database management system, and a communications module, as well as several types of graphics and drawing capabilities. Each of the modules has an intuitive, easy-to-learn interface to assist you in doing your work. Information can be easily transferred between the modules, a feature that expands the usefulness of the package.

The **word processor** has a sufficient number of features to meet most users' needs. With it you can do the following:

Create textual documents.

Save, retrieve, and print created documents.

Preview full-page layouts before they are printed.

Insert and delete characters, lines, and paragraphs within a document.

Move parts of a document by "cut and paste" operations.

Format paragraphs, controlling such parameters as spaces between lines, left and right margins, left and right justification of text, centering of text, tab settings, and indentation.

Format characters and strings of characters by having them appear as bold, underlined, or italicized.

Place text above or below the line as superscripts or subscripts.

Insert page headers and footers, with automatic page numbering.

Use a variety of text font styles and sizes.

Check spelling.

Incorporate graphics within documents.

Figure 2.1 shows a document produced by using the Works word processing module together with its drawing capabilities. Such visually appealing combinations of text and graphics can be created with very little effort in Works. These drawing capabilities are also available for use in the spreadsheet module of Works.

A Works **database** is a file of records on a disk that contain related information about a person, object, or any other entity of interest. With the Works database module, it is easy to:

Organize and store information in files.

Design a file's records.

Modify the design of the records after the database has been created.

Modify the contents of existing records.

Delete stored information.

Retrieve stored information in formats that aid in answering questions about the data.

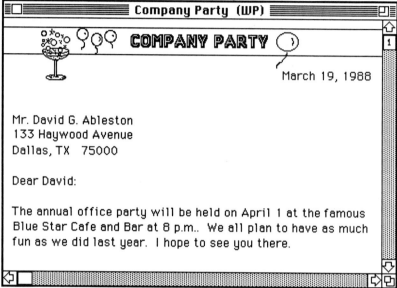

**Figure 2.1.** A Sample Word Processing Document Using Works' Text and Drawing Capabilities.

Works can be used to create a database form to allow input or display of a record. Alterations to the form design are easy to make. Figure 2.2 shows a simple form for an employee database for a hypothetical company. It can be used for entering information that is to be stored in the database. Data on individual employees can also be retrieved and displayed using the form.

Information entered into the database using the form can also be viewed in a table format, which is more convenient for some situations. Figure 2.3 shows the table display format for several employees. Data for additional employees can also be entered into the file using the table form.

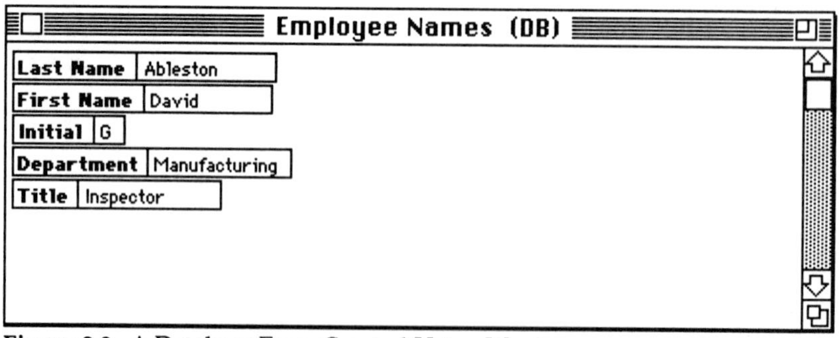

**Figure 2.2.** A Database Form Created Using Works.

| Last Name | First Name | Initial | Department | Title |
|---|---|---|---|---|
| Ableston | David | G | Manufacturing | Inspector |
| Highmaster | Jonathon | A | Marketing | Salesman |
| Jasper | Thomas | I | Marketing | Salesman |
| Siththe | Bernard | R | Grounds | Gardener |
| Zebbley | Arthur | P | Accounting | Clerk |

**Figure 2.3.** A Portion of a Table for a Database.

The **mail merge** feature of Works combines records in a database with a word processing document. This feature could be used to produce automatically a copy of the letter in Figure 2.1 for each employee, personalized with the person's name and address. This can save much time if there are many employees.

The Works **spreadsheet** can be used to:

Perform almost any computation that is normally done using a calculator.

Perform calculations that depend on logical functions that would normally require a computer program.

Use a wide range of built-in functions to perform arithmetic, logical, financial, and statistical calculations.

Display the results of calculations in a number of different formats.

Chart the results of calculations using bar charts, line charts, or pie charts.

Automatically adjust its calculations and the corresponding charts when data are changed.

Various accounting applications such as accounts receivable, accounts payable, balance sheets, payroll, and profit and loss statements are easy to do with a spreadsheet. Some other applications are inventory, grade calculations, budget modeling, simple statistics, and some scientific calculations.

An example Works worksheet is illustrated in Figure 2.4. In this worksheet, some budget calculations have been carried out. These calculations are made using simple formulas that are entered for one sample calculation of a particular type and then are copied (replicated) to produce the additional calculations of the same type.

| | A | B | C | D |
|---|---|---|---|---|
| | | **Budget (SS)** | | |
| 1 | | | | |
| 2 | | Amount | Percentage | |
| 3 | Rent | $450.00 | 27.52% | |
| 4 | Car | $240.00 | 14.68% | |
| 5 | Food/Entertainment | $480.00 | 29.36% | |
| 6 | Insurance/Medical | $175.00 | 10.70% | |
| 7 | Utilities | $190.00 | 11.62% | |
| 8 | Miscellaneous | $100.00 | 6.12% | |
| 9 | | | | |
| 10 | Total | $1635.00 | 100.00% | |
| 11 | | | | |

**Figure 2.4.** A Sample Works Worksheet.

An important capability of Works is its ability to present worksheet data in a visual or graphical form, such as is shown in Figure 2.5.  Data tables and graphs produced from worksheets can be easily transferred to word processing documents.

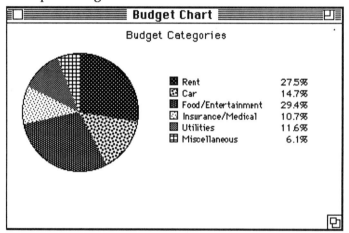

**Figure 2.5.** A Pie Chart of Expenses from the Sample Spreadsheet.

Several Works windows can be open simultaneously as shown in Figure 2.6.  (The maximum number that can be open is 10.) The type of window is identified by the abbreviation in parentheses after the name of the window: (WP) for a word processing document, (DB) for a database, and (SS) for a spreadsheet. *Employee Pay* (SS) is the active window in the figure.

The windows in Figure 2.6 have been arranged so that a portion of each can be seen, but normally, one window would be covering the others. A special menu, **Window**, can be used to switch quickly between the open windows.  This is shown in Figure 2.7, in which the *Employee Names* window has been selected. This feature makes it easy to examine and select information in a window for transfer to another window. For example, you might wish to transfer data from a database to a spreadsheet in order to do some calculations.

| | **File** | **Edit** | **Window** | **Select** | **Format** | **Options** | **Chart** | **Ma** |
|---|---|---|---|---|---|---|---|---|

| | | | | | | | | |
|---|---|---|---|---|---|---|---|---|
| | | | **Company Party (WP)** | | | | | |
| | | | **Employee Names (DB)** | | | | | |
| | | | **Employee Pay (SS)** | | | | | |

| **A** | **B** | **C** | **D** | **E** | **F** | **G** |
|---|---|---|---|---|---|---|
| st Name | First Name | Initial | Title | Rate | Hours | Gross Pay |
| leston | David | G | Inspector | $9.00 | 45 | $405.00 |
| ghmaster | Jonathon | A | Salesman | $7.50 | 55 | $412.50 |
| sper | Thomas | I | Salesman | $12.00 | 48 | $576.00 |
| hthe | Bernard | R | Gardener | $6.25 | 40 | $250.00 |
| bbley | Arthur | P | Clerk | $7.30 | 42 | $306.60 |

**Figure 2.6.** Three Open Works Windows.

| | **File** | **Edit** | **Window** | **Select** | **Format** | **Options** | **Chart** | **Ma** |
|---|---|---|---|---|---|---|---|---|

**Show Clipboard**

**Help**  ⌘?

**Employee Pay (SS) 3K**
**Employee Names (DB) 1K**
**Company Party (WP) 2K**

| **A** | **B** | | | | **F** | **G** |
|---|---|---|---|---|---|---|
| st Name | First Nan | | | | Hours | Gross Pay |
| leston | David | | | | 45 | $405.00 |
| ghmaster | Jonathon | | | | 55 | $412.50 |
| sper | Thomas | | | | 48 | $576.00 |
| hthe | Bernard | | | | 40 | $250.00 |
| bbley | Arthur | P | Clerk | $7.30 | 42 | $306.60 |

**Figure 2.7.** The **Window** Menu with *Employee Names(DB)* Selected.

Finally, Works has a **communications module** that allows your computer to communicate with other computers. The Works *Communications Settings* dialog box is shown in Figure 2.8. Clicking on various buttons in this dialog box will allow you to configure your computer to communicate with another computer. You will learn the meaning of some of these items in Chapter 7.

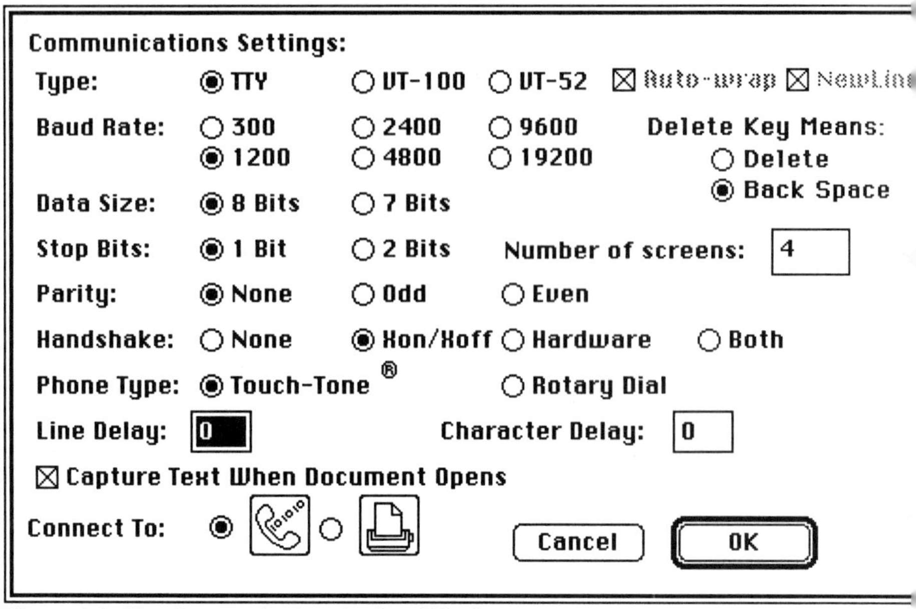

**Figure 2.8.** The *Communications Settings* Window.

# LESSON 1

# STARTING WORKS

After completing this lesson, you will be able to:

❏ Start the Works program.

*Special Note:* In several of the lessons in this chapter, you will be asked to work with a folder named *Chapter2* which contains all the sample documents discussed in the earlier *Works Overview* section of the chapter. Your instructor will provide this folder for you to copy to your *MyDisk* disk that you initialized and worked with in Chapter 1.

## DISTINGUISHING AMONG DIFFERENT COMPUTER CONTEXTS

When you first boot the computer, you are interacting with the computer at the **context** that we refer to as the desktop. By a context in the computer we mean the set of commands or operations that you are allowed to issue. When you use the computer in the desktop context, for example, some of the operations available to you include moving a folder from one position to another on the desktop, opening a folder to see what is in it, creating a new folder, naming a folder, and so on. For each of these actions you communicate commands to the computer through a series of manipulations of the mouse pointer and appropriate pressing of the mouse button. For example, to move a folder, you point to it and then drag it to the position you desire.

When you open the Works application, you are presented with a different context. In this context you are able to issue commands to write letters and documents, draw simple figures, calculate values, and so forth. To issue these commands to the computer, you perform manipulations of the mouse that are similar to those you performed on the desktop. However, their results will be different because you issued these commands in the Works context.

This perspective brings us to a centrally important principle about communicating with computers. To have the computer do what you want, *you* must first *place the computer in the proper context*, so that it interprets your instruction the way you wish. For example, if you are in the desktop context, you cannot directly draw pictures on the screen. To draw pictures on the screen, you must set the context to Works. Alternatively, while you are in the Works context you cannot move a folder around on the desktop or copy a document from one disk to another. Each different component of Works that we study in this text has its own context, just as the desktop has its context.

## CONTEXTS VIEWED AS DEFINING A LANGUAGE

To understand communicating with the computer, it is valuable to think of each context as defining a language through which we communicate our wishes to the computer. A language consists of symbols and a set of rules as to how we can combine the symbols. For example, in our natural language we may think of the symbols as being words and the rules being English grammar.

Whenever we learn a new language we must learn the symbols (*vocabulary*) and the rules of forming sentences (*grammar*). The rules that allow us to combine symbols together in a language are called collectively the **syntax** of the language. Note that symbols inherently have no meaning of their own. The symbol "Fox" has no intrinsic meaning. That is, the letters "F" followed by "o" followed by "x" do not by themselves intrinsically represent an animal. We have learned to associate the animal with this grouping of letters—this symbol. **Semantics** in language refers to the process of attaching meaning to symbols. Just as in learning a foreign language, to learn to use a computer application such as Works to solve problems for us, we must learn both the semantics and the syntax of the language that Works defines.

## OPENING WORKS

In this lesson, you will learn how to move from the desktop into the Works context. If you have a network with a file server, you will learn how to access the file server disk to gain access to an application. The steps required to access the Works program will be different depending on the Macintosh configuration and environment in which you are working. We cover the three basic environments and configurations below; choose the one appropriate for you.

## USING WORKS WITH A FLOPPY DISK-BASED COMPUTER

If your computer has a hard disk or the software is resident on a file server, skip to the next section. If your Macintosh has only floppy drives, you will need to obtain a boot disk as well as a disk that contains the Works application (we will refer to this latter disk as the *Works* disk).

- Boot your system following the steps of Lesson 1 of Chapter 1. Close any open windows by clicking their *Close Boxes*.
- Into the second drive, insert the *Works* disk.

- Open the *Works* disk by double clicking its icon. (It may already be open.)
- You may find the *Microsoft Works* icon (shown in Figure 2.9) present when you open the *Works* disk. If this is not the case, look for a folder titled *Works Folder* (or something similar with *Works* in its title) and open it. Scroll as necessary until you see the *Microsoft Works* icon.

**Figure 2.9.** *Microsoft Works* Icon.

- Double click the *Microsoft Works* icon to bring the Works context into execution. You will see a window presented similar to that shown in Figure 2.10. Henceforth you will be issuing commands to Works as opposed to the desktop.

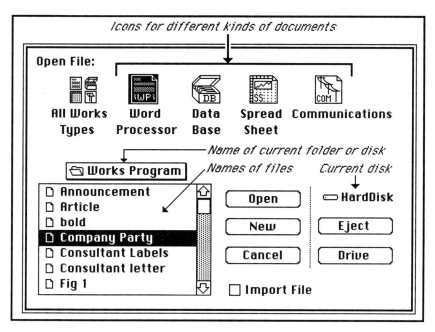

**Figure 2.10.** Example *Starting Works* Dialog Box.

You have now completed the portion of Lesson 1 appropriate for your environment, and you may proceed to Lesson 2. If you must terminate your work at this point and return later, skip to Lesson 7 to see how to quit the Works program.

# USING WORKS WITH A HARD DISK-BASED COMPUTER

If your computer is configured with a hard disk, then you will likely find the Works applications in a folder on the hard disk. Perform the following.

- Boot the computer using the instructions contained in Lesson 1 of Chapter 1.

- Open the hard disk by double clicking its icon. (It may already be open.)

- You may find the *Microsoft Works* icon (shown in Figure 2.9) present when you open the hard disk. If this is not the case, look for a folder titled *Works Folder* (or something similar with *Works* in its title) and open it. Scroll as necessary until you see the *Microsoft Works* icon.

- Double click the *Microsoft Works* icon to bring the Works context into execution. You will see a window presented similar to that shown in Figure 2.10. Henceforth you will be issuing commands to Works as opposed to the desktop.

You have now completed the portion of Lesson 1 appropriate for your environment, and you may proceed to Lesson 2. If you must terminate your work at this point and return later, skip to Lesson 7 to see how to quit the Works program.

# USING WORKS ON A FILE SERVER NETWORK

If your computer is attached to a network it is possible that you have a file server disk that is to be used for accessing Works.

- Boot the system using the steps you took in Lesson 1 of Chapter 1.

- Select the *Chooser* operation from the **Apple** menu. The **Apple** menu has the icon of an Apple and appears to the left of **File** in the main menu bar.

- A dialog box similar to that shown in Figure 2.11 will appear. Note that the actual icons and/or names may appear somewhat different from those shown here.

- Click on the icon named *AppleShare*. In the box titled *Select a file server:* a list of the file servers to which your computer may connect will appear. In Figure 2.11 there is only one whose name is *Furman Apple Server*. If your dialog box shows more than one server, you will have been told by your instructor or laboratory manager which server to access. Move the mouse pointer into this box and click on the appropriate file server name. This name will become highlighted as shown in Figure 2.11.

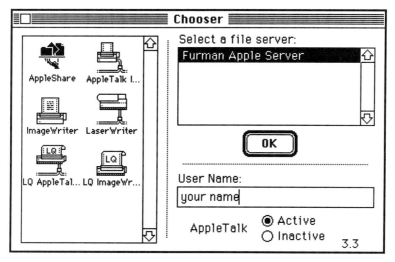

**Figure 2.11.** Illustration of the *Chooser* Dialog Box.

- You will have been given a user name for accessing the network by your instructor or the laboratory manager. Click in the box titled *User Name* and type in the name you were told to use. Then click the *OK* button.

- A dialog box such as that shown in Figure 2.12 will appear. Your user name as entered above will also be shown in the box titled *Name:*. Click on either the *Guest* or *Registered User* button as indicated by your instructor. If your instructor indicates it to be necessary, an appropriate password (obtained from your instructor) must be entered into the box titled *Password:*.

**Connect to the file server "Furman Apple Server" as:**

○ Guest
● Registered User

Name: |your name
Password: |        |  (Scrambled)

( Cancel )   ( Set Password )   ( OK )

v2.0.1

**Figure 2.12.** Illustration of the Sign-On Process to Use a File Server.

- When the appropriate information has been entered into the dialog box, click the *OK* button. A dialog box similar to that of Figure 2.13 will be presented. If the file server you selected has more than one disk drive you will see the name of each drive displayed.

- Select the name indicated by your instructor by clicking it.

- Then click *OK*.

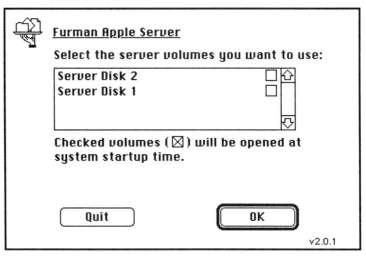

**Figure 2.13.** Illustration of Selecting a Server Disk.

- You will now be returned to the desktop and a new icon will appear in the disk area to the right side of the screen, such as shown in Figure 2.14. In this example the icon is titled *Server Disk 1*. From now on you may use this file server disk just like any other disk.

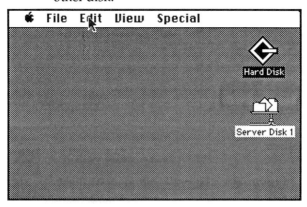

**Figure 2.14.** Illustration of the *Server Disk 1* Icon.

- Open the file server disk icon by double clicking it.

- You may find the *Microsoft Works* icon (shown in Figure 2.9) present when you open the file server disk. If this is not the case, look for a folder titled *Works Folder* (or something similar with *Works* in its title) and open it. Scroll as necessary until you see the *Microsoft Works* icon.

* Double click the *Microsoft Works* icon to bring the Works context into execution. You will see a window presented similar to that shown in Figure 2.10. Henceforth you will be issuing commands to Works as opposed to the desktop.

You have now completed the portion of Lesson 1 appropriate for your environment, and you may proceed to Lesson 2. If you must terminate your work at this point and return later, skip to Lesson 7 to see how to quit the Works program.

# NAVIGATING THE FILE SYSTEM FROM WITHIN WORKS

After completing this lesson, you will be able to:

❑ Open Works documents stored in any folder.

❑ Save Works documents in the folder of your choice

In the preceding chapter, we discussed in detail the nature of the hierarchical file system that you will be using on the Macintosh computer. You learned the basic techniques needed for managing and navigating within file hierarchies from the desktop context. To use the Works software package effectively, you will also need to understand how to navigate within this hierarchical file system when you are in the Works context.

In the desktop context, you may move from one disk to another by selecting the icon of interest and then double clicking to open a window to the disk to see its contents. When you are in Works, however, you cannot see the desktop. Thus, to manipulate documents in Works (that is, to open them or to decide where in the file structure your work will be stored), you must make use of the **File** menu *Open, Save,* or *Save As* commands.

These commands provide almost the same flexibility for navigating within the file system hierarchy as you have in the desktop context. However, you must manipulate the folders and disks in a slightly different way than you used on the desktop. For example, to switch from one disk to another disk within an application, you must use the *Drive* option presented in the dialog box that results from either the *Open, Save,* or *Save As* commands under the **File** menu as opposed to clicking a disk icon as you would on the desktop.

The *Open, Save,* and *Save As* commands present slightly different dialog boxes. In the discussion and examples that follow, we will use the *Save*

*As* dialog box, but the ideas can be easily transferred to the other kinds of dialog boxes. Note that the *Save* operation will present a dialog box only if the document has not been previously saved, that is, only if it is currently untitled. Otherwise the document will be saved over the previous version using the same path name.

A typical *Save As* dialog box is illustrated in Figure 2.15. The current context shown is the *Chapter2* folder. This is equivalent to having *Chapter2* as the active window on the desktop. Note that the contents of the folder are listed in the scroll area to the left of the dialog box. (We shall term this area the *scroll window*.) Note also the name of the current disk, *MyDisk*, above the *Eject* button at the right-hand side of the dialog box. If you were to type in a name for the document at this point and then click the *Save* button, the document would be saved in the *Chapter2* folder on *MyDisk*.

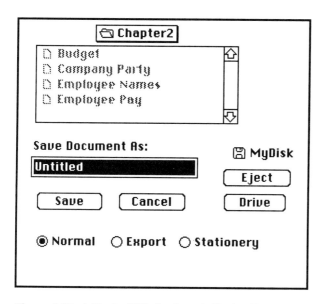

**Figure 2.15.** A Typical Works *Save As* Dialog Box.

We can pull down a menu that will show all the folders in the current complete path name for the folder that is "active." This is illustrated in Figure 2.16. By selecting a folder or disk from this menu, you can set a new active context.

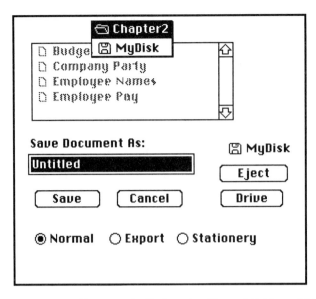

**Figure 2.16.** Viewing the Path to the *Chapter2* Folder within Works.

If we drag down to *MyDisk* and release the button, the names appearing will be those of the files and folders on that disk. This is illustrated in Figure 2.17. Thus, we have moved up one level in the hierarchy to the *MyDisk* level. If you were to type in a name for the document at this point and then click the *Save* button, the document would be saved at the disk level on *MyDisk*.

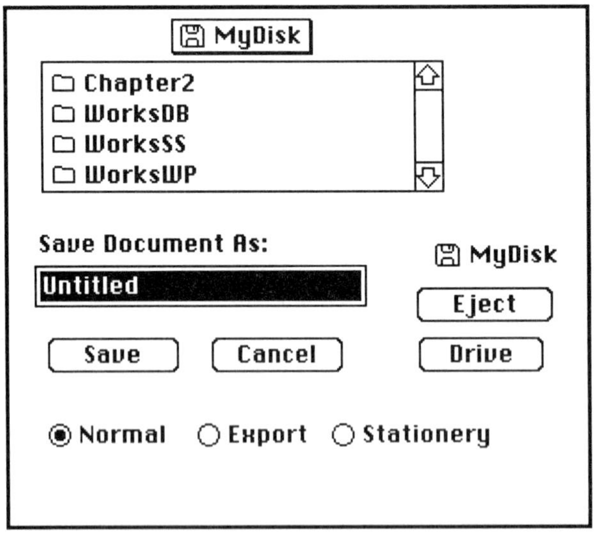

**Figure 2.17.** Moving up One Level to the *MyDisk* Context.

To move down in the hierarchy it is only necessary to open one of the folders shown displayed in the scroll window. For example, if we now double click on the *Works DB* folder in the scroll window of Figure 2.17, the screen of Figure 2.18 will appear. Thus, we have moved down one level in the hierarchy; the context is now set to be inside the *Works DB* folder.

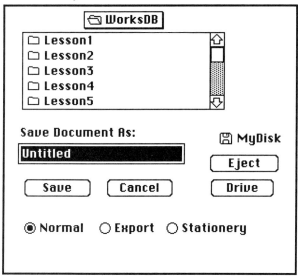

**Figure 2.18.** Moving Down into the *Works DB* Context.

By double clicking one of the folders displayed in the scroll window (such as the *Lesson1* folder), we would move down another level. If you were then to type in a name for the document and click the *Save* button, the document would be saved in the *Lesson1* folder inside the *Works DB* folder on *MyDisk*.

The *Drive* button within the *Open, Save,* or *Save As* command dialog boxes allows you to choose the disk from which you will read your file or to which you will store your file. By successively clicking on the *Drive* button you can select *any* of the disk drives attached to the computer. The choices also would include network file server disks, if you had allocated them previously.

The *Eject* button in this dialog box allows you to exchange the disk in a floppy disk drive. Thus, you may choose which disk you will use from your entire collection of disks. The *Eject* button will be shown dimmed if a hard disk drive is the drive selected, as it is not possible to eject the disk of a hard disk drive.

In summary, you may move at will up, down, and horizontally in the overall hierarchical file structure such as that shown in Figure 1.30. When you wish to move up in the hierarchy, pull down the menu from the folder icon shown above the scroll window and select a folder or disk at a higher level in the hierarchy. All folders and files available in the current context will be shown to you in the scroll window. When you wish to go deeper into the hierarchy, open a folder within the scroll window by double clicking on its icon symbol. Any possible context within the entire file system hierarchy can be reached by issuing commands of these two kinds and by changing the active disk using the *Drive* command.

To practice using the hierarchical file system within the Works context perform the following.

- Enter the Works context by double clicking the *Works* icon. (If you are continuing directly from Lesson 1, the Works program will already be open.)

- In the dialog box displayed you will see the name of the disk (and folder, assuming the program is inside a folder) containing the Works program, as illustrated in Figure 2.19.

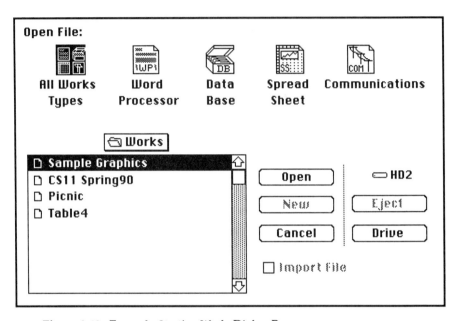

**Figure 2.19.** Example *Starting Works* Dialog Box.

- Insert the disk *MyDisk* into a floppy drive on your computer. (If you are using a computer with only floppy disk drives, you may first have to eject a disk.)

- Your disk should now become the active disk. (If your disk had already been inserted prior to starting Works, you could make your disk the active disk by repeatedly clicking on the *Drive* button in the dialog box until the disk drive holding your disk is selected.)

- In the scroll window of the dialog box you should see a list of folders displayed such as those shown in Figure 2.17. Double click the *Chapter2* name and a dialog box like the one in Figure 2.20 will be presented.

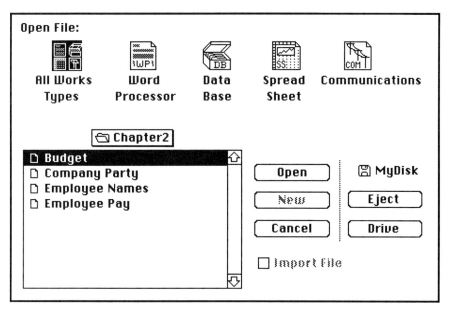

Figure 2.20. Works Open Dialog Box with the Folder *Chapter2* Active.

- Double click the *Company Party* name. This opens the word processing document *Company Party*, and you are presented with the window shown in Figure 2.21. (If you are using a computer with only floppy disk drives, you may be requested to swap disks. Perform these swaps as requested.)

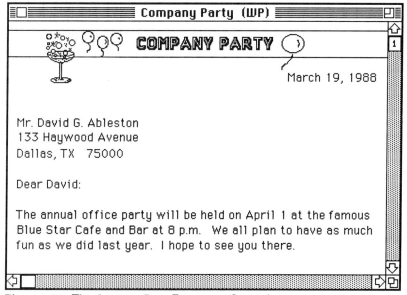

Figure 2.21. The *Company Party* Document Opened.

In the next section of this lesson you will save a copy of the *Company Party* document on your disk. Perform the following.

- Choose *Save As* from the **File** menu of Works WP. A dialog box will be presented. It will be similar to the one shown in Figure 2.15, but the file name *Company Party* will appear instead of *Untitled*.

- Pull down the path menu from the *Chapter2* folder as illustrated in Figure 2.16, selecting *MyDisk* as the new hierarchy level.

- Now edit the document name *Company Party* (just as you did icon names in Chapter 1) so that it reads *Company Party Backup*.

- Click *Save*. A copy of the document *Company Party* will now be saved by the new name *Company Party Backup* at the disk level on your disk. Notice that the name of the document you now have in your active window is *Company Party Backup*. Any time you save a document under a new name, the newly named copy becomes the active open document.

- Close the active document by clicking in its window's *Close Box*. You will then be returned to the Works starting dialog box (see Figure 2.10). In this dialog box you can observe that the document *Company Party Backup* is indeed stored on your disk.

You have now completed Lesson 2, and you may proceed to Lesson 3. If you must terminate your work at this point and return later, skip to Lesson 7 to see how to quit the Works program.

# ACCESSING AND MODIFYING A WORKS WP DOCUMENT

After completing this lesson, you will be able to:

❏ Access an existing word processing document.

❏ Make changes in paragraph justification within the document.

❏ Make changes in the ruler settings within the document.

❏ Save the modified document under a different name.

In this lesson, you will open an existing Works word processing document, make some simple modifications to that document, and then save the document under a different name. The purpose here is not to teach you details about Works WP, but just to give you a quick introduction to the "look and feel" of this module. Chapter 3 provides a thorough introduction to Works WP.

- If you are continuing directly from Lesson 2, you will have the Works program open with your disk the active disk. If you are starting this lesson from scratch, open the Works program and then insert your disk into a floppy drive. In either case you should see a screen like the one illustrated in Figure 2.22.

- Double click the name *Chapter2* in the scroll box, selecting the folder *Chapter2* as the active folder.

- Double click the *Company Party* name. This opens the word processing document *Company Party* and you are presented with the window shown in Figure 2.21.

- To change the line spacing in the main paragraph of the letter, first move the I-beam pointer into that paragraph and click.

- Now pull down the **Format** menu and drag to the *Spacing* selection. You will notice that when you select *Spacing*, a new submenu appears to the right. Move the mouse pointer directly right into the submenu and then drag down to the *Double* selection and release. Your document should now look similar to Figure 2.23.

- Examine some of the other submenus included under the **Format** menu. As you will see in Chapter 3, you will use this menu and its submenus often when creating your own word processing documents.

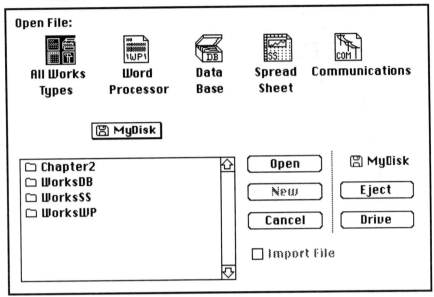

**Figure 2.22.** The Works *Starting Works* Dialog Box for Lesson 3.

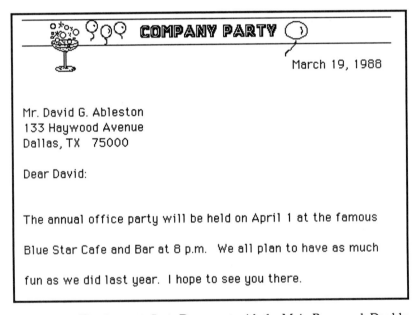

**Figure 2.23.** The *Company Party* Document with the Main Paragraph Double Spaced.

- At the top of your document window, you may see a ruler. If the ruler is not visible, select the *Show Ruler* command from the **Format** menu to display it.

- Rulers are used to set tab stops and align margins for paragraphs. Each paragraph in a Works WP document has its own unique ruler. Make sure the blinking insertion pointer is still located within the main paragraph of the letter. If it is not, place it there by moving the I-beam pointer inside the paragraph and clicking.

- You should have a ruler similar to that shown in Figure 2.24. Notice the location of the right margin marker at 5 1/2 in.

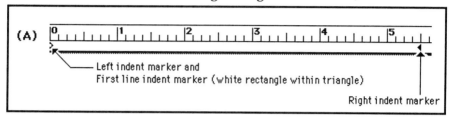

Figure 2.24. The Ruler for the Main Paragraph of the *Company Party* Document.

- Use the mouse to select and drag the right indent marker to the 6 1/2 in. location. Your document should now look similar to the one shown in Figure 2.25

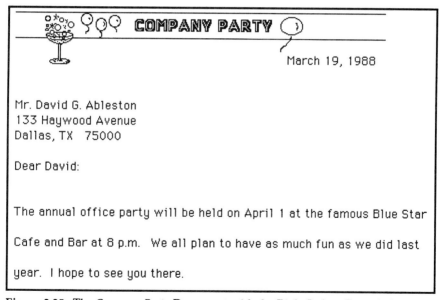

Figure 2.25. The *Company Party* Document with the Right Indent Extended.

In the next section of this lesson you will save a copy of the modified *Company Party* document inside the *Chapter2* folder contained on your disk. Perform the following.

- Choose *Save As* from the **File** menu of Works WP. A dialog box will be presented. It will be similar to the one shown in Figure 2.15, but the file name *Company Party* will appear instead of *Untitled*.

- Edit the document name *Company Party* (just as you did icon names in Chapter 1) so that it reads *Company Party Modified*.

- Click *Save*. A copy of the document *Company Party* will now be saved by the new name *Company Party Modified* in the *Chapter2* folder on your disk. Notice that the name of the document you now have in your active window is *Company Party Modified*. (Recall that any time you save a document under a new name, the newly named copy becomes the active open document.)

- Close the active document by clicking in its window's *Close Box*. You will then be returned to the Works starting dialog box (see Figure 2.10). In this dialog box you can observe that the document *Company Party Modified* is indeed stored in your *Chapter2* folder.

You have now completed Lesson 3, and you may proceed to Lesson 4. If you must terminate your work at this point and return later, skip to Lesson 7 to see how to quit the Works program.

# ACCESSING AND MODIFYING A WORKS DB DOCUMENT

After completing this lesson, you will be able to:

❏ Access an existing database.

❏ View the database data using both a form and a list display.

❏ Make changes in the database data.

❏ Change the layout of the database entry/display form.

❏ Save the modified database under a different name.

In this lesson, you will open an existing Works database, make some simple modifications to the database, and then save the database under a different name. The purpose here is not to teach you details about Works DB, but just to give you a quick introduction to the "look and feel" of this module. Chapter 4 will provide a thorough introduction to Works DB.

- If you are continuing directly from Lesson 3, you will have the Works program open with the *Chapter2* folder of your disk the active folder. If you are starting this lesson from scratch, open the Works program, insert your disk into a floppy drive, and then select *Chapter2* as the active folder by double clicking its name. In either case you should see a screen like the one illustrated in Figure 2.26.

- Double click the *Employee Names* name. This opens the database *Employee Names*, and you are presented with the window shown in Figure 2.27.

- Select the *Show List* command from the **Format** menu to change the appearance of the database to be similar to that shown in Figure 2.28.

- Place the selection pointer over the field containing the *Title* for employee Zebbley and click. This should produce a window like Figure 2.28. Notice that the record number (5) appears in the box to the left of the edit bar at the top of the window and the contents of the field selected ("Clerk") appears in the right box of the edit bar.

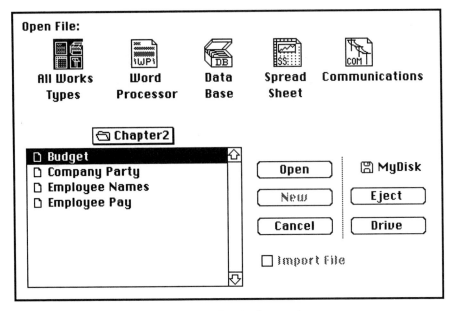

**Figure 2.26.** The *Starting Works* Dialog Box for Lesson 4.

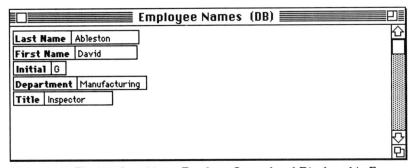

**Figure 2.27.** The *Employee Names* Database Opened and Displayed in Form Mode.

- Move the pointer into the right-hand box of the edit bar and notice that it changes to an I-beam pointer. Move it to a point just to the right of the text string *Clerk* and click to place the insertion pointer (blinking straight line) at that point. The situation is illustrated in Figure 2.28.

| 5 | | Clerk | | |

| Last Name | First Name | Initial | Department | Title |
|-----------|-----------|---------|------------|-------|
| Ableston | David | G | Manufacturing | Inspector |
| Highmaster | Jonathon | A | Marketing | Salesman |
| Jasper | Thomas | I | Marketing | Salesman |
| Siththe | Bernard | R | Grounds | Gardener |
| Zebbley | Arthur | P | Accounting | Clerk |

Employee Names (DB)

**Figure 2.28.** Preparing to Modify the *Title* Data for an Employee.

- Now press the *Delete* key five times to erase the text *Clerk,* and then type in the title *Auditor.* Click the *Check* box (✔) to make this change in the database itself. Your window should now look exactly like Figure 2.29.

| 5 | | Auditor | | | |

Employee Names (DB)

| Last Name | First Name | Initial | Department | Title | |
|-----------|-----------|---------|------------|-------|---|
| Ableston | David | G | Manufacturing | Inspector | |
| Highmaster | Jonathon | A | Marketing | Salesman | |
| Jasper | Thomas | I | Marketing | Salesman | |
| Siththe | Bernard | R | Grounds | Gardener | |
| Zebbley | Arthur | P | Accounting | Auditor | |
| | | | | | |
| | | | | | |

**Figure 2.29.** The Revised Database.

- Select the *Show Form* command from the **Format** menu to change the appearance of the database to be similar to that shown in Figure 2.27.

The underlying data in the database is unchanged by the mode (*Form* or *List*) that we choose for viewing it. The *List* mode is convenient when you wish to view many records together, and the *Form* mode is convenient for viewing records one at a time and especially for entering new data into the database. In fact, the form can be redesigned to make the data entry more naturally match written forms from which the data are transcribed. If the pointer is moved over the name of a field, it turns into a hand symbol, as shown in Figure 2.30. The field can then be dragged to a new position on the form.

- Try moving one or more of the fields in this way.

Employee Names (DB)

| Last Name | Zebbley |
| First Name | Arthur |
| Initial | P |
| Department | Accounting |
| Title | Auditor |

**Figure 2.30.** Preparing to Move a Field on an Entry/Display Form.

- Use the technique just described to configure the form as shown in Figure 2.31.

Employee Names (DB)

| Last Name | Zebbley | First Name | Arthur | Initial | P |

| Department | Accounting |

| Title | Auditor |

**Figure 2.31.** The Redesigned Form.

In the next section of this lesson you will save a copy of the *Employee Names* database inside the *Chapter2* folder contained on your disk. Perform the following.

- Choose *Save As* from the **File** menu of Works DB. A dialog box will be presented. It will be similar to the one shown in Figure 2.15, but the file name *Employee Names* will appear instead of *Untitled*.

- Edit the database name *Employee Names* so that it reads *Employee Names Modified*.

- Click *Save*. A copy of the database *Employee Names* will now be saved by the new name *Employee Names Modified* in the *Chapter2* folder on your disk.

- Close the active document by clicking in its window's *Close Box*. You will then be returned to the Works starting dialog box (see Figure 2.10). In this dialog box you can observe that the document *Employee Names Modified* is indeed stored in your *Chapter2* folder.

You have now completed Lesson 4, and you may proceed to Lesson 5. If you must terminate your work at this point and return later, skip to Lesson 7 to see how to quit the Works program.

# ACCESSING AND MODIFYING A WORKS SS DOCUMENT

After completing this lesson, you will be able to:

❏ Access an existing spreadsheet document.

❏ Make changes in some of the data used and observe the way the spreadsheet automatically recalculates its values.

❏ Make changes in the data used and observe the way spreadsheet charts are automatically adjusted.

❏ Save the modified spreadsheet document under a different name.

In this lesson, you will open an existing Works spreadsheet, make some simple modifications to the spreadsheet, and then save the spreadsheet under a different name. The purpose here is not to teach you details about Works SS, but just to give you a quick introduction to the "look and feel" of this module. Chapter 5 will provide a thorough introduction to Works SS.

- If you are continuing directly from Lesson 4, you will have the Works program open with the *Chapter2* folder of your disk the active folder. If you are starting this lesson from scratch, open the Works program, insert your disk into a floppy drive, and then select *Chapter2* as the active folder by double clicking its name. In either case you should see a screen like the one illustrated in Figure 2.26.

- Double click the *Budget* name. This opens the spreadsheet *Budget*, and you are presented with the window shown in Figure 2.32.

- A pie chart has been created to graph the percentages spent for various budget categories. To access the chart, select the *Draw Chart* command from the **Chart** menu. Then double-click the chart name *Budget Chart* in the scroll box that is presented. This action will cause the chart to be displayed in a window (on top of the spread-sheet window).

- Move (drag by the *Title Bar*) and resize the chart window and the spreadsheet window (drag the grow boxes in their lower right corners) so that your screen has an appearance similar to that shown in Figure 2.33.

| | A | B | C | D | E |
|---|---|---|---|---|---|
| 1 | | | | | |
| 2 | | Amount | Percentage | | |
| 3 | Rent | $450.00 | 27.52% | | |
| 4 | Car | $240.00 | 14.68% | | |
| 5 | Food/Entertainment | $480.00 | 29.36% | | |
| 6 | Insurance/Medical | $175.00 | 10.70% | | |
| 7 | Utilities | $190.00 | 11.62% | | |
| 8 | Miscellaneous | $100.00 | 6.12% | | |
| 9 | | | | | |
| 10 | Total | $1635.00 | 100.00% | | |
| 11 | | | | | |
| 12 | | | | | |

Budget (SS)

**Figure 2.32.** The *Budget* Spreadsheet Opened.

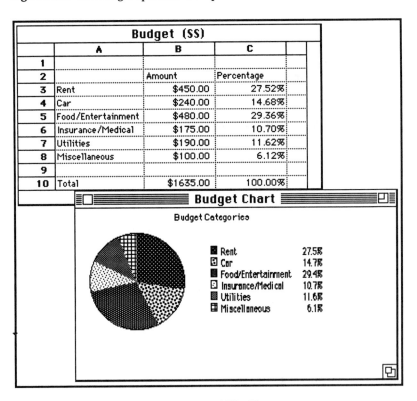

**Figure 2.33.** The *Budget* Spreadsheet and Pie Chart.

- Click the *Close Box* in the chart window to close that window.
- Place the selection pointer over cell B8 in the spreadsheet and click. This should produce a spreadsheet window like Figure 2.34. The contents of the cell selected will appear in the right-hand portion of the edit bar.

- Move the pointer into the right-hand box of the edit bar and notice that it changes to an I-beam pointer. Move it to a point just to the right of the text string *100* and click to place the insertion pointer (blinking straight line) at that point.

- Now press the *Delete* key three times to erase the text *100* and then type in the number *500*. Click the *Check* box (✔) to make this change in the spreadsheet itself. Your spreadsheet window should now look exactly like Figure 2.34. Notice that the value *500* is format-ted in dollar notation automatically in the spreadsheet itself.

| | A | B | C | D | E |
|---|---|---|---|---|---|
| | | | Budget (SS) | | |
| 1 | | | | | |
| 2 | | Amount | Percentage | | |
| 3 | Rent | $450.00 | 22.11% | | |
| 4 | Car | $240.00 | 11.79% | | |
| 5 | Food/Entertainment | $480.00 | 23.59% | | |
| 6 | Insurance/Medical | $175.00 | 8.60% | | |
| 7 | Utilities | $190.00 | 9.34% | | |
| 8 | Miscellaneous | $500.00 | 24.57% | | |
| 9 | | | | | |
| 10 | Total | $2035.00 | 100.00% | | |
| 11 | | | | | |
| 12 | | | | | |

**Figure 2.34.** The *Budget* Spreadsheet after a Change in the *Miscellaneous* Amount.

- Now select the *Draw Chart* command from the **Chart** menu. Then double click the chart name *Budget Chart* in the scroll box that is presented. This action will again cause the chart to be displayed in a window. Your screen will now look like Figure 2.35. Notice that the chart appears in the same position and has the same size as it was when it was last closed. Notice also that the chart has been automatically updated to include the new values calculated when the *Miscellaneous* amount was changed to $500. Close the chart window.

In the next section of this lesson you will save a copy of the *Budget* spreadsheet inside the *Chapter2* folder contained on your disk. Perform the following.

- Choose *Save As* from the **File** menu of Works SS. A dialog box will be presented. It will be similar to the one shown in Figure 2.15, but the file name *Budget* will appear instead of *Untitled*.

- Edit the spreadsheet name *Budget* so that it reads *Budget Modified*.

- Click *Save*. A copy of the spreadsheet *Budget* will now be saved by the new name *Budget Modified* in the *Chapter2* folder on your disk.

- Close the active document by clicking in its window's *Close Box*. You will then be returned to the Works starting dialog box (see Figure 2.10). In this dialog box you can observe that the document *Budget Modified* is indeed stored in your *Chapter2* folder.

You have now completed Lesson 5, and you may proceed to Lesson 6. If you must terminate your work at this point and return later, skip to Lesson 7 to see how to quit the Works program.

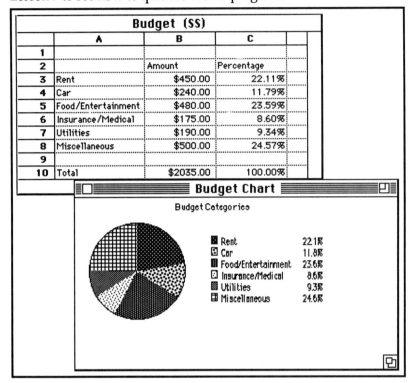

**Figure 2.35.** The Revised *Budget* Spreadsheet and Chart.

LESSON 6 _____

# USING THE WORKS HELP FEATURE

After completing this lesson, you will be able to:

❑ Access the Works *Help* scroll box.

❑ Locate the entry of interest in the *Help* scroll box by using the Works Help mouse pointer within various Works contexts.

In this lesson, you will see how to use the on-line Works *Help* file. You must have a Works document open in order to access the *Help* file. There are two ways to access this file. One is by selecting the *Help* command from the **Window** menu. This action will place you at the beginning of the *Help* file for the module you are currently in. You can then scroll through the *Help* window presented to find the information you seek. A second method of access is to first open the *Help* window as just described and use the special *Help* pointer (?) to then select the command about which you have a question. You choose the command just as if you wish to execute it, but the action that is taken is to present you with the *Help* window positioned at the point where information about the command is found. We will illustrate these techniques by using a spreadsheet document, but they can be applied identically for the other types of Works documents

- If you are continuing directly from Lesson 5, you will have the Works program open with the *Chapter2* folder of your disk the active folder. If you are starting this lesson from scratch, open the Works program, insert your disk into a floppy drive, and then select *Chapter2* as the active folder by double clicking its name. In either case you should see a screen like the one illustrated in Figure 2.26.

- Double click the *Budget* name. This opens the spreadsheet *Budget*, and you are presented with the window shown in Figure 2.32.

- Now select the *Help* command from the **Window** menu. You should see a screen like the one shown in Figure 2.36.

- Scroll the *Help* window to examine some of its contents.

- Move the mouse pointer to the menu bar and notice that it has changed to the shape of a question mark (?). Use the pointer to select the command *Set Cell Attributes* from the **Format** menu. This action will produce the *Help* window shown in Figure 2.37.

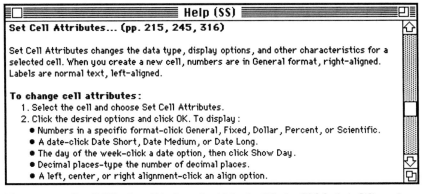

| Budget (SS) | | | | | | |
|---|---|---|---|---|---|---|
| | A | B | C | D | E | F |
| 1 | | | | | | |
| 2 | | Amount | Percentage | | | |
| 3 | Rent | $450.00 | 27.52% | | | |
| 4 | Car | $240.00 | 14.68% | | | |
| 5 | Food/Entertainment | $480.00 | 29.36% | | | |
| 6 | Insurance/Medical | $175.00 | 10.70% | | | |
| 7 | Utilities | | | | | |
| 8 | Miscellaneo | | | | | |

Help (SS)

**Spreadsheet**

Help provides information about commands for the tool you're using. To get Help for a different tool, open a file in that tool, and then choose Help.

**If you're not sure which command you need help with:**
√ Scroll the window to find the information you need.

**If you know the command name:**
1. Move the pointer outside the Help window.
2. Choose the command from its menu. Help displays information about the command.

**To quit using Help:**
√ Click the close box in the Help window's title bar.

**Figure 2.36.** Scroll Window Displayed within the Works SS Module When the *Help* Command Is Selected from the **Window** Menu.

Help (SS)

**Set Cell Attributes... (pp. 215, 245, 316)**

Set Cell Attributes changes the data type, display options, and other characteristics for a selected cell. When you create a new cell, numbers are in General format, right-aligned. Labels are normal text, left-aligned.

**To change cell attributes:**
1. Select the cell and choose Set Cell Attributes.
2. Click the desired options and click OK. To display:
   ● Numbers in a specific format-click General, Fixed, Dollar, Percent, or Scientific.
   ● A date-click Date Short, Date Medium, or Date Long.
   ● The day of the week-click a date option, then click Show Day.
   ● Decimal places-type the number of decimal places.
   ● A left, center, or right alignment-click an align option.

**Figure 2.37.** Scroll Window Displayed within the Works SS Module When the *Set Cell Attributes* Command Is Selected from the **Format** Menu Using the Help (?) Pointer.

- Now use the **?** pointer to select the command *Draw Chart* from the **Chart** menu. This action will produce the *Help* window shown in Figure 2.38.

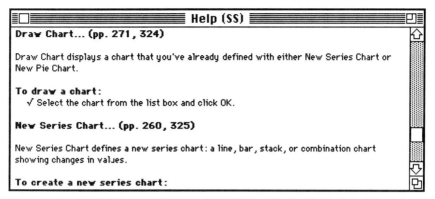

**Figure 2.38.** Scroll Window Displayed within the Works SS Module When the *Draw Chart* Command Is Selected from the **Chart** Menu Using the Help (?) Pointer.

- Finally use the **?** pointer to select the command *Save As* from the **File** menu. This action will produce the *Help* window shown in Figure 2.39.

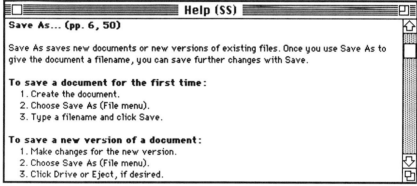

**Figure 2.39.** Scroll Window Displayed within the Works SS Module When the *Save As* Command Is Selected from the **File** Menu Using the Help (?) Pointer.

- Close the *Help* window by clicking its *Close Box*.
- Close the active document by clicking in its window's *Close Box*. You will then be returned to the Works starting dialog box (see Figure 2.10).

## LESSON 7

# QUITTING WORKS

After completing this lesson, you will be able to:

❑ Quit the Works program.

❑ Make a Works Desktop file to save a particular configuration of Works windows for quick access in a later Works session.

In this lesson, you will see how to quit the Works program and, if you desire, save specific window configurations to be opened and displayed automatically when you return to Works later.

- If you are continuing directly from Lesson 6, you will have the Works program open with the *Chapter2* folder of your disk the active folder. If you are starting this lesson from scratch, open the Works program, insert your disk into a floppy drive, and then select *Chapter2* as the active folder by double clicking its name.In either case you should see a screen like the one illustrated in Figure 2.26.

- To quit Works from this configuration (with all documents closed), simply select the *Quit* command from the **File** menu.

- Restart Works. Make your disk the active disk and double click the *Chapter2* folder name. You will again be presented with a screen like the one illustrated in Figure 2.26.

- Double click the name *Budget* to open the *Budget* spreadsheet. When it is open, change the *Miscellaneous* amount in cell B8 to $400 (see Lesson 5 if you need help with this step).

- Select the *Open* command from the **File** menu. Double click the name *Company Party* to open the *Company Party* word processing document.

- Now both the spreadsheet *Budget* and the word processing document *Company Party* are open. You can switch from document to document by selecting the one you desire from the **Window** menu. Try this to see how it works.

- Select the *Quit* command from the **File** menu.

- You will be asked if you wish to save the changes made to *Budget*. Answer *No*. Both *Budget* and *Company Party* will be closed automatically. Note that you were not asked about *Company Party* because no changes had been made to it.

- Restart Works. Make your disk the active disk and double click the *Chapter2* folder name. You will again be presented with a screen like the one illustrated in Figure 2.26.

- Double click the name *Budget* to open the *Budget* spreadsheet.

- Select the *Open* command from the **File** menu. Double click the name *Company Party* to open the *Company Party* word processing document.

- Select the *Make Works Desktop* command from the **File** menu. This action allows you to create a document that you can use later to open Works with the same documents and windows open as you have open at present. You will get a dialog box (similar to a *Save As* dialog box) in which you are asked to name this document. Accept the default name *Works Desktop* and click *Save*.

- Now select the *Quit* command from the **File** menu.

- Locate the icon shown in Figure 2.40 in your *Chapter2* folder on your disk. Double-click the icon. Observe that this causes Works to be opened and the two documents *Budget* and *Company Party* to be opened as well. Use the **Window** menu to switch between the documents to verify this. You can save as many Works Desktop files as you wish (under different names, of course), so that you can open any configuration of Works documents you desire with a single double click. Once you have created a Works Desktop file and then modify the documents involved, you need not create another Works Desktop file; the modified documents will be automatically opened when the previous Works Desktop icon is double clicked.

- Quit Works once again by selecting the *Quit* command from the **File** menu.

- Shut down your computer following the directions given in Lesson 1 of Chapter 1.

**Figure 2.40.** The *Works Desktop* Icon.

# 3

# USING WORKS WP

When you have completed the Works WP tutorial you will be able to:

- ❏ Create, enter, and save a WP document.
- ❏ Edit a WP document.
- ❏ Employ different fonts, font sizes and styles in your WP documents.
- ❏ Change paragraph alignment, line spacing, and indentation.
- ❏ Use tabs for formatting.
- ❏ Check spelling within your WP documents.
- ❏ Search and replace text within your WP documents.
- ❏ Create and use macros.
- ❏ Use the Works drawing tools.
- ❏ Create headers and footers for Works documents.
- ❏ Set page margins for Works documents.
- ❏ Preview documents on screen before printing.
- ❏ Print Works documents.
- ❏ Incorporate graphics into WP documents.

## TUTORIAL OUTLINE

CHAPTER 3. USING WORKS WP

# WHAT IS WORKS WP?

Works WP is a word processing program designed to allow you to prepare documents. With Works WP you can compose any document that would ordinarily be written by using pencil and paper or using a typewriter.

Works WP is both easy to use and powerful enough for preparing documents of moderate complexity. It is more than sufficient for most correspondence, business reports, and papers for school assignments. With Works you can do the following.

Create word processing documents.

Save, retrieve, and print created documents.

Preview full-page layouts before they are printed.

Insert and delete characters, lines, and paragraphs within a document.

Move parts of a document by "cut and paste" operations.

Format paragraphs, controlling parameters such as spaces between lines, left and right margins, left and right justification of text, centering of text, tab settings, and indentation.

Format characters and strings of characters by having them appear as bold, underlined, or italicized.

Place text above or below the line as superscripts or subscripts.

Insert page headers and footers, with automatic page numbering.

Use a variety of text font styles and sizes.

Check spelling.

Incorporate graphics within documents.

Figure 3.1 shows a document produced by using the Works WP module. Such visually appealing combinations of text and graphics can be created with very little effort within Works.

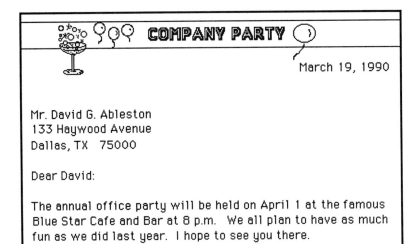

March 19, 1990

Mr. David G. Ableston
133 Haywood Avenue
Dallas, TX  75000

Dear David:

The annual office party will be held on April 1 at the famous
Blue Star Cafe and Bar at 8 p.m.  We all plan to have as much
fun as we did last year.  I hope to see you there.

**Figure 3.1.** A Simple Word Processing Document Using Works' Text and
Drawing Capabilities.

# OVERVIEW OF WORD PROCESSING CONCEPTS

In this section we examine some word processing concepts that apply to
almost any word processing system.  You should note that there are many
similarities between using a word processor and using a typewriter, but
there are also many differences because of the flexibility that is possible
with a computer.

Working with a word processor can be divided into six major functions
as follows.

Creating a document.

Saving a document.

Entering text.

Editing text.

Formatting text.

Printing a document.

These functions will be discussed as if they were independent, but in
practice you can use them in many sequences, jumping back and forth
between them as is convenient.

Creating a document refers to giving a command, *New* in Works WP,
to cause a new document to be created.  This document is ready to receive
the information that you enter through the keyboard or other input device.

The document is stored in the volatile RAM and will be lost unless it is saved.

In Works WP, a document is saved in nonvolatile form as a disk file by giving a command, *Save* or *Save As*. The first time the document is saved, you will be asked to give a name to the document. Select a meaningful name, one that will help you remember the contents of the document.

Entering text involves using the keyboard to type the document. If you make an error during the typing and notice the error immediately, you can use the *Delete* (or *Backspace*) key to correct the error. Otherwise, it can be corrected during the edit phase.

**Wordwrap.** An important feature associated with entering text is *wordwrap*. When a word is typed that would extend beyond the right margin, it is moved (wrapped) to the beginning of the next line. In Figure 3.2, part (A) shows the word *demonstrating* extending beyond the right margin. Thus, it is automatically moved to the next line as shown in part (B). Actually, as soon as the *a* in *demonstrating* is typed, the partial word moves to the next line because even the partial word will not fit on the line. Part (C) shows the appearance of the text after several lines have been entered. The *Return* (or *Enter*) key has not been pressed during the entry of these sentences. Note that this feature of a word processor differs from an ordinary typewriter on which you must use a carriage return at the end of each line. When using a word processor, you will press the *Return* key *only* when you wish to start a new paragraph.

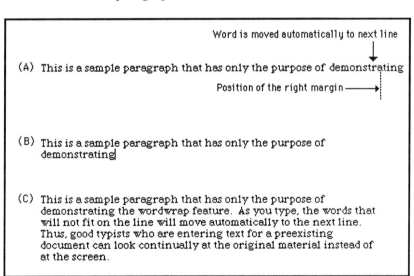

**Figure 3.2.** Illustration of the Wordwrap Feature.

**Paragraph.** A paragraph in a word processing document consists of the lines typed between pressing the *Return* key. In other words, pressing the *Return* key ends a paragraph. It is very important that you follow this convention because a paragraph is automatically reformatted when, for example, ruler margins are reset, line spacing is changed, text is added, or text is deleted — but only the text within the affected paragraph is altered. Hence, you will not want to have carriage returns embedded in what you think of as a single paragraph, because the word processor will treat such text as multiple paragraphs.

When the *Return* key is pressed, an **invisible control character** (i.e., a character that does not show on the printed document) is entered into the text to serve as a symbol for the end of a paragraph. Many other invisible control characters are entered to serve as signals that some action is to be taken by the word processor. For example, pressing the *Tab* key, which moves the typing location to preset column positions, enters a control character whose purpose is to position the text at some specified column position. Many of the actions that cause changes in the formatted appearance of the text will be entered in the document as invisible control characters.

Conversely, deleting an invisible character may change the appearance of the text. For example, deleting a blank space at the end of a paragraph may remove the *Return* mark and cause the paragraph to become part of the next paragraph, assuming all of the formatting of the next paragraph. Some word processors have a command to cause the invisible characters to be displayed in the text on the screen, which is valuable in many formatting situations.

Editing a document is the process of modifying a previously entered document. Editing changes the content of the document in some way. For example, new text can be entered in a document at any location by placing the insertion pointer at the desired location and then typing the text. Any text entered will take on the character formatting of the text at the insertion point. Existing text can be replaced by selecting the text (highlighting) by dragging and typing the new word as shown for the word *good* in part A of Figure 3.3. Part B shows the result of typing the word *excellent* while the word *good* is highlighted.

This example illustrates an important idea. To perform various operations during editing, the procedure is to *select and then do*. *Select* defines the object to be operated on. *Do* defines the operation to be performed. When editing is discussed for Works WP, you will see many applications of *select and then do*.

Copying is accomplished by selecting the text to be copied, using the *Copy* command that places a copy on the Clipboard, placing the pointer at the location where the copy is to be inserted, and giving the *Paste* command. Both the *Copy* and *Cut* commands place a copy of the selected text on the Clipboard. Details will be described a little later.

**Formatting.** Formatting a document is the process of changing the appearance of the text. Note that formatting changes only the appearance of the document; there is not a change in the content of the document as is the case with editing.

```
(A)   This is a sample paragraph that has only the purpose of
      demonstrating the wordwrap feature. As you type, the words that
      will not fit on the line will move automatically to the next line.
      Thus, [good] typists who are entering text for a preexisting
      document can look continually at the original material instead of
      at the screen.

(B)   This is a sample paragraph that has only the purpose of
      demonstrating the wordwrap feature. As you type, the words that
      will not fit on the line will move automatically to the next line.
      Thus, excellent typists who are entering text for a preexisting
      document can look continually at the original material instead of
      at the screen.
```

**Figure 3.3.** Illustration of the Selection Process.

There are two basic kinds of formatting: character and paragraph formatting. **Character formatting** is concerned with changing the appearance of an individual character or sequence of characters. A document can use different character fonts, styles, or sizes for emphasis or to create visual interest. Figure 3.4 shows examples of character fonts that can be used, character style names with corresponding examples, and character sizes with corresponding examples. Fonts are also available for foreign alphabets such as Greek, Russian, Hebrew, and so on.

Character formatting is also used to create superscripts and subscripts. Superscript characters are raised above the normal position for a character in a line and are often used for footnote reference numbers. For example, the "2" in "Totals$^2$" is a superscript. Subscript characters are below the normal position for a character in a line. For example, the "i" in "$V_i$" is a subscript. Both superscripts and subscripts are used often in mathematical notation.

**Paragraph formatting** is used to change the features associated with entire paragraphs. For example, you may customize paragraph margins, line spacing, justification (alignment of text along one or both margins), first line indenting, tabs, and other features for each paragraph. Thus, paragraphs with almost any desired appearance are possible.

Of course, all word processors provide ways to print documents. A document is not changed by printing a copy. During the time that the document is being printed, you may not be able to use the computer for anything else. However, if your network provides for spooling of the documents to be printed, once your document is **spooled** (i.e., copied to the file server), you will be able to continue work even though the printing may not be finished.

| Character Fonts | Character Style | Example |
|---|---|---|
| Chicago | Plain Text | wordwrap |
| Courier | **Bold** | **wordwrap** |
| Geneva | *Italic* | *wordwrap* |
| New York | Underline | wordwrap |
| Venice | Outline | wordwrap |
| | Shadow | wordwrap |

| Character Size | Example |
|---|---|
| 9 Point | wordwrap |
| 10 Point | wordwrap |
| 12 Point | wordwrap |
| 14 Point | wordwrap |
| 18 Point | wordwrap |
| 24 Point | wordwrap |

**Figure 3.4.** Sample Character Fonts, Styles, and Sizes.

A *Page Setup* (or equivalent) command is used to set the major features of a page such as page height, page length, margins, and the locations of footnotes. The page margins and the paragraph margins (properly called the paragraph indents) have slightly different meanings. The **page margin** is measured from the edge of the page and is set using the *Page Setup* command. The **paragraph indent** is measured from the location of the page margin. Hence, changing the page margins will change the indents correspondingly. In addition, the first line of a paragraph may also be indented. These features are illustrated in Figure 3.5.

Using a word processor is a relatively natural activity for most people. This is the result of the success of the designers of a word processor in translating normal actions with a typewriter into commands for the word processor. The most common action is entering text, and this process is as efficient as possible; pressing a key on the keyboard is all that is necessary. Features analogous to the physical cut and paste actions, with scissors and rubber cement, that are used in revising typewritten documents will normally appear as *Cut* and *Paste* commands. Your intuition will often suffice for finding and using a word processing command. Note that you do not have to master all features of a word processing language to use a word processor. As you write more complex documents, you can learn the necessary new commands to accomplish your goals.

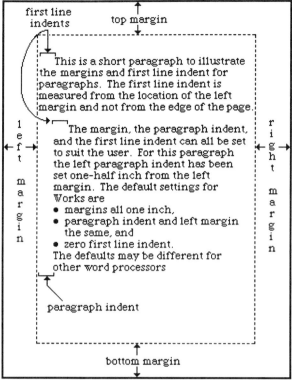

first line indents

top margin

This is a short paragraph to illustrate the margins and first line indent for paragraphs. The first line indent is measured from the location of the left margin and not from the edge of the page.

The margin, the paragraph indent, and the first line indent can all be set to suit the user. For this paragraph the left paragraph indent has been set one-half inch from the left margin. The default settings for Works are
- margins all one inch,
- paragraph indent and left margin the same, and
- zero first line indent.
The defaults may be different for other word processors

left margin

right margin

paragraph indent

bottom margin

**Figure 3.5.** Organization of a Word Processing Document Page.

# CREATING, ENTERING, AND SAVING A WP DOCUMENT

After completing this lesson, you will be able to:

❏ Create a word processing document.

❏ Enter text into a document.

❏ Save a document.

## CREATING A NEW WP DOCUMENT

To create a new word processing document, perform the following.

• Insert your disk that contains the folder *Works WP* (which in turn contains folders *Lesson1*, *Lesson2*, etc.) that you created in Lesson 5 of Chapter 1. If you have not completed that lesson, do so before beginning this lesson. We will store various documents to be created in this chapter in the folders *Lesson1*, *Lesson2*, and so on.

• Open Works by double clicking the *Works* icon.

• Begin the process of creating a Works WP document by double clicking the word processing icon, which is highlighted in Figure 3.6. Alternately, you could highlight the word processing icon, and select the *New* command in the **File** menu.

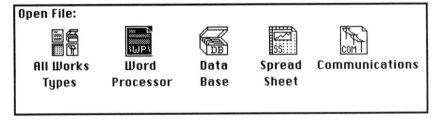

**Figure 3.6.** Module Icons Displayed After Works Is Opened.

• Examine the initial Works WP window, which has the appearance shown in Figure 3.7.

The window contains two pointers: a blinking vertical line called the **insertion pointer** which is the point at which text is entered, and the **I-beam pointer**, a nonblinking pointer whose position is controlled by the mouse. As text is entered, the insertion pointer will move along to indicate the new location for entering text. The I-beam is used to move the insertion pointer to any position in previously typed text. The I-beam pointer may not be visible initially, but it will appear as soon as you move the mouse.

At the top of the window is a ruler that shows the current format for paragraphs. A full description of how to read a ruler and to modify its settings to structure paragraphs within your document will be given later; here you will make one simple adjustment. Each paragraph has its own ruler which determines its indent settings and tabs. Rulers can be hidden by selecting the *Hide Ruler* command from the **Format** menu. Hiding the rulers allows more text to be displayed in the window.

- The right indent marker, the black triange located at 6 inches in Figure 3.7, is normally at 6.5 inches. Drag the right indent marker to 6 inches as shown in Figure 3.7

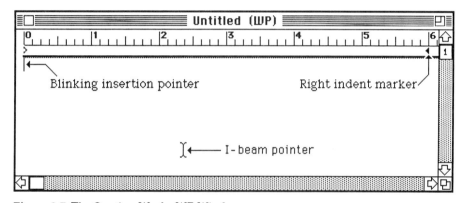

**Figure 3.7.** The Starting Works WP Window.

# ENTERING TEXT

To enter information in the window, you type just as you would with a typewriter. Remember that the *Return* key should be pressed *only* when you reach the end of a paragraph. To create a blank line between paragraphs, press the *Return* key an extra time at the end of a paragraph. Each additional pressing of the *Return* key will insert an additional blank line.

In this part of the lesson you are to enter the text that is shown in Figure 3.8. You are to type it exactly as you see it. (The text is 10 point New York font.) Do not be concerned if the lines you type end with different words from those shown in the box. As you type, if you make an error and notice it immediately, use the *Delete* key to backspace and delete characters. Then type the word correctly. If you discover an error after typing several subsequent words, ignore the error for now. Later during the editing of the document, you can correct these errors.

Perform the following.

- If the right indent marker is not at 6.0 inches, drag it to that location.

- Set the font to New York by selecting it from the **Font** submenu under the **Format** menu.  Set the font size to 10 by accessing it in the **Size** submenu.

Document line:

- Type the first line that contains the word *Document*.  Press the *Return* key to make the first line a paragraph.

- Press the *Return* key again to leave a blank line.

Main paragraph:

- Type the body of the document shown in Figure 3.8 from *A word processor* through *including:*.  Press the *Return* key to end the paragraph.

- Press the *Return* key again to leave a blank line.

Numbered paragraphs:

- Type the line that starts with the number 1.  At the end of the line after the period, press the *Return* key to make it a paragraph.

- Type the line that starts with the number 2.  At the end of the line after the period,  press the *Return* key to make it a paragraph.

- Type the line that starts with the number 3.  After the period, do not press the *Return* key, so that the insertion point remains at the end of the line.

## SAVING A DOCUMENT

The title bar for the document you have just created contains *Untitled (WP)*. This means that you have not yet saved and named the document.  The *WP* indicates that this is a word processing document as opposed to the other possible kinds of documents in Works.  Selecting the *Save* or *Save As* command from the **File** menu allows you to save the document with whatever name you wish in whatever position within your disk hierarchy you wish.

Perform the following.

- Insert your disk into a floppy disk drive.

- Select the *Save As* command in the **File** menu.

- Navigate until your disk is the active disk.  A dialog box similar to that shown in Figure 3.9.  Open the *Works WP* folder that you created in Lesson 5 of Chapter 1.

- Now open the *Lesson1* folder found inside the *Works WP* folder.

- Type the name *Practice1<your initials>* into the *Save Document As:* information box.  For example, if your name is John Doe, you would type the name *Practice1JD*, as shown in Figure 3.9.

- Click the *Save* button on the dialog box to save the document.

You have now completed Lesson 1.  If you do not wish to proceed directly to the next lesson, quit Works by clicking the *Close Box* of the document and then selecting the *Quit* command from the **File** menu, clean up the desktop, and shut down your computer.

---

Document

A word processor such as that found in Works can change the way that you think about writing a document. Creating a WP paper is less trouble than ordinary typing because errors can be corrected properly as they occur. It is however during the revising of a document that word processing really shines. Revising becomes a satisfying manipulating activity instead of a time-consuming retyping job. Learning to use a word processor is well worth the time required. A document can be modified in many ways, including:

1. Inserting new word, lines, or paragraphs.
2. Copying or moving blocks of information to new locations.
3. Changing the format of the entire document or the format of various paragraphs.

---

**Figure 3.8.** Text to Be Entered into a Works Word Processing Document.

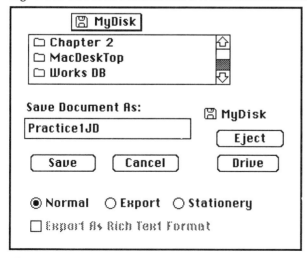

**Figure 3.9.** The Dialog Box for Saving a Works Document.

# LESSON 2

# EDITING A DOCUMENT

After completing this lesson, you will be able to:

❏ Insert text into a document.

❏ Select text to be moved and/or deleted in a document.

❏ Move text in a document.

❏ Delete text in a document.

Almost all important documents must be edited several times before a final version is obtained. Thus, learning the techniques for editing will be very important to you. Recall that editing can be done at any time after text has been entered; it is not necessary to wait until the first draft has been completed. Ordinarily, errors should be corrected as soon as they are discovered.

To edit text, the first step is to move the insertion pointer to the location of the text to be edited. Use the mouse to position the I-beam pointer at the position of interest and click. The insertion pointer then moves to the new location. With the insertion pointer in the proper location, a number of different editing operations can be performed.

## INSERTING TEXT

*Note:* In the work to be described to you in this chapter, the lines in the sample document (Figure 3.8) are counted starting with the first nonblank line and blank lines are not counted. Of course, if your document's lines are not exactly the same length as the document shown in the figures, you will need to make the necessary adjustments in line numbers to find particular text being referenced.

- If it is not already open, open your document *Practice1<your initials>* in the folder *Lesson1*, which is in the folder *Works WP* on your disk.

To insert text at the position of the insertion pointer, simply begin typing. The text inserted can be as short as a single character or as long as many paragraphs. Suppose, for example, that you decide that the words *Correcting a* should be inserted at the beginning of the first line of the document *Practice1*. To do this, perform the following.

- Move the I-beam to just before the word *Document* in the first line, as shown in Figure 3.10, and click to move the insertion pointer there. Of course, your I-beam pointer may not appear originally at the same location as shown in Figure 3.10.

- Now type the words, *Correcting a*. These words will be inserted before the word *Document*, as shown in Figure 3.11. Notice that the insertion pointer is then located immediately after the inserted words.

```
Document

A word processor such as that found in Works can change the way that you
think about writing a document. Creating a WP paper is less trouble than
ordinary typing because errors can be corrected properly as they occur. It is
however during the revising of a document that word processing really
shines. Revising becomes a satisfying manipulating activity instead of a time-
consuming retyping job. Learning to use a word processor is well worth the
time required. A document can be modified in many ways, including:

1. Inserting new word, lines, or paragraphs.
2. Copying or moving blocks of information to new locations.
3. Changing the format of the entire document or the format of various
paragraphs|                    ⌉[◄──── I-beam pointer
```

**Figure 3.10.** Moving the Insertion Pointer by Moving the I-beam Pointer.

- In lines 4 and 5, which start with *ordinary* and *however*, respectively, insert commas around the word *however* by moving the insertion pointer to immediately after *is* at the end of line 4, clicking, typing a comma, then moving the insertion pointer to immediately after *however*, at the beginning of line 5, clicking, and typing the second comma.

- In line 8, which starts with *time* insert the words *and effort* between the words *time* and *required* by performing the following. Move the insertion pointer to immediately after *time* and click. Type *and effort*. Put a blank space before *and*. Your document should now be similar to the one in Figure 3.11.

```
Correcting a Document

A word processor such as that found in Works can change the way that you
think about writing a document. Creating a WP paper is less trouble than
ordinary typing because errors can be corrected properly as they occur. It is,
however, during the revising of a document that word processing really
shines. Revising becomes a satisfying manipulating activity instead of a time-
consuming retyping job. Learning to use a word processor is well worth the
time and effort required. A document can be modified in many ways,
including:

1. Inserting new word, lines, or paragraphs.
2. Copying or moving blocks of information to new locations.
3. Changing the format of the entire document or the format of various
paragraphs.
```

**Figure 3.11.** Example of Inserting Text.

## SELECTING TEXT

Selecting text is a key process for both editing and formatting. In particular, it is the first step in replacing, deleting, copying, moving text, or modifying the format of the text. Because selecting text is so important, you will practice several selection techniques in this part of the lesson. In Works WP, selected text is shown highlighted on the screen.

Probably the most frequently used technique for selecting is dragging. By dragging you can select any portion of a word, a word, several consecutive words, lines, or even the entire document. In this part, you will first use the method to select several consecutive words. Then you will use the method to select parts of words. Finally, you will select multiple lines.

Perform the following.

- Using the I-beam, point to the beginning of the text to be selected; for this example, point to the location just before *as* in the second line of the document.

- Click to place the insertion pointer in the desired location.

- Hold down the mouse button and drag the I-beam to the end of the text to be selected; for this example, drag to the end of *found*, as shown in Figure 3.12.

- Once the desired text is selected (highlighted), release the mouse button.

> A word processor such as that found in Works can change the way that you
> think about writing a document. Creating a WP paper is less trouble than
> ordinary typing because errors can be corrected properly as they occur. It is,

Figure 3.12. Selecting a Phrase by Dragging.

- Click once to deselect the text.

- Next place the pointer between the *a* and *s* in *as*, click, and drag to just before the *d* in *found*. The selected text should appear as shown in Figure 3.13.

> A word processor such as that found in Works can change the way that you
> think about writing a document. Creating a WP paper is less trouble than
> ordinary typing because errors can be corrected properly as they occur. It is,

Figure 3.13 Selecting an Arbitrary Sequence of Characters by Dragging.

- Click to deselect the text.

To select larger sections of text, place the I-beam just before the beginning of the text to be selected, and then drag the I-beam down the region between the left edge of the window and the left margin. As the I-beam moves down this region, the lines will become selected. When you reach the bottom of the window, additional text will scroll upward automatically and become selected.

Perform the following.

- Move the I-beam to above the body of the document (before the second line of text) as shown in Figure 3.14.

- Click to place the insertion point at the location of the I-beam.

- Drag the pointer down the left edge of the document as shown in Figure 3.14. In this process a common problem is to select more text (or less text) than is desired, but don't panic if this happens to you. As long as you have not released the mouse button, the I-beam can be moved back up (or down) the window, deselecting lines or words. Be careful to not release the mouse button until you have selected exactly the text of interest.

- Click to deselect the text.

Word Selection Using Double Clicking:

- Move the pointer so that it is anywhere within the word *found* in the second line of text.

- Double click — be careful not to move the mouse as you double click. The word *found* will be selected. If you make a mistake and select the wrong word, click again to deselect the word. Then try again to select *found*.

- Point to the word *think* at the beginning of the third line of the text and double click. The word *think* is selected and the word *found* is deselected.

- Practice this technique by moving the pointer to various words and double clicking. Each time the current word should become selected and the previously selected word should become deselected.

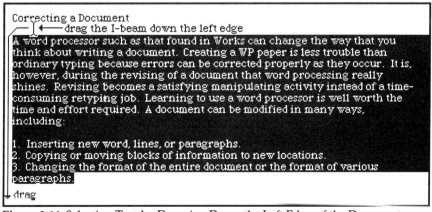

**Figure 3.14.** Selecting Text by Dragging Down the Left Edge of the Document.

Multiple Word Selection Using Shift-Click:

- Select the first word, *ordinary*, in the fourth line of the document by double clicking.

- Press the *Shift* key and hold it down.

- Extend the selection by clicking the word *typing*, clicking the word *because*, and clicking the word *errors*. During this process, do not release the *Shift* key.

- Release the *Shift* key. The document should have the appearance shown in Figure 3.15. Note that the blank after the word *errors* has also been selected.

- Click to deselect the words.

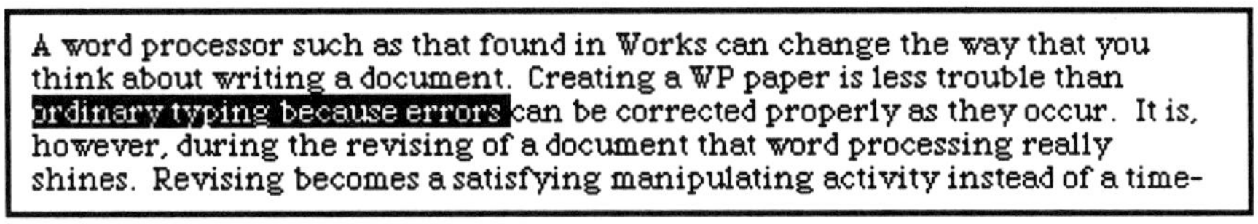

> A word processor such as that found in Works can change the way that you think about writing a document. Creating a WP paper is less trouble than `ordinary typing because errors` can be corrected properly as they occur. It is, however, during the revising of a document that word processing really shines. Revising becomes a satisfying manipulating activity instead of a time-

**Figure 3.15.** Selection of Multiple Words Using the Shift-Click Method.

Entire Line Selection Using the Left-Edge Method:

- Move the I-beam pointer to the region between the left edge of the window and the left margin. The pointer will change to an arrow. Move the arrow so that it is located beside the line to be selected and click. Notice that the entire line beside the arrow becomes selected, as shown in Figure 3.16.

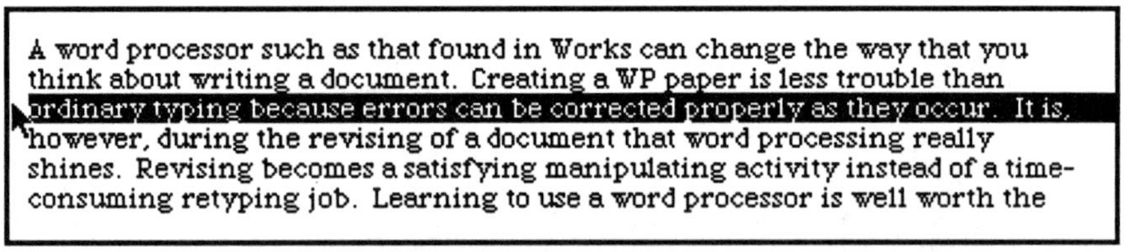

> A word processor such as that found in Works can change the way that you think about writing a document. Creating a WP paper is less trouble than ordinary typing because errors can be corrected properly as they occur. It is, however, during the revising of a document that word processing really shines. Revising becomes a satisfying manipulating activity instead of a time-consuming retyping job. Learning to use a word processor is well worth the

**Figure 3.16.** Selecting a Line Using the Arrow Pointer in the Left Edge of the Document.

Entire Paragraph Selection Using the Left-Edge Method:

- Move the I-beam pointer to the region between the left edge of the window and the left margin, as was done in the last step. You can select a paragraph rapidly by proceeding as just described for selecting a line, but instead of clicking, double click. Observe that the entire paragraph to the right of the arrow becomes selected.

Entire Document Selection Using the *Select All* Method:

- Choose the *Select All* command in the **Edit** menu. The entire document will become selected.

- Click to remove the selection.

After the completion of the previous steps, compare your document with Figure 3.17. If there are any differences other than the placement of the words on a line, revise the document to make it have the same content as Figure 3.17.

---

Correcting a Document

A word processor such as that found in Works can change the way that you think about writing a document. Creating a WP paper is less trouble than ordinary typing because errors can be corrected properly as they occur. It is, however, during the revising of a document that word processing really shines. Revising becomes a satisfying manipulating activity instead of a time-consuming retyping job. Learning to use a word processor is well worth the time and effort required. A document can be modified in many ways, including:

1. Inserting new word, lines, or paragraphs.
2. Copying or moving blocks of information to new locations.
3. Changing the format of the entire document or the format of various paragraphs.

---

**Figure 3.17.** The *Practice1* Document after Insertion and Selection Practice.

# DELETING TEXT

There are two basic ways of deleting text. The simplest way to delete a small amount of text is to use the *Delete* (or *Backspace*) key. For larger amounts of text, it is usually more convenient to first select the text, using one of the techniques just discussed, and then apply whichever of the following three methods is most appropriate for what you wish to accomplish.

**Deleting Selected Text without Saving a Copy.** Press the *Delete* (or *Backspace*) key. The selected text is deleted. If you have made a mistake, you can recover the deleted text by selecting the *Undo* command in the **Edit** menu. The *Undo* command works only if no other actions have been taken after the deletion. Alternately, the *Clear* command of the **Edit** menu can be used, to clear (i.e., delete) the selected text. Again, the *Undo* command can be used to recover the deleted text if this is desired.

**Deleting Selected Text and Saving a Copy on the Clipboard.** Select the *Cut* command from the **Edit** menu. The selected text is deleted and a copy of it is saved on the *Clipboard*. This allows the text to be pasted into the document (or another document) at another position.

**Deleting Text by Replacing It.** If you wish to replace the selected text with alternate text, you can type in the new text or paste the new text from the Clipboard (this latter action assumes, of course, that you have already placed the desired new text on the Clipboard with a *Copy* or *Cut* command). The selected text will be deleted automatically and replaced by new text.

To practice these techniques, perform the following.

- In line 2 double click the word *Works* to select it.

- Press the *Delete* key. The word *Works* is deleted and the text shifts to fill the empty space.

- Before taking any other action, select the *Undo* command from the **Edit** menu. Line 2 will be returned to its original condition. *Undo* can be used after any editing activity provided there has been no other intervening action.

- In line 2 select the words *Works can change* using the dragging technique.

- Select the *Cut* command from the **Edit** menu. The selected text is cut from the document and placed on the *Clipboard*. Note that the remaining text shifts to fill the empty space.

- Select the *Show Clipboard* command from the **Window** menu. When the *Clipboard* window is displayed, note that it contains the text that was cut from the document. Close the Clipboard window.

- With the insertion pointer at the location from which the text was cut, select the *Paste* command from the **Edit** menu. The words *Works can change* are pasted back into the document, which rearranges to resume the form that it had before the *Cut* command.

- In line 2 use the shift-click method to select the words *such as that found*.

- Select the *Clear* command from the **Edit** menu. These words are removed from the text, which is then rearranged.

- Immediately select the *Undo* command from the **Edit** menu. The document will be returned to the form that it had before the *Clear* command was executed. If you accidentally performed some action before selecting *Undo* the command would fail. If this happened to you, type in the deleted words.

- In line 4 change the word *properly* to the word *easily* by highlighting *proper* (drag over *proper*) and then typing *easi*. The selected portion of the word is shown in Figure 3.18.

A word processor such as that found in Works can change the way that you think about writing a document. Creating a WP paper is less trouble than ordinary typing because errors can be corrected properly as they occur. It is, however, during the revising of a document that word processing really shines. Revising becomes a satisfying manipulating activity instead of a time-consuming retyping job. Learning to use a word processor is well worth the time and effort required. A document can be modified in many ways, including:

**Figure 3.18.** Preparing to Replace *properly* with *easily*.

## MOVING TEXT

In writing documents, it is often desirable to move a block of text to another location to achieve greater clarity, better visual impact, or better document organization. It is easy to move text using the cut and paste technique in Works which is analogous to the process of using scissors and tape with typed documents. The procedures are as follows.

**Cut and Paste Technique.**

Select the text block of interest using any of the text selection methods.

Choose the *Cut* command of the **Edit** menu. The selected text will be deleted from the document, and a copy will be placed on the Clipboard.

Move the insertion pointer to the location where the text is to be inserted.

Select the *Paste* command from the **Edit** menu. The text on the Clipboard will be pasted into the document immediately following the insertion point. The text is left unchanged on the Clipboard, so it could also be pasted in other locations in the document.

You will now practice these ideas by moving a word to another location. Then you will move an entire sentence to another position.

Move a word:

• Select the word *easily* (and the blank space that follows it) in line 4 of the sample document.

• Choose the *Cut* command from the **Edit** menu.

- Move the insertion pointer to before the word *corrected* in the same line.

- Select the *Paste* command from the **Edit** menu. (You may have to adjust the spacing by inserting and/or deleting a space.)

Move a sentence:

- In lines 7 and 8, use the dragging method to select the sentence that starts with *Learning to use*.

- Choose the *Cut* command from the **Edit** menu.

- Move the insertion pointer to the end of the document.

- Press the *Return* key twice to insert one blank line and place the insertion pointer in a new paragraph.

- Select the *Paste* command from the **Edit** menu. The document should now have the appearance shown in Figure 3.19. If your text is different, make appropriate corrections.

- After all the changes have been made and your document is identical to that in the box, choose the *Save As* command to save the document with the name *Practice2<your initials>* in the folder *Lesson2*, which is in the folder *Works WP* on your disk.

You have now completed Lesson 2. If you do not wish to proceed directly to the next lesson, quit Works by clicking the *Close Box* of the document and then selecting the *Quit* command from the **File** menu, clean up the desktop, and shut down your computer.

---

Correcting a Document

A word processor such as that found in Works can change the way that you think about writing a document. Creating a WP paper is less trouble than ordinary typing because errors can be easily corrected as they occur. It is, however, during the revising of a document that word processing really shines. Revising becomes a satisfying manipulating activity instead of a time-consuming retyping job. A document can be modified in many ways, including:

1. Inserting new word, lines, or paragraphs.
2. Copying or moving blocks of information to new locations.
3. Changing the format of the entire document or the format of various paragraphs.

Learning to use a word processor is well worth the time and effort required.

---

**Figure 3.19.** The Document after Moving Text.

# CHARACTER FORMATTING

After completing this lesson, you will be able to:

❑ Change the font used within a document or for selected characters.

❑ Change the style and size of selected characters.

## CHANGING FONTS

When you first start Works WP, the font is set to Geneva font. As you type the document, you can change to another font at any time by pointing to the **Font** submenu. Note the black triangle to the right of some of the menu choices in the **Format** menu. This is a signal that these menu choices are actually submenus. Whenever such a choice is highlighted, its submenu is displayed. To select a command from the submenu, drag the pointer directly to the right (or left, as the case may be) into the submenu, then drag down to the desired choice before releasing the mouse button. This process is illustrated for the **Font** submenu in Figure 3.20. The new font will apply only to newly entered text; the previously typed text will not be affected. The font of previously entered text may also be changed by first selecting the text and then choosing a different font from the **Font** submenu. Figure 3.21 shows the form of several fonts. Note that the example sentence occupies different line lengths for different fonts. This is due to the difference in the design of the characters in different fonts. Also note that different fonts have quite different visual impact. You can use this feature to make documents convey your ideas more effectively. As a general rule, however, documents that have only a few different fonts are more appealing visually than documents that employ multiple fonts.

Perform the following.

• Open your *Practice2<your initials>* document in the folder *Lesson2* within the *Works WP* folder on your disk.

• Choose the *Select All* command from the **Edit** menu. The entire document should become highlighted.

• Choose the **Font** submenu from the **Format** menu.

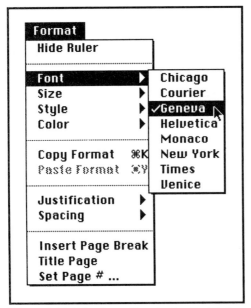

**Figure 3.20.** Selecting a Font in the *Font* Submenu.

| Font | Sample Sentence |
|------|----------------|
| Chicago | **You may use different fonts in a document.** |
| Courier | You may use different fonts in a document. |
| Geneva | You may use different fonts in a document. |
| Helvetica | You may use different fonts in a document. |
| Monaco | You may use different fonts in a document. |
| New York | You may use different fonts in a document. |
| Times | You may use different fonts in a document. |
| Venice | You may use different fonts in a document. |

**Figure 3.21.** A Sample Sentence Using Different Fonts.

- Drag to select the *Times* font. (If *Times* is not installed on your machine, select any font other than *New York*.) The font will be changed for the entire document.

- Click to deselect the document. Your document should have the appearance shown in Figure 3.22.

- Use the *Save As* command to save the modified document by the name *Practice3<your initials>* in the folder *Lesson3* in your folder *Works WP*. Close your document.

Correcting a Document

A word processor such as that found in Works can change the way that you think about writing a document. Creating a WP paper is less trouble than ordinary typing because errors can be easily corrected as they occur. It is, however, during the revising of a document that word processing really shines. Revising becomes a satisfying manipulating activity instead of a time-consuming retyping job. A document can be modified in many ways, including:

1. Inserting new word, lines, or paragraphs.
2. Copying or moving blocks of information to new locations.
3. Changing the format of the entire document or the format of various paragraphs.

Learning to use a word processor is well worth the time and effort required.

**Figure 3.22.** *Practice2* with the Font *Times*.

## CHANGING STYLE AND SIZE

Interest and visual impact can sometimes be added to a document by changing the style and character size in some portion of the document. Earlier, we discussed how to change fonts; changing style and size is accomplished in essentially the same way. To change the style of a portion of text, select the text, and then select the style from the **Style** submenu of the **Format** menu. Figure 3.4 given earlier shows the styles available in Works WP. Of course, more than one style can appear in the same document.

The size of text is changed by selecting from the **Size** submenu of the **Format** menu. In Figure 3.4 the word *wordwrap* is shown in various sizes. The usual size for text is 10 or 12 points. It is easy to experiment with the fonts, styles, and character sizes to see if they improve a document. If a combination is not found that pleases you, converting the text back to its original format takes only a few seconds.

If a document contains too many fonts, styles, and character sizes, the document becomes cluttered, which detracts from its appearance. In general, you should use these character formatting capabilities sparingly. Perform the following.

- Open your document *Practice2<your initials>* in the folder *Lesson2* in the folder *Works WP* on your disk.

- Choose the *Select All* command from the **Edit** menu. The entire document should now be highlighted.

- Choose the **Style** submenu from the **Format** menu and choose the *Bold* command. The style of each character in the document should change, and the document should still be highlighted.

- Choose the **Size** submenu from the **Format** menu and choose the 12 Point size. The size of each character in the document should change, and the document should still be highlighted.

123

- Click anywhere to deselect the document.

- Examine the document carefully. It should have the approximate appearance of the document shown in Figure 3.23.

- Use the *Save As* command to save the modified document by the name *Practice4<your initials>* in the folder *Lesson3* in your folder *Works WP*. Close your document.

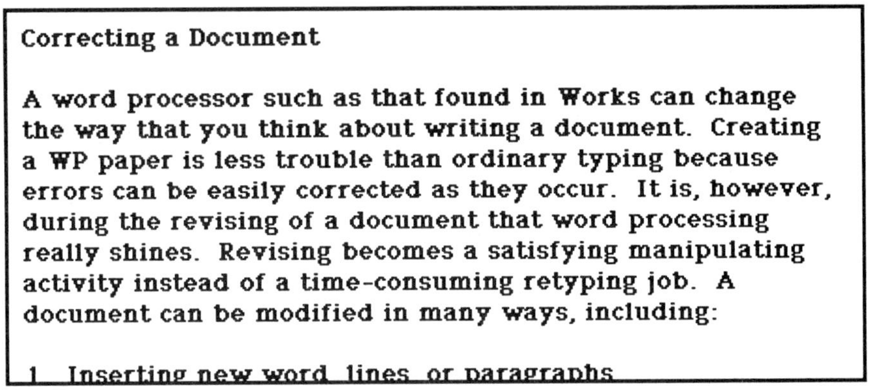

---

**Correcting a Document**

A word processor such as that found in Works can change the way that you think about writing a document. Creating a WP paper is less trouble than ordinary typing because errors can be easily corrected as they occur. It is, however, during the revising of a document that word processing really shines. Revising becomes a satisfying manipulating activity instead of a time-consuming retyping job. A document can be modified in many ways, including:

1  Inserting new word lines or paragraphs

---

Figure 3.23. *Practice2* with Bold Style and 12 Point Characters.

You have now completed Lesson 3. If you do not wish to proceed directly to the next lesson, quit Works by selecting the *Quit* command from the **File** menu, clean up the desktop, and shut down your computer.

# PARAGRAPH FORMATTING

After completing this lesson, you will be able to:

❑ Set the format of paragraphs using the ruler.

❑ Set the format of paragraphs using the *Copy Format* command.

❑ Change the justification and line spacing of paragraphs.

## USING PARAGRAPH RULERS

Rulers are used to set the indents and tabs for individual paragraphs. *The settings displayed on a ruler always refer to the paragraph in which the insertion point is located.* This formatting information is stored as an invisible character at the end of a paragraph. Thus, deleting the "blank space" at the end of a paragraph may change the format of the paragraph.

On a ruler two small black triangles show the locations of the left and the right indents. In addition, there is a smaller black rectangle that shows how the first line of a paragraph will be indented. If all the lines of the paragraph have the same left indenting, both the left indent marker and the first line indenting marker will be at the same location. In this case, the first line indicator becomes a small white rectangle within the left indent marker. This situation is demonstrated in Figure 3.24 part (A).

The three markers (left indent, right indent, and first line indent) can be moved along the ruler by dragging them to the desired location. In Figure 3.24 (B), the first line indent marker has been dragged to cause the first line to be indented 0.5 in. Marker settings that will produce a left hanging first line are shown in Figure 3.24(C). Notice that the first line indent marker is to the left of the left margin marker.

Perform the following.

- Open your document *Practice2<your initials>* in the folder *Lesson2* in the folder *Works WP* on your disk.

- Point anywhere in the main paragraph that begins on line 2 and click to place the insertion pointer within that paragraph.

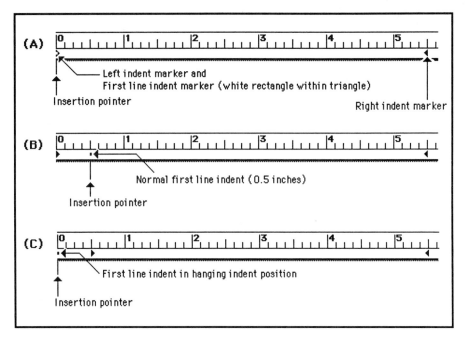

**Figure 3.24.** Examples of the Ruler and Its Markers.

- If the ruler is not showing, choose the *Show Ruler* command from the **Format** menu. Recall that the ruler displays only formatting information about the current paragraph (i.e., the paragraph currently containing the insertion pointer).

- On the ruler, point to the right margin indicator and drag it to 5.5 in.

- On the ruler, point to the first line indent marker and drag it to 0.5 in. You may have to try this several times before you succeed.

- Examine the resulting paragraph, which is shown in Figure 3.25. The first line of the paragraph is indented, and the right edge of all lines in the paragraph is 5.5 in. Notice that the formatting of the paragraph in line 1 has not been modified.

- With the insertion pointer still within the second paragraph, drag the first line indent marker to 0.0 in. on the ruler and drag the left margin indicator to 0.5 in. These changes produce a hanging indent, as shown in Figure 3.26.

- Use the *Save As* command to save the modified document by the name *Practice5<your initials>* in the folder *Lesson4* in your folder *Works WP*. Close your document.

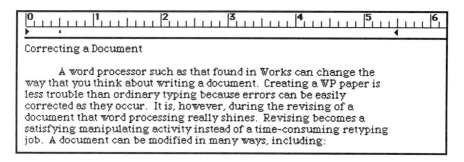

Figure 3.25. Paragraph 2 with First Line Indent of 0.5 In. and Right Margin at 5.5 In.

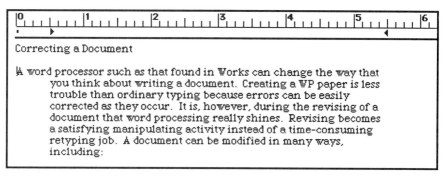

Figure 3.26. An Example of the Hanging Indent Technique.

## COPYING PARAGRAPH FORMATS

Remember that when the *Return* key is pressed, the current paragraph is ended and a new paragraph is started. All the formatting information of the first paragraph (e.g., indents, tabs, spacing, and justification) becomes associated with the new paragraph. This is valuable because adjacent paragraphs tend to have similar formats, and it would be inefficient to have to reset all the format parameters for each new paragraph.

In a similar way, occasions arise when you need to use a format that is found in a paragraph in some nonadjacent part of the document. One option is to reset all the format parameters manually, but it is usually faster to use the *Copy Format* command.

Perform the following.

- Open your document *Practice2<your initials>* in the folder *Lesson2* in the folder *Works WP* on your disk.

- Place the insertion pointer anywhere in the first paragraph by pointing and clicking.

- Drag the first line indent marker to 0.5 in. The text moves to the right to conform to the new format.

127

- Choose the *Copy Format* command in the **Format** menu.

- Select all the paragraphs following this one using the dragging method.

- Choose the *Paste Format* command in the **Format** menu. The formatting information is then pasted into each of the selected paragraphs. All the text in these paragraphs is rearranged to conform to the new format.

- Click anywhere to deselect the paragraphs.

- Compare your results with that shown in Figure 3.27. Redo your work as necessary to obtain a document similar to that shown in the figure.

- Use the *Save As* to save the modified document by the name *Practice6<your initials>* in the folder *Lesson4* in your folder *Works WP*. Close your document.

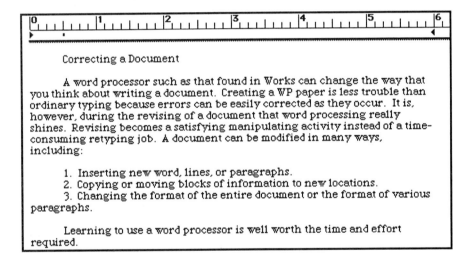

Figure 3.27. *Practice2* after Changing the Format of the Paragraphs.

## CHANGING PARAGRAPH JUSTIFICATION

The term *justification of text* refers to the alignment of the text along one or both sides of the paragraph indents. The **Justification** submenu under the **Format** menu contains four commands for controlling justification for a paragraph. *Left*, if selected, produces an aligned left indent with a jagged right indent. This is the justification style seen in most typewritten letters. *Justified* causes alignment of text at both the left and right indents. It is seen in books and other typeset documents. *Centered* causes text to be centered between the indents and is useful for titles. *Right* causes the text to be jagged along the left indent and smooth along the right indent, which is sometimes useful for special effects. Examples of the kinds of justification are given in Figure 3.28.

If you wish to change the justification for a paragraph, place the insertion pointer in that paragraph, then access and execute the appropriate *Justification* command from the **Justification** submenu. To change the justification for several paragraphs, or perhaps for the entire document, select the text of interest and then proceed as just described for a paragraph.

---

(A) Left justified, jagged right indent

Enclosed is a summary of our conversation of May 12, including a description of the work we would perform and the cost of each item. If we are in agreement, the survey could begin in two weeks.

(B) Justified, both indents even

Enclosed is a summary of our conversation of May 12, including a description of the work we would perform and the cost of each item. If we are in agreement, the survey could begin in two weeks.

(C) Centered
SUMMARY OF CONVERSATION
May 12

(D) Right justified, jagged left indent

Enclosed is a summary of our conversation of May 12, including a description of the work we would perform and the cost of each item. If we are in agreement, the survey could begin in two weeks.

---

**Figure 3.28.** Examples of the Application of the Justification Commands.

Perform the following.

- Open your document *Practice2<your initials>* in the folder *Lesson2* in the folder *Works WP* on your disk.

- Place the insertion pointer anywhere in the second paragraph.

- Choose the **Justification** submenu from the **Format** menu and select the *Justified* command. The text will rearrange so that the words in this paragraph are aligned smoothly along the edges defined by the left and right indent markers.

- Compare your paragraph with that shown in Figure 3.29.

- Leave the document window on the screen and do the work described in the next part.

---

Correcting a Document

A word processor such as that found in Works can change the way that you think about writing a document. Creating a WP paper is less trouble than ordinary typing because errors can| be easily corrected as they occur. It is, however, during the revising of a document that word processing really shines. Revising becomes a satisfying manipulating activity instead of a time-consuming retyping job. A document can be modified in many ways, including:

---

**Figure 3.29.** *Practice2* with the Second Paragraph Justified.

## CHANGING PARAGRAPH LINE SPACING

To change the line spacing in the paragraph in which the insertion pointer is located, access the **Spacing** submenu in the **Format** menu. You can then select the desired line spacing, and the paragraph will immediately rearrange to have the indicated spacing. If you wish to change the spacing for several paragraphs, or perhaps for the entire document, select the text of interest and then proceed as described for a paragraph.

Perform the following.

- If the insertion pointer is not already in the second paragraph, place it anywhere in the second paragraph.

- Choose the **Spacing** submenu from the **Format** menu and select the *Double* command. The text will rearrange so that the lines in this paragraph are double spaced, that is, have a blank line between nonblank lines.

- Compare your paragraph with that shown in Figure 3.30.

- Use the *Save As* to save the modified document by the name *Practice7<your initials>* in the folder *Lesson4* in your folder *Works WP*. Close your document.

## PUTTING IT ALL TOGETHER

In this part of the lesson you will make changes to the *Practice2<your initials>* document using a number of the techniques described in previous sections. Consequently, you should see how the formatting techniques blend in producing a document.

---

Correcting a Document

A word processor such as that found in Works can change the way that you think about writing a document. Creating a WP paper is less trouble than ordinary typing because errors can be easily corrected as they occur. It is, however, during the revising of a document that word processing really shines. Revising becomes a satisfying manipulating activity instead of a time-consuming retyping job. A document can be modified in many ways, including:

---

**Figure 3.30.** *Practice2* with the Second Paragraph Double Spaced and Justified.

Perform the following.

- Open your document *Practice2<your initials>* in the folder *Lesson2* in the folder *Works WP* on your disk.

Modify the title line:

- Center line 1 by proceeding as follows. Click anywhere in the line to position the insertion pointer. Select the **Format** menu, drag to the **Justification** submenu, and select the *Center* command. The phrase should now be centered.

- Make line 1 bold by proceeding as follows. Highlight the words "Correcting a Document" on line 1 by pointing to the beginning of the phrase, clicking, and dragging to the end of the phrase. Select the **Format** menu, drag to the **Style** submenu, and select the *Bold* command.

Modify the main paragraph:

- Give the second paragraph a first line indent of 0.5 inches by performing the following. Click anywhere in the paragraph to position the insertion pointer.

- Point to the first line indent marker, which is a white rectangle in the left margin indicator, and drag the marker to 0.5 in. It is likely that you will move the left margin indicator instead of the first line indent marker. If that is the case, move the indicator back to its original position and repeat the moving process. After some practice you will be able to move the desired marker.

- Make the first paragraph justified at both margins by selecting the **Format** menu, the **Justification** submenu, and the *Justified* command.

131

Modify the numbered paragraphs:

- Make the numbered comments have a hanging left indent with the first line 0.5 in. from the margin and subsequent lines indented an additional 0.25 in. by performing the following.  Select all the numbered paragraphs by moving the insertion pointer to just before the 1, dragging the pointer down the margin until all the lines of the numbered paragraphs are highlighted.

- With the paragraphs highlighted, set the left indent marker to 0.5 in., and set the first line indent marker to 0.25 in.  See Figure 3.26 for an example.

- Obtain properly aligned indents between the numbers and the indented text by deleting blank spaces between the numbers and the text and then pressing the tab key.

Modify the last paragraph:

- Give the final paragraph a first line indent of 0.5 in., and make it justified at both margins.  Your document should now be identical to the text shown in Figure 3.31.  If your text is different, make appropriate corrections.

Save the document:

- After all the changes have been made, use the *Save As* command of the **File** menu to save the document with the name *Practice8<your initials>* in the folder *Lesson4* in the folder *Works WP* on your disk. Close the document after saving it.

You have now completed Lesson 4.  If you do not wish to proceed directly to the next lesson, quit Works by selecting the *Quit* command from the **File** menu, clean up the desktop, and shut down your computer.

---

**Correcting a Document**

A word processor such as that found in Works can change the way that you think about writing a document. Creating a WP paper is less trouble than ordinary typing because errors can be easily corrected as they occur.  It is, however, during the revising of a document that word processing really shines. Revising becomes a satisfying manipulating activity instead of a time-consuming retyping job.  A document can be modified in many ways, including:

1. Inserting new word, lines, or paragraphs.
2. Copying or moving blocks of information to new locations.
3. Changing the format of the entire document or the format of various paragraphs.

Learning to use a word processor is well worth the time and effort required.

---

**Figure 3.31.** The *Practice8* Document.

# USING TABS FOR FORMATTING

After completing this lesson, you will be able to:

❑ Set tabs on the ruler.

❑ Use left, right, decimal, and center tabs.

❑ Create a table using tabs.

## UNDERSTANDING THE TYPES OF TABS

Tab stops are used to skip horizontally across a line and to produce precise alignment of text on successive lines. Works has four kinds of tab stops: left, right, decimal, and center tab stops. The shapes of the tab stops are shown in Figure 3.32.

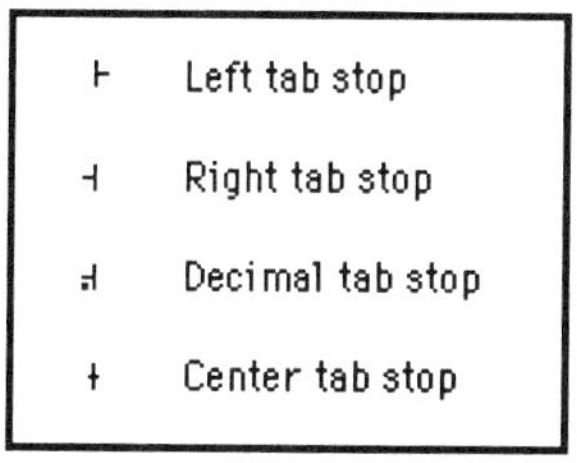

| | |
|---|---|
| ├ | Left tab stop |
| ┤ | Right tab stop |
| ┧ | Decimal tab stop |
| ┼ | Center tab stop |

Figure 3.32. The Shapes of the Works Tab Stops.

The types of tabs have the following properties.

**Left Tabs.** Left tabs cause the left edge of the tabbed text to be anchored at the position of the tab. Subsequent characters will be entered to the right of the tab position.

**Right Tabs.** Right tabs cause the right edge of the tabbed text to be anchored at the position of the tab. Subsequent characters will force the text to the left of the tab.

**Decimal Tabs.** Decimal tabs cause numbers entered to be aligned with the decimal points at the position of the tab. A string of characters entered at a decimal tab will have its right edge anchored at the tab position until a

133

decimal (period) is entered; once the decimal point is entered, the left edge of succeeding characters will be anchored at the tab position.

**Center Tabs.** Center tabs cause the tabbed text to be centered about the tab mark.

## PLACING AND CHANGING TABS

To place a left tab stop you point to the ruler at the desired location of the tab and click. The symbol for a left tab stop will appear on the ruler. You can point to the tab and drag it to any desired location.

Entering a left tab in this way has an important side effect. In every new document, left tabs are placed by default every 0.5 in. across the ruler; these default tabs are *invisible*. When you place a new tab, the invisible default tabs to the left of the entered tab are *erased automatically*. Erasure of the default tabs may cause the text to be rearranged in some surprising manner, but if this happens, do not panic. Merely insert new tabs in the location of those erased by pointing at the desired locations on the ruler and clicking.

You can alter the type of a tab by clicking it. When a left tab is clicked, it turns into a right tab. When a right tab is clicked, it turns into a decimal tab. When a decimal tab is clicked, it turns into a center tab. When a center tab is clicked, it turns into a left tab.

Perform the following.

- Open Works and create a new word processing document.

- If the ruler is not visible, choose the *Show Ruler* command from the **Format** menu.

Left tab:

- Point to just below the 3 in. marker on the ruler and click. A left tab stop will be placed at this location. If you missed the desired location, drag the tab until it is located at 3 in.

- Press the *Tab* key and type $5,678.94. Notice that the dollar sign, which is the leftmost character of the amount, is anchored at the left tab stop.

- Press the *Return* key twice to obtain a blank line.

Right tab:

- Click the symbol for the left tab stop on the ruler. It becomes the symbol for a right tab stop.

- Press the *Tab* key and type $5,678.94. Notice that the 4, which is the rightmost character of the amount, is anchored at the right tab stop, and that text moves left as additional letters are typed.

- Press the *Return* key twice to obtain a blank line.

Decimal tab:

- Click the symbol for the right tab stop on the ruler. It becomes the symbol for a decimal tab stop.

- Press the *Tab* key and type $5,678.94. Notice that the decimal is anchored at the location of the decimal tab.

- Press the *Return* key twice to obtain a blank line.

Center tab:

- Click the symbol for the decimal tab stop on the ruler. It becomes the symbol for the center tab stop.

- Press the *Tab* key and type $5,678.94. Notice that the characters in the amount are centered at the location of the center tab stop.

- Compare your result with that shown in Figure 3.33. If any of the amounts have different locations from those shown in the figure, change your document to make it look like the figure.

- Save your document by the name *TabPractice<your initials>* in the folder *Lesson5* inside the folder *Works WP* on your disk. Close the document.

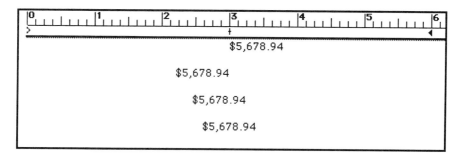

**Figure 3.33.** Illustration of the Use of the Works Tab Stops.

## USING TABS IN CREATING A TABLE

In this section you will use tabs to create the table shown in Figure 3.34. Take a look now at this table to see what you will be creating. Perform the following.

- Create a new word processing document.

- If the ruler is not visible, choose the *Show Ruler* command from the **Format** menu. Note that the ruler is marked in 1/8 (= 0.1275) in. intervals.

- Drag the right indent marker to 5.5 inches.

- Create a blank line by pressing the *Return* key.

Place tabs for the heading line:

- Place left tab stops at 0.375 (3/8) in., 2 in., 3.25 (3 1/4) in., and 4.375 (4 3/8) in. by pointing and clicking at these locations in the ruler. The ruler should now look like the following.

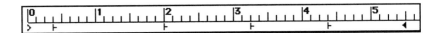

Create the heading line:

- Choose the *12 Point* command from the **Size** submenu of the **Format** menu.

- Select the *Bold* command from the **Style** submenu of the **Format** menu.

- Press the *Tab* key and type the heading *Item*.

- Press the *Tab* key and type the heading *Unit Cost*.

- Press the *Tab* key and type the heading *Number*.

- Press the *Tab* key and type the heading *Total*.

- Turn off the bold style by selecting the *Bold* command once again from the **Style** submenu of the **Format** menu.

- Press the *Return* key twice to obtain a blank line.

Set the tabs for the body of the table:

- Drag the left tab stop that is at 4.375 (4 3/8) in. to 4.75 (4 3/4) in. Double click the tab to change it into a decimal tab stop.

- Drag the left tab stop that is at 3.25 (3 1/4) in. to 3.75 (3 3/4) in. Click the tab to change it into a right tab stop.

- Drag the left tab stop that is at 2.0 in. to 2.5 in. Double click the tab to change it into a decimal tab stop. The ruler should now look like the following.

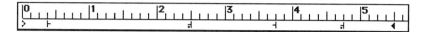

First line of the body of the table:

- Press the *Tab* key to position the insertion pointer for the first line of the table.

- Type *Micro disks* and press the *Tab* key.

- Type *1.80* and press the *Tab* key.

- Type *200* and press the *Tab* key.

- Type *360.00* and press the *Return* key.

Second line of the body of the table:

- Press the *Tab* key to position the insertion pointer for the second line of the table.

- Type *Printer ribbons* and press the *Tab* key.

- Type *7.00* and press the *Tab* key.

- Type *15* and press the *Tab* key.

- Type *105.00* and press the *Return* key.

Third line of the body of the table:

- Press the *Tab* key to position the insertion pointer for the third line of the table.

- Type *Paper, printer* and press the *Tab* key.

- Type *21.10* and press the *Tab* key.

- Type *6* and press the *Tab* key.

- Type *126.60* and press the *Return* key twice to obtain a blank line.

Set the tabs for the totals line:

- Drag the tabs at 0.375 in. and 3.75 in. off the ruler.

- Double click the decimal tab stop at 2.5 in. to change it into a left tab stop.

- Drag your new left tab stop located at 2.5 in. to 2.25 in.. The ruler should now look like the following.

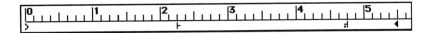

Totals line:

- Press the *Tab* key to advance the insertion pointer to the tab at 2.25 inches.

- Choose the *Bold* command from the **Style** submenu in the **Format** menu.

- Type *Total*.

- Choose the *Bold* command again from the **Style** submenu in the **Format** menu to turn off the bold style.

- Press the *Tab* key and type *591.60*. Now your document should look exactly like Figure 3.34. If it does not, make changes until you obtain the desired format.

Save the document:

- Use the *Save As* command to save the document with the name *Table<your initials>* in the folder *Lesson5* inside folder *Works WP* on your disk. Close the document.

| Item | Unit Cost | Number | Total |
|------|-----------|--------|-------|
| Micro disks | 1.80 | 200 | 360.00 |
| Printer ribbons | 7.00 | 15 | 105.00 |
| Paper, printer | 21.10 | 6 | 126.60 |
| | Total | | 591.60 |

**Figure 3.34.** Using Tabs in Creating a Table.

You have now completed Lesson 5. If you do not wish to proceed directly to the next lesson, quit Works by selecting the *Quit* command from the **File** menu, clean up the desktop, and shut down your computer.

# LESSON 6

# CHECKING SPELLING

After completing this lesson you will be able to:

- ❑ Select options for spelling checking.
- ❑ Find and correct misspelled words in a document.
- ❑ Add words to the dictionary.
- ❑ Create specialized document dictionaries.

## CREATING A DOCUMENT TO USE FOR SPELLING CHECKING

In this section of the lesson you will modify your *Practice8<your initials>* document so that it contains spelling errors. In subsequent sections of the lesson, you will check spelling using this document. Perform the following.

- Open your document *Practice8<your initials>* in the folder *Lesson4* inside the folder *Works WP* on your disk.

- In line 2 change the word *processor* to *processer*.

- In line 3, change the word *think* by interchanging the last two letters to obtain *thikn*.

- In line 4, change the word *errors* by deleting the *o* to obtain *errrs*.

- In line 6, change the word *satisfying* by deleting the *y* to obtain *satisfing*.

- In line 13, which is the last sentence of the document, change the word *processor* to *processer*. Insert the word *the* before the word *time* to obtain consecutive occurrences of *the*.

- Compare your document with Figure 3.35 to see if you have made the requested changes. To help you identify the changes, each has been underlined in the figure. If your document differs, correct it.

- Save the document with the name *Practice8sp<your initials>* in the folder *Lesson6* in the *Works WP* folder. This will make it possible for you to use it repeatedly for spelling checking practice if you desire. Do not close the document.

---

**Correcting a Document**

A word processer such as that found in Works can change the way that you thikn about writing a document. Creating a WP paper is less trouble than ordinary typing because errrs can be easily corrected as they occur. It is, however, during the revising of a document that word processing really shines. Revising becomes a satisfing manipulating activity instead of a time-consuming retyping job. A document can be modified in many ways, including:

1. Inserting new word, lines, or paragraphs.
2. Copying or moving blocks of information to new locations.
3. Changing the format of the entire document or the format of various paragraphs.

Learning to use a word processer is well worth the the time and effort required.

---

**Figure 3.35.** The *Practice8* Document Containing Errors for Spelling Checking.

## SELECTING OPTIONS FOR SPELLING CHECKING

Examine the options listed on the dialog box shown in Figure 3.37. Options to be applied during the checking of spelling have an x in the box beside the option. To select or deselect an option, click in the box for the option to obtain an x or a blank box as desired.

If the *Double word* errors option is selected, adjacent occurrences of the same word will be displayed as an error. These errors are surprisingly difficult to detect during the reading of a document. Recall that an example of a double word error was introduced into your document *Practice8sp<your initials>*.

If the *Homonyms* errors option is selected, a word will be displayed as a possible error if there is another word with the same pronunciation but different meaning and spelling. You would select the correct version of the word. There are a surprising number of frequently used homonyms in English, so choosing this option may appreciably slow the spelling checking process.

To select the options to be used in checking the spelling of a document perform the following.

- Choose the *Options* command from the **Spell** menu, which is shown in Figure 3.36.

- Choose all the options as shown in Figure 3.37 and then click *OK*.

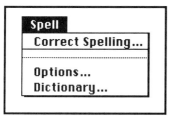

Figure 3.36. The Spell Menu.

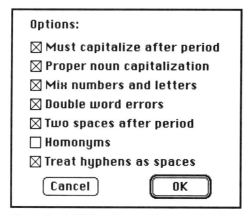

Figure 3.37. Dialog Box for Options Available in Works Spelling Checking.

## FINDING AND CORRECTING MISSPELLED WORDS IN A DOCUMENT

In this part of the lesson you will find and correct the errors that were introduced into document *Practice8sp<your initials>*. You may find that your document contains spelling errors that were not made intentionally and that are not discussed in the following. If that should occur, correct these errors also.

**Techniques for Correcting Spelling.** When Works determines that an error in spelling has occurred (which means the word was not found in the current Works dictionary), the misspelled word will be highlighted in the document, and a dialog box will be displayed, as illustrated in Figure 3.38.

The scroll box to the left (labeled *Suggestions* in Figure 3.38) in the dialog box will serve one of two functions and have one of two different names, depending on which of the following situations applies:

If the *View Suggestions* button has been selected and a misspelled word is discovered, suggested replacements will be displayed in the scroll box, which then assumes the name *Suggestions*.

If the *View Dictionary* button on the dialog box has been selected and a misspelled word is discovered, the contents of the dictio-

141

nary which are nearest in spelling to the misspelled word will be displayed in the scroll box, which is then renamed *Dictionary*.

If the word discovered *is* actually misspelled, there are several ways to proceed. To correct the spelling you can use editing techniques on the word shown in the *Replace With* box. Alternately, you can click the word having the correct spelling if it appears in the *Suggestions* scroll box. When you have the correctly spelled word in the *Replace With* box, you click the *Replace* button. The correctly spelled word will replace the incorrectly spelled word in the document. In many instances, the correctly spelled version of the word will be placed automatically in the *Replace With* box.

**Handling Correctly Spelled Words.** As noted above, the spelling checker will highlight any word not in its dictionary and display a dialog box as illustrated in Figure 3.38. If the word is actually correctly spelled and you would like to include it in the dictionary for future spell checking, click the *Add* button on the dialog box. If the word is correctly spelled but you do not want to add it to the dictionary, click the *Skip* button.

If the *Homonyms* option has been chosen, as the document is processed various homonyms are highlighted. When a homonym is discovered, alternate spelling or spellings will appear in an *Alternate Spellings* dialog box. You may then select the proper word or keep the current word by clicking the appropriate buttons.

**Figure 3.38.** *Spelling Checker* Dialog Box.

Perform the following.

- Use the *Save As* command to save the current document (*Practice8sp<your initials>*) with the name *Practice9<your initials>* in the folder *Lesson6* inside folder *Works WP* on your disk.

- Place the insertion pointer at the beginning of the document *Practice9<your initials>* by pointing and clicking.

- Select the *Correct Spelling* command from the **Spell** menu. A dialog box may be displayed asking you to locate the dictionary. If this happens, use the standard navigation techniques to locate the dictionary (most likely in a folder named *Works* — or perhaps *inside* a folder in the *Works* folder) and double click. The spelling checker will now move through your document from the location of the insertion pointer to the end of the document, highlighting every word that might contain an error. Whenever a possible error is found, a dialog box is displayed to allow appropriate action to be taken.

Make the corrections:

- Correct the spelling of *processer* by clicking on *View Suggestions*, selecting the correct spelling from the *Suggestions* scroll box (if it is not already selected for you) and then clicking *Replace* when the correct spelling is placed in the *Replace With* box.

- In a similar manner, correct the spelling of *thikn* when it appears in the *Unknown* box.

- Click the *Skip* button when *WP* in line 3 appears in the *Unknown* box.

- Correct the spelling of *errrs* in line 4 when it appears in the *Unknown* box. Note that the correct spelling will be preselected in the *Dictionary* scroll box and also placed in the *Replace With* box.

- Click *Replace* to correct the spelling.

- Correct the spelling of *satisfing* in line 6 when it appears in the *Unknown* box.

- Click *View Suggestions*. Note that no suggested spelling appears.

- Click *View Dictionary* and locate the correct spelling. Click the correct spelling in the *Dictionary* scroll box, and then click *Replace*.

- Click the *Skip* button when *retyping* in line 7 is highlighted.

- Correct the spelling of *processer* again (in line 13) when it appears in the *Unknown* box.

- When *the the* in line 13 is highlighted, click the *Replace* button. The dialog box for this situation is shown in Figure 3.39.

Create a special document dictionary:

Note: You must have Works 2.00a or a later version to complete the last part of this lesson. If the dialog box described below does not appear, skip to the last step of the lesson.

- When the end of the document is reached, a dialog box will be displayed having the message: *Do you want Works to remember which words were skipped for future use?* Click the *Yes* button and the skipped words will be saved in a document having the same name as your open document, but with the extension *.dict*. In this case the document dictionary will be named *Practice9<your initials>.dict*.

Once you create a document dictionary, when you subsequently perform spelling checking on the document, you will be asked whether you wish to use the document dictionary (along with the main Works dictionary).

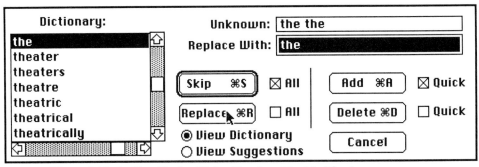

**Figure 3.39.** *Spelling Checker Dialog Box for a Double Word.*

Save the document:

- Use the *Save* command to save the document. Close the document, and quit Works. Open the folder *Lesson6* in the folder *Works DB* on your disk. Locate the skipped words dictionary *Practice9<your initials>.dict* in this folder.

You have now completed Lesson 6. If you do not wish to proceed directly to the next lesson, clean up the desktop and shut down your computer.

# SEARCHING AND REPLACING TEXT

After this lesson you will be able to:

❑ Find text anywhere in a document using the *Find* command.

❑ Find and replace text anywhere in a document using the *Replace* command.

Suppose in a long document you need to find a word or phrase that might occur in several locations. You might also want to replace the found text with new text in some instances. A manual search in which you read the document is both inefficient and very error prone. With a manual search in a long document, it is almost certain that you will miss some occurrences of the word or phrase. Works WP provides a special search feature to help with this problem.

## FINDING TEXT

In this part of the lesson you will use the previously prepared document *Practice8<your initials>* as text for investigating the features of the *Find* command. The *Find* command is found in the **Search** menu as illustrated in Figure 3.40. When the *Find* command is executed, the dialog box shown in Figure 3.41 is displayed. Before beginning the activities of this lesson, we will examine the choices on this dialog box.

```
Search
Find...          ⌘F
Replace...       ⌘R
...............................
Go To Page #...  ⌘G
```

**Figure 3.40.** The **Search** Menu.

The box titled *Find What* holds the word or phrase of interest. An entry in this box can be up to 80 characters in length.

You would click the box before *Match Whole Words Only* if you are interested only in whole words. For example, if the word *Figure* is in the *Find What* box, and you click the *Match Whole Words Only* box, the word *Figures* would not be an exact match because of the *s* on the end, and it would not be found. It *would* be found if the *Match Whole Words Only* box is not clicked.

You would click the box *Check Upper/Lowercase* if you want the case of the characters to be significant. For example, if the word *Figure* is in the *Find What* box and the *Check Upper/Lowercase* box is clicked, the word *figure* would not be found because its first character does not have the same case as the entered word *Figure*.

You would click the *Find Next* button to begin the search from the current location of the insertion pointer. When a match is found, the document is displayed with the word highlighted. The *Find* dialog box stays on the screen. If an occurrence is found that is not of interest, you would click the *Find Next* button again to continue the search. At the end of the document a message will be displayed that no more occurrences of the word could be found.

You would click the *Cancel* button to stop the find process and return to work on the text. Normally, this will be done when an occurrence of the word has been found that needs modification. The *Find* dialog box will disappear from the screen, and the text containing the highlighted word will continue to be displayed.

Notice the two buttons located just under the *Find What* in Figure 3.41. The symbols in these buttons represent tab markers and paragraph markers, respectively. If one of these buttons is checked, then clicking the *Find Next* button causes a search for the appropriate marker.

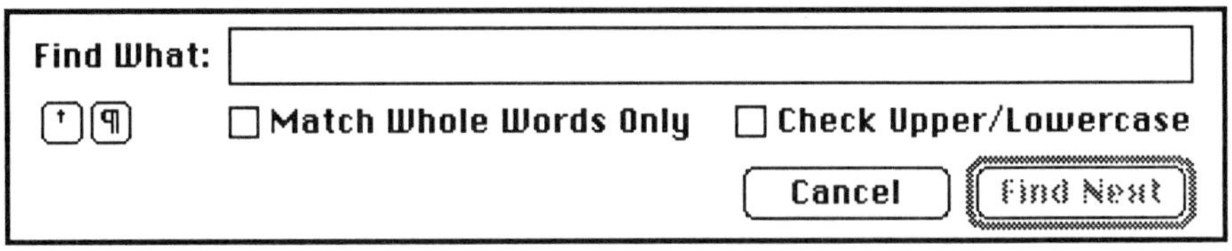

| Find What: | |
|---|---|
| ⬚ ⬚     ☐ Match Whole Words Only    ☐ Check Upper/Lowercase | |
| | Cancel    Find Next |

**Figure 3.41.** The *Find* Dialog Box.

Perform the following.

- Open the document *Practice8<your initials>* in the *Lesson4* folder in the *Works WP* folder on your disk.

- Select the *Find* command from the **Search** menu. The dialog box shown in Figure 3.41 will be displayed.

Search for *it*:

- Type the word *it* into the *Find What* dialog box.

- Click the *Find Next* button. A search for *it* will begin. The first occurrence of *it* is found embedded in the word *writing* as is shown in Figure 3.42.

---

**Correcting a Document**

A word processor such as that found in Works can change the way that you think about writing a document. Creating a WP paper is less trouble than ordinary typing because errors can be easily corrected as they occur. It is, however, during the revising of a document that word processing really shines. Revising becomes a satisfying manipulating activity instead of a time-consuming retyping job. A document can be modified in many ways, including:

---

**Figure 3.42.** First Occurrence of *it* in the Document.

- Click the *Find Next* button repeatedly until the *All Occurrences* dialog box is displayed. Notice that two other occurrences of *it* are discovered before the dialog box is displayed.

- Click the *OK* button. The *All Occurrences* dialog box will disappear. The document window will be displayed with no highlighted areas. The insertion pointer will be at the position at which the search for *it* began, that is, the beginning of the document.

Search for *it* as a whole word:

- Again, select the *Find* command from the **Search** menu. The dialog box shown in Figure 3.41 will be displayed.

- Notice that the word *it* already appears in the *Find What* dialog box. Generally, when the *Find* command is given, the most recently used search phrase is automatically displayed in the dialog box.

- Click the *Match Whole Words Only* box.

- Click the *Find Next* button. The word *It* in line 4 of the document is highlighted. Embedded occurrences of *it* as were found in *writing* before are now skipped.

- Click the *Find Next* button. The *All Occurrences* dialog box is displayed immediately because there is only one occurrence of *it* as a whole word within the document.

- Click the *OK* button. The *All Occurrences* dialog box will disappear. The document window will be displayed with no highlighted areas. The insertion pointer will be at the position at which the search for the word *it* as a whole word began, that is, the beginning of the document.

Search for *it* as a whole word, case sensitive:

- Select the *Find* command from the **Search** menu. The dialog box shown in Figure 3.41 will be displayed.

- Notice that the word *it* already appears in the *Find What* dialog box.

- If it is not already selected, click the *Match Whole Words Only* box.

- Click the *Check Upper/Lowercase* box.

- Click the *Find Next* button. A dialog box is displayed immediately explaining that the word was not found because the only occurrence of *it* as a word within the document starts with capital *I*. Thus, the occurrence *It* does not match *it* as typed in the *Find What* box.

- Click the *OK* button. The dialog box will disappear, and the document window will be displayed with no highlighted areas.

Search for tab markers:

- Select the *Find* command from the **Search** menu. The dialog box shown in Figure 3.41 will be displayed.

- Click the button for the tab marker. The symbol representing a tab will be placed automatically in the *Find What* box, and the *Find Next* button will switch from dimmed to bold.

- Turn off the *Match Whole Words Only* and *Check Upper/Lowercase* boxes.

- Click the *Find Next* button. A search for a tab marker will begin. Recall that in *Practice8<your initials>*, the only tabs used were after the number in each of the numbered paragraphs at the end of the document. The first of these tabs will be found and highlighted as shown in Figure 3.43. Because a tab marker is an invisible character, no character is shown within the highlighted block.

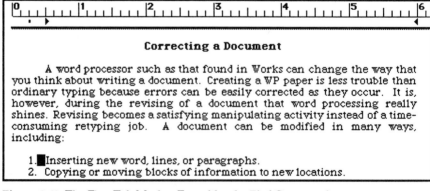

**Correcting a Document**

A word processor such as that found in Works can change the way that you think about writing a document. Creating a WP paper is less trouble than ordinary typing because errors can be easily corrected as they occur. It is, however, during the revising of a document that word processing really shines. Revising becomes a satisfying manipulating activity instead of a time-consuming retyping job. A document can be modified in many ways, including:

1. Inserting new word, lines, or paragraphs.
2. Copying or moving blocks of information to new locations.

**Figure 3.43.** The First Tab Marker Found by the *Find* Command.

- Click the *Find Next* button repeatedly until the dialog box of Figure 3.44 is displayed. Notice that two additional tab markers are discovered in the numbered paragraphs before the dialog box is displayed. In this dialog box the search phrase will always be displayed between the quotation marks.

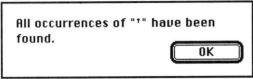

**All occurrences of "†" have been found.**

OK

**Figure 3.44.** The *All Occurrences* Dialog Box of the *Find* Command.

- Click the *OK* button. The *All Occurrences* dialog box will disappear. The document window will be displayed with no areas highlighted. The insertion pointer will be at the position at which the search for tab markers began, that is, the beginning of the document.

Search for paragraph markers:

- Select the *Find* command from the **Search** menu. The dialog box shown in Figure 3.41 will be displayed.

- Click the button for the paragraph marker. The symbol representing a paragraph marker will be placed automatically in the *Find What* box.

- Click the *Find Next* button. A search for a paragraph marker will begin. Recall that in *Practice8<your initials>* the *Return* key was pressed numerous times to create paragraphs and to create blank lines as paragraphs. When a paragraph marker is found, the area from the marker to the end of the line becomes highlighted. Because a paragraph marker is an invisible character, no character is shown within the highlighted block. The highlighting for the paragraph marker at the end of the title line is shown in Figure 3.45.

**Correcting a Document**

A word processor such as that found in Works can change the way that you think about writing a document. Creating a WP paper is less trouble than ordinary typing because errors can be easily corrected as they occur. It is, however, during the revising of a document that word processing really shines. Revising becomes a satisfying manipulating activity instead of a time-consuming retyping job. A document can be modified in many ways, including:

**Figure 3.45.** Highlighted Area after a Paragraph Marker.

- Click the *Find Next* button repeatedly until the *All Occurrences* dialog box is displayed. (Notice that many paragraph markers are discovered before this dialog box is displayed.)

- Click the *OK* button. The *All Occurrences* dialog box will disappear. The document window will be displayed with no highlighted areas. The insertion pointer will be at the position at which the search for paragraph markers began, that is, the beginning of the document.

## REPLACING TEXT

The operation of the *Replace* command is quite similar to that of the *Find* command except that the found word or phrase can be replaced (or not replaced) with a new word or phrase.

Examine the *Replace* dialog box shown in Figure 3.46. The *Find What* box, the tab and paragraph marker buttons, and the *Match Whole Words Only* and *Check Upper/Lowercase* boxes have the same functions as in the *Find* dialog box.

The *Replace With* box is to contain the text, up to 80 characters, that is to replace the text in the *Find What* box when it is found. The *Replace All* button is to be clicked if you want to replace all occurrences of the found text. These operations will be carried out without the intervention of the user. The *Replace, then Find*, *Replace*, and *Find Next* buttons allow the user to examine each occurrence of the found text and replace the text or not before finding the next occurrence of the text.

Perform the following.

- If it is not already there, place the insertion pointer at the beginning of the *Practice8<your initials>* document.

- Select the *Replace* command of the **Search** menu. The dialog box shown in Figure 3.46 will be displayed.

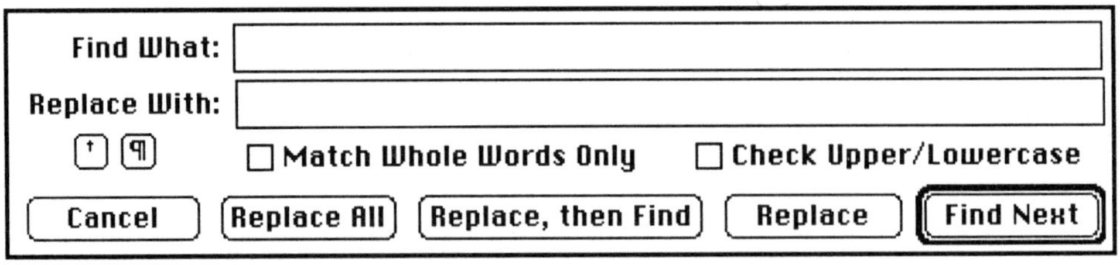

| Find What: | |
|---|---|
| Replace With: | |

[↑] [¶] ☐ Match Whole Words Only ☐ Check Upper/Lowercase

( Cancel ) ( Replace All ) ( Replace, then Find ) ( Replace ) (( Find Next ))

**Figure 3.46.** The *Replace* Dialog Box.

Replace all occurrences of *the*:

- Type *the* in the *Find What* box and *THE* in the *Replace With* box. Do not click the *Match Whole Words Only* button.

- Click the *Replace All* button. The replacement process takes place without operator intervention and produces the document shown in Figure 3.47. The insertion pointer is automatically placed at its original location at the beginning of the document *Practice8<your initials>*.

---

### Correcting a Document

A word processor such as that found in Works can change THE way that you think about writing a document. Creating a WP paper is less trouble than ordinary typing because errors can be easily corrected as THEy occur. It is, however, during THE revising of a document that word processing really shines. Revising becomes a satisfying manipulating activity instead of a time-consuming retyping job. A document can be modified in many ways, including:

1. Inserting new word, lines, or paragraphs.
2. Copying or moving blocks of information to new locations.
3. Changing THE format of THE entire document or THE format of various paragraphs.

Learning to use a word processor is well worth THE time and effort required.

---

**Figure 3.47.** *Practice8<your initials>* after Replacement of All Occurrences of *the*.

- Examine the document. Notice that all occurrences of *the* both whole words and parts of words have been replaced by *THE*.

*Note:* The *Replace All* command should be used with caution! If occurrences of the text string you wish to replace appear in places you have not anticipated, this command will introduce mistakes into your document. Usually, these kinds of mistakes cannot be easily remedied or even found. It is usually better (even though it does take a little more time) to use the *Replace, then Find* and *Find Next* commands, so that you can evaluate each occurrence of the text string for yourself and decide whether to replace or go on to the next occurrence without replacing.

Save the document:

- Use the *Save As* command to save the document with the name *Practice10<your initials>* in the folder *Lesson7* inside folder *Works WP* on your disk. Close the document.

You have now completed Lesson 7. If you do not wish to proceed directly to the next lesson, quit Works by selecting the *Quit* command from the **File** menu, clean up the desktop, and shut down your computer.

*NOTE TO THE READER:* The final four lessons of this chapter demonstrate some features of Works that are common to more than one of the Works modules. In these lessons, the emphasis will be placed on using these features with the Works WP module, but additional examples will be given later when the other Works modules are examined.

# USING THE DRAWING TOOLS

After completing this lesson you will be able to:

❑ Use the Works drawing tools.

❑ Use the **Fill Pattern** and **Fill Line** menus.

❑ Create Works drawings.

## DRAWING CONCEPTS

As you learned in Chapter 2, Works contains a number of drawing features. These features are available in both the word processing and spreadsheet modules (Works WP and Works SS). The *Draw On* command of the **Edit** menu is executed to make the drawing features available in either the word processor or the spreadsheet module. Similarly, to exit the drawing mode, the *Draw Off* command from the **Edit** menu is executed.

In Works, each object drawn can be thought of as existing on a separate transparent sheet. More recently drawn objects may obscure earlier drawn objects that exist on previous sheets. There are techniques to make the objects transparent so they do not hide previous objects. In addition, you will be able to change the order of the sheets after they are created.

When the *Draw On* command is executed, the tool palette shown in Figure 3.48 is displayed along the left side of the window. The tool palette can be moved to any other location as desired by pointing to the word *Tools* and dragging. To select a tool to be used in creating a drawing, point to the tool and click. The drawing tools are represented by icons that suggest their functions.

The selection tool is used for selection and movement of one or many objects in a drawing; the text tool allows you to enter alphabetic characters; the straight line, freehand, vertical/horizontal line, and arc tools are all line drawing tools; and the remaining tools are for drawing frequently occurring shapes. Some techniques for using these tools will now be covered in more detail.

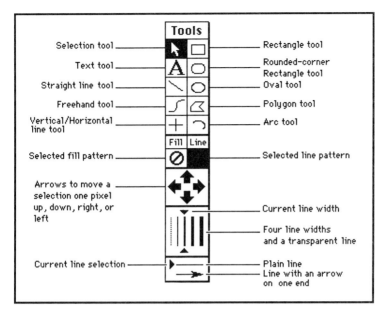

**Figure 3.48.** The Works Drawing Tools.

**Selection Tool.** The selection tool is represented by the pointer arrow icon. To select a graphics object, choose the selection tool, then use the selection pointer arrow to point to the object of interest and click. Alternately, you can click and drag a selection rectangle (which is displayed with dotted lines) to surround the object(s) of interest; when the mouse button is released the object will be selected. When an object is selected, small boxes called *handles* will appear at the corners and on the sides of the object. To move the selected object, place the pointer on the object (not on a handle), and drag the object to the desired location. The size of a selected object can be changed by pointing to a handle and dragging. Figure 3.49 shows two examples of changing the size of a rectangle.

**The Freehand Tool.** The freehand tool is used to make drawings employing techniques similar to those you would make with a pencil or brush in normal drawing. If you click the freehand icon, the pointer assumes a crosshair shape. Move the pointer to the desired starting location for your figure. Then hold down the mouse button and drag the crosshair to draw the desired figure. You will probably need considerable practice to be able to control accurately the motion of the mouse (and hence the crosshair). When you release the mouse button, the figure will be displayed in a selected state, ready to be moved or resized as described above. To continue drawing you must again select a drawing tool.

When an object created using the freehand tool is selected, a number of handles will appear and the object may be "resized" in a number of directions, as illustrated in Figure 3.50.

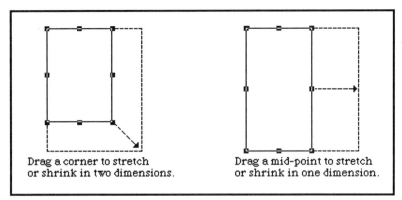

**Figure 3.49.** Changing the Size of a Rectangle.

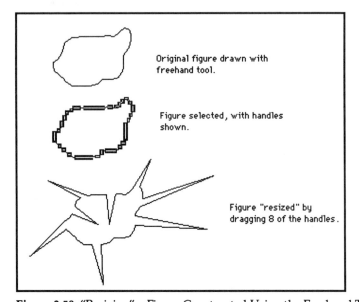

**Figure 3.50.** "Resizing" a Figure Constructed Using the Freehand Tool.

**The Line Tool.** The line tool is used to draw a straight line between any two points. When this tool icon is clicked, the pointer again becomes a small crosshair. Point to the first location, drag to the second location, keeping the button depressed, and then release the button to create a line between the two locations. The line will appear in a selected state with a handle at either end. It may be moved or resized as before. Notice that resizing by dragging an end of the line allows it to be rotated, keeping the other end fixed. If the line tool is selected again, note that whenever the crosshair is touching a line, it is white. This feature allows you to align separately created lines perfectly. The use of the line tool to draw a triangle is shown in Figure 3.51.

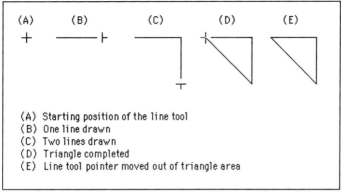

(A)  Starting position of the line tool
(B)  One line drawn
(C)  Two lines drawn
(D)  Triangle completed
(E)  Line tool pointer moved out of triangle area

**Figure 3.51.** Use of the Line Tool to Draw a Triangle.

**The Vertical/Horizontal Line Tool.** The vertical/horizontal line tool operates in a way quite similar to the line tool. The difference is that the vertical/horizontal line tool will allow only vertical or horizontal lines to be drawn. The **arc tool** functions in essentially the same way as the line tool, with an arc being drawn to connect the starting and ending mouse positions.

You can cause an arrowhead to be placed on the end of any straight line to be drawn by selecting the *arrowed line* choice at the bottom of the tool palette before selecting your line draw tool. Alternatively, you can place an arrowhead at the end of a line already drawn by first selecting the line, then clicking the *arrowed line* at the bottom of the tool palette. In this same way, you can change an arrowed line to a plain line by selecting the line, then clicking the *plain line* choice from the tool palette. Note that for any of the drawing tools, the line width may be changed in a similar way by choosing the desired width from the tool palette.

**Fill Patterns.** A drawing may be filled with a pattern. To do this select the drawing by clicking it, and click the desired pattern in the **Fill Pattern** menu; then the drawing will be filled with the pattern. If the drawing selected does not form a closed figure, the fill pattern will be placed in a position to close the figure's boundary. A portion of the **Fill Pattern** menu is shown in Figure 3.52. Lines may also have different patterns, which can be obtained from the **Fill Line** menu. (The **Fill Pattern** and **Fill Line** menus contain the same patterns.) The special pattern, ⊘, which is found in both menus, makes the drawing or line transparent. This pattern should always be used for drawings that overlay text, and it may be used to allow obscured objects to be seen. Note that the currently selected fill and line patterns are displayed in the tool palette, as shown in Figure 3.48.

**Additional Drawing Tools.** The remaining drawing tools make it easy to paint simple figures such as rectangles and ovals. Each type of figure can

**155**

be filled with the various patterns available in the **Fill Pattern** menu. To draw a rectangle, click the **rectangle tool** and the pointer becomes a crosshair identical to that used for the line tool. Place the crosshair at a location that is to be a corner of the rectangle, and drag to the diagonally opposite corner. Releasing the mouse button stops the drawing of the rectangle. The rectangle will be filled with the currently selected pattern. The pattern can be changed after the rectangle is drawn by first selecting the rectangle and then selecting the desired pattern from the **Fill Pattern** menu as discussed above. Figure 3.53 illustrates this procedure. The **rounded-corner** and **oval tools** function in exactly the same manner as the rectangle tool.

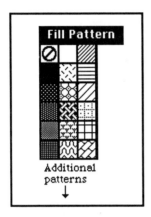

**Figure 3.52.** A Portion of the **Fill Pattern** Menu.

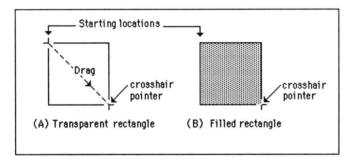

**Figure 3.53.** Drawing Hollow and Filled Rectangles.

The **polygon tool** allows you to easily draw various polygons (closed figures having straight lines for their sides). To draw a polygon, select the polygon tool and place the crosshair at the starting point. Click once, then move the crosshair to the termination point of the first side of your figure and click again. When you click, the line you just drew will be completed, but instead of being returned to the selection tool (as would be the case if you were using the line tool), the selected tool remains the polygon tool. Simply move the tool to the point where your second side will terminate. Then click the mouse button to complete the second side of your polygon. Continuing in this manner you can easily complete the figure. When you have finished your figure (note that it does not have to be a true polygon, because it does not have to be closed), double click to complete the figure and return to the selection tool, leaving your figure selected.

**The Text Tool.**  The text tool allows you to type alphabetic characters into a drawing.  The size and style of these characters can be selected by choosing the appropriate option(s) in the **Font**, **Size**, and **Style** submenus found under the **Format** menu just as is done within Works WP.  Editing is also performed exactly as it is in Works WP.

## USING THE DRAWING TOOLS

In this part of the lesson you will create simple drawings using the Works drawing tools.  The examples are intended to illustrate techniques and not to produce a meaningful drawing; you will do that later in the Practice Projects.  Your work should resemble that shown in the diagrams, but it does not have to be identical.  Perform the following.

- Open Works and create a new WP document.

- Select the *Draw On* command from the **Edit** menu.

- Drag the drawing tool palette to the lower right of your document window.

Draw a closed figure having points:

- Select the freehand tool and use it to create a simple closed figure similar to the one shown earlier in the top portion of Figure 3.50.

- Select the figure by pointing at its outline and clicking.

- Experiment with "resizing" the figure.

- If the object is not selected, select it.  Practice moving the object by dragging it to different locations on the screen.  This can be tricky because you must point to the outline of the object but not to a handle.

- Finally, when you have mastered moving the object, press the delete key to erase it.  (Note that the object must be selected for this latter operation.)

Draw a figure having multiple objects:

In this part of the lesson, you will use the rectangle, oval, and arc tools to create the drawing elements shown in Figure 3 54

- Select the rectangle tool by pointing at it and clicking. If the transparent fill symbol, 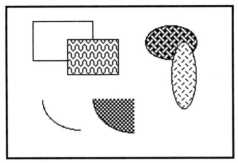, is not displayed on the drawing palette, select it from the **Fill Pattern** menu.

**Figure 3.54.** The Drawing to be Constructed.

- Draw the first rectangle (the one with its upper left corner nearest to the upper left corner of the drawing).

- Select the rectangle tool and select the fill pattern shown in the second rectangle from the **Fill Pattern** menu. The appropriate fill pattern should now be displayed on the tools palette.

- Draw the second rectangle.

- Select the oval tool and select the appropriate fill pattern as shown in the first oval (the one "underneath" the other oval).

- Draw the first oval.

- Select the oval tool and select the appropriate fill pattern for the second oval.

- Draw the second oval.

- Select the arc tool.

- Choose the transparent fill pattern.

- Draw the leftmost arc and click to deselect the arc.

- Select the arc tool.

- Draw the second arc and, while it is selected, choose a fill pattern. Your drawing should now be similar to Figure 3.54.

- Save the document as *Drawing1<your initials>* in the *Lesson8* folder in the *Works WP* folder on your disk.

Copy a drawing having multiple objects:

- Choose the selection tool from the drawing tools palette.

- Point to a location above and to the left of the multi-object figure you have just created.

- Press the mouse button and drag the pointer in a downward diagonal until the entire figure is enclosed in a dashed rectangle. Release the mouse button. All the objects in the figure should have handles to indicate that they are selected. If not all the objects have been selected, try again until you do select all of them.

- Select the *Copy* command from the **Edit** menu. A copy of the figure will be placed on the *Clipboard*.

- Select the *Paste* command from the **Edit** menu. A copy of the figure will be pasted onto the current document. The copy of the figure may obscure a portion of the original figure, but because the copy is still selected, it can be moved.

- Point to any point within the body of one of the selected objects and drag the figure to below the original version of the figure. Notice that all the objects move as a unit because of the way they were selected.

Change the newly created figure:

In this section of the lesson you will modify the copy of the figure so that it looks like Figure 3.55 and then save it.

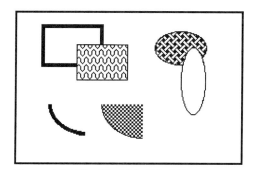

**Figure 3.55.** The First Modified Drawing.

- Select the first rectangle (the transparent rectangle) and click the widest line width indicator on the drawing tools palette. This will cause the width of the line defining the rectangle to increase.

- Select the first arc (the one without the fill pattern) and click the widest line width indicator on the drawing tools palette to cause the width of the arc to increase.

159

- Select the oval on top and select the "plain" fill pattern from the **Fill Pattern** menu. Your version of the figure should now resemble that shown in Figure 3.55.

- Use the *Save As* command to save your document as *Drawing2<your initials>* in folder *Lesson8* in the folder *Works WP* on your disk.

Change the order of appearance of objects:

- Resize the larger oval and the transparent rectangle so they appear as they do in Figure 3.56.

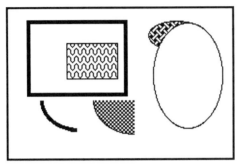

**Figure 3.56.** The Drawing with the Oval and Rectangle Modified.

- Select the smaller rectangle and move it so that your figure now looks like the one shown in Figure 3.57.

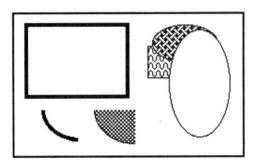

**Figure 3.57.** The Drawing Modified by Moving the Small Rectangle.

- Select the larger oval by clicking over its boundary.

- Execute the *Send to Back* Command in the **Format** menu.

- Select the smaller rectangle by clicking over its boundary.

- Execute the *Send to Back* Command in the **Format** menu.

- Select the larger oval by clicking over its boundary.

- Execute the *Bring to Front* Command in the **Format** menu.

- With the larger oval still selected, choose the transparent fill pattern from the **Fill Pattern** menu.  Your figure should now look like the one in Figure 3.58.

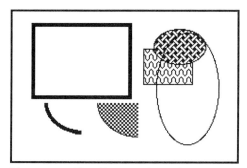

**Figure 3.58.** The  Drawing Modified by Moving the Small Rectangle.

- Use the *Save As* command to save your document as *Drawing3<your initials>* in folder *Lesson8* in the folder *Works WP* on your disk.

Create some polygons:

- Use the polygon tool to create the two figures shown in Figure 3.59.  Place these drawings below or to the side of the previous drawings on your page.  Use the transparent pattern for the first figure.  Remember that you must double click to complete the figure.

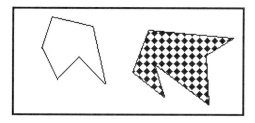

**Figure 3.59.** A Drawing Illustrating the Polygon Tool.

- Use the *Save As* command to save your document as *Drawing4<your initials>* in folder *Lesson8* in the folder *Works WP* on your disk.  Close your document.

You have now completed Lesson 8.  If you do not wish to proceed directly to the next lesson, quit Works by selecting the *Quit* command from the **File** menu, clean up the desktop, and shut down your computer.

# INCORPORATING GRAPHICS INTO WORKS WP DOCUMENTS

After completing this lesson you will be able to:

❏ Use the drawing features of Works with WP documents.

❏ Use drawings from other drawing packages with Works WP documents.

## USING DRAWING WITH WORKS WP DOCUMENTS

Recall that drawing in Works takes place on a transparent sheet that overlays the text page of the document. Thus, drawings and changes to drawings have no effect on the text of the document that it overlays. However, when a drawing is placed over or near a portion of text, the drawing is associated with the text. For example, if lines are added or deleted so that text must be moved vertically within the document, all drawings move with their associated text. However, if text is moved horizontally, text and drawings may lose their association. As an example, you will insert a graphic object into the table shown in Figure 3.34 and then observe the behavior of the object as the table is modified.

Perform the following.

- Open the document that you saved as *Table<your initials>* in the folder *Lesson5* in your *Works WP* folder.

Create a box around the total:

- Select the *Draw On* command from the **Edit** menu.

- Select the rectangle tool from the drawing tools palette.

- Make the rectangle transparent, by selecting (if necessary) the transparent symbol from the **Fill Pattern** menu.

- Draw a rectangle around the value of the total to emphasize it. Your table should look approximately like that shown in Figure 3.60. If necessary, move and resize the rectangle.

| Item | Unit Cost | Number | Total |
|------|-----------|--------|-------|
| Micro disks | 1.80 | 200 | 360.00 |
| Printer ribbons | 7.00 | 15 | 105.00 |
| Paper, printer | 21.10 | 5 | 126.60 |
| Total | | | 591.60 |

**Figure 3.60.** Enhancing a Table with Graphics.

Modify the table.

- Select the *Draw Off* command from **Edit**. Delete the blank line between the column headings and the first line of data. Notice that the rectangle moves up with its associated text.

- Place the insertion pointer at the end of the heading line and press the *Return* key twice to reinsert the blank line just removed and one additional blank line. Notice that the rectangle moves down with its associated text.

- Place the insertion pointer at the end of the second line of data (after the 105.00) and press the *Return* key to insert a blank line. Notice that the rectangle and its associated text moved down.

- Pressing the *Tab* key as necessary, type the following data into the blank line: *Tape, printer, 10.00, 1, 10.00*. Notice the rectangle and its associated text did not move.

- Change the value of the total to *601.60*. Notice the rectangle and its associated text did not move. The table should now look like the Figure 3.61.

| Item | Unit Cost | Number | Total |
|------|-----------|--------|-------|
| Micro disks | 1.80 | 200 | 360.00 |
| Printer ribbons | 7.00 | 15 | 105.00 |
| Tape, printer | 10.00 | 1 | 10.00 |
| Paper, printer | 21.10 | 6 | 126.60 |
| Total | | | 601.60 |

**Figure 3.61.** The Table Modified.

- Place the insertion pointer in the total line.

- Point to the decimal tab at 4.75 inches in the ruler and drag the tab to 4.0 in Notice that the rectangle and the value of the total are no longer aligned properly.

- Select the *Draw On* command from the **Edit** menu, select the rectangle, and move it into proper alignment.

- Use the *Save As* command to save the document with the name *Table2<your initials>* in the folder *Lesson9* inside your *Works WP* folder.

- Select *Draw Off* and move the decimal tab back to 4.75 inches.

- Now select *Draw On* and realign the rectangle over the text.

Enhance the document with another rectangle:

- Select the rectangle tool from the drawing tools palette.

- Make the rectangle transparent, by selecting (if necessary) the transparent symbol from the **Fill Pattern** menu.

- Draw a rectangle around the entire table to emphasize it. Your table should look approximately like that shown in Figure 3.62. If necessary, move and resize the rectangle.

- Use the *Save As* command to save the document with the name *Table3<your initials>* in the folder *Lesson9* inside your *Works WP* folder.

| Item | Unit Cost | Number | Total |
|---|---|---|---|
| Micro disks | 1.80 | 200 | 360.00 |
| Printer ribbons | 7.00 | 15 | 105.00 |
| Tape, printer | 10.00 | 1 | 10.00 |
| Paper, printer | 21.10 | 6 | 126.60 |
| | Total | | 601.60 |

**Figure 3.62.** The Table with a Second Rectangle.

Enhance the document with additional graphics:

(You are going to create the drawing at the top of the page illustrated in Figure 3.63.)

- Select the *Draw Off* command from the **Edit** menu.

- Place the insertion pointer at the top of your document and press the *Return* key seven times to place some blank lines above your table. Your graphics objects (rectangles) should move down with the table text. If they do not, select *Draw On* and position them correctly.

- Select the *Draw On* command from the **Edit** menu.

- Select the text tool from the drawing tools palette.

- Access the **Font** submenu in the **Format** menu and select *Chicago* font (if this font is not available select another font).

- Access the **Size** submenu in the **Format** menu and select *18 point*.

- Place the insertion pointer near the top of your page and click to create a text field.

- Type *Computer Supplies for May*. Resize, if necessary, so that the text is all on one line. To do this, use the Selection tool.

- Select the oval tool from the drawing tools palette.

- Select transparent from the **Fill Patterns** menu.

- Draw an oval around the text *Computer Supplies for May* that you just entered; see Figure 3.63.

- When you are satisfied with the position and size of the oval (and with it still selected), choose the ▦ pattern from the **Fill Pattern** menu.

- With the oval still selected, execute the *Send to Back* command from the **Format** menu.

- Reposition the oval and the text inside it if necessary so that your document looks like the one shown in Figure 3.63. To move both objects (the oval and the text field) at once, you will need to use the shift-click method to select them both, and then drag by the boundary of the oval.

- Use the *Save As* command to save the document with the name *Table4<your initials>* in the folder *Lesson9* inside your *Works WP* folder. Close the document.

**Computer Supplies for May**

| Item | Unit Cost | Number | Total |
|---|---|---|---|
| Micro disks | 1.80 | 200 | 360.00 |
| Printer ribbons | 7.00 | 15 | 105.00 |
| Tape, printer | 10.00 | 1 | 10.00 |
| Paper, printer | 21.10 | 6 | 126.60 |
| | Total | | 601.60 |

**Figure 3.63.** The Table with a Additional Graphics Enhancement.

The next section of this lesson requires that:

You have access to a drawing package (MacPaint, SuperPaint, or some similar package).

You have some expertise at using the drawing package.

If these conditions are true for you, proceed to the next section. However, if either of the above two conditions do not hold, you have now completed Lesson 9, and you may proceed to the Lesson 10 if you desire. If you do not wish to proceed directly to the next lesson, quit Works, clean up the desktop, and shut down your computer.

## USING GRAPHICS FROM OTHER SOFTWARE PACKAGES

There will be times when you would like to include within your documents graphics objects that are too complex to be created with the Works drawing tools alone. In these instances the picture might first be prepared with a program such as MacPaint or SuperPaint. For example, the champagne glass in the company party invitation letter shown in Figure 3.1 is quite tedious to create with the Works tools because the glass must be drawn as many objects that must be assembled much like a picture puzzle to produce the appearance of a single object.

Assuming that you have adequate knowledge of a painting program, you could prepare the company letter as follows. If you have experience with and access to a painting program, try this activity on your own.

- Open a new Works word processing document.

- Type the letter shown in Figure 3.1.

- Use the Works drawing tools to create the horizontal lines and the balloons.

- Save the document as *PartyLetter<your initials>* in the *Lesson9* folder inside the *Works WP* folder on your disk.

- Open your painting program.

- Prepare the champagne glass using the painting program.

- Select and copy the champagne glass painting to the Clipboard.

- Exit the painting program.

- Open the document *PartyLetter<your initials>* that you saved earlier.

- Move the I-beam pointer to the location where the insertion of the champagne glass painting is to occur.

- Click the mouse button to set the insertion point to this location.

- Paste the contents of the Clipboard into the document at the insertion point by selecting the *Paste* command of the **File** menu. Once you have pasted the painting into Works, it becomes an object that may be edited (moved, resized, deleted) just like the graphics objects created within Works itself.

- Position the champagne glass so your letter looks like the one in Figure 3.1.

- Save the document. Close the document.

You have now completed Lesson 9. If you do not wish to proceed directly to the next lesson, quit Works, clean up the desktop, and shut down your computer.

# PAGE FORMATTING AND DOCUMENT PRINTING

After completing this lesson you will be able to:

❑ Format pages in Works documents.

❑ Set page margins for Works documents.

❑ Set and remove manual page breaks in Works WP documents.

❑ Create headers and footers for Works WP documents.

❑ Preview documents on screen before printing.

❑ Print Works documents.

## PAGE SETUP

Recall from Lesson 6 of Chapter 1 that the specification of various parameters for printing (such as page margins, page size, orientation, and other special effects) is done by accessing the *Page Setup* command in the **File** menu. Theparticular options available in the *Page Setup* dialog box will depend on what context you are in when the command is executed and what printer you have allocated in the *Chooser* dialog box.

Practice using the *Page Setup* command from within Works by doing the following activities.

• Open the document *Table4<your initials>* in the folder *Lesson9* inside your *Works WP* folder.

• Use the *Chooser* command in the **Apple** menu to select an Image-Writer printer if you have more than one kind of printer available.

• Select the *Page Setup* command from the **File** menu.

Set print parameters:

• Select the *Vertical* orientation (the icon that shows the image of an upright man on a page coming from a printer).

• Select *US Letter* for the paper.

- If paper width is not 8.5 in. and paper height is not 11 in., change them to be so.

- Set all margins to 1 in. Your dialog box should now be as shown in Figure 3.64. Note the two boxes titled *Header* and *Footer*. The purposes of these boxes and the details of how to use them are presented in a later section of this lesson.

- Click the *OK* button.

- Use the *Save As* command to save the document as *Table5<your initials>* in the folder *Lesson10* inside your *Works WP* folder. Save the document.

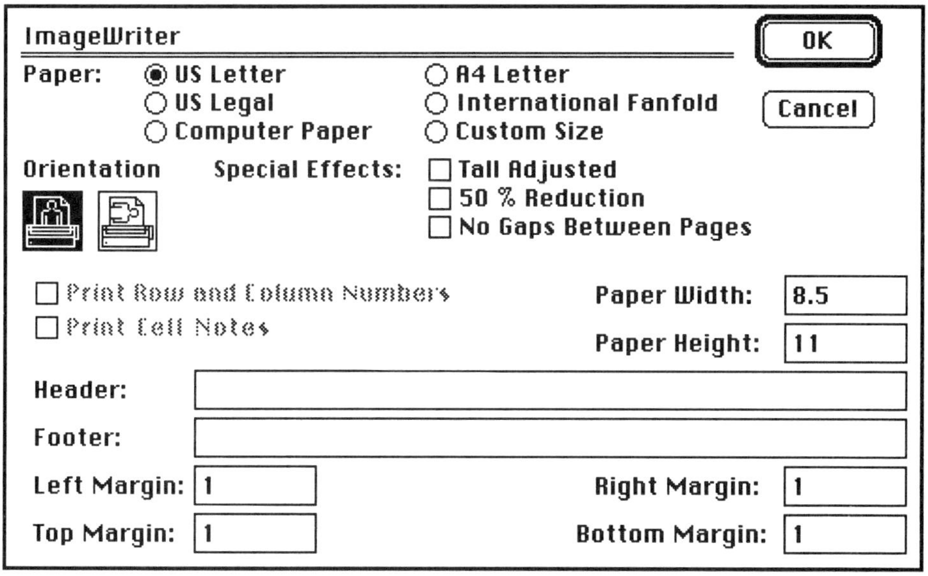

---

**ImageWriter**            [ **OK** ]

Paper:   ● US Letter      ○ A4 Letter
         ○ US Legal      ○ International Fanfold    [ Cancel ]
         ○ Computer Paper      ○ Custom Size

Orientation      Special Effects:   ☐ Tall Adjusted
                            ☐ 50 % Reduction
                            ☐ No Gaps Between Pages

☐ Print Row and Column Numbers      Paper Width:   | 8.5 |
☐ Print Cell Notes      Paper Height:   | 11 |

Header:   [_____]

Footer:   [_____]

Left Margin: | 1 |      Right Margin: | 1 |

Top Margin: | 1 |      Bottom Margin: | 1 |

**Figure 3.64.** The *Page Setup* Window for the ImageWriter.

---

Examine the LaserWriter Page Setup dialog box:

- Use the *Chooser* command in the **Apple** menu to select a Laser-Writer printer if you have one available. If you do not have such a printer available in the Chooser dialog box, close the dialog box and skip to the next section: *Print Preview*.

- Select the *Page Setup* command from the **File** menu.

- Examine the dialog box. It should look similar to the one shown in Figure 3.65. Note that there are some additional options compared to the ImageWriter *Page Setup* dialog box, and that some of the items in the ImageWriter *Page Setup* dialog box are not present in the LaserWriter *Page Setup* dialog box. This is because of the different characteristics and capabilities of the two kinds of printers.

169

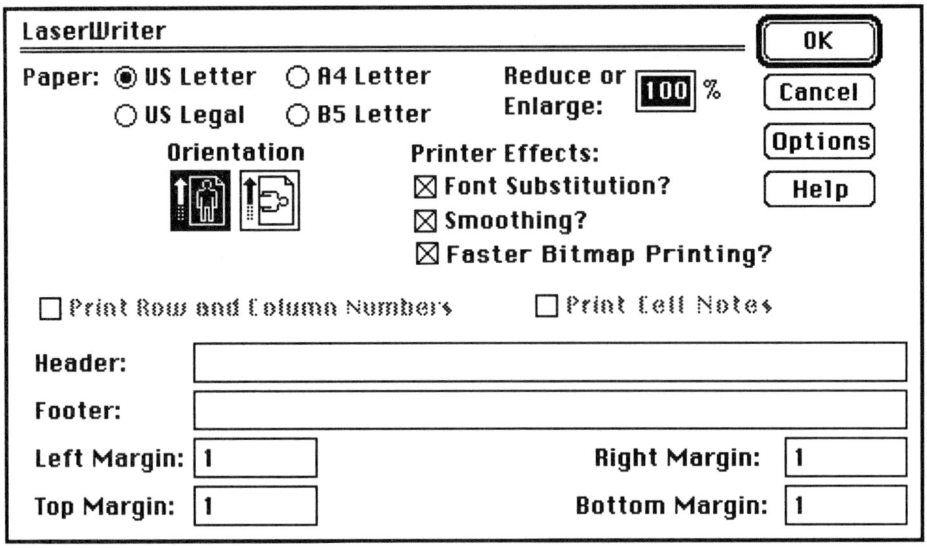

```
┌──────────────────────────────────────────────────────────────────────────┐
│ LaserWriter                                                    ╭────────╮  │
│ ═══════════════════════════════════════════════════════════   │   OK   │  │
│ Paper: ● US Letter   ○ A4 Letter    Reduce or ┌────┐ %        ╰────────╯  │
│        ○ US Legal    ○ B5 Letter    Enlarge:  │100 │          ╭────────╮  │
│            Orientation         Printer Effects: └────┘        │ Cancel │  │
│            ┌──┐ ┌──┐            ⊠ Font Substitution?          ╰────────╯  │
│            │  │ │  │            ⊠ Smoothing?                  ╭─────────╮ │
│            └──┘ └──┘            ⊠ Faster Bitmap Printing?     │ Options │ │
│                                                              ╰─────────╯ │
│      ☐ Print Row and Column Numbers     ☐ Print Cell Notes   ╭────────╮  │
│                                                              │  Help  │  │
│  Header:  ┌──────────────────────────────────────────────╮  ╰────────╯  │
│           └──────────────────────────────────────────────┘              │
│  Footer:  ┌──────────────────────────────────────────────┐              │
│           └──────────────────────────────────────────────┘              │
│  Left Margin: ┌───┐              Right Margin: ┌───┐                     │
│               │ 1 │                            │ 1 │                     │
│  Top Margin:  │ 1 │              Bottom Margin:│ 1 │                     │
│               └───┘                            └───┘                     │
└──────────────────────────────────────────────────────────────────────────┘
```

Figure 3.65. The *Page Setup* Window for the LaserWriter.

## PRINT PREVIEW

The *Print Preview* option of the *Print* command allows a user to examine the layout of a document before printing it. Because printing is time consuming, it is a good idea to preview the appearance of a document on the screen before actually printing it. If any problems are discovered, the document can be reformatted as desired. After any changes, use *Print Preview* again. When you are satisfied with the form of the document, the actual printing can be done.

The *Print Preview* option can be used with word processing, spreadsheet, and database documents. In all cases the *Print* command of the **File** menu is selected, which causes a *Print* dialog box to be displayed as is illustrated for the ImageWriter printer in Figure 3.66. Notice the *Print Preview* box in the lower left-hand corner. Clicking this box causes the print preview mode to be used instead of actually printing the document.

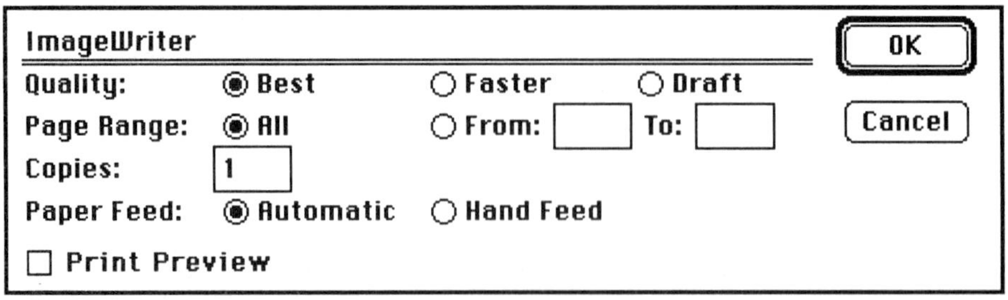

```
┌──────────────────────────────────────────────────────────────────────────┐
│ ImageWriter                                                    ╭────────╮  │
│ ═══════════════════════════════════════════════════════════   │   OK   │  │
│ Quality:      ● Best      ○ Faster      ○ Draft               ╰────────╯  │
│ Page Range:   ● All       ○ From: ┌────┐  To: ┌────┐          ╭────────╮  │
│ Copies:       ┌───┐               └────┘      └────┘          │ Cancel │  │
│               │ 1 │                                           ╰────────╯  │
│               └───┘                                                       │
│ Paper Feed:   ● Automatic ○ Hand Feed                                     │
│ ☐ Print Preview                                                           │
└──────────────────────────────────────────────────────────────────────────┘
```

Figure 3.66. *Print* Dialog Box for the ImageWriter.

When a document is examined using the *Print Preview* feature, a window such as that shown in Figure 3.67 is displayed. When the pointer is moved over the page being displayed, it will assume the form of a magnifying glass. Clicking will cause the area under it to be displayed in normal size. The pointer then becomes a hand, which can be used to move the page to view different areas. Double clicking will return you to the full page view. The *Previous* button moves to the previous page and the *Next* button moves to the next page. The *Print* button will initiate actual printing of the document, and the *Cancel* button returns you to the document in Works WP proper.

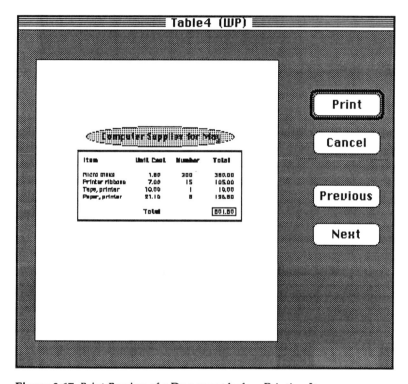

**Figure 3.67.** *Print Preview* of a Document before Printing It.

Examine the document *Table5<your initials>* using the print preview feature by the following steps.

- With your document *Table5<your initials>* open, use the *Chooser* command in the **Apple** menu to select an ImageWriter printer.

- Select the *Print* command from the **File** menu.

- Click the *Print Preview* box, then click the *OK* button. A reduced-sized page will be displayed that shows the location of the text for the page above the page break.

171

- Move the pointer over the page so that it assumes the shape of a small magnifying glass. Click to see a full-sized version of the page.

- Notice that the pointer has changed to the shape of a hand. Drag the page in the window using this tool.

- Return to the page preview view of the page by double clicking while the pointer is over the page.

- Return to the normal window by clicking the *Cancel* button.

## HEADERS AND FOOTERS

A *header* is a special line of text that appears as the top line of each page. A Works header appears in the area reserved for the top margin and does not reduce the area for entering text. It also does not show on the screen as a document is entered; it appears only on the printed document. A header may contain such information as a title, a page number, and a date. A *footer* is like a header except it is printed at the bottom of a page.

Recall that the page setup screens, Figures 3.64 and 3.65, contain boxes titled *Header* and *Footer*. Any information entered in these blocks will be treated as a header or a footer. Special sequences of characters starting with an & is used to specify details of the format. The special formatting characters are elements of the language syntax and do not show when a header of footer is printed. Figure 3.68 shows the characters and their meanings.

It is possible to prevent headers and footers from being printed on a document's first page. This is done by declaring the first page to be a title page. To do so, you must select the *Title Page* command in the **Format** menu. Then the header will be printed on the second and all following pages, and the displayed page numbers, if included, will start with 2.

```
&L  Align at the left margin
&C  Center between the margins
&R  Align at the right margin

&P  Print the page number
&D  Print the current date
&T  Print the current time
&F  Print the document name

&B  Print in bold
&I  Print in italic
&&  Print an "&"
```

**Figure 3.68.** Formatting Characters for Works Headers and Footers.

Perform the following.

- With your document *Table5<your initials>* open, select the *Page Setup* command from the **File** menu.

- Enter the following into the *Header* box:

    &L&BAce Consultants&R&D

    The meanings of the parts of the header are:

    &L causes the title to be left justified.

    &B causes the title to be bold.

    *Ace Consultants* is the title.

    &R causes the next item to be right justified.

    &D causes the date to be printed.

- Enter the following into the *Footer* box:

    &CPage&P

    The meanings of the parts of the footer are:

    &C causes the next item to be centered.

    *Page* is to be printed.

    &P causes the current page number to be printed.

- Click the *OK* button.

Check header and footer in Print Preview:

- Select the *Print* command from the **File** menu.

- Click the *Print Preview* box, then click the *OK* button. A reduced-sized page will be displayed that shows the page with header and footer included. This is illustrated in Figure 3.69.

- Move the pointer over the page so that it assumes the shape of a small magnifying glass. Click to see a full-sized version of the page.

- Drag the page in the window using the hand tool so that you can observe the header and footer.

- Return to the page preview view of the page by double clicking while the pointer is over the page.

- Return to the normal window by clicking the *Cancel* button.

- Save the document.

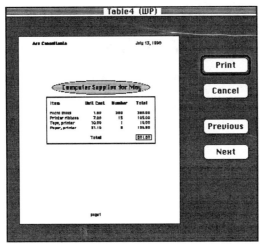

**Figure 3.69.** *Print Preview* of a Document Showing Header and Footer.

## PRINTING DOCUMENTS

Documents are printed in Works by selecting the *Print* command from the **File** menu while the desired document is open and in the active window. When the *Print* command is executed, a *Print* dialog box will be presented. The exact form of this dialog box will depend on what kind of printer has most recently been chosen in the *Chooser* dialog box. The *Print* dialog box for the ImageWriter was shown in Figure 3.66 and the *Print* dialog box for the ImageWriter is shown in Figure 3.70. Printing is initiated by clicking the *OK* box after the appropriate parameters have been set.

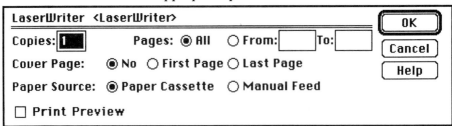

**Figure 3.70.** *Print* Dialog Box for the LaserWriter.

For the ImageWriter, the print quality can be selected by clicking the appropriate box. Note that the draft quality is fastest, but character styles, fonts, graphics, and formatting information are sacrificed to obtain printing speed, and so this option is seldom chosen.

For both printers a single page only or a given sequence of pages in the document can be printed. To print a sequence of pages, you would place the pointer in the *From* box, enter the starting page number, tab to the *To* box, and enter the ending page number. If you desire to print a single page, you place the number of the page in both the *From* and *To* boxes. If no entries are placed in the *From* and *To* boxes, the entire document will be printed. You can print more than one copy of the document (or the selected pages) by entering the number of copies desired in the *Copies* box.

Perform the following.

- With your document *Table5<your initials>* open, use the *Chooser* command in the **Apple** menu to select an ImageWriter printer.

- Execute the *Print* command from the **File** menu.

- Select *Best* for print quality.

- Click *OK* to initiate the printing.

- When the printing is complete, you will be returned to your document window. Close your document.

## PAGE BREAKS

As you type a Works WP document, the text is automatically divided into pages. The division between pages is shown by a dotted line across the screen. The vertical scroll box contains the page number of the text displayed in the window.

Occasionally the automatic page break produces an unsatisfactory result such as dividing a short table between two pages or making the last line of a paragraph the first line at the top of the next page. You can override the automatic page break by inserting manual page breaks using the *Insert Page Break* command in the **Format** menu. To insert a manual page break, place the insertion pointer at the location of the desired page break and then select the *Insert Page Break* command.

A manual page break will be signaled by a dashed line across the window instead of a dotted line. Once a manual page break is entered, Works WP will automatically reposition the page breaks for pages that follow. To remove a manual page break, place the insertion pointer at the beginning of the line *following* the dashed line that represents the manual page break and select the *Remove Page Break* command of the **Format** menu. *This command will appear in the pull-down menu only when the insertion pointer is properly positioned.*

Perform the following.

- Open your document *Practice2<your initials>* in the folder *Lesson 2* in the folder *Works WP* on your disk.

- Place the insertion pointer at the beginning of the fifth line of the practice document by pointing and clicking. If your document is like that shown in Figure 3.19, the insertion point will be immediately to the left of the word *however*.

- Choose the *Insert Page Break* command from the **Format** menu. A dashed line will be drawn above the insertion pointer and across the page to indicate the manual page break. See Figure 3.71.

Examine in Print Preview:

- Select the *Print* command from the **File** menu.

- Click the *Print Preview* box and then click the *OK* button. A reduced sized page will be displayed that shows the location of the text for the page above the page break.

- Click the *Next* button to see the location of the text for the page that follows the page break.

- Return to the normal window by clicking the *Cancel* button.

- Place the insertion point before the word *however*, which is in the line below the manual page break indicator. If your document looks different, place the insertion pointer at the beginning of the line below the manual page break indicator.

- Choose the *Remove Page Break* command from the **Format** menu. The dashed line will disappear.

- Examine the document with the print preview feature, which will demonstrate that the page break is gone.

- Close your document without saving the changes.

---

Correcting a Document

A word processor such as that found in Works can change the way that you think about writing a document. Creating a WP paper is less trouble than ordinary typing because errors can be easily corrected as they occur. It is, however, during the revising of a document that word processing really shines. Revising becomes a satisfying manipulating activity instead of a time-consuming retyping job. A document can be modified in many ways, including:

---

**Figure 3.71.** An Example of a Manual Page Break.

You have now completed Lesson 10. If you do not wish to proceed directly to the next lesson, quit Works, clean up the desktop, and shut down your computer.

# CREATING AND USING MACROS

After this lesson you will be able to:

❑ Define a Works WP macro.

❑ Use a Works WP macro to perform a useful repetitious activity.

A Works macro is a recorded sequence of keystrokes that can be played back at any later time to duplicate the initially recorded keystroke sequence. Thus, macros are valuable in Works to automate frequently occurring, repetitive tasks. In this lesson you are to assume that tables of the kind shown earlier in Figure 3.34 must be prepared frequently. The data in the table are different from one instance to another, but the column headings and tab markers are always the same. You will record a macro to create the headings and set the tabs.
Perform the following.

- Open Works and create a new word processing document.

Record the macro:

- Set the font to *New York* by selecting it from the **Font** submenu of the **Format** menu.

- Select font size *12 points* by selecting it from the **Size** submenu of the **Format** menu.

- Drag any displayed tabs off the ruler to obtain tabs in their preset default positions. (In this particular case there will be no displayed tabs because you are working with a new document, and you can skip this step. Normally, you would be creating a macro within an existing document.)

- Select the *Macros On* command from the **Macro** menu, which is shown in Figure 3.72.

- Select the *Start Recording* command from the **Macro** menu  A dialog box will be displayed that requires you to enter the name of a key for executing the macro and allows you to enter a description of the macro. The dialog box for the sample macro is shown in Figure 3.73.

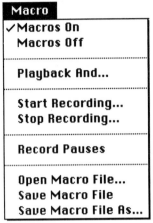

Figure 3.72. The **Macro** Menu.

- Enter a name, *h*, for the key (*h* stands for *heading*).

- Press the *Tab* key and then enter the word description of the macro, *headings for table*, as shown in Figure 3.73.

- Click the *Record* button to start the recording. If you were to click the *Record pauses* box, all the pauses you make in creating the macro would be recorded as part of the macro. Then playing the macro would take as long as you took to create it.

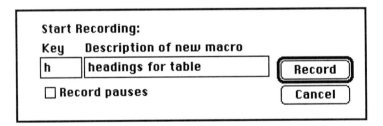

Figure 3.73. The *Start Recording* Dialog Box.

- Create a blank line by pressing the *Return* key.

- Place left tab stops at 0.375 (3/8), 2, 3.25, and 4.375 (4 3/8) in. by pointing and clicking at these locations in the ruler.

- Turn on bold font by selecting the *Bold* command from the **Style** submenu of the **Format** menu.

- Type the column headings by:

  - Pressing the *Tab* key and typing **Item.**

  - Pressing the *Tab* key and typing **Unit Cost.**

  - Pressing the *Tab* key and typing **Number.**

  - Pressing the *Tab* key and typing **Total.**

- Turn off the bold font by selecting the *Bold* command once again from the **Style** submenu of the **Format** menu.

- Press the *Return* key twice to obtain a blank line.

- Place the tabs for the contents of the table by performing the following.

  - Drag the left tab at 2 in. to 2.5 in. and click it twice to change it into a decimal tab.

  - Drag the left tab at 3.25 in. to 3.75 in. and click it to change it into a right tab.

  - Drag the tab at 4.25 in. to 4.75 in. and click it twice to change it into a decimal tab.

- Press the *Tab* key to position the insertion pointer for the first line of the table.

- Select the *Stop Recording* command in the **Macro** menu.

- Click the *Stop* button on the dialog box that is displayed.

- Select the *Save Macro File As* command from the **Macro** menu. A dialog box will be displayed in which the default name for the macro file, Microsoft Works(keys), is displayed in the *Save As* box.

- Navigate through the file system until your folder *Lesson11* inside the folder *Works WP* is the active folder.

- Click the *Save* button. The macro file will be stored in your folder *Lesson11* and will be represented by the icon shown in Figure 3.74.

**Figure 3.74.** The *Macro File* Icon.

- Close your current document without saving it.

A macro can be played any time the *Macros On* command is active (i.e., checked). If you forget the name of the macro, the *Playback* command of the **Macro** menu displays the description and corresponding key of the available macros.

Play the macro:

- Create a new word processing document by selecting the *New* command from the **File** menu.

- Select *Macros On* from the **Macro** menu.  Then select *Open Macro File* from the same menu.  Navigate to your *Lesson11* folder and open the file *Microsoft Works(Keys)*.

- Press the *Option* and *h* keys at the same time.  You should obtain the result shown in Figure 3.75.

- Now use the *Tab* and *Return* keys to put the data shown in Figure 3.34 into your table.

- Save the document as *MacroTable<your initials>* in the folder *Lesson11* in your *Works WP* folder.  Close the document.

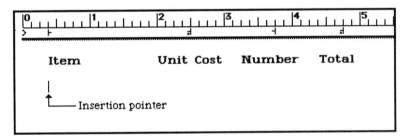

**Figure 3.75.** Result of Executing the Sample Macro.

You have now completed Lesson 11 and this chapter.  If you do not wish to proceed directly to the Practice Projects, quit Works, clean up the desktop, and shut down your computer.

# PRACTICE PROJECTS

## PROJECT 1

In this project, you will create a document like the one shown in Figure 3.76. This will involve the use of Works graphics and a number of the WP features. Step by step instructions will be given, but they will not be as detailed as the tutorial material.

1.  Create a folder on your disk and name it *WPProject1*.

2.  Open Works WP to get a new untitled document. Save the document inside the folder *WPProject1* under the name *Picnic<your initials>*.

Create the drawing:

> *Note:* Of course it isn't necessary for you to reproduce the drawing exactly as it appears in Figure 3.76. Follow the steps below to create your own "version" of the drawing.

3.  Select the *Draw On* command from the **Edit** menu. Next select the pattern for the tree top (consult Figure 3.76) from the **Fill Pattern** menu. Now select the freehand tool and draw the tree top at the top of your document. Select the transparent pattern from the **Fill Pattern** menu.

4.  Select the line tool and draw the straight sides of the tree trunk. Note that you will have to reselect the tool once you complete one side of the trunk. Now select the freehand tool once again and draw the base of the tree trunk.

5.  Use the freehand tool to draw the horizon and mountain ridges in the background of the drawing. Save your document.

6.  Select the pattern for the picnic blanket from the **Fill Pattern** menu. Then select the polygon tool and draw the blanket. Remember you must double click to complete the figure.

7.  Select the black pattern for the vacuum bottle base from the **Fill Pattern** menu, and then use the rectangle tool to construct the base. Use the white pattern and the rectangle tool to construct the two smaller rectangles making up the lid for the bottle.

8. Use the rounded rectangle tool and the arc tool to create the picnic basket. Remember to select the transparent pattern before starting to draw the handle. Create the arc for the handle in two parts, starting at the basket and moving to the top middle of the handle, then from that point to the other side of the basket. If you make errors, recall that you can delete any object by selecting it and then pressing the *Delete* key.

9. Select and use the freehand tool to draw the flower. Use the text tool to write the *Be There!* message — use size 18 font and *Shadow* style. Finish the drawing by placing the straight line at its bottom to separate it from the text to follow. Save your document.

Enter the text:

10. Select *Draw Off* command from the **Edit** menu. Press the *Return* key a number of times until the text insertion pointer is below the line marking the bottom of the drawing.

11. Set the right margin marker at 6.5 inches. (You may have to select the *Show Ruler* command from the **Format** menu to display the ruler.) Select the Geneva font from the **Font** submenu under the **Format** menu.

12. Select the *Center* command from the **Justification** submenu under the **Format** menu, size 18 font from the *Size* submenu, and both the *Shadow* and *Bold* commands from the **Style** submenu (you will need to access the **Style** menu twice to do this). Type *Memo* for the heading, and press *Return*.

13. Select the *Left* command from the **Justification** submenu under the **Format** menu, size 12 font from the **Size** submenu, and the *Normal* command from the **Style** submenu. Type the *To* and *From* lines, and press *Return* twice. Select the words *To* and *From* and make them bold by selecting the *Bold* command from the **Style** submenu.

14. Click at the bottom of your document to move the insertion pointer to the last line of the document. Now set the first line indent at 0.5 inches in the paragraph ruler. Type the first paragraph of the memo and press *Return*. Save your document.

Enter the table:

15. Prepare for typing the table heading by placing left tab stops at 1.5, 3, and 4.5 inches in the ruler. Select both the *Underline* and *Bold* commands from the **Style** submenu. Tab once and type *Time;* tab again and type *Place;* tab once more and type *Event*. Press *Return.*

16. Prepare for typing the table body by placing a right tab stop at 2.125 (2 and 1/8) inches, and left tab stops at 2.875 (2 and 7/8) and 4.25 inches in the ruler. Select the *Normal* command from the **Style** submenu. Using the *Tab* key where appropriate, type in the body of the table and then press *Return* twice.

17. Finish your document by typing in the last paragraph.

18. Save your document and quit Works.

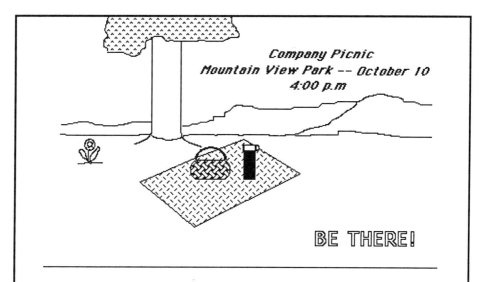

*Company Picnic*
*Mountain View Park -- October 10*
*4:00 p.m*

BE THERE!

Memo

**To:** All Employees
**From:** The Big Cheese

    I have planned a company picnic and hope that all of you will be able to attend. The volunteer Picnic Committee has been hard at work, and the event promises to be filled with exictement and fun for all. The schedule is as follows:

| Time | Place | Event |
|---|---|---|
| 9:00 a.m. | Shelter #1 | Welcome |
| 9:30 a.m. | Field #1 | Sack Races |
| 11:00 a.m. | Field #3 | Volley Ball |
| 12:00 noon | Shelter #1 | BarBQ Lunch |
| 2:00 p.m. | Field #1 | Greased Pig Chase |
| 3:00 p.m. | Shelter #2 | Pie Eating Contest |
| All Day | Lake | Swimming and Boating |

My family and I look forward to seeing you and your family there!

Figure 3.76. Project 1 Document

## PROJECT 2

In this project you will enter a short resume for Jonathon Henry Doe as shown in Figure 3.77. The major construct in this document is a hanging indent in which the first line of a paragraph extends to the left of the remaining lines of the paragraph. Step by step instructions will be given, but they will not be as detailed as the tutorial material.

1.  Create a folder on your disk and name it *WPProject2*.

2.  Open Works WP to get a new untitled document. Save the document inside the folder *WPProject2* under the name *Resume<your initials>*.

Enter the heading:

3.  The document shown in Figure 3.77 is in *New York* font; so begin by selecting New York font from the **Font** submenu (under the **Format** menu). Also select the *Center* command from the **Justification** submenu and the *Bold* command from the **Style** submenu. Set the right paragraph indent at 6 inches.

4.  Type the name, address, and phone number on separate lines as shown in Figure 3.79. The name should be 14 points, and the address and phone number should be 12 points each. After typing the phone number, press the *Return* key three times to insert two blank lines.

5.  Select the *Draw On* command from the **Edit** menu. Place the two horizontal lines in the document (see Figure 3.77) by using the line tool. Select the *Draw Off* command. Save the document.

Enter the resume body:

6.  Click at the bottom of the document to place the insertion pointer in the last line of the document. To set up the hanging indent for the remaining paragraphs, drag the left margin marker (the triangle) to 1.5 inches on the ruler, leaving the first line indent (the rectangle) at 0 inches. It make take several tries to properly drag the margin marker away from the first line indent.

7.  Set the justification to *Left*. Make the font size *10 Points*. Type the paragraphs as shown in Figure 3.77. Use the *Tab* key after typing the paragraph identifiers; this will move the insertion pointer to line up with the rest of the paragraph. Save the document.

8.  One by one, select the paragraph identifiers on the left margin by dragging. Then choose the *Bold* command from the **Style** submenu.

9.  Save your document and quit Works.

# Jonathon Henry Doe

**264 Cedar Street   Washington, DC   20004**
**Telephone: (202)-555-3309**

| | |
|---|---|
| **Education:** | Bachelor of Arts in Business Administration, Highly Political University, Washington, DC, June 1991. Graduated Magna Cum Laude. |
| | Hilltop High School, Washington , DC, June 1987. Graduated first in a class of 503. |
| **Honors:** | Eta Theta Epsilon, honorary business fraternity. National Merit Scholar. Full tuition scholarship, Highly Political University, 1987-1991. Roosevelt Scholar, Highly Political University, 1990-1991. Listed in Who's Who Among Students in American Colleges and Universities. |
| **Experience:** | Student intern, U.S. Senate, Staff member for Senator McQuail, 1988-1989. Responsible for managing office accounts. |
| | Junior Accountant, Arthur Johnson and Company. Assisted with internal auditing,1989-1990. |
| | MacDonald's. Performed all routine duties such as taking orders, cleaning the restaurant, and helping prepare food. Summers 1986 and 1987. |
| **Special Skills:** | 32 semester hours of accounting courses. |
| | 16 semester hours of computer science courses. |
| | Experience with microcomputer software including MicroSoft Works, MacPaint, and Excel.  Have designed a database for Senator McQuail's office.  Own a Macintosh computer. |

**Figure 3.77.**  Resume to be Produced.

## PROJECT 3

In this project you will use a number of the features of the Works word processing system to create the relatively complex document displayed in Figures 3.78a, 3.78b, and 3.78c. Rulers will be used throughout the document to change the margins and tabs. Take a look at Figures 3.78a - 3.78c to see what you are going to create.

1.  Create a folder on your disk and name it *WPProject3*.

2.  Open Works WP to get a new untitled document. Save the document inside the folder *WPProject3* under the name *Annual Report<your initials>*.

3.  The document shown in Figures 3.78 was entered using New York font, so select this font in the **Font** submenu under the **Format** menu. If that font is not available to you, select Geneva font instead. If you use Geneva font, note that the lines in your document and the document shown in Figures 3.78 will have different numbers of words. Do not be concerned with this; all actions described will work the same no matter which font you use. Drag the right margin indicator to 6.125 (6 and 1/8) inches.

Enter the document title:

4.  The title of the document is to be centered, bold, and 14 points. Select the *Center* command from the **Justification** submenu under the **Format** menu. Select the *Bold* command from the **Style** submenu, and then select the *14 Point* command from the **Size** submenu.

5.  Type the first line of the title, press the *Return* key, and type the second line of the title. Press the *Return* key three times to obtain two blank lines. If your title does not appear as shown in Figure 3.78a, make corrections before you proceed. If the title is not bold or is not the correct size, select the title by dragging, and make the corrections by accessing the appropriate submenu.

---

# Acme National Corporation
# Annual Report

**To the Shareholders:**

Acme National's financial results for 1991 reflect a return to the strong earnings for which the Corporation has historically been known. Earnings for the year totaled $43.8 million, a 38% improvement over the $31.7 million reported for 1990. Primary earnings per share increased to $2.02 versus $1.42 last year. On a fully diluted basis, per share earnings for 1991 were $2.00, up 41% from $1.42 in 1990.

The Corporation's financial performance was highlighted by substantial growth in the loan and investment securities portfolios, which contributed to a 10% increase in net income in 1991. Our profitability as measured by return on average assets reached 1.0% in 1991 despite the significant growth of assets during the year. Return on average equity also showed substantial improvement, growing from 12.10% in 1990 to 15.27% this year.

We enter 1992 well positioned for continued growth and profitability in the years to come. With the continued support of our shareholders, customers, and employees, we look forward to facing the challenges of the future.

**Quality of Customer Service:**

Within the financial services industry, customers have many choices on where to do business, no matter where they live. Today you can open accounts by mail or over the telephone. Why then does a customer choose one financial institution over another? The number one reason, according to research, is the quality of service delivered to that customer. Our President has noted [1]:

> *There is nothing magic about quality service. It simply means treating the customer the same way you want to be treated. And it means doing it every day.*

**Figure 3.78a.** Document to be Produced — Part 1.

Your corporation is serious about the service it delivers, and it has established high standards of service.  The satisfaction of our customers is measured on a routine basis, and our performance is subjected to rigorous examination.  Quality service must become routine.

**Sales:**

While an aggressive personal selling program has been viewed in the past as a luxury in institutions of our type, the companies that are going to continue to be successful can no longer adopt this viewpoint. Changes in competition clearly indicate that those successful institutions will be the ones that do the best selling job with both their existing customers and their new ones.

To accomplish this goal, management must be committed to a sales mentality; personnel must be well trained in product knowledge and selling skills; sales goals must be established for individuals and products; the results must be measured; and superior performance must be rewarded.  These steps are in place and will be cornerstone strategies for many years to come.  Henry Masters, Vice President for Sales and Services, has noted[2]:

> *A large part of the solution to continued high performance is to become even more sales and marketing oriented.*

**Earnings Summary:**

Net income was up 42% in 1991.  Over the past five years, primary earnings per share have increased at a compound growth rate of 10%.  Table 1 shows the components of primary earnings for the past three years, as well as the per share change for each component.

**Figure 3.78b.** Document to be Produced — Part 2.

Table 1: Components of Primary Earnings Per Share[3]

| | 1991 | 1990 | Per Share Increase (Decrease) | 1989 |
|---|---|---|---|---|
| Interest income | $18.95 | $18.27 | $ .68 | $15.21 |
| Interest expense | 10.05 | 10.14 | (.09) | 8.62 |
| Net interest income | 8.90 | 8.13 | .77 | 6.59 |
| Provision for losses | .82 | .63 | .19 | .32 |
| | 8.08 | 7.50 | .58 | 6.27 |
| Non-interest income | 2.97 | 2.66 | .31 | 1.94 |
| Non-interest expense | 8.56 | 8.66 | (.10) | 6.00 |
| Income before taxes | 2.49 | 1.50 | .99 | 2.21 |
| Applicable taxes | .47 | .07 | .40 | .33 |
| Preferred dividends | | .01 | (.01) | .04 |
| Net income | $ 2.02 | $ 1.42 | $ .60 | $ 1.84 |

----

[1] Herman S. Harmon, President, Acme National Corporation, Annual Stockholders Meeting, 1990.

[2] Mr. Henry R. Masters, Executive Vice President, Acme National Corporation, An Address to the AMA, February, 1988.

[3] Adjusted for the two-for-one stock split in the form of a 100% stock dividend on September 1, 1990.

**Figure 3.78c.** Document to be Produced — Part 3.

Enter the heading *To the Shareholders:*

6. Set the justification to *Left* by accessing the **Justification** submenu under the **Format** menu. Change the size to 12 point using the **Size** submenu. Note that the *Bold* style is still in effect, because it was inherited from the previous paragraph. Type the heading. Save the document.

Enter the first three body paragraphs::

7. Press the *Return* key twice and then drag the first line indent (the small rectangle which appears white inside the left margin marker at present) to 0.5 inches on the displayed ruler. Select the *Normal* command from the **Style** submenu. Select *Justified* from the **Jus-**

tification submenu. You are now prepared to enter the first three body paragraphs.

8. Type those paragraphs. After each paragraph press the *Return* key twice to obtain a blank line. Press the *Return* key three times after you finish the third paragraph to obtain two blank lines before the next heading line. Your document should now look something like the one shown in Figure 3.79. Save the document.

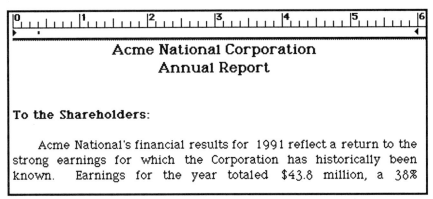

**Figure 3.79.** Document with Title, First Heading, and First Paragraph Entered.

Enter the section *Quality of Customer Service:*

9. Prepare for entering the heading *Quality of Customer Service:* by copying the format of the line containing the heading *To the Shareholders:*. To accomplish this, place the insertion pointer anywhere in the line containing the heading *To the Shareholders:*, then select the command *Copy Format* in the **Format** menu. Move the insertion pointer back to the last line on your page and select the *Paste Format* command from the **Format** menu.

10. Now enter the heading *Quality of Customer Service:*. Next, select the text you just entered by dragging and then execute the *Bold* command in the **Style** submenu.

11. Prepare for entering the paragraph beginning with *Within the financial services* by clicking at the end of the line to deselect the text, and then executing the *Normal* command in the **Style** submenu. Press the *Return* key twice.

12. Next copy the format of the paragraph beginning with *We enter 1992*. To accomplish this, place the insertion pointer anywhere in that paragraph, then select the command *Copy Format* in the **Format** menu. Move the insertion pointer back to the last line on your page and select the *Paste Format* command from the **Format** menu.

13. Now enter the paragraph beginning with *Within the financial services.* At the end of the paragraph between the word *noted* and the colon, type 1. Highlight the 1, and make it a superscript by selecting the *Superscript* command of the **Style** submenu. Move the pointer to the end of the paragraph and press the *Return* key twice. Save the document.

14. Enter the indented, italicized paragraph. To do so, drag *both* the left margin and first line indent markers to 1 inch. Drag the right indent to 5.5 inches. Select the *Italic* command of the **Style** submenu. Type the paragraph. Press *Return* twice.

15. Copy the format from the paragraph beginning with *Within the financial services* to the last paragraph in your document (see step 12 if you need to review this action). With the insertion pointer in the last paragraph of the document, enter the paragraph beginning with *Your corporation is serious.* Save the document.

Enter more text:

16. The remaining part of the document shown in Figure 3.78b involves no new constructions, and so the details for entering it will not be given. If necessary, review the steps given earlier to complete this part of the project. Use the *Copy Format* command wherever possible to save time and effort and ensure consistency.

17. Your document should now look like the parts shown in Figures 3.78a and 3.78b. If there are any differences, correct them before going on. Save the document.

Enter Table 1:

18. In this step you will create the table shown in Figure 3.78c. This involves setting tabs on rulers, and using the tabs to place the text of the table. To enter the title *Table1: Components of Primary Earnings per Share*[3] of the document, first move the first line indent to 0 inches and select *Center* from the **Justification** submenu. Type the figure title. At the end of the title, type the number 3 and press *Return* twice. Now go back and make the 3 a superscript using the method given in step 13. When this is done, move the insertion pointer back to the last line in your document.

19. Now you will create the column heading *Per Share*. Set a left tab at 2.5 inches by pointing and clicking. Press the *Tab* key, select the *Underline* command from the **Style** submenu. Press the *Space* bar approximately 20 times to produce a leading underline; then type the column heading *Per Share*. Press the *Space* bar until the underline is near the right indent. Select the *Normal* command from

the **Style** submenu. Press the *Return* key twice. The situation is illustrated in Figure 3.80. Save the document.

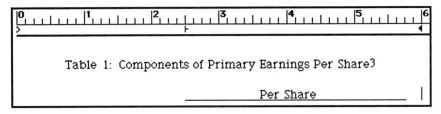

**Figure 3.80.** Beginning the Table on Page 3 of the Document.

20. To enter the heading *Increase* do the following. Drag the tab at 2.5 inches to 4.3125 inches. Type the heading and press the *Return* key. The table before the *Return* key is pressed is shown in Figure 3.81.

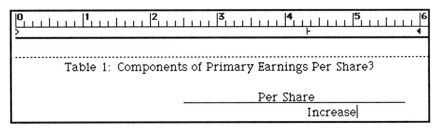

**Figure 3.81.** Entering the Heading Increase in the Table.

21. To enter the column headings proceed as follows. Set left tabs at 2.5625, 3.4375, 4.25, and 5.3125 inches as shown in Figure 3.82. Press the *Tab* key. Select the *Underline* command from the **Style** submenu. Press the *Space* bar, type the heading *1991,* and press the *Space* bar one time. Pressing the *Tab* key to position the remaining headings, enter them as shown in Figure 3.82. Save the document.

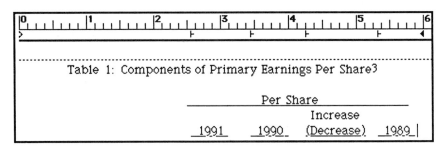

**Figure 3.82.** Entering the Column Headings in the table.

22. You are now ready to enter the rows of the table. Proceed as follows. Click each of the left tabs twice to change them into decimal tabs. Drag the tabs to 2.875, 3.75, 4.75, and 5.625 inches as shown in Figure 3.83. Type the entry *Interest income;* press the *Tab* key and type $18.95; press the *Tab* key and type $18.27; press the *Tab* key and type $ .68; and press the *Tab* key and type $15.21. Repeat this process for each of the rows containing numbers.

23. For the rows of the table that contain lines (e.g., see the row near the bottom of Figure 3.83), press the *Tab* key, select the *Underline* command of the **Style** submenu, and press the *Space* bar 5 times. Tab to the next position in the row and again press the *Space* bar 5 times. Repeat this for the remaining two tab positions. Save the document.

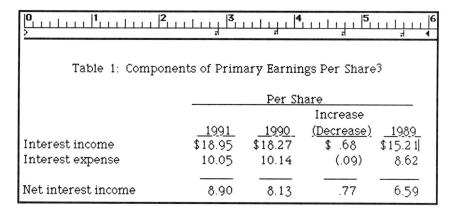

Table 1: Components of Primary Earnings Per Share[3]

| | Per Share | | | |
|---|---|---|---|---|
| | 1991 | 1990 | Increase (Decrease) | 1989 |
| Interest income | $18.95 | $18.27 | $ .68 | $15.21 |
| Interest expense | 10.05 | 10.14 | (.09) | 8.62 |
| | ——— | ——— | ——— | ——— |
| Net interest income | 8.90 | 8.13 | .77 | 6.59 |

**Figure 3.83.** Entering the Body of the Table.

Enter the footnotes:

24. The footnotes should be entered near the bottom of the page. Insert blank lines as needed, and enter a short line of underlines. Below the line type each footnote number and its corresponding reference. Use a left hanging indent as shown in Figure 3.84. Select each footnote number and make it a superscript. Your final result should have the form of Figure 3.84 which shows the first footnote.

---

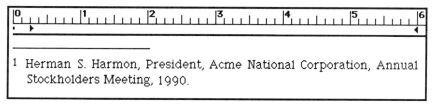

[1] Herman S. Harmon, President, Acme National Corporation, Annual Stockholders Meeting, 1990.

**Figure 3.84.** Entering the Footnotes.

25. Use the Works *Spelling Checking* feature to check the spelling in your document. Do not add any names to the dictionary.

26. Use the *Search/Replace* feature of Works to replace all occurrences of the word *employees* within your document with the phrase *dedicated employees*.

27. Save your document and quit Works.

# 4

# USING WORKS DB

When you have completed the Works DB tutorial you will be able to:

❏ Create a database template.

❏ Enter and edit data using a database form.

❏ Modify the definition of a database.

❏ View database data in a variety of ways.

❏ Insert, delete, and copy database records.

❏ Select and retrieve specified information from a database.

❏ Create database reports.

❏ Create a computed field in a database.

❏ Create merged Works word processing and database documents.

## TUTORIAL OUTLINE

# WHAT IS WORKS DB?

The main purpose of a database management system such as Works DB is to allow a user to "manage" information. By "managing" information, we mean the abilities to:

> Organize and store information in files.

> Update and/or delete stored information.

> Retrieve stored information.

There are many uses or applications of Works DB, including:

> Business information (customers, inventories, suppliers, accounting data).

> General information (sources of articles, government statistics).

> Personal information (record keeping, home library, telephone and address lists).

> Scientific information (journal article information, experimental data).

**Files.** You can think of the kind of information to be kept in a database as being the same kind of information that might be kept in a file cabinet. For example, a drawer in a company's file cabinet might contain folders on all the customers for that company. A single folder would then contain information about an individual customer. Works DB is an electronic equivalent of the file cabinet. The name database file is given to the collection of information in the electronic database.

Just as a manager of the accounts for a company must determine the kind of information to be stored in each of the file folders, the creator of a Works DB database must organize data in a manner that will allow Works DB to manage the information efficiently and flexibly. This means that we must decide what information we wish to store and the **formats** (arrangement and type of data) that will be used for its storage.

**Records.** Electronic database files are organized into smaller units called records. Once we decide what kinds of data are to be stored in a file, the actual data are placed in records within the file. Each record will hold one complete set of information about a particular object of the type associated with the file. For example, if the file holds information about students, then a record in that file holds information about some *particular student*. Because information in a record is about some particular student, it is called related information. The specific categories of information stored in each record are called the fields or attributes of the record. A Works database file is composed of a collection of such records. The diagram of Figure 4.1 illustrates this organization for a hypothetical *Student* file.

| Field Names | | | |
|---|---|---|---|
| Name | Address | Phone | Class |
| Joe Jones | 123 Hanes Dorm | 4-4554 | Freshman |
| Mary Smith | 33 Wren Dorm | 4-3321 | Sophomore |
| Rick Hall | 12 Gayle Dorm | 4-9999 | Senior + |
| Susan Dell | 10 Frat Row #1 | 3-1001 | Junior |

**Figure 4.1.** File Organization Illustrated.

Works DB will generate default entry forms that allow convenient entry of the information so that it may be stored in a Works DB file. These forms also allow convenient display and printing of the information stored in a Works DB file. The default entry form also can be modified, and thus we can control the appearance of the data if desired.

Abilities to retrieve records from a database that satisfy some selection criteria are included in Works DB. For example, we can retrieve information about all students in the Freshman class. Works DB also allows us to extract data from specified fields for all the records meeting some selection criterion. Thus, we could find the names of all students who are in the Freshman class. We will learn about each of these kinds of operations in this tutorial and why these operations are useful for solving problems of general interest to us.

# CREATING A DATABASE

After completing this lesson, you will be able to:

❑ Define a Works database table.

❑ Save a database document.

❑ Set field attributes.

❑ Quit Works DB.

❑ Open a saved database.

## LESSON BACKGROUND

Before we can create a Works DB file, we must make decisions about the following:

1. We must first define a template that *categorizes* the various kinds of information to be held in our database. Think of this template as the headings of a table that would contain the information relevant to our interest. We will want to choose each column heading of the table to have a name that captures the *essence* of the information contained within that column. For our example, we will create a database containing information about customer orders for a local company. The categories of information about our orders are: *Last Name, First Name, Phone, Date, Time, Order,* and *Amount.* Time and date of the order are important because of the company's guaranteed 24-hour service policy. These categories become the column headings (also termed fields) of our example database table, as shown in Figure 4.2. Each row in the table holds information about a *single* customer's order. As we will see shortly, this table structure will translate directly into a Works DB database template.

2. For each of the column headings defined in step 1, we must also define the *type* of data that will be contained in that column. Because Works DB allows different kinds of operations on data, dependent on its type, we must decide the type based on our intended manipulation of the information. For example, if we wish to perform arithmetic on the values

in a column, we need to define the type of the data as *numeric*. Every entry in a given column must be of the *same* type. The types available in Works DB are *text* (useful for names, addresses, cities, and so forth), *numeric* (useful for information such as numbers and currency that will be processed using arithmetic operations), *date* (useful when month, day, and year are required), and *time* (when hours and minutes are required). In Works DB the process of choosing the type of data for each field is called *setting the field attributes*. For the example database to be discussed in this lesson, we will choose the following types of information for each column:

| Column Heading | Type of Data in That Column |
|---|---|
| Last Name | Text |
| First Name | Text |
| Phone | Text |
| Date | Date |
| Time | Time |
| Order | Numeric |
| Amount | Numeric |

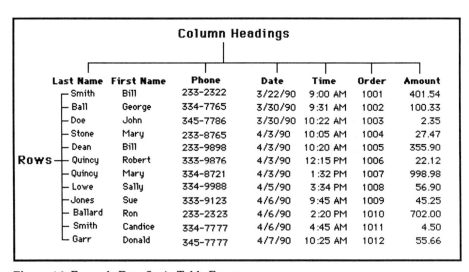

Figure 4.2. Example Data Set in Table Format.

## DEFINING WORKS DATABASE TABLES

In this section you will create a Works DB database table (template) and enter data into the database. Performing this work will teach you to start Works DB, set the field attributes for your database, save a Works database, open an existing Works database, and quit Works. As you read this tutorial, you should perform the indicated actions using your computer.

The database table will have the column headings: *Last Name, First Name, Phone, Date, Time, Order,* and *Amount,* as illustrated in Figure 4.2.

To begin the process of creating a Works database perform the following.

- Insert your disk that contains the folder *Works DB* (which in turn contains folders *Lesson1, Lesson2,* etc.) that you created in Lesson 6 of Chapter 1. If you have not completed that lesson, do so before beginning this lesson. We will store various versions of the databases to be created in this chapter in the folders *Lesson1, Lesson2,* and so on.

- Open Works by double clicking the *Works* icon.

- Open Works DB by double clicking the *Data Base* icon shown highlighted in Figure 4.3. The dialog box in Figure 4.4 should then be displayed.

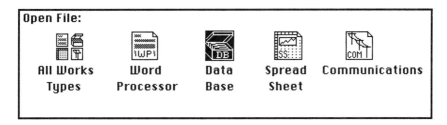

Figure 4.3. Module Icons Displayed after Works Is Opened.

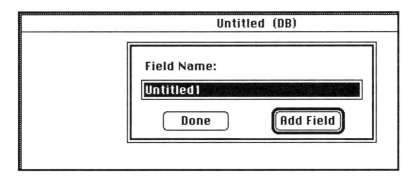

Figure 4.4. Startup Screen for Defining a Works Database.

201

You are now ready to define the column headings (field names) of information for your database table.  Recall from Figure 4.2 that these are *Last Name, First Name, Phone, Date, Time, Order,* and *Amount*.  They will be entered in this order.

Enter the column headings:

- Type in *Last Name,* the name of the first field.  (As you type, the information will be displayed in the field shown highlighted in Figure 4.4.)

- Click the *Add Field* button.  You are now presented with another dialog box like the one shown in Figure 4.4.

- Type in *First Name,* the name of the second field.

- Click the *Add Field* button.  Each time you click this button, you will be presented with a dialog box like the one shown in Figure 4.4.

- Type in *Phone,* the name of the third field.

- Click the *Add Field* button.

- Type in *Date,* the name of the fourth field.

- Click the *Add Field* button.

- Type in *Time,* the name of the fifth field.

- Click the *Add Field* button.

- Type in *Order,* the name of the sixth field.

- Click the *Add Field* button.

- Type in *Amount,* the name of the seventh field.

- Click the *Add Field* button.  You are again presented with a dialog box like the one shown in Figure 4.4.

- Click *Done.*  This choice indicates to Works DB that there are no more fields to be defined for the database.  The resulting screen is shown in Figure 4.5.

```
┌─────────────────────────────────────────────────────────┐
│ ▤▢▤▤▤▤▤▤▤▤▤▤▤▤▤▤▤ Untitled (DB) ▤▤▤▤▤▤▤▤▤▤▤ │
│                                                             │
│ ┌────────────┬──────────┐                                  │
│ │ Last Name  │          │                                  │
│ ├────────────┼──────────┤                                  │
│ │ First Name │          │                                  │
│ ├───────────┬┴──────────┤                                  │
│ │ Phone     │           │                                  │
│ ├─────────┬─┴───────────┤                                  │
│ │ Date    │             │                                  │
│ ├─────────┼─────────────┤                                  │
│ │ Time    │             │                                  │
│ ├────────┬┴─────────────┤                                  │
│ │ Order  │              │                                  │
│ ├────────┴┬─────────────┤                                  │
│ │ Amount  │             │                                  │
│ └─────────┴─────────────┘                                  │
└─────────────────────────────────────────────────────────┘
```

**Figure 4.5.** Definition of the *Orders* Database Fields Completed.


## SETTING FIELD ATTRIBUTES

Once you have entered all the field names, you will select each field in turn and set its attributes. A set of suitable data types for the fields in our example is as follows.

| Field Name | Data Type |
|------------|-----------|
| Last Name | Text |
| First Name | Text |
| Phone | Text |
| Date | Date, short |
| Time | Time |
| Order | Numeric, no decimal digits |
| Amount | Numeric, two digits to the right of the decimal |

The default **data type** is text, and so in this case it is not necessary for you to explicitly set the data type for *Last Name, First Name,* or *Phone.* You need to execute the *Set Field Attributes* command for text attributes only if you wish to change some of the other features shown in the dialog box in Figure 4.6. These features include setting the alignment of text to be either left justified, right justified, or centered, and setting the text style to bold and/or underline.

Perform the following for each of the database fields.

Last Name:

- Click the *Last Name* field in your *Database Definition* window to select it.

- Execute the *Set Field Attributes* command under the **Format** menu. This selection will produce the dialog box shown in Figure 4.6.

- Observe that the type *Text* and alignment *Left* are preselected as shown by the darkened circles in the dialog box presented.

- These are the settings we desire, so click the *OK* button. The *Database Definition* window will reappear.

Because the default settings for *First Name* and *Phone* are correct, those fields may be skipped.

Date:

- Click the *Date* field in your *Database Definition* window to select it.

- Execute the *Set Field Attributes* command under the **Format** menu. This will produce another dialog box similar to that shown in Figure 4.6.

- Click the *Date* button in the left column of the dialog box. Additional buttons will be displayed for *Short, Medium,* and *Long* dates. Click the *Short* date button. (A *Set Field Attributes* dialog box for *Date* is shown in Figure 4.18 should you wish to consult it at this time.)

- Click the *OK* button.

Time:

- Click the *Time* field in your *Database Definition* window to select it.

- Execute the *Set Field Attributes* command under the **Format** menu.

- Click the *Time* button in the left column of the resulting dialog box.

- Click the *OK* button.

Order:

- Click the *Order* field in your *Database Definition* window to select it.

- Execute the *Set Field Attributes* command under the **Format** menu.

- Click the *Numeric* button in the left column of the resulting dialog box.

- Type a zero into the *Decimal Places* box. Notice that this box is already preselected for keyboard input.

- Click the *OK* button.

Amount:

- Click the *Amount* field in your *Database Definition* window to select it.

- Execute the *Set Field Attributes* command under the **Format** menu.

- Click the *Numeric* button in the left column of the resulting dialog box.

- Click the *OK* button. (We will take the other defaults: the *Fixed* button in the *Display* column and 2 in the *Decimal Places* box.)

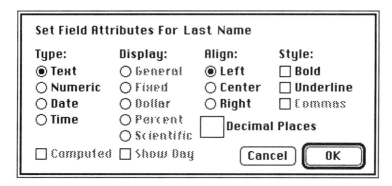

**Figure 4.6.** Dialog Box for Defining Attribute Data Type.

## SAVING THE DATABASE

Save the definition of the database by performing the following.

- Select the *Save As* command of the **File** menu.

- Navigate through the file system using the methods described in Lesson 5 of Chapter 1 until you are inside the folder on your disk named *Lesson1* contained in the folder *Works DB*.

- Enter *Orders<your initials>* as the name of the document in the dialog box.

- Click the *Save* button.

The database with name *Orders<your initials>* has now been saved inside the folder named *Lesson1* within the folder *Works DB*.

## QUITTING WORKS DB

Now that you have created and saved a Works database you will learn to exit Works DB.

- Select *Quit* from the **File** menu. Because you have made no changes to the database since it was last saved to disk, you will be returned to the desktop. If you had made changes since the last *Save* operation, Works would ask if you wished to save the current changes. If you clicked *Yes*, the currently displayed database (now only stored in RAM) would replace the one on disk. If you clicked *No*, then the database stored on disk would remain exactly as it was before you began the current session and the displayed database now stored in RAM would be erased.

From the desktop, verify that you have stored the *Orders<your initials>* database to disk as follows.

- Open your disk icon by double clicking its icon.

- Open the folder *Works DB* on your disk by double clicking it.

- Now open the folder *Lesson1* by double clicking it.

- You should now observe that the *Orders<your initials>* icon as shown in Figure 4.7 (for initials JHD) is present.

If you cannot find the *Orders<your initials>* database, try using the *Find File* option under the **Apple** menu to help you locate the file. When you locate it, place it into the *Lesson1* folder within the *Works DB* folder on your disk.

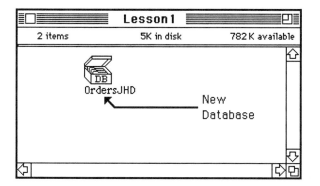

**Figure 4.7.** Saved *OrdersJHD* Database in *Lesson1* Folder.

## OPENING AN EXISTING DATABASE

From the desktop, open the *Orders<your initials>* database by performing the following.

- Find the icon for the *Orders<your initials>* database on your disk. Double click it. Works will be started, and the *Orders<your initials>* database form of Figure 4.5 will be displayed.

- Close the database and return to the desktop.

Open an existing database from within Works:

- Open *Works* by double clicking its icon.

- Select *Works Data Base* by single clicking its icon.

- Navigate through the file system until the name *Orders<your initials>* appears in the scroll rectangle.

- Double click the name *Orders<your initials>*. Your *Orders<your initials>* database form will now appear.

You have now completed Lesson 1. If you do not wish to continue to the next lesson, you should quit Works, clean up the desktop, and shut down your computer.

# ENTERING DATABASE DATA AND SIMPLE EDITING

After completing this lesson you will be able to:

❏ Rearrange a form.

❏ Enter data into a form.

❏ Edit the data in the database.

## FORMS

The window shown in Figure 4.5 is called a **form**. The form was created automatically as the names of the fields were entered during the steps in Lesson 1. As you created the definition of the database, you probably noticed the form being drawn in the upper left-hand part of the window as the name of each field was entered. A form can be used to enter data into a database table one row at a time. A form can also be used to display information in a database one row at a time. The appearance of the information on the form can be altered by rearranging the structure of the form.

## REARRANGING A FORM

In this section you will alter the appearance of the form created in Lesson 1. Perform the following.

- If not already open, open the *Orders<your initials>* database stored in the folder *Lesson1* contained in the *Works DB* folder on your disk. The database form of Figure 4.8 should appear.

- Execute the *Save As* command from the **File** menu.

- Navigate through your disk hierarchy and save the database *Orders<your initials>* in the folder *Lesson2* contained in the *Works DB* folder.

- Place the mouse pointer over the field *Last Name* and it will turn into a hand symbol, as shown in Figure 4.8.

- Drag, noting that the position of the field in the form follows the mouse.  This feature allows you to place field blocks in the form.  Experiment by moving the fields into the positions shown in Figure 4.9.

Alter the size of a field box:

- Place the pointer on the right-hand edge of the *Phone* field box.  The pointer will change into the symbol ✛.

- Dragging will stretch or shrink the size of the block.  Experiment by changing the size of the blocks.

- Rearrange the locations and sizes of the fields to obtain a form similar to the one shown in Figure 4.9.

- Save your database.

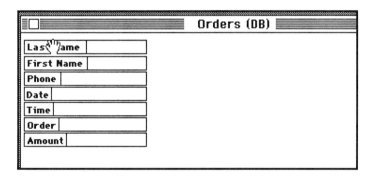

**Figure 4.8.** Preparing to Move a Field Block within a Form.

**Figure 4.9.** Reformatted Form.

## ENTERING DATA INTO A FORM

On your screen, notice the number (1 in this case) in the upper left corner. This is the record number of the currently displayed record.  It tells you that the blank record on the screen is record number 1.

Use the form to enter records into the database:

- Select the *Last Name* data field by clicking anywhere inside it.  The field should become highlighted as shown in Figure 4.9.

- Type in the customer name *Smith* from the first row of data shown in Figure 4.2.

- Press *Tab* and the *First Name* data field will be selected.  Type in the name *Bill* from the first row of Figure 4.2.

- Press *Tab* and the *Phone* data field will be selected.  Type in the phone number 233-2322 from the first row of Figure 4.2.

- Press *Tab* and the *Date* data field will be selected.  Type in the date data *3/22/90* from the first row of Figure 4.2.

- Press *Tab* and the *Time* data field will be selected.  Type in the time data *9:00 AM* from the first row of Figure 4.2.

- Press *Tab* and the *Order* data field will be selected.  Type in the order number *1001* from the first row of Figure 4.2.

- Press *Tab* and the *Amount* data field will be selected.  Type in the amount *401.54* from the first row of Figure 4.2.

The form should now have the appearance shown in Figure 4.10.

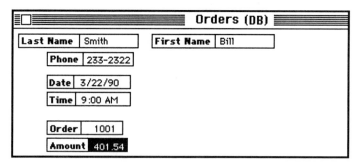

**Figure 4.10.** Form Containing the First Record of the Database.

- Press *Tab*.  A new blank record form is displayed for additional data entry.

- Enter the data for the remaining rows of Figure 4.2 using the sequence of steps just followed for the first row of data. *Note*: If you notice that you have made a typing error and you have not yet pressed *Tab* you may backspace to correct the error. If you notice errors in a previously entered field, do not worry; you may use the methods of the next section to correct them.

- When all the records have been entered, select *Save* from the **File** menu. Your *Orders<your initials>* database complete with data will now be saved to your disk.

## EDITING DATA USING A FORM

If you find a mistake in a previously typed field on a form, you correct the error by first finding the record that contains the error and then selecting the field containing it (by clicking anywhere in the field). The data in that field will be displayed in the *Edit Bar* at the top of the screen, as shown in Figure 4.11. The usual word processing functions such as selecting by dragging, deleting, and inserting text can be applied to the data displayed in the *Edit Bar*.

Let us assume in this step that the *Amount* for record 1 has been discovered to be incorrect. Suppose for a moment that the number 501.54 should have been entered instead of 401.54. To correct the value perform the following.

- You may scroll through the records in the database by using the *Scroll Bar* displayed at the right of the form. Drag the *Scroll Box* in the *Scroll Bar* to the top position of the *Scroll Bar*. Verify that the data in the first record is now displayed in the form.

- Select the *Amount* field of the first record by clicking. The window shown in Figure 4.11 should be displayed. Notice that the information in the field has been displayed in an *Edit Bar* immediately below the menu bar.

- Move the pointer to the *Edit Bar*. Within the *Edit Bar* the pointer becomes an *I-beam*, $\mathcal{I}$.

- Drag the I-beam pointer across the leftmost 4 so that the 4 becomes highlighted, and type 5. The contents of the *Edit Bar* should now read *501.54*. (Notice that the contents of the *Amount* field in the record form has not yet changed.)

- To place the modified amount into the form click the *Accept Box* just to the left of the *Edit Bar* (alternately, you could press the *Return* key). If you make mistakes during the editing process, you can click the *Cancel Box* just to the left of the *Accept Box* to revert to the earlier value.

- With the *Amount* field selected, move the pointer into the *Edit Bar*. Experiment with the selection techniques that you used with the word processor.

- Return the contents of the *Amount* field of record 1 to *401.54* using the methods discussed above. Be sure to check the *Accept Box* when you finish editing.

You have now completed Lesson 2. If you do not wish to continue to the next lesson, you should quit Works, clean up the desktop, and shut down your computer.

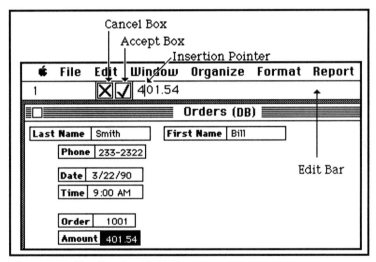

**Figure 4.11.** The Database Edit Bar.

# MODIFYING THE DEFINITION OF A DATABASE

After completing this lesson you will be able to:

❏ Change the name of a field.

❏ Add a new field to a database.

❏ Delete a field from a database.

## LESSON BACKGROUND

As your needs for information change, the information stored in a database may become inadequate, and it may become necessary to increase the number of fields in the database, or to change the database definition in some other way. In this lesson you will learn how to modify the database created in Lessons 1 and 2. It is important for you to realize that this modification can be done at anytime. If, for example, your database contains several thousand rows of information, you can still use the methods described here.

Let us assume that as a result of using your database, you discover that it is essential that a new data field be added to hold the date that an order is picked up by the customer. Because there are now two dates, the date the order was placed and the date the order was picked up, you must be careful to use column headings that clearly identify the dates. For this lesson you are to assume that the *Date* column heading is to be changed to *OrderDate*, and the new field is to be called *DatePickedUp*. In addition, assume that you wish to delete the *Time* information because it is not being used and is thus wasting valuable space on the disk. In summary the changes to be made are

Change the name of field *Date* to *OrderDate*.

Create a new field named *DatePickedUp*.

Delete the field named *Time*.

213

## CHANGING THE NAME OF A FIELD

To change the name of the *Date* field perform the following.

- If it is not already open, open the *Orders<your initials>* database stored in the folder *Lesson2* contained in the *Works DB* folder on your disk.

- Execute the *Save As* command from the **File** menu. Navigate through your disk hierarchy and save the database *Orders<your initials>* in the folder *Lesson3* contained in the *Works DB* folder.

- The form of Figure 4.10 will now be displayed (with no fields highlighted).

- Select the *Date* field by pointing to it and clicking.

- Execute the *Change Field Name* command of the **Edit** menu. A dialog box will be displayed.

- Type the new field name *OrderDate* into the text field on the dialog box. You should now have a display that is similar to Figure 4.12.

- Click the *OK* button. The name displayed on the form will change to *OrderDate*.

- If necessary, drag the right edge of the *Order Date* field so that the entire date is displayed.

- Save your database by choosing the *Save* command from the **File** menu.

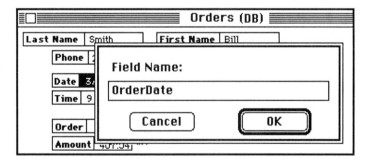

**Figure 4.12.** Dialog Box for Changing the Name of a Field.

## ADDING A NEW FIELD

To add the *DatePickedUp* field perform the following.

- Execute the *Add New Field* command from the **Edit** menu.

- Type the name of the new field, *DatePickedUp,* into the text field of the dialog box as shown in Figure 4.13.

- Click the *Add Field* button. Resize the new field and drag it to the bottom of the display so that your form for the new database resembles that shown in Figure 4.14.

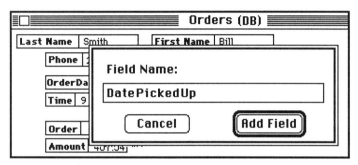

**Figure 4.13.** Dialog Box for Adding a New Field to a Database.

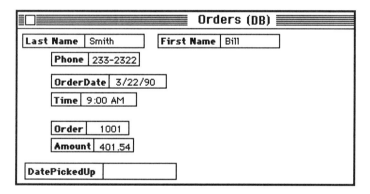

**Figure 4.14.** The Database Form after Adding the *DatePickedUp* Field.

# DELETING A FIELD

To delete the *Time* field perform the following.

- Select the *Time* field by clicking.

215

- Execute the *Delete Field* command from the **Edit** menu. The field and all the data stored in it will be removed from the database. The field and its data can be restored, if desired, by using immediately the *Undo* command of the **Edit** menu. The form that results from deleting the field should resemble that shown in Figure 4.15.

- Do not save these last changes. Quit Works, and answer *No* when asked if you wish to save the changes to *Orders<your initials>*.

You have now completed Lesson 3. If you do not wish to continue to the next lesson, you should clean up the desktop, and shut down your computer.

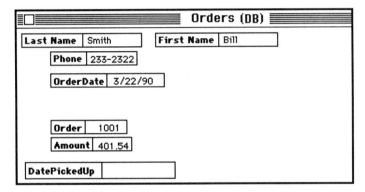

**Figure 4.15.** The Database Form after Deleting the *Time* Field.

# VIEWING DATABASE DATA

After completing this lesson, you will be able to:

❏ View the data in a form display.

❏ View the data in a list display.

❏ Change the appearance of the data.

❏ View the data in sorted order.

## SELECTING BETWEEN FORM AND LIST DISPLAYS

Thus far we have considered only the forms display mode of Works DB. However, there are actually two ways that may be used to view and/or edit data in a Works database. As we have seen, in the forms display mode only a single data record may be viewed at one time on the screen. Alternatively, it is possible to view a Works database directly as a table. This latter display mode is termed the list display mode.

Choose the list display:

• If it is not already open, open the *Orders<your initials>* database stored in the folder *Lesson3* contained in the *Works DB* folder on your disk.

• Execute the *Save As* command from the **File** menu. Navigate through your disk hierarchy and save the database *Orders<your initials>* in the folder *Lesson4* contained in the *Works DB* folder.

• Select *Show List* from the **Format** menu. The screen should be similar to that shown in Figure 4.16. Note that some of the data at the right of the screen may not be visible. All the data can be viewed as in Figure 4.16 by changing the widths of the fields, which we will do shortly.

- Execute the *Show Form* command from the **Format** menu. The display should now appear similar to that shown in Figure 4.10.

Change the data space for a field:

- Select *Show List* from the **Format** menu.

- Move the mouse pointer to the dividing grid line between the *OrderDate* and *Time* data field names. The pointer changes to a double horizontal arrow. You can now stretch (or reduce) the size of the *OrderDate* data field.

- Drag the mouse to the left to reduce the field width of the *OrderDate* field.

- Use this technique to make your list display look like the one in Figure 4.16.

Note that the display mode in effect at the time the database is last saved will determine the mode of display when a Works database is reopened.

## VIEWING DATA IN A FORM DISPLAY

Practice viewing data in a form display by performing the following.

- Select the *Show Form* command from the **Format** menu.

- Select the *Last Name* field by clicking anywhere in it.

- By pressing the *Tab* key, note that you may move forward to each successive field. Select the *Amount* field of the first record using this method.

- By holding down the *Shift* key while pressing the *Tab* key, note that you may move backward through each successive field. Select the *Last Name* field again using this method.

- Move to the next record by repeatedly pressing the *Tab* key. Note that when you are in the last data field of a record and press the *Tab* key, you will move automatically to the first data field of the next record in the database; that record is then shown in place of the one you were previously viewing.

- Move back to the *Last Name* field of the previous record by holding down the *Shift* key and pressing the *Tab* key repeatedly.

- You may also use the *Scroll Bar* to select which record you are viewing. Position the pointer into the *Scroll Arrow* at the bottom of the *Scroll Bar* to the right of the form and click. Verify that the record number is increased by one for each click made.

- Click in the *Scroll Arrow* at the top of the *Scroll Box*. Verify that the record number is decreased by one for each click made.

- Drag the *Scroll Box* up and down in the *Scroll Bar* and release it at various points. Note the effect on the record number. Use this technique to locate record 6.

- Return to record 1 using this same technique.

You may move to any field in any record of the database in the forms display mode using the techniques you have just practiced.


## VIEWING DATA IN A LIST DISPLAY

There are many times when you may wish to view more than one record (row) of data at once. The list display mode can be used for this purpose and for data entry as well. Explore viewing data in the list mode with the following.

- Select the *Show List* command from the **Format** menu. A display of the format shown in Figure 4.16 will be shown.

- Practice moving forward and backward through the fields and records by pressing either the *Tab* or *Return* key and then also holding down the *Shift* key while pressing either the *Tab* or *Return* key. The *Tab* allows you to move forward to the next data field in a given row. When *Shift* is pressed with *Tab*, you will move back one field position. The *Return* key will take you to the *next record* and leave you in the same field. When *Shift* is pressed with *Return*, you will move to the same field of the previous record.

- You can also use the mouse in the usual way to select new fields for entry by moving the pointer inside the field and clicking. Try this for several fields.

- You may also use the *Scroll Bar* to the right of the display to scroll forward or back in the database. To practice the use of the scroll bar for this purpose, you may have to make your window smaller (in the vertical dimension), so that not all the records can be viewed at once. Try this, and then return the window to its former size.

| Last Name | First Name | Phone | OrderDa | Time | Order | Amount |
|-----------|-----------|---------|---------|----------|------|--------|
| Smith | Bill | 233-2322 | 3/22/90 | 9:00 AM | 1001 | 401.54 |
| Ball | George | 334-7765 | 3/30/90 | 9:31 AM | 1002 | 100.33 |
| Doe | John | 345-7786 | 3/30/90 | 10:22 AM | 1003 | 2.35 |
| Stone | Mary | 233-8765 | 4/3/90 | 10:05 AM | 1004 | 27.47 |
| Dean | Bill | 233-9898 | 4/3/90 | 10:20 AM | 1005 | 355.90 |
| Quincy | Robert | 333-9876 | 4/3/90 | 12:15 PM | 1006 | 22.12 |
| Quincy | Mary | 334-8721 | 4/3/90 | 1:32 PM | 1007 | 998.98 |
| Lowe | Sally | 334-9988 | 4/5/90 | 3:34 PM | 1008 | 56.90 |
| Jones | Sue | 333-9123 | 4/6/90 | 9:45 AM | 1009 | 45.25 |
| Ballard | Ron | 233-2323 | 4/6/90 | 2:20 PM | 1010 | 702.00 |
| Smith | Candice | 334-7777 | 4/6/90 | 4:45 AM | 1011 | 4.50 |
| Garr | Donald | 345-7777 | 4/7/90 | 10:25 AM | 1012 | 55.66 |

Orders (DB)

**Figure 4.16.** Displaying Data in List Format.

- You can remove the grid lines shown in Figure 4.16 by deselecting (just release the button over the command) *Show Grid* under the **Format** menu. The display resulting from these actions is shown in Figure 4.17. To display the grid again, you select *Show Grid* under the **Format** menu.

| Last Name | First Name | Phone | OrderDate | Time | Order | Amount |
|-----------|-----------|---------|-----------|----------|------|--------|
| Smith | Bill | 233-2322 | 3/22/90 | 9:00 AM | 1001 | 401.54 |
| Ball | George | 334-7765 | 3/30/90 | 9:31 AM | 1002 | 100.33 |
| Doe | John | 345-7786 | 3/30/90 | 10:22 AM | 1003 | 2.35 |
| Stone | Mary | 233-8765 | 4/3/90 | 10:05 AM | 1004 | 27.47 |
| Dean | Bill | 233-9898 | 4/3/90 | 10:20 AM | 1005 | 355.90 |
| Quincy | Robert | 333-9876 | 4/3/90 | 12:15 PM | 1006 | 22.12 |
| Quincy | Mary | 334-8721 | 4/3/90 | 1:32 PM | 1007 | 998.98 |
| Lowe | Sally | 334-9988 | 4/5/90 | 3:34 PM | 1008 | 56.90 |
| Jones | Sue | 333-9123 | 4/6/90 | 9:45 AM | 1009 | 45.25 |
| Ballard | Ron | 233-2323 | 4/6/90 | 2:20 PM | 1010 | 702.00 |
| Smith | Candice | 334-7777 | 4/6/90 | 4:45 AM | 1011 | 4.50 |
| Garr | Donald | 345-7777 | 4/7/90 | 10:25 AM | 1012 | 55.66 |

Orders (DB)

**Figure 4.17.** List Display with No Grid.

## CHANGING THE APPEARANCE OF THE DATA

The appearance of the data in either the list or forms viewing modes can be altered using *Set Field Attributes* in the **Format** menu.

Observe the effect of using *Set Field Attributes*:

- Click the *OrderDate* field to select it.

- Select the *Set Field Attributes* command in the **Format** menu. The resulting dialog box is shown in Figure 4.18.

- Click the *Long* button under *Display* and click the *Right* button under *Align*; then click *OK*. The appearance of the display will be similar to that shown in Figure 4.19 (you will have to increase the width of the *OrderDate* field to see the complete display). Notice that the month has changed from a number into the corresponding word for the month, and the text is moved to align with the right margin of the field space.

- To make your display look more like the one in Figure 4.19, select the *Time* field.

- Select the *Set Field Attributes* command under the **Format** menu and set the *Align* to *Right*.

- Click *OK* and compare your display to the one shown in Figure 4.19.

- Save your database.

```
╔══════════════════════════════════════════════════╗
║ Set Field Attributes For OrderDate                 ║
║                                                    ║
║ Type:        Display:      Align:       Style:     ║
║ ○ Text       ○ Short       ○ Left       ☐ Bold     ║
║ ○ Numeric    ○ Medium      ○ Center     ☐ Underline║
║ ◉ Date       ◉ Long        ◉ Right      ☐ Commas   ║
║ ○ Time                                             ║
║                          ┌──┐ Decimal Places       ║
║                          └──┘                       ║
║ ☐ Computed ☐ Show Day    ( Cancel ) (( OK ))       ║
╚══════════════════════════════════════════════════╝
```

**Figure 4.18.** The *Set Field Attribute* Dialog Box.

| Last Name | First Name | Phone | OrderDate | Time | Order | Amount |
|-----------|-----------|---------|----------------|----------|-------|--------|
| Smith | Bill | 233-2322 | March 22, 1990 | 9:00 AM | 1001 | 401.54 |
| Ball | George | 334-7765 | March 30, 1990 | 9:31 AM | 1002 | 100.33 |
| Doe | John | 345-7786 | March 30, 1990 | 10:22 AM | 1003 | 2.35 |
| Stone | Mary | 233-8765 | April 3, 1990 | 10:05 AM | 1004 | 27.47 |
| Dean | Bill | 233-9898 | April 3, 1990 | 10:20 AM | 1005 | 355.90 |
| Quincy | Robert | 333-9876 | April 3, 1990 | 12:15 PM | 1006 | 22.12 |
| Quincy | Mary | 334-8721 | April 3, 1990 | 1:32 PM | 1007 | 998.98 |
| Lowe | Sally | 334-9988 | April 5, 1990 | 3:34 PM | 1008 | 56.90 |
| Jones | Sue | 333-9123 | April 6, 1990 | 9:45 AM | 1009 | 45.25 |
| Ballard | Ron | 233-2323 | April 6, 1990 | 2:20 PM | 1010 | 702.00 |
| Smith | Candice | 334-7777 | April 6, 1990 | 4:45 AM | 1011 | 4.50 |
| Garr | Donald | 345-7777 | April 7, 1990 | 10:25 AM | 1012 | 55.66 |

*Orders (DB)*

**Figure 4.19.** The List Display with *Long* Display Selected for the *OrderDate* Field.

221

Observe the effect of using other options in the **Format** menu:

- Point to the **Format** menu and drag to the *Font* submenu.

- Drag to any font other than the one that is now checked and release the mouse button. Figure 4.20 shows the result of changing the font to *New York*. (This font may not show up as an option in your menu. If not, choose another font.) Notice that we have also displayed the grid again in Figure 4.20.

- Experiment by selecting other fonts and other sizes.

Return the database to a form similar to its original appearance:

- Select Geneva font and *9 points* for the size. Both these options are found in the **Format** menu.

- Select the *OrderDate* field, and select the *Set Field Attributes* in the **Format** menu. Click the *Short* button under *Display* and click *OK*.

- Save your database by selecting the *Save* command from the **File** menu.

## VIEWING THE DATA IN SORTED ORDER

Records may be sorted by executing the *Sort* command under the **Organize** menu as follows.

- Click the *Last Name* field of one of the records to select the field to be used for sorting the records.

- Select the *Sort* command of the **Organize** menu. A dialog box similar to the one shown in Figure 4.21 is displayed.

- Click the *A to Z* button. Because *Last Name* is a text type, you have the two choices *From A to Z* and *From Z to A*. Finally, click the *OK* button to execute the *Sort* command.

- Examine the records in the database to check that they are in alphabetical order based on *Last Name*.

- Save your database by selecting the *Save* command from the **File** menu.

| Last Name | First Name | Phone | OrderDate | Time | Order | Amount |
|-----------|------------|-------|-----------|------|-------|--------|
| Smith | Bill | 233-2322 | March 22, 1990 | 9:00 AM | 1001 | 401.54 |
| Ball | George | 334-7765 | March 30, 1990 | 9:31 AM | 1002 | 100.33 |
| Doe | John | 345-7786 | March 30, 1990 | 10:22 AM | 1003 | 2.35 |
| Stone | Mary | 233-8765 | April 3, 1990 | 10:05 AM | 1004 | 27.47 |
| Dean | Bill | 233-9898 | April 3, 1990 | 10:20 AM | 1005 | 355.90 |
| Quincy | Robert | 333-9876 | April 3, 1990 | 12:15 PM | 1006 | 22.12 |
| Quincy | Mary | 334-8721 | April 3, 1990 | 1:32 PM | 1007 | 998.98 |
| Lowe | Sally | 334-9988 | April 5, 1990 | 3:34 PM | 1008 | 56.90 |
| Jones | Sue | 333-9123 | April 6, 1990 | 9:45 AM | 1009 | 45.25 |
| Ballard | Ron | 233-2323 | April 6, 1990 | 2:20 PM | 1010 | 702.00 |
| Smith | Candice | 334-7777 | April 6, 1990 | 4:45 AM | 1011 | 4.50 |
| Garr | Donald | 345-7777 | April 7, 1990 | 10:25 AM | 1012 | 55.66 |

*Orders (DB)*

**Figure 4.20.** The Database in List Form Using the New York Font.

**Sort the Document on This Field:**
**Last Name**

◉ **From A to Z**
○ **From Z to A**

○ From 0 to 9
○ From 9 to 0

○ Chronological
○ Reverse Chronological

[ Cancel ]     [ OK ]

**Figure 4.21.** Dialog Box for the *Sort* Command.

   You have now completed Lesson 4. If you do not wish to continue to the next lesson, you should quit Works, clean up the desktop, and shut down your computer.

# MORE EDITING OF DATABASE DATA

After completing this lesson, you will be able to:

❏ Edit data using split screens.

❏ Insert a new record into a database.

❏ Copy a record in a database.

❏ Copy information in a database.

❏ Delete a record from a database.

## USING SPLIT SCREENS

It is often desirable to compare database records that are not located close to one another in the table. It is also often the case that database records are too long to fit on a screen. Works DB provides a convenient and flexible method for viewing, comparing, and editing data in different parts of a database. This is accomplished through the use of split screen list displays.

To display the *Orders<your initials>* database with a horizontally split screen, perform the following.

- If not already open, open the *Orders<your initials>* database stored in the folder *Lesson4* contained in the *Works DB* folder on your disk.

- Execute the *Save As* command from the **File** menu. Navigate through your disk hierarchy and save the database *Orders<your initials>* in the folder *Lesson5* contained in the *Works DB* folder.

- If your display is not in list mode, select the *Show List* command of the **Format** menu.

- Locate the *Split Rectangle* (the dark rectangle located at the top of the vertical *Scroll Bar*). When the cursor is placed over this rectangle it changes into two horizontal lines with upward and downward pointing arrows. Drag the *Split Rectangle* from the top of the vertical scroll bar to a point midway down the vertical scroll bar. You will obtain a display similar to that shown in Figure 4.22, in which the screen has been split into two separate list displays.

Notice that each display now has its own *Scroll Bar*. These scroll bars are independent of each other, and the *entire database* is available in each display. Hence any two sections of the database can be viewed simultaneously.

- Drag the scroll bars to demonstrate to yourself that any record in the database can be viewed in either display.

- Drag the *Split Rectangle* back up to the top of the *Scroll Bar*. Notice that the display returns to a single list display.

- Now, return the display to the appearance shown in Figure 4.22.

| Last Name | First Name | Phone | OrderDate | Time | Order | Amount |
|-----------|-----------|----------|-----------|----------|-------|--------|
| Garr | Donald | 345-7777 | 4/7/90 | 10:25 AM | 1012 | 55.66 |
| Jones | Sue | 333-9123 | 4/6/90 | 9:45 AM | 1009 | 45.25 |
| Lowe | Sally | 334-9988 | 4/5/90 | 3:34 PM | 1008 | 56.90 |
| Quincy | Robert | 333-9876 | 4/3/90 | 12:15 PM | 1006 | 22.12 |
| Quincy | Mary | 334-8721 | 4/3/90 | 1:32 PM | 1007 | 998.98 |
| Smith | Bill | 233-2322 | 3/22/90 | 9:00 AM | 1001 | 401.54 |
| Smith | Candice | 334-7777 | 4/6/90 | 4:45 AM | 1011 | 4.50 |
| Stone | Mary | 233-8765 | 4/3/90 | 10:05 AM | 1004 | 27.47 |
| Dean | Bill | 233-9898 | 4/3/90 | 10:20 AM | 1005 | 355.90 |
| Doe | John | 345-7786 | 3/30/90 | 10:22 AM | 1003 | 2.35 |
| Garr | Donald | 345-7777 | 4/7/90 | 10:25 AM | 1012 | 55.66 |
| Jones | Sue | 333-9123 | 4/6/90 | 9:45 AM | 1009 | 45.25 |
| Lowe | Sally | 334-9988 | 4/5/90 | 3:34 PM | 1008 | 56.90 |
| Quincy | Robert | 333-9876 | 4/3/90 | 12:15 PM | 1006 | 22.12 |
| Quincy | Mary | 334-8721 | 4/3/90 | 1:32 PM | 1007 | 998.98 |
| Smith | Bill | 233-2322 | 3/22/90 | 9:00 AM | 1001 | 401.54 |
| Smith | Candice | 334-7777 | 4/6/90 | 4:45 AM | 1011 | 4.50 |
| Stone | Mary | 233-8765 | 4/3/90 | 10:05 AM | 1004 | 27.47 |

*Orders (DB)*

**Figure 4.22.** Horizontal Split Screen Database List Display.

Split the screen horizontally:

- The dark rectangle at the left end of the *Horizontal Scroll Bar* is also a *Split Rectangle*. Drag the *Horizontal Split Rectangle* from the left end of the original *Horizontal Scroll Bar* to a point at the middle of the *Horizontal Scroll Bar*. Your screen should look something like that shown in Figure 4.23. The screen is now split both horizontally and vertically.

- Scroll the screens using both the *Vertical* and *Horizontal Scroll Boxes.*

These displays are related to each other in the sense that if you use one of the vertical screen scroll boxes, both the horizontal screens are scrolled on the appropriate vertical side of the screen. Similarly, if you use a horizontal screen scroll box, both the vertical screens are scrolled in the appropriate horizontal side of the screen. This is done so that when you look at a row completely across the screen, you are always looking at data from the *same* row in the database. In a similar manner, a column (even though it is split vertically) always represents data for the *same* field. Selected fields are available for editing in the data display bar at the top of the screen, just as is the case when you are using a single screen display.

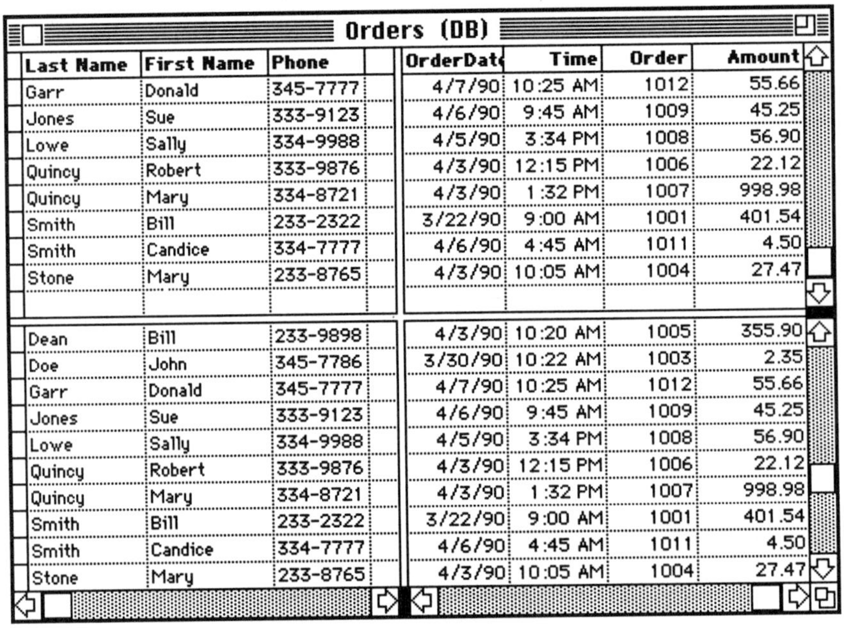

| Last Name | First Name | Phone | OrderDate | Time | Order | Amount |
|-----------|------------|----------|-----------|-----------|------|--------|
| Garr | Donald | 345-7777 | 4/7/90 | 10:25 AM | 1012 | 55.66 |
| Jones | Sue | 333-9123 | 4/6/90 | 9:45 AM | 1009 | 45.25 |
| Lowe | Sally | 334-9988 | 4/5/90 | 3:34 PM | 1008 | 56.90 |
| Quincy | Robert | 333-9876 | 4/3/90 | 12:15 PM | 1006 | 22.12 |
| Quincy | Mary | 334-8721 | 4/3/90 | 1:32 PM | 1007 | 998.98 |
| Smith | Bill | 233-2322 | 3/22/90 | 9:00 AM | 1001 | 401.54 |
| Smith | Candice | 334-7777 | 4/6/90 | 4:45 AM | 1011 | 4.50 |
| Stone | Mary | 233-8765 | 4/3/90 | 10:05 AM | 1004 | 27.47 |
| Dean | Bill | 233-9898 | 4/3/90 | 10:20 AM | 1005 | 355.90 |
| Doe | John | 345-7786 | 3/30/90 | 10:22 AM | 1003 | 2.35 |
| Garr | Donald | 345-7777 | 4/7/90 | 10:25 AM | 1012 | 55.66 |
| Jones | Sue | 333-9123 | 4/6/90 | 9:45 AM | 1009 | 45.25 |
| Lowe | Sally | 334-9988 | 4/5/90 | 3:34 PM | 1008 | 56.90 |
| Quincy | Robert | 333-9876 | 4/3/90 | 12:15 PM | 1006 | 22.12 |
| Quincy | Mary | 334-8721 | 4/3/90 | 1:32 PM | 1007 | 998.98 |
| Smith | Bill | 233-2322 | 3/22/90 | 9:00 AM | 1001 | 401.54 |
| Smith | Candice | 334-7777 | 4/6/90 | 4:45 AM | 1011 | 4.50 |
| Stone | Mary | 233-8765 | 4/3/90 | 10:05 AM | 1004 | 27.47 |

Orders (DB)

**Figure 4.23.** A Four-Display Split Screen.

- Scroll the windows so that the record for Sally Lowe is visible in all four windows.

- Select the name *Lowe* by clicking.

Notice that *Lowe* is highlighted in all four displays, as demonstrated in Figure 4.24. It is important to understand that with split screen displays, the database data duplication that you are viewing is for display only. That is, the database itself is not duplicated. When you select that data item, it is highlighted simultaneously in all four displays. Likewise, if you were to edit the data in the data display bar, the changes would be immediately reflected in all four displays.

| Last Name | First Name | Phone | | Last Name | First Name | Phone | |
|---|---|---|---|---|---|---|---|
| Garr | Donald | 345-7777 | | Garr | Donald | 345-7777 | |
| Jones | Sue | 333-9123 | | Jones | Sue | 333-9123 | |
| Lowe | Sally | 334-9988 | | Lowe | Sally | 334-9988 | |
| Quincy | Robert | 333-9876 | | Quincy | Robert | 333-9876 | |
| Quincy | Mary | 334-8721 | | Quincy | Mary | 334-8721 | |
| Smith | Bill | 233-2322 | | Smith | Bill | 233-2322 | 3 |
| Smith | Candice | 334-7777 | | Smith | Candice | 334-7777 | |
| Stone | Mary | 233-8765 | | Stone | Mary | 233-8765 | |
| Dean | Bill | 233-9898 | | Dean | Bill | 233-9898 | |
| Doe | John | 345-7786 | | Doe | John | 345-7786 | 3 |
| Garr | Donald | 345-7777 | | Garr | Donald | 345-7777 | |
| Jones | Sue | 333-9123 | | Jones | Sue | 333-9123 | |
| Lowe | Sally | 334-9988 | | Lowe | Sally | 334-9988 | |
| Quincy | Robert | 333-9876 | | Quincy | Robert | 333-9876 | |
| Quincy | Mary | 334-8721 | | Quincy | Mary | 334-8721 | |
| Smith | Bill | 233-2322 | | Smith | Bill | 233-2322 | 3 |
| Smith | Candice | 334-7777 | | Smith | Candice | 334-7777 | |
| Stone | Mary | 233-8765 | | Stone | Mary | 233-8765 | |

*Title bar:* Orders (DB)

**Figure 4.24.** Viewing Multiple Copies of the Same Data.

- To remove the horizontal splitting of the display, drag the *Horizontal Split Rectangle* to the left end of the *Horizontal Scroll Bar* and release.

- Drag the *Vertical Split Rectangle* to the top of the *Vertical Scroll Bar* and release. Your display should appear as a single list display.

## INSERTING A RECORD

You can insert a record anywhere in the database. For example, to insert a record before the record for Sally Lowe, perform the following.

- Display the database using the *Show List* command of the **Format** menu.

- Select any field in the row of the database containing the name *Sally Lowe*.

- Select the *Insert Record* command from the **Edit** menu. An empty record will be inserted before the record containing the name *Sally Lowe*.

227

- Click the *Last Name* field in the empty row.

- Type *Kelly* in the *Last Name* field and press the *Tab* key.

- Type *Brad* in the *First Name* field and press the *Tab* key.

- Type *234-1211* in the *Phone* field and press the *Tab* key.

- Type *4/7/90* in the *OrderDate* field and press the *Tab* key.

- Type *8:42 AM* in the *Time* field and press the *Tab* key.

- Type *1013* in the *Order* field and press the *Tab* key.

- Type *55.66* in the *Amount* field. Click the *Accept* box. The newly inserted record should now have the appearance shown in Figure 4.25.

- Save your database by selecting the *Save* command from the **File** menu.

| | | | | | Orders (DB) | | |
|---|---|---|---|---|---|---|---|
| Last Name | First Name | Phone | OrderDate | Time | Order | Amount | |
| Ball | George | 334-7765 | 3/30/90 | 9:31 AM | 1002 | 100.33 | |
| Ballard | Ron | 233-2323 | 4/6/90 | 2:20 PM | 1010 | 702.00 | |
| Dean | Bill | 233-9898 | 4/3/90 | 10:20 AM | 1005 | 355.90 | |
| Doe | John | 345-7786 | 3/30/90 | 10:22 AM | 1003 | 2.35 | |
| Garr | Donald | 345-7777 | 4/7/90 | 10:25 AM | 1012 | 55.66 | |
| Jones | Sue | 333-9123 | 4/6/90 | 9:45 AM | 1009 | 45.25 | |
| Kelly | Brad | 234-1211 | 4/7/90 | 8:42 AM | 1013 | 55.66 | |
| Lowe | Sally | 334-9988 | 4/5/90 | 3:34 PM | 1008 | 56.90 | |
| Quincy | Robert | 333-9876 | 4/3/90 | 12:15 PM | 1006 | 22.12 | |
| Quincy | Mary | 334-8721 | 4/3/90 | 1:32 PM | 1007 | 998.98 | |
| Smith | Bill | 233-2322 | 3/22/90 | 9:00 AM | 1001 | 401.54 | |
| Smith | Candice | 334-7777 | 4/6/90 | 4:45 AM | 1011 | 4.50 | |
| Stone | Mary | 233-8765 | 4/3/90 | 10:05 AM | 1004 | 27.47 | |

Figure 4.25. The Database after Inserting a Record.

## COPYING A RECORD

Occasionally, you may find it convenient to copy an entire record and insert it into the database. For example, suppose that Bill Dean's order is a standing order that is to be filled every month. You could enter the next order for him by copying his record and then modifying the fields that change value.

To illustrate perform the following.

- Click the *record selector* box for the record containing data for *Bill Dean*. This box is the small rectangular box at the extreme left end of the record to the left of the *Last Name* field that contains the name *Dean*. The entire record will become highlighted to indicate that it is selected.

- Select the *Copy* command from the **Edit** menu. A copy of the record is now on the *Clipboard*.

- Click the record selector box for the record containing *John Doe*. This record immediately follows Bill Dean's record in the database. The entire row for this record will become highlighted.

- Select the *Paste* command from the **Edit** menu. The copy of the record will be inserted immediately before the record for *John Doe*. See Figure 4.26.

- Select the *OrderDate* field of this record by clicking in it.

- Type *5/6/90* for the *OrderDate* field and press the *Tab* key.

- Type *9:15 AM* for the *Time* field and press the *Tab* key.

- Type *1014* for the *Order* field and press the *Tab* key.

- Type *44.60* for the *Amount* field and click the *Accept Box*. The final result is shown in Figure 4.27.

- Save your database by selecting the *Save* command from the **File** menu.

| Last Name | First Name | Phone | OrderDate | Time | Order | Amount |
|-----------|-----------|----------|-----------|----------|-------|--------|
| Ball | George | 334-7765 | 3/30/90 | 9:31 AM | 1002 | 100.33 |
| Ballard | Ron | 233-2323 | 4/6/90 | 2:20 PM | 1010 | 702.00 |
| Dean | Bill | 233-9898 | 4/3/90 | 10:20 AM | 1005 | 355.90 |
| Dean | Bill | 233-9898 | 4/3/90 | 10:20 AM | 1005 | 355.90 |
| Doe | John | 345-7786 | 3/30/90 | 10:22 AM | 1003 | 2.35 |
| Garr | Donald | 345-7777 | 4/7/90 | 10:25 AM | 1012 | 55.66 |
| Jones | Sue | 333-9123 | 4/6/90 | 9:45 AM | 1009 | 45.25 |
| Kelly | Brad | 234-1211 | 4/7/90 | 8:42 AM | 1013 | 55.66 |
| Lowe | Sally | 334-9988 | 4/5/90 | 3:34 PM | 1008 | 56.90 |
| Quincy | Robert | 333-9876 | 4/3/90 | 12:15 PM | 1006 | 22.12 |
| Quincy | Mary | 334-8721 | 4/3/90 | 1:32 PM | 1007 | 998.98 |
| Smith | Bill | 233-2322 | 3/22/90 | 9:00 AM | 1001 | 401.54 |

Orders (DB)

Figure 4.26. A Copied Record after Inserting It into the Database.

| Last Name | First Name | Phone | OrderDate | Time | Order | Amount |
|-----------|------------|-------|-----------|------|-------|--------|
| Ball | George | 334-7765 | 3/30/90 | 9:31 AM | 1002 | 100.33 |
| Ballard | Ron | 233-2323 | 4/6/90 | 2:20 PM | 1010 | 702.00 |
| Dean | Bill | 233-9898 | 4/3/90 | 10:20 AM | 1005 | 355.90 |
| Dean | Bill | 233-9898 | 5/6/90 | 9:15 AM | 1014 | 44.60 |
| Doe | John | 345-7786 | 3/30/90 | 10:22 AM | 1003 | 2.35 |
| Garr | Donald | 345-7777 | 4/7/90 | 10:25 AM | 1012 | 55.66 |
| Jones | Sue | 333-9123 | 4/6/90 | 9:45 AM | 1009 | 45.25 |
| Kelly | Brad | 234-1211 | 4/7/90 | 8:42 AM | 1013 | 55.66 |
| Lowe | Sally | 334-9988 | 4/5/90 | 3:34 PM | 1008 | 56.90 |
| Quincy | Robert | 333-9876 | 4/3/90 | 12:15 PM | 1006 | 22.12 |
| Quincy | Mary | 334-8721 | 4/3/90 | 1:32 PM | 1007 | 998.98 |
| Smith | Bill | 233-2322 | 3/22/90 | 9:00 AM | 1001 | 401.54 |

**Orders (DB)**

**Figure 4.27.** Modified Record for Bill Dean.

## COPYING BLOCKS OF INFORMATION

You may find it convenient to copy information within the database to other fields. For example, suppose that you wish to enter four records into the database for the date 5/6/90. Perform the following.

- Click the *OrderDate* field for the new record just entered for Bill Dean (this field contains 5/6/90).

- Select *Copy* from the **Edit** menu. The text *5/6/90* is now on the *Clipboard*.

- Select the *OrderDate* field of the first blank row at the end of the database by clicking. You many need to use the *Scroll Arrows* to position the database appropriately.

- Select the *Paste* command from the **Edit** menu. The data on the *Clipboard* will be pasted into the field.

- Select the *OrderDate* field of the next blank row and paste the data into it. There are now two copies of these data appended to the end of the database.

- Click the *OrderDate* field in which you first pasted the date and drag to the second *OrderDate* field in which you pasted the date. The situation is shown in Figure 4.28.

- Select the *Copy* command from the **Edit** menu.

- Click the blank *OrderDate* field just below those you copied in the last two steps.

- Select the *Paste* command from the **Edit** menu. The copied data will be pasted into the *OrderDate* fields of two records. The result is shown in Figure 4.29.

The method you have just used for copying and pasting data can be repeated as many times as you wish.

| Last Name | First Name | Phone | OrderDate | Time | Order | Amount |
|---|---|---|---|---|---|---|
| Smith | Bill | 233-2322 | 3/22/90 | 9:00 AM | 1001 | 401.54 |
| Smith | Candice | 334-7777 | 4/6/90 | 4:45 AM | 1011 | 4.50 |
| Stone | Mary | 233-8765 | 4/3/90 | 10:05 AM | 1004 | 27.47 |
| | | | 5/6/90 | | | |
| | | | 5/6/90 | | | |
| | | | | | | |

Orders (DB)

**Figure 4.28.** The Database after Selecting Two Rows of Date Data.

| Last Name | First Name | Phone | OrderDate | Time | Order | Amount |
|---|---|---|---|---|---|---|
| Smith | Bill | 233-2322 | 3/22/90 | 9:00 AM | 1001 | 401.54 |
| Smith | Candice | 334-7777 | 4/6/90 | 4:45 AM | 1011 | 4.50 |
| Stone | Mary | 233-8765 | 4/3/90 | 10:05 AM | 1004 | 27.47 |
| | | | 5/6/90 | | | |
| | | | 5/6/90 | | | |
| | | | 5/6/90 | | | |
| | | | 5/6/90 | | | |

Orders (DB)

**Figure 4.29.** The Database after Pasting Two Rows of Date Data.

# DELETING A RECORD

There are two methods for deleting an entire record from the database using a list display.

Method 1. Deleting and leaving a blank record:

- Select *John Doe's* record by clicking in the record selector box to the left of the first field.

- Delete the data in the row data by executing the *Clear* command from the **Edit** menu. A blank record is left in the database as shown in Figure 4.30. A copy of the deleted record is **not** placed on the *Clipboard*.

| Last Name | First Name | Phone | OrderDate | Time | Order | Amount |
|-----------|-----------|---------|-----------|----------|-------|--------|
| Ball | George | 334-7765 | 3/30/90 | 9:31 AM | 1002 | 100.33 |
| Ballard | Ron | 233-2323 | 4/6/90 | 2:20 PM | 1010 | 702.00 |
| Dean | Bill | 233-9898 | 4/3/90 | 10:20 AM | 1005 | 355.90 |
| Dean | Bill | 233-9898 | 5/6/90 | 9:15 AM | 1014 | 44.60 |
|  |  |  |  |  |  |  |
| Garr | Donald | 345-7777 | 4/7/90 | 10:25 AM | 1012 | 55.66 |
| Jones | Sue | 333-9123 | 4/6/90 | 9:45 AM | 1009 | 45.25 |
| Kelly | Brad | 234-1211 | 4/7/90 | 8:42 AM | 1013 | 55.66 |
| Lowe | Sally | 334-9988 | 4/5/90 | 3:34 PM | 1008 | 56.90 |

Orders (DB)

**Figure 4.30.** The Database after Using the *Clear* Command on Record 5.

- Restore John Doe's record by selecting the *Undo* command in the **Edit** menu.

Method 2. Deleting and not leaving a blank record:

- Select Bill Dean's second record (record 4) by dragging through its fields or by clicking in the record selection box to the left of the first entry.

- Delete the data in the row data by executing the *Cut* command from the **Edit** menu. The record is removed from the database, as shown in Figure 4.31. A copy of the record deleted is placed on the *Clipboard*.

- Quit Works, but **do not** save the changes made to your database since the last *Save* was executed. (Click *No* in the dialog box presented when you select *Quit*.)

You have now completed Lesson 5. If you do not wish to continue to the next lesson, you should clean up the desktop and shut down your computer.

| Last Name | First Name | Phone | OrderDate | Time | Order | Amount |
|-----------|-----------|---------|-----------|----------|-------|--------|
| Ball | George | 334-7765 | 3/30/90 | 9:31 AM | 1002 | 100.33 |
| Ballard | Ron | 233-2323 | 4/6/90 | 2:20 PM | 1010 | 702.00 |
| Dean | Bill | 233-9898 | 4/3/90 | 10:20 AM | 1005 | 355.90 |
| Doe | John | 345-7786 | 3/30/90 | 10:22 AM | 1003 | 2.35 |
| Garr | Donald | 345-7777 | 4/7/90 | 10:25 AM | 1012 | 55.66 |
| Jones | Sue | 333-9123 | 4/6/90 | 9:45 AM | 1009 | 45.25 |
| Kelly | Brad | 234-1211 | 4/7/90 | 8:42 AM | 1013 | 55.66 |
| Lowe | Sally | 334-9988 | 4/5/90 | 3:34 PM | 1008 | 56.90 |
| Quincy | Robert | 333-9876 | 4/3/90 | 12:15 PM | 1006 | 22.12 |

Orders (DB)

**Figure 4.31.** The Database after Using the *Cut* Command on Record 4.

# SELECTING AND DISPLAYING INFORMATION

After completing this lesson, you will be able to:

❑ Select records satisfying some condition from a database.

❑ Save the records selected.

## LESSON BACKGROUND

An important characteristic of any database management system is the ease and flexibility with which it allows you to retrieve stored information. In this section you will learn how to make information retrievals using record selection criteria in Works DB. By using record selection criteria you will be able to retrieve only those records in the database that meet certain criteria that you specify. We begin by defining a new database that will be used for the examples in the remainder of this chapter.

## EXAMPLE DATABASE

Suppose you are the program manager of radio station WWIN, which plays a variety of types of music during a week, with music sets grouped in many different ways. Hence, it is very desirable to automate the selection of the various musical sets that you must program. You decide to place information about WWIN's sizable record collection in a Works DB database. Using this database, you can easily find what records of a given type are available in the station. In this way you can plan the week's music segments and have your assistant collect the appropriate records and deliver them to the appropriate D.J. in a timely manner.

Suppose you decide that the following fields are important ones for your purposes: *Title, Artist, Label, Year Released, Highest Rating Attained on WWIN's Chart*, and *Music Type*. As a consequence, you might lay out the following record format:

| Title | Artist | Label | YearRel | HighestR | Type |
|-------|--------|-------|---------|----------|------|

A sample list display from such a database is shown in Figure 4.32.

| Title | Artist | Label | YearRel | HighestR | Type |
|-------|--------|-------|---------|----------|------|
| Baby Come Back | Player | RSO | 1977 | 3 | Rock1 |
| Both Sides Now | Judy Collins | Electra | 1967 | 8 | Folk1 |
| The Way We Were | Barbara Striesand | Columbia | 1974 | 1 | Pop2 |
| Greenback Dollar | Kingston Trio | Capital | 1964 | 8 | Folk1 |
| Killing Me Softly | Roberta Flack | Atlantic | 1973 | 1 | Rock1 |
| You've Got a Friend | Carole King | A & M | 1971 | 3 | Rock1 |
| Only Yesterday | Carpenters | A & M | 1973 | 5 | Rock1 |
| Baby Love | The Supremes | Motown | 1967 | 1 | Rock2 |
| Reunited | Peaches and Herb | Polydor | 1978 | 1 | Rock2 |
| Material Girl | Madonna | Sire | 1984 | 1 | Rock3 |
| The Next Time I Fall | Peter Cetera | Warner Bros. | 1986 | 3 | Rock3 |
| We Are the World | "Many" | Columbia | 1985 | 1 | Rock1 |
| We Built this City | Starship | Grunt | 1985 | 1 | Rock3 |
| It's a Heartache | Bonnie Tyler | RCA | 1978 | 10 | Rock3 |
| The Boxer | Simon & Garfunkel | Columbia | 1968 | 3 | Rock4 |
| Blowin in the Wind | Bob Dylan | Columbia | 1964 | 1 | Folk2 |
| Chances Are | Johnny Mathis | Columbia | 1965 | 10 | Pop1 |

**WWIN Record Collection (DB)**

**Figure 4.32.** List Display of the Example Database.

## CREATING THE EXAMPLE DATABASE

Perform the following.

- Insert your disk containing the folder *Works DB*.

- Open Works DB.

- Define the example database using the techniques described in Lesson 1. The data type for all fields is text.

- Type the data shown in Figure 4.32 into the database. You will probably find it more convenient once the fields are defined to use the list display mode to enter the data rather than the form display mode.

- Save the database by the name *WWINRecordCollection<your initials>* in the *Lesson6* folder contained in the *Works DB* folder on your disk.

Later we will see that it is a good idea to have a backup copy of your database saved. To do this, perform the following steps.

- Select the *Save As* command from the **File** menu, and save a copy of your database under the name *WWINBackup<your initials>* in your *Lesson6* folder contained in the *Works DB* folder on your disk.

- When this *Save As* operation is completed you will have the *WWINBackup<your initials>* database open on your screen. Close this database, and then open the original *WWINRecordCollection<your inititals>* database again.

## SELECTING RECORDS

### EXAMPLE

As a first example retrieval, you will select from all records in the database only those that were released in 1978.

To retrieve these records perform the following.

- If not already the case, display the database using the *Show List* command of the **Format** menu.

- Choose the *Record Selection* command from the **Organize** menu. When this command is chosen, the dialog box shown in Figure 4.33 is displayed. Notice that the database field names are listed in the scroll rectangle to the left of the screen and a list of comparison operators appears in the scroll rectangle to the right. We will refer to those two boxes as the *Record Selection* boxes. Values to be used in completing a selection rule are entered into the rectangle labeled *Record Comparison Information*.

- Click *YearRel* in the list of field names.

- Click the *equals* in the list of operations.

- Type *1978* in the *Record Comparison Information* box. The result is shown in Figure 4.34.

- Click the *Select* button to cause the records to be selected. The selected records are shown in Figure 4.35. Because there are two records with *YearRel* = 1978 in the example database, these two records are displayed when the command is executed.

## SAVING SELECTED SUBSETS

Works DB allows you to save any selected subset of records as a database with its own name. In fact you can also delete some fields from the selected subset of records before saving it. To delete a field, display the subset of records on the screen and then select the field to be deleted by clicking on any entry in its column. *Caution: You should not delete a field that is used in the record selection condition; if you do, the record selection will be canceled.* Assuming you have chosen a field that is not included in the record selection condition, choose the *Delete Field* command from the **Edit** menu. You can delete as many such fields as you choose in this manner.

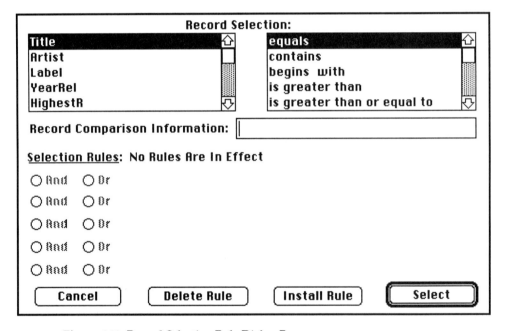

Figure 4.33. Record Selection Rule Dialog Box.

Save the subset database you selected above using the following steps.

- Select the *Save As* command from the **File** menu.

- The dialog box should show that you are positioned inside the folder *Lesson6* within the *Works DB* folder on your disk. If you are not in this position, navigate until you are.

- Click the *Save Selected Records Only* option.

- Type the name of your new database, *WWIN Sub1<your initials>*, in the dialog box.

- Click the *Save* button.

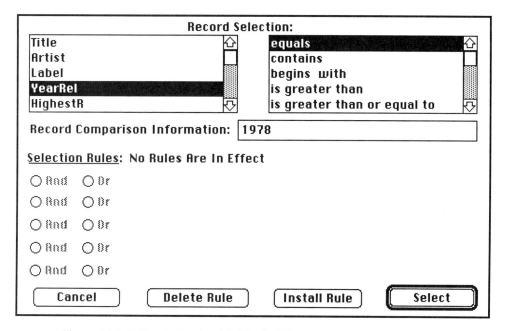

**Figure 4.34.** A Simple Retrieval in Works DB.

| Title | Artist | Label | YearRel | HighestR | Type |
|-------|--------|-------|---------|----------|------|
| Reunited | Peaches and Herb | Polydor | 1978 | 1 | Rock2 |
| It's a Heartache | Bonnie Tyler | RCA | 1978 | 10 | Rock3 |

*WWIN Record Collection (DB)*

**Figure 4.35.** Display of Results from Retrieval of Figure 4.34.

When a subset database is saved, the original database is left intact, as long *as you do not save the changes to your original database when you exit Works DB*. You will need to be **very cautious** when extracting and saving subsets of databases to ensure that the original database remains unchanged. In fact, it is a good idea to use the *Save As* command to save a duplicate of the original database under a different name (as we did at the beginning of this lesson) before you begin the construction of a subset database.

- Select the *Show All Records* command from the **Organize** menu to verify that the original database is the one you are currently working with.

- Close the *WWINRecordCollection<your inititals>* database, but **do not save the changes made**.

- Open the *WWINSub1<your initials>* database and then execute a *Show All Records* command from the **Organize** menu to verify that it contains only the records selected previously.

- Close the *WWINSub1<your initials>* database.

You have now completed Lesson 6. If you do not wish to continue to the next lesson, you should quit Works, clean up the desktop, and shut down your computer.

# MULTIPLE CONDITION RECORD SELECTIONS

After completing this lesson, you will be able to:

❏ Use logical operators in selections.

❏ Use multiple condition record selections.

## LOGICAL OPERATORS

The logical operators AND and OR can be used with the comparison operators to produce more complex retrieval criteria. Note that in the example above the value in field *YearRel* for each record was compared with 1978 to see if they were equal. The result of this comparison is then either *True* or *False*. Only those records for which this comparison results in *True* were displayed. The AND and OR operators combine results for two such condition comparisons to produce a *True* or *False* value for the single combined condition. Ultimately records selected for display must have their selection criteria evaluate to *True*.

The way in which these operators combine truth values is given in Figure 4.36; the tables in this figure are called **truth tables**. Here imagine that x is a *True* or *False* value resulting from one of the comparison operations, such as, "Does the value in field *YearRel* equal *1978*?" Similarly, imagine that y is a *True* or *False* value resulting from one of the comparison operations, such as, "Is the value in field *HighestR* less than or equal 5?" Notice that AND is *True* only when both of its argument conditions are *True*, and OR is *True* when either (including both) of its argument conditions is *True*.

You may construct more complex conditions by using combinations of the AND and OR operations. For conditions involving the combination of several logical operators, you can construct a truth table to find the value of the condition for all the possible values of the constituent conditions. Consider the example given in Figure 4.37, where the retrieval conditions are represented by x, y, and z. Notice that because there are three logical variables involved, there are eight different combinations of *True* and *False* values for those variables. The column y OR z is performed first because of the parentheses. After the result of $y$ OR $z$ is determined, the result of the AND operator is placed in the last column.

| Operator | Truth Value of Result | | |
|----------|------|------|------|
| | x | y | x AND y |
| | True | True | True |
| | True | False | False |
| x AND y | False | True | False |
| | False | False | False |
| | | | |
| | x | y | x OR y |
| | True | True | True |
| x OR y | True | False | True |
| | False | True | True |
| | False | False | False |

**Figure 4.36.** Truth Tables Defining the Basic Logical Operators.

| Evaluating x AND (y OR z) | | | | |
|------|------|------|------|------|
| x | y | z | y OR z | x AND (y OR z) |
| True | True | True | True | True |
| True | True | False | True | True |
| True | False | True | True | True |
| True | False | False | False | False |
| False | True | True | True | False |
| False | True | False | True | False |
| False | False | True | True | False |
| False | False | False | False | False |

**Figure 4.37.** Evaluating a Condition Involving Multiple Logical Operators.

Perform the following using pencil and paper.

- Make a table like the one in Figure 4.37 to evaluate the condition ($x$ AND $y$) OR $z$. Here the parentheses mean to evaluate $x$ AND $y$ first, then apply the OR operator to the result of that and $z$.

- Compare the result with Figure 4.37. You will notice that the two criteria $x$ AND ($y$ OR $z$) and ($x$ AND $y$) OR $z$ have different results in their tables. Hence, if we write the condition $x$ AND $y$ OR $z$ without parentheses, it can be interpreted in two different ways, depending on the order in which the operators AND and OR are applied.

In Works DB the operator AND has precedence over the operator OR. This means that whenever AND and OR operators are used together in a selection criterion, the AND operators will all be evaluated first (left to right in the expression) followed by the OR operators. For example, the expression $x$ OR $y$ AND $z$ would be interpreted in Works DB as if it had been written as $x$ OR ($y$ AND $z$), so that the AND is done first. We will see some implications of this precedence rule in our later examples.

## MULTIPLE CONDITION SELECTION CRITERIA

- Open the *WWINRecordCollection<your inititals>* database stored in the folder *Lesson6* contained in the *Works DB* folder on your disk.

- Execute the *Save As* command from the **File** menu. Navigate through your disk hierarchy and save the database *WWINRecordCollection<your inititals>* in the folder *Lesson7* contained in the *Works DB* folder.

### EXAMPLE 1

In this lesson you will use multiple conditions for selecting records. As a first example, suppose you want all records in the *WWINRecordCollection<your inititals>* that are both of *Type* Rock1 and have a *HighestR* of less than 5. A more concise way of stating the desired selection is

Select all records from *WWINRecordCollection<your inititals>* where

$Type$ = Rock1 AND HighestR < 5.

Here *Type* = Rock1 is the first comparison to make and *HighestR* < 5 is the second comparison to make. You then wish to AND these two conditions together to form the rule to be used for extracting records.

Perform the following to make the selection.

- Choose the command *Record Selection* from the **Organize** menu.

Form the first condition *Type = Rock1*:

- In the *Record Selection* boxes, click the *Type* field (you'll have to scroll to display it) in the left box and click the *equals* in the right box.

- Type *Rock1* into the *Record Comparison Information* box.

- Click the *Install Rule* button. The first part of the rule has now been defined. In general after the first part of a rule has been entered, you can click on either OR or AND. A combination rule built in this way can have *up to six constituent rules* (up to five logical operators).

Combine the first comparison with the second using AND:

- Click the *And* button in the first row of *And* and *Or* buttons.

- In the *Record Selection* boxes, click the *HighestR* field in the left box, and click the *is less than* (scroll to display it) operation in the right box.

- Type *5* into the *Record Comparison Information* box. Figure 4.38 shows the *Record Selection* dialog box after all these steps have been completed.

- Click the *Select* button to cause the records satisfying this rule to be displayed. The list display that results is shown Figure 4.39. Check the records displayed to verify that each satisfies the retrieval criteria.

Save the subset database you selected above:

- Select the *Save As* command from the **File** menu.

- Click the *Save Selected Records Only* option in the dialog box that is displayed.

- Type the name of your new database, *WWINSub2<your initials>*.

- Click the *Save* button.

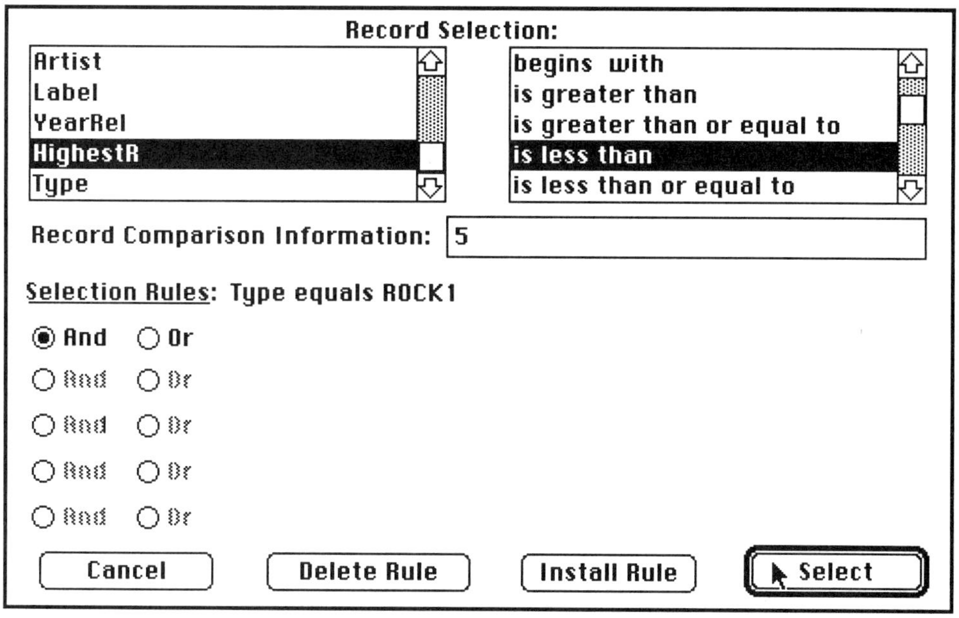

**Record Selection:**

| | | |
|---|---|---|
| Artist | | begins with |
| Label | | is greater than |
| YearRel | | is greater than or equal to |
| **HighestR** | | **is less than** |
| Type | | is less than or equal to |

**Record Comparison Information:** 5

**Selection Rules: Type equals ROCK1**

◉ And  ○ Or

○ And  ○ Or

○ And  ○ Or

○ And  ○ Or

○ And  ○ Or

[ Cancel ]   [ Delete Rule ]   [ Install Rule ]   [ ▶ Select ]

**Figure 4.38.** A Simple AND Rule Being Constructed.

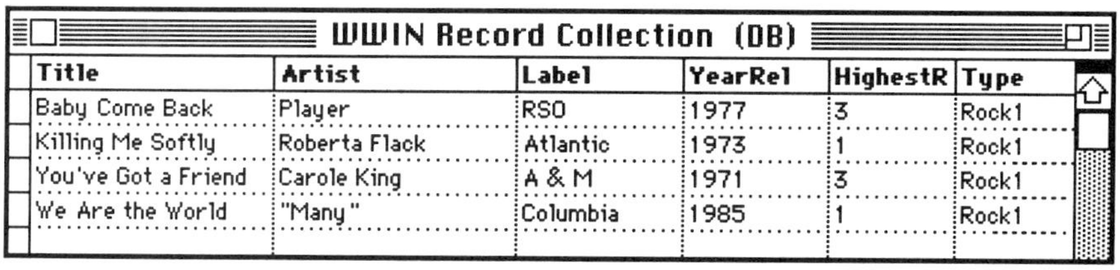

### WWIN Record Collection (DB)

| Title | Artist | Label | YearRel | HighestR | Type |
|---|---|---|---|---|---|
| Baby Come Back | Player | RSO | 1977 | 3 | Rock1 |
| Killing Me Softly | Roberta Flack | Atlantic | 1973 | 1 | Rock1 |
| You've Got a Friend | Carole King | A & M | 1971 | 3 | Rock1 |
| We Are the World | "Many" | Columbia | 1985 | 1 | Rock1 |

**Figure 4.39.** The List Display of Records Selected in Figure 4.38.

**EXAMPLE 2**

Now as a second example, suppose you want to produce a list of all the records that were released between 1975 and 1985 (inclusive) or achieved a number one WWIN rating no matter when they were released. In a more concise form the selection is:

Select all records from *WWINRecordCollection<your inititals>* where

$(YearRel >= 1975$ AND $YearRel <= 1985)$ OR $HighestR = 1$.

As the Record Selection dialog box is being completed, note carefully how the AND precedence over OR is being used in the selection process. Perform the following to make the selection.

• Choose the command *Record Selection* from the **Organize** menu.

243

- Click the *Delete Rule* button twice to clear the current selection rule.

Form the first condition *YearRel >= 1975*.

- In the *Record Selection* boxes, click the *YearRel* field in the left box and click the *is greater than or equal to* operation in the right box.

- Type *1975* into the *Record Comparison Information* box.

- Click the *Install Rule* button. The first part of the rule has now been defined.

AND with second condition *YearRel <= 1985*:

- Click the *And* button in the first row of *And* and *Or* buttons.

- In the *Record Selection* boxes, click the *YearRel* field in the left box and click the *is less than or equal to* operation in the right box.

- Type *1985* into the *Record Comparison Information* box.

- Click the *Install Rule* button. The second part of the rule has now been defined.

OR with third condition *HighestR = 1*:

- Click the *Or* button in the second row of *And* and *Or* buttons.

- In the *Record Selection* boxes, click the *HighestR* field in the left box, and click the *equals* operation in the right box.

- Type *1* into the *Record Comparison Information* box.

- Click the *Install Rule* button. The third part of the rule has now been defined. Figure 4.40 shows the *Record Selection* dialog box after all these steps have been completed. (*Note:* Installing the most recent selection condition is optional.)

- Click the *Select* button to display the records selected. The list display that results is shown in Figure 4.41. Check the records displayed to see that each satisfies the retrieval selection criteria.

- Verify that the information displayed is correct by manually evaluating the selection criteria for each record in the database shown in Figure 4.32 and determining whether or not that record meets the selection criteria.

Save the subset database you selected above:

- Select the *Save As* command from the **File** menu.

- Click the *Save Selected Records Only* option in the dialog box.

- Type the name of your new database, *WWINSub3<your initials>*.

- Click the *Save* button.

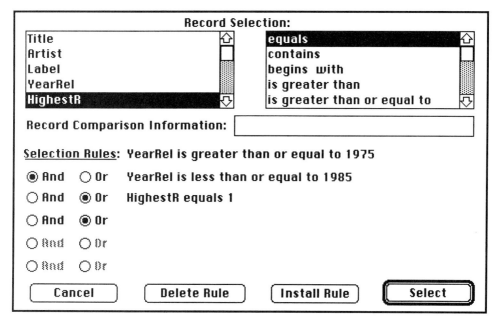

**Figure 4.40.** Selection with an AND and an OR Condition.

| Title | Artist | Label | YearRel | HighestR | Type |
|---|---|---|---|---|---|
| Baby Come Back | Player | RSO | 1977 | 3 | Rock1 |
| The Way We Were | Barbara Striesand | Columbia | 1974 | 1 | Pop2 |
| Killing Me Softly | Roberta Flack | Atlantic | 1973 | 1 | Rock1 |
| Baby Love | The Supremes | Motown | 1967 | 1 | Rock2 |
| Reunited | Peaches and Herb | Polydor | 1978 | 1 | Rock2 |
| Material Girl | Madonna | Sire | 1984 | 1 | Rock3 |
| We Are the World | "Many" | Columbia | 1985 | 1 | Rock1 |
| We Built this City | Starship | Grunt | 1985 | 1 | Rock3 |
| It's a Heartache | Bonnie Tyler | RCA | 1978 | 10 | Rock3 |
| Blowin in the Wind | Bob Dylan | Columbia | 1964 | 1 | Folk2 |

*WWIN Record Collection (DB)*

**Figure 4.41.** List Display of Records Selected in Figure 4.35.

EXAMPLE 3

As a final example in this lesson, suppose you want to produce a list of all records having type *Rock1* whose highest rating was either *1* or *3*. The attempt to do this with the selection criterion shown in Figure 4.42 will fail. Can you see why?

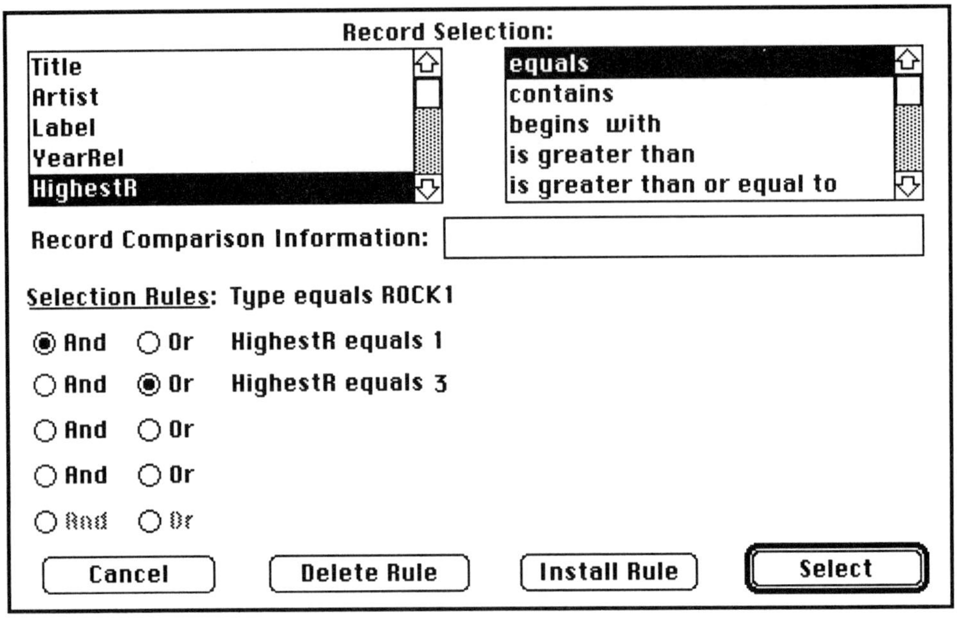

**Figure 4.42.** An Incorrect Retrieval for all *Rock1* Type Records whose Highest Rating Was 1 or 3.

The retrieval in Figure 4.42 is equivalent to the following selection because of the precedence of AND over OR.

Select all records from *WWINRecordCollection<your inititals>* where

(*Type* = Rock1 AND *HighestR* = 1) OR *HighestR* = 3.

Look at the above retrieval closely to see why it does not produce the desired list. The list that it does produce is shown in Figure 4.43. Verify by manually checking the database in Figure 4.32 that the data shown there is that produced by the above selection. Notice that it is not the list you desired, because it includes some records that are not of type *Rock1*.

| Title | Artist | Label | YearRel | HighestR | Type |
|-------|--------|-------|---------|----------|------|
| Baby Come Back | Player | RSO | 1977 | 3 | Rock1 |
| Killing Me Softly | Roberta Flack | Atlantic | 1973 | 1 | Rock1 |
| You've Got a Friend | Carole King | A & M | 1971 | 3 | Rock1 |
| The Next Time I Fall | Peter Cetera | Warner Bros. | 1986 | 3 | Rock3 |
| We Are the World | "Many" | Columbia | 1985 | 1 | Rock1 |
| The Boxer | Simon & Garfunkel | Columbia | 1968 | 3 | Rock4 |

WWIN Record Collection (DB)

**Figure 4.43.** List Display Produced by the Retrieval of Figure 4.42.

The correct retrieval is given in Figure 4.44. It is equivalent to the following (again because of the precedence of AND over OR).

Select all records from *WWINRecordCollection<your inititals>* where

(*Type* = Rock1 AND *HighestR* = 1)

OR

(*Type* = Rock1 AND *HighestR* = 3)

Perform the following to make the selection.

- Choose the command *Record Selection* from the **Organize** menu.

- Click the *Delete Rule* button three times to clear the previous selection rule.

Form the first comparison *Type* = *Rock1*:

- In the *Record Selection* boxes, click the *Type* field in the left box and click the *equals* operation in the right box.

- Type *Rock1* into the *Record Comparison Information* box.

- Click the *Install Rule* button. The first part of the rule has now been defined.

AND with the second comparison *HighestR* = 1:

- Click the *And* button in the first row of *And* and *Or* buttons.

247

- In the *Record Selection* boxes click the *HighestR* field in the left box and click the *equals* operation in the right box.

- Type *1* into the *Record Comparison Information* box.

- Click the *Install Rule* button. The second part of the rule has now been defined.

Form the OR with the third comparison *Type = Rock1*:

- Click the *Or* button in the second row of *And* and *Or* buttons.

- In the *Record Selection* boxes, click the *Type* field in the left box and click the *equals* operation in the right box.

- Type *Rock1* into the *Record Comparison Information* box.

- Click the *Install Rule* button. The third part of the rule has now been defined.

Form the AND with the last comparison *HighestR = 3*:

- Click the *And* button in the third row of *And* and *Or* buttons.

- In the *Record Selection* boxes, click the *HighestR* field in the left box and click the *equals* operation in the right box.

- Type *3* into the *Record Comparison Information* box.

- Click the *Install Rule* button. The fourth part of the rule has now been installed. Figure 4.44 shows the *Record Selection* dialog box after all these steps have been completed.

- Click the *Select* button to cause the selection to be done. The list display that results is shown Figure 4.45. Check the records displayed to see that they satisfy the retrieval selection criterion.

- Verify that the information is correct by manually evaluating the selection criteria for the records from the database shown in Figure 4.32.

Save the subset database you selected above:

- Select the *Save As* command from the **File** menu.

- Click the *Save Selected Records Only* option in the dialog box.

- Type the name of your new database, *WWINSub4<your initials>*.

- Click the *Save button.*

Recall that you must be careful not to save only the selected subset of your database in place of your entire database. Execute the following carefully.

- Quit Works, but **do not** save the changes made to your database. Click *No* in the dialog box presented after you select *Quit*.

You have now completed Lesson 7. If you do not wish to continue to the next lesson, you should clean up the desktop and shut down your computer.

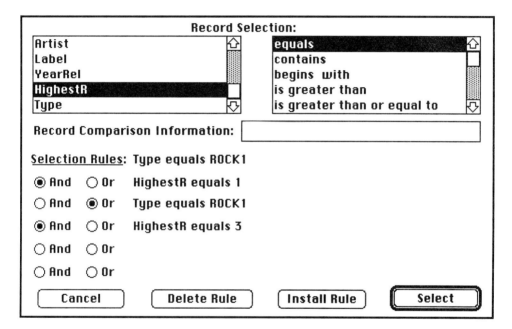

**Figure 4.44.** Correct Version of Retrieval Attempted in Figure 4.42.

| Title | Artist | Label | YearRel | HighestR | Type |
|-------|--------|-------|---------|----------|------|
| Baby Come Back | Player | RSO | 1977 | 3 | Rock1 |
| Killing Me Softly | Roberta Flack | Atlantic | 1973 | 1 | Rock1 |
| You've Got a Friend | Carole King | A & M | 1971 | 3 | Rock1 |
| We Are the World | "Many" | Columbia | 1985 | 1 | Rock1 |

WWIN Record Collection (DB)

**Figure 4.45.** List Display for the Retrieval of Figure 4.44.

# CREATING DATABASE REPORTS

After completing this lesson, you will be able to:

❑ Create and save reports.

❑ Use the Report Definition screen.

❑ Remove unwanted fields from the report.

❑ Preview and print a report.

## CREATING AND SAVING REPORTS

Use of the record selection features in Works as discussed in Lessons 6 and 7 allows selective retrieval of information from the database. In this lesson you will use the *WWINRecordCollection<your inititals>* database to retrieve information from the database and create a report summarizing that information. In creating a report you will first need to define the rules to be used to select the data of interest. These rules coupled with the format of the report you wish to generate are termed the *report specifications*.

Report specifications that you create during a session are automatically saved if the database is saved. Saved report specifications result in the inclusion of all updated information in a database report produced at a later time. The maximum number of reports that can be saved is eight. When you have eight report specifications saved and wish to save an additional report, one of the eight already saved must first be deleted.

## REPORT DEFINITION SCREEN

The goal for this portion of the lesson is to create a report that contains the *Title, Artist, YearRel, HighestR,* and *Type* for songs that are of type *Rock1* or *Rock2*.

Perform the following.

- If not already open, open the *WWINRecordCollection<your inititals>* database stored in the folder *Lesson7* contained in the *Works DB* folder on your disk.

- Execute the *Save As* command from the **File** menu. Navigate through your disk hierarchy and save the database *WWINRecordCollection<your inititals>* in the folder *Lesson8* contained in the *Works DB* folder.

- Be sure that *Show All Records* is selected in the **Organize** menu.

- Display the database using the *Show List* command of the **Format** menu.

- Begin the record selection process by selecting the *Record Selection* command from the **Organize** menu.

Form first comparison *Type = Rock1*:

- In the *Record Selection* boxes, click the *Type* field in the left box and click the *equals* operation in the right box.

- Type *Rock1* into the *Record Comparison Information* box.

- Click the *Install Rule* button. (The first part of the rule has now been defined.)

Form OR with second comparison:

- Click the *Or* button.

- In the *Record Selection* boxes, click the *Type* field in the left box and click the *equals* operation in the right box.

- Type *Rock2* into the *Record Comparison Information* box.

- Click the *Install Rule* button. (The second part of the rule has now been defined.)

- Click the *Select* button to select the desired records from the database.

Next obtain the Report Window:

- Select the *New Report* command from the **Report** menu. A screen similar to the one shown in Figure 4.46 will be displayed. Notice the presence of a new menu, **TotalsPage** on the menu bar. You will understand its purpose in the next lesson.

The selection rules that have been entered are displayed on the report definition screen. At the bottom of the report definition screen (notice the database list display window in the background in Figure 4.46) are shown the records that will appear in the report. The small triangle at the left edge of the ruler marks the **left margin** of the report, and a similar symbol near the right edge of the ruler marks the **right margin**. The width of the report can be controlled by dragging the right margin marker.

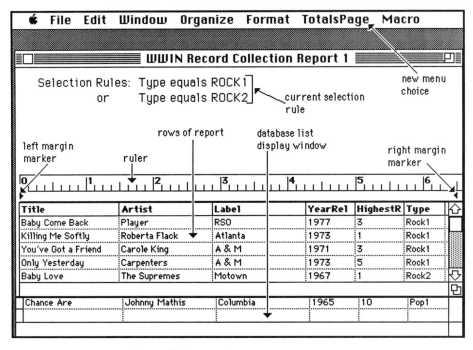

**Figure 4.46.** A Report Definition Screen.

## REMOVING UNWANTED FIELDS IN A REPORT

Examine the column headings for the report shown in Figure 4.46. Notice that the *Label* field is within the report area as defined by the positions of the *left margin* and *right margin* markers. However, recall that the *Label* field is not supposed to be part of the report because the report will include only the information in the *Title, Artist, YearRel, HighestR,* and *Type* fields. In this section of the lesson, you will remove the *Label* field from the report area.

Perform the following.

- Move the *Label* field to the right of the *right margin* marker by moving the pointer over the box containing the name of the field so the pointer takes the shape of a hand. Then drag the field name past the last field to appear in the database, in this case the *Type* field.

• Adjust the *right margin* marker so that it is located at the right edge of the *Type* field, thus excluding the *Label* field from the report. Your window should resemble Figure 4.47. (Note that the *right margin* marker is now to the left of the field *Label*.)

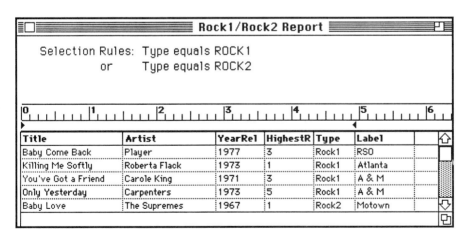

**Figure 4.47.** Moving a Field to the Right.

• Rename the report by selecting the *Change Report Title* command from the **Edit** menu and typing *Rock1/Rock2 Report* into the dialog box. The resulting report definition window is shown in Figure 4.48.

**Figure 4.48.** A Report Definition with the Field Named Label Excluded.

The report *Rock1/Rock2 Report* is now ready to be previewed.

## PREVIEWING AND PRINTING A REPORT

You may observe how a report will appear when printed without actually printing it. This process is called previewing a report. Because printing a database report may take a considerable amount of time if the report is large, you may save a considerable amount of time by critically previewing the report before printing. If some aspect of the report is not as you want it, you can alter the report and preview it again. Print the report only when you are satisfied that it is correct.

Perform the following.

- Select the *Print* command of the **File** menu.

- If the *Print Preview* button located in the lower left-hand corner of the *Print* dialog box does not already contain an x, click it. Click the *Print* (or *OK*) box. A preview window will be displayed in which an entire page containing the report will be shown exactly as it would be printed. (The size is reduced, however, to allow a full page to appear on a Macintosh screen.)

- Move the pointer to within the reduced page. The pointer will become a magnifying glass.

- Move the magnifying glass to within the report and click. You will then see the report in full size. The result is shown in Figure 4.49.

- Reduce the size of the page by clicking the *Close* box or by double clicking the hand that is displayed when the window is full size. (The buttons *Next* and *Previous* allow scrolling through a multiple page report one page at a time.)

- Click the *Print* button to initiate printing the report. (Make sure you have selected a proper printer using Chooser.)

- When the printing is completed, close the report window by clicking its *Close* box.

- Save your database by selecting the *Save* command from the **File** menu.

You have now completed Lesson 8. If you do not wish to continue to the next lesson, you should clean up the desktop and shut down your computer.

| Title | Artist | YearRel | HighestR | Type |
|-------|--------|---------|----------|------|
| Baby Come Back | Player | 1977 | 3 | Rock1 |
| Killing Me Softly | Roberta Flack | 1973 | 1 | Rock1 |
| You've Got a Friend | Carole King | 1971 | 3 | Rock1 |
| Only Yesterday | Carpenters | 1973 | 5 | Rock1 |
| Baby Love | The Supremes | 1967 | 1 | Rock2 |
| Reunited | Peaches and Herb | 1978 | 1 | Rock2 |
| We Are the World | "Many" | 1985 | 1 | Rock1 |

**Figure 4.49.** The *Rock1/Rock2 Report* as Shown on the *Print Preview* Display.

LESSON 9 _____

# TOTALS AND SUBTOTALS IN REPORTS

_____

After completing this lesson, you will be able to:

❑ Compute totals and subtotals automatically.

❑ Use the **TotalsPage** menu.

## TOTALS AND SUBTOTALS

To demonstrate the ability of Works DB to calculate automatic totals, it will be necessary to add a data field that could be meaningfully summed. Let us suppose that you have notes indicating how many times a given record has been played on the air. Let us add a field to our database to contain this information.

Perform the following.

- If not already open, open the *WWINRecordCollection<your inititals>* database stored in the folder *Lesson8* contained in the *Works DB* folder on your disk.

- Execute the *Save As* command from the **File** menu. Navigate through your disk hierarchy and save the database *WWINRecordCollection<your inititals>* in the folder *Lesson9* contained in the *Works DB* folder.

- Select the *Show List* command from the **Format** menu and the *Show All Records* command from the **Organize** menu.

- Select the command *Add New Field* under the **Edit** menu. Name the new field *TimesAired* and it will be added to the database.

- Type the information shown in Figure 4.50 into the *TimesAired* field of the database.

- Save your database by selecting the *Save* command from the **File** menu.

| Title | Artist | Label | YearRel | HighestR | Type | TimesAired |
|-------|--------|-------|---------|----------|------|------------|
| Baby Come Back | Player | RSO | 1977 | 3 | Rock1 | 100 |
| Both Sides Now | Judy Collins | Electra | 1967 | 8 | Folk1 | 20 |
| The Way We Were | Barbara Streisand | Columbia | 1974 | 1 | Pop2 | 110 |
| Greenback Dollar | Kingston Trio | Capitol | 1964 | 8 | Folk1 | 30 |
| Killing Me Softly | Roberta Flack | Atlanta | 1973 | 1 | Rock1 | 50 |
| You've Got a Friend | Calole king | A & M | 1971 | 3 | Rock1 | 45 |
| Only Yesterday | Carpenters | A & M | 1973 | 5 | Rock1 | 100 |
| Baby Love | The Supremes | Motown | 1967 | 1 | Rock2 | 100 |
| Reunited | Peaches and Herb | Polydor | 1978 | 1 | Rock2 | 200 |
| Material Girl | Madonna | Sire | 1984 | 1 | Rock3 | 150 |
| The Next Time I Fall | Peter Cetera | Warner Bros. | 1986 | 3 | Rock3 | 80 |
| We Are the World | "Many" | Columbia | 1985 | 1 | Rock1 | 60 |
| We Built this City | Starship | Grunt | 1985 | 1 | Rock3 | 300 |
| It's a Heartache | Bonnie Tyler | RCA | 1978 | 10 | Rock3 | 50 |
| The Boxer | Simon & Garfunkel | Columbia | 1968 | 3 | Rock4 | 240 |
| Blowin in the Wind | Bob Dylan | Columbia | 1964 | 1 | Folk2 | 100 |
| Chances Are | Johnny Mathis | Columbia | 1965 | 10 | Pop1 | 120 |

The window title bar reads: **WWIN Record Collection (DB)**

**Figure 4.50.** The New Field, *TimesAired*, with Data Added.

## SUMMING FIELD VALUES

In this section you will use the **TotalsPage** menu to create a new report by obtaining the sum of the number of times records of type *Rock1* and *Rock2* were aired. This involves summing the *TimesAired* field for the rows selected in your database retrieval.

Perform the following.

- Choose *New Report* from the **Report** menu. A *Report Definition* window will appear.

- Select the *Record Selection* command of the **Organize** menu. If the selection rule

*Type* equals *Rock1* OR *Type* equals *Rock2*

appears, click on the *Select* button. (If another selection rule is in effect when you access the *Record Selection* command, click on the *Delete Rule* button until the message *No Rules Are In Effect* is displayed. Then install the selection rule above and click on the *Select* button.)

- The *Report Definition Window* should now display only the selected records. Choose *Change Report Title* from the **Edit** menu. Enter the name *AirTime Report* in the dialog box presented. The title bar should now display *AirTime Report*.

- To move the *TimesAired* field in the report so that it comes immediately after the *Artist* field as shown in Figure 4.51, click on the field name and drag to the position shown.

- With the *TimesAired* field still selected (it should still appear highlighted), choose *Sum This Field* from the **TotalsPage** menu.

- Select the *Print* command from the **File** menu. Be sure the *Print Preview* box is selected (has an x in it). Click *Print* (or *OK*). Figure 4.52 shows the report that is displayed.

- Close the report window by clicking its *Close* box.

- Save your database by selecting the *Save* command from the **File** menu.

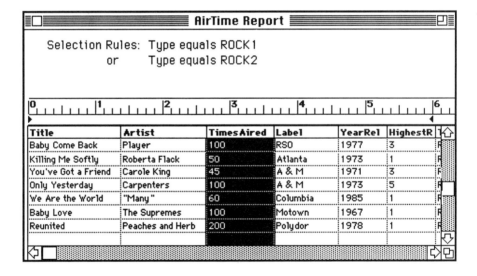

**Figure 4.51.** Preparing to Choose *TimesAired* for Summing.

## SUBTOTAL OF FIELD VALUES

In the final part of this lesson you will learn to compute subtotals in a report. As an example, the separate totals of the *TimesAired* field for each type *Rock1* and *Rock2* will be obtained. To obtain useful subtotals, however, it is first necessary to sort the records on the field of interest so that all entries of the same kind are grouped together for the subtotal.

| AirTime Report | | | | |
|---|---|---|---|---|
| **Title** | **Artist** | **TimesAired** | **YearRel** | **HighestR** |
| Baby Come Back | Player | 100 | 1977 | 3 |
| Killing Me Softly | Roberta Flack | 50 | 1973 | 1 |
| You've Got a Friend | Carole King | 45 | 1971 | 3 |
| Only Yesterday | Carpenters | 100 | 1973 | 5 |
| We Are the World | "Many" | 60 | 1985 | 1 |
| Baby Love | The Supremes | 100 | 1967 | 1 |
| Reunited | Peaches and Herb | 200 | 1978 | 1 |
| | | 655 | | |

**Figure 4.52.** The *AirTime* Report Showing the Sum of the TimesAired for Selected Records.

- The *WWINRecordCollection<your inititals>* database should be open. If it is not, open it. The full database should appear. If it does not, choose *Show All Records* under the **Organize** menu.

- Click on the field name *Type*. The entire column should become highlighted.

- Choose *Sort* from the **Organize** menu. Click the *A to Z* button and then click the *OK* button. Records of the same *Type* should now be grouped together in the display.

- Choose *Select Report* from the **Report** menu. Select *AirTime Report* from the resulting dialog box.

- Click on the field name *Type*. The entire column should become highlighted.

- Execute the command *Take a Subtotal on Field Change* under the **TotalsPage** menu.

259

- Select the *Print* command from the **File** menu.

- Click the *Print Preview* button if an *x* does not already appear there. Click the *Print* (or *OK*) button. Examine the preview screen to verify that you see a display similar to that in Figure 4.53.

- Select *Cancel* to return to the report display. Then close the report window by clicking its *Close* box.

- Save your database by selecting the *Save* command from the **File** menu.

You have now completed Lesson 9. If you do not wish to continue to the next lesson, you should quit Works, clean up the desktop and shut down your computer.

| AirTime Report 2 | | | |
|---|---|---|---|
| **Title** | **Artist** | **Times Aired** | **Type** |
| Baby Come Back | Player | 100 | Rock1 |
| Killing Me Softly | Roberta Flack | 50 | Rock1 |
| You've Got a Friend | Carole King | 45 | Rock1 |
| Only Yesterday | Carpenters | 100 | Rock1 |
| We Are the World | "Many" | 60 | Rock1 |
| | | 355 | |
| | | | |
| Baby Love | The Supremes | 100 | Rock2 |
| Reunited | Peaches and Herb | 200 | Rock2 |
| | | 300 | |
| | | | |
| | | 655 | |

**Figure 4.53.** The Report Produced by the Command *Take a Subtotal on Field Change.*

# LESSON 10

# COMPUTED FIELDS AND FUNCTIONS

After completing this lesson, you will be able to:

❑ Create a computed field.

❑ Enter a formula into a database field.

## LESSON BACKGROUND

There are a number of arithmetic and logical functions that can be used with database *computed* fields. The available functions can be accessed using the *Paste Function* choice from the **Edit** menu. Functions used in a database computed field cannot relate to more than one record at a time and can use only other fields in the same record. A more complete discussion of the functions available will be postponed until the chapter on the Works spreadsheet. Some readers may wish to postpone the reading of this subsection until they have studied the spreadsheet chapter. For now, a single example will be presented illustrating the use of a computed field with two of the more important logical functions, the IF and AND logical functions.

## CREATING A COMPUTED FIELD

The example illustrates the use of the IF and AND logical functions in the *WWINRecordCollection<your inititals>* database. Suppose that you would like to keep track of records that have been played too infrequently according to some criteria set up by the WWIN station manager. In particular, suppose the manager says a record has been underplayed if it was rated 1, 2, 3, or 4 and was played fewer than 100 times. We will add a computed field, *UnderPlayed*, to the database to identify which records were underplayed and how badly they missed the 100 play times criterion.

Perform the following.

- If not already open, open the *WWINRecordCollection<your inititals>* database stored in the folder *Lesson9* contained in the *Works DB* folder on your disk.

- Execute the *Save As* command from the **File** menu. Navigate through your disk hierarchy and save the database *WWINRecordCollection<your inititals>* in the folder *Lesson10* contained in the *Works DB* folder.

- Be sure that *Show All Records* is selected in the **Organize** menu.

- Display the database using the *Show List* command of the **Format** menu.

- Select the *Add Field* command from the **Edit** menu.

- Type *Underplayed* into the *Field Name* box as shown in Figure 4.54.

- Click the *Add Field* button to add the field to the database definition.

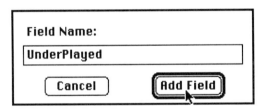

**Field Name:**

UnderPlayed

Cancel     Add Field

**Figure 4.54.** Adding a Field to the Database.

- Select the new field in the database window.

- Select the *Set Field Attributes* command from the **Format** menu.

- Click the *Numeric, Fixed,* and *Right* buttons on the dialog box.

- Type 0 into the *Decimal Places* box.

- Click the *Computed* box in the lower left corner. The resulting dialog box should be the same as shown in Figure 4.55.

- Click the *OK* button to return to the database window. The *Edit Bar* will display an equal sign, indicating that a formula to compute the values for the computed field may now be entered.

```
┌──────────────────────────────────────────────────────────────┐
│  Set Field Attributes For UnderPlayed                          │
│                                                                │
│  Type:          Display:        Align:        Style:           │
│  ○ Text         ○ General       ○ Left        ☐ Bold           │
│  ⦿ Numeric      ⦿ Fixed         ○ Center      ☐ Underline      │
│  ○ Date         ○ Dollar        ⦿ Right       ☐ Commas         │
│  ○ Time         ○ Percent      ┌─┐                             │
│                 ○ Scientific   │0│ Decimal Places              │
│                                └─┘                             │
│  ☒ Computed  ☐ Show Day       ( Cancel )  ( ( OK ) )           │
└──────────────────────────────────────────────────────────────┘
```

Figure 4.55. Defining the Computed Field, *UnderPlayed*.

# ENTERING A FORMULA

In this section you will enter the formula

$$=IF(AND(HighestR < 5, TimesAired < 100), 100 - TimesAired, 0)$$

into the *UnderPlayed* field of the first record. The formula causes a value to be computed and placed in the *UnderPlayed* field of every record of the database. There are two steps in the evaluation of this formula. First, the AND function is evaluated. Then depending on the result (*True* or *False*), one of two possible values is returned by the IF function. The meaning of the above formula is as follows. For a given record if both the value of *HighestR* is less than 5 and the value of *TimesAired* is less than 100, the result placed in the field is 100 - *TimesAired*. Otherwise, the value placed in the field is zero. For example, in the *Carole King* record of the database:

*HighestR* = 3 and

*TimesAired* = 45

Thus, the value of the AND function is TRUE.

So *UnderPlayed* = 100 - 45 = 55.

Perform the following to enter the computed field formula.

- With the equal sign already appearing in the *Edit Bar*, type the remainder of the formula,

IF(AND(*HighestR* < 5, *TimesAired* < 100), 100 - *TimesAired*, 0)

into the *Edit Bar*. Your formula should appear as shown in Figure 4.56. If it does not, alter the entry as necessary until it is correct.

- Click the *Accept* box. The above calculation will be made automatically for all the records in the *UnderPlayed* field of the database. Results similar to Figure 4.56 should be displayed.

- Save your database by selecting the *Save* command from the **File** menu.

- Quit Works.

You have now completed Lesson 10. If you do not wish to continue to the next lesson, you should clean up the desktop and shut down your computer.

| 1 | | | =If(And(HighestR<5,TimesAired<100),100-TimesAired,0) | | | | | |
|---|---|---|---|---|---|---|---|---|
| **WWIN Record Collection (DB)** | | | | | | | | |
| | **Artist** | **Label** | **YearRel** | **HighestR** | **Type** | **Times Aired** | **UnderPlayed** | |
| y | Judy Collins | Electra | 1967 | 8 | Folk1 | 20 | 0 | |
| ar | Kingston Trio | Capital | 1964 | 8 | Folk1 | 30 | 0 | |
| Vind | Bob Dylan | Columbia | 1964 | 1 | Folk2 | 100 | 0 | |
| | Johnny Mathis | Columbia | 1965 | 10 | Pop1 | 120 | 0 | |
| ere | Barbara Striesand | Columbia | 1974 | 1 | Pop2 | 110 | 0 | |
| ck | Player | RSO | 1977 | 3 | Rock1 | 100 | 0 | |
| ly | Roberta Flack | Atlanta | 1973 | 1 | Rock1 | 50 | 50 | |
| riend | Carole King | A & M | 1971 | 3 | Rock1 | 45 | 55 | |

**Figure 4.56.** Entering the Formula for Computing the Computed Field Values.

# MERGING WORKS DATABASE AND WORD PROCESSING DOCUMENTS

After completing this lesson you will be able to:

❏ Merge database fields into a word processing document.

❏ View database data in a word processing document.

❏ Format the database fields in a word processing document.

❏ Take actions to correct a *NOT ON DESKTOP* error.

❏ Print a merged document.

## MERGING DATABASE FIELDS

Works DB databases can be used as sources of data for inclusion into Works WP documents. Suppose you want to produce a word processing document that will list the customers in our example database *Orders<your initials>* from Lessons 1 through 5, together with related information about their orders. The steps required to create such a document follow.

In this section you will produce a word processing document containing database fields positioned as shown in Figure 4.57. Notice that the name of the database itself is a part of the field names. By using these complete path names, Works makes it possible to insert data from several different databases into the same word processing document.

Perform the following.

• Open the *Orders<your initials>* database stored in the folder *Lesson5* contained in the *Works DB* folder on your disk.

- Execute the *Save As* command from the **File** menu. Navigate through your disk hierarchy and save the database *Orders<your initials>* in the folder *Lesson11* contained in the *Works DB* folder.

- Select the *New* command from the **File** menu and then choose the *WP* icon from the resulting dialog box to get a new word processing document. Save it as *MergeDoc<your initials>* in your folder *Lesson11* contained in the *Works DB* folder.

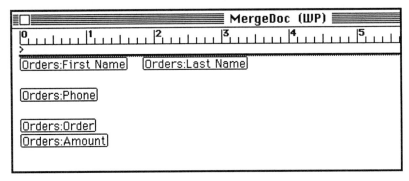

**Figure 4.57.** Data Field Names Inserted and Positioned within the Word Processing Document.

Enter the Merge *First Name* and *Last Name* Fields:

- Execute the *Prepare to Merge* command under the **Edit** menu, and you will be presented with the dialog box shown in Figure 4.58.

- Select *First Name* in the *Select Merge Field* and click the *Merge* button to place *First Name* in the word processing document at the position of the insertion pointer.

- Execute *Show Field Names* in the **Edit** menu.

- Press the space bar a few times. Execute the *Prepare to Merge* command under the **Edit** menu. Select *Last Name* in the *Select Merge Field* and click the *Merge* button to place *Last Name* in the word processing document at the position of the insertion pointer.

- Press the *Return* key twice to insert a blank line in the word processing document and to position the insertion pointer for the next field.

Enter the Merge *Phone* Field:

- Execute the *Prepare to Merge* command under the **Edit** menu, and you will be presented with the dialog box shown in Figure 4.58.

- Select *Phone* in the *Select Merge Field* and click the *Merge* button to place the *Phone* field in the word processing document at the position of the insertion pointer.

- Press the *Return* key twice to insert a blank line in the word processing document and to position the insertion pointer for the next field.

Enter the Merge *Order* Field:

- Execute the *Prepare to Merge* command under the **Edit** menu.

- Select *Order* in the *Select Merge Field* and click the *Merge* button to place *Order* in the word processing document at the position of the insertion pointer.

- Press the *Return* key to move to the next line in the word processing document.

Enter the Merge *Amount* Field:

- Execute the *Prepare to Merge* command under the **Edit** menu.

- Select *Amount* in the *Select Merge Field* and click the *Merge* button to place *Amount* in the word processing document at the position of the insertion pointer.

- Save your document.

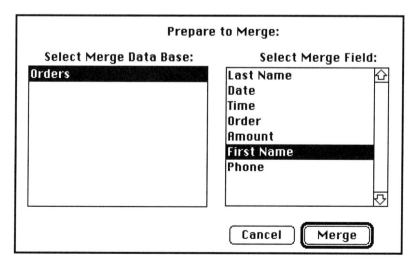

**Figure 4.58.** Dialog Box for Preparing a Print Merge.

267

## VIEWING THE DATABASE DATA IN A WORKS WP DOCUMENT

After the database fields have been inserted into the word processing document, you can view the word processing document with data inserted into the fields.

Perform the following.

- Execute the *Show Field Data* command from the **Edit** menu. This causes the data from the currently selected database record in *Orders<your initials>* to be displayed, as is demonstrated in Figure 4.59.

- Execute *Show Field Names* in the **Edit** menu to return to the situation shown in Figure 4.57.

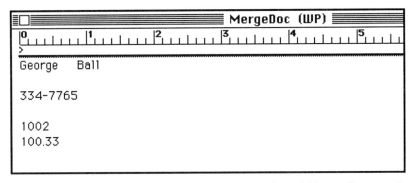

**Figure 4.59.** Displaying Database Data Using the *Show Field Data* Command.

## FORMATTING THE DATABASE FIELDS IN A WORKS WP DOCUMENT

Once the field names are inserted and positioned, you can format the display of these items in all the ways that you can format other word processing text. For example, you can use italics, different fonts, various font sizes, and so on. You can also add descriptive labels. Figure 4.60 gives an example of such formatting. Notice in Figure 4.61 that the formatting shows even after you have selected *Show Field Names* from the **Edit** menu.

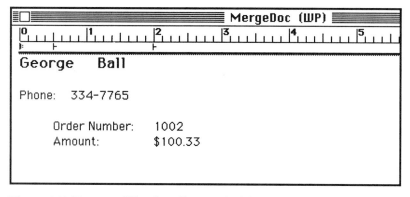

**Figure 4.60.** Formatted Database Data in the Word Processing Document.

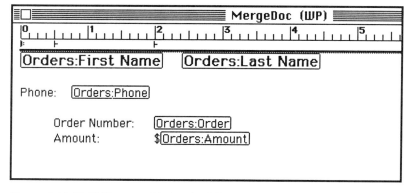

**Figure 4.61.** Field Names with Applied Formatting Indicated.

Perform the following to format the document as shown in Figures 4.60 and 4.61.

- Display the document using the *Show Field Data* command of the **Edit** menu if the data are not already displayed in this form.

Format the Name line:

- Move the insertion pointer to the beginning of the document.

- Select the data in the *First Name* and *Last Name* fields, *George Ball* in Figure 4.60.

- Select *18 Point* command from the **Size** submenu of the **Format** menu.

- Select the *Bold* command from the **Style** submenu of the **Format** menu. The *First Name* and *Last Name* fields should now be 18 points and bold.

Format the Phone, Order, and Amount lines:

- Move the insertion pointer in front of the *Phone* field and type the text *Phone:* then press the *Tab* key.

- Select the lines containing the *Order* and *Amount* fields. Place a left tab at .5 in. by pointing to the ruler at that position and clicking. Also place a left tab at 2.0 in. by pointing to that position on the ruler and clicking.

- Format the line containing the *Order* field by placing the insertion pointer immediately to the left of the *Order* field; press the *Tab* key twice to move the *Order* field to its final location. Place the insertion pointer at .5 in. (at the first tab) and type the text *Order Number:* to complete the formatting.

- Format the line containing the *Amount* field by placing the insertion pointer immediately to the left of the *Amount* field; press the *Tab* key twice to move the *Amount* field to its final location. Place the insertion pointer immediately in front of the *Amount* field and type a $. Now, place the insertion pointer at .5 in. (at the first tab) and type the text *Amount:* to complete the formatting.

- Save your document.

Your document should now look like Figure 4.60.

## NOT ON DESKTOP ERROR

For database information to be accessible to the word processing document, the appropriate database must be opened. If you should open the word processing document (which has been saved and named *MergeDoc<your initials>*) without opening the database, you will receive error messages similar to those shown in Figure 4.62. Although it did not happen in this example, an error message may wrap to the next line. This wrapping is simply a consequence of the length of the error message and does not indicate how the actual data will be displayed. Once the appropriate database is opened, these messages will disappear and the document will be in one of the forms shown earlier in Figures 4.60 and 4.61.

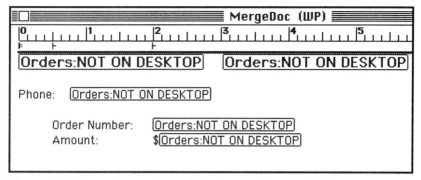

**Figure 4.62.** Attempting to Access Data from an Unopened Database.

# PRINTING A MERGED WORKS WP AND DB DOCUMENT

To print the word processing document with all the database data included, perform the following.

- Choose a printer as described in Lesson 4 of Chapter 1.

- Make sure that both the word processing document and the database document are open.

- Select the *Print Merge* command from the **File** menu. The records will now be printed.

- Select the *Print Preview* option and then click the *Print* (or *OK*) button.

- Use the *Next* and *Previous* buttons to see various versions of the document.

- Click *Cancel* to return to the document.

*For each record in the database, a complete copy of the word processing document is printed.* If a subset of the database records is selected in the database document (as was done in Lesson 6), then only the data from the selected records will be printed.

You have now completed Lesson 11 and this chapter. You should quit Works, clean up the desktop, and shut down your computer.

# PRACTICE PROJECTS

## PROJECT 1

In this project you will implement a Works DB version of the database structure defined in Figure 4.63, which is designed to keep swimming meet records. After loading some data into the database, you will be asked to write selection criteria to display certain records, and to create and print several reports from the database. Detailed instructions will not be given. If you have questions about an operation or task, see the appropriate lesson in this chapter.

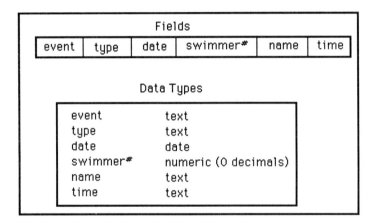

**Figure 4.63.** Project 1 Database Structure.

1. Create a folder on your disk and name it *DBProject1*.

2. Define the database of Figure 4.63 in Works DB. Remember to set the data types for the nontext fields.

3. Save the database as *SwimTimes<your initials>* in your folder *DBProject1*.

4. Resize the data field areas to hold the appropriate data, and enter the data given in Figure 4.64 into the database. Save your database at various intervals during this process.

| event | type | date | swimmer # | name | time |
|---|---|---|---|---|---|
| | | | | SwimTimes (DB) | |
| 100 Freestyle | Men | 2/10/89 | 112 | Bill Jones | 0:54.62 |
| 100 Freestyle | Men | 2/10/89 | 143 | Adam Wilmer | 0:53.44 |
| 100 Freestyle | Women | 2/10/89 | 232 | Jan Polanski | 0:58.12 |
| 100 Freestyle | Women | 2/10/89 | 211 | Carmen Smith | 0:59.11 |
| 100 Breast | Women | 3/13/89 | 232 | Jan Polanski | 1:14.67 |
| 100 Breast | Women | 3/13/89 | 211 | Carmen Smith | 1:13.55 |
| 100 Breast | Men | 3/13/89 | 112 | Bill Jones | 1:06.79 |
| 100 Butterfly | Men | 4/12/89 | 143 | Adam Wilmer | 0:55.71 |
| 100 Butterfly | Men | 4/12/89 | 112 | Bill Jones | 0:55.78 |
| 100 Backstroke | Men | 4/12/89 | 155 | Frank Klinger | 0:58.45 |
| 100 Backstroke | Women | 5/23/89 | 211 | Carmen Smith | 1:07.23 |
| 100 Freestyle | Men | 5/23/89 | 122 | Ramon Ryser | 0:53.12 |
| 100 Freestyle | Women | 5/23/89 | 232 | Jan Polanski | 0:58.71 |
| 100 Freestyle | Men | 5/23/89 | 112 | Bill Jones | 0:52.11 |
| 100 Breast | Women | 6/17/89 | 254 | Mary Thomas | 1:14.19 |
| 100 Breast | Women | 6/17/89 | 211 | Carmen Smith | 1:14.04 |
| 100 Backstroke | Women | 6/17/89 | 267 | Gwen Holden | 1:08.01 |
| 100 Backstroke | Women | 6/17/89 | 232 | Jan Polanski | 1:07.88 |
| 100 Butterfly | Men | 6/17/89 | 143 | Adam Wilmer | 0:55.03 |
| 100 Butterfly | Women | 6/17/89 | 232 | Jan Polanski | 1:03.92 |
| 100 Butterfly | Women | 6/17/89 | 254 | Mary Thomas | 1:04.07 |

**Figure 4.64.** Project 1 Database Data.

5. Construct a selection criterion to list records for all men's freestyle data sorted by increasing times. Recall that to sort on any field, you first select that field and then execute the *Sort* command from the **Organize** menu. The resulting data are shown in Figure 4.65.

| event | type | date | swimmer # | name | time |
|---|---|---|---|---|---|
| 100 Freestyle | Men | 5/23/89 | 112 | Bill Jones | 0:52.11 |
| 100 Freestyle | Men | 5/23/89 | 122 | Ramon Ryser | 0:53.12 |
| 100 Freestyle | Men | 2/10/89 | 143 | Adam Wilmer | 0:53.44 |
| 100 Freestyle | Men | 2/10/89 | 112 | Bill Jones | 0:54.62 |

**Figure 4.65.** Data Produced by the Record Selection of Step 5.

6. Construct a selection criterion to list records for all women's breaststroke data recorded for March 13, 1989, sorted by increasing times. The resulting data are shown in Figure 4.66.

| event | type | date | swimmer # | name | time |
|---|---|---|---|---|---|
| 100 Breast | Women | 3/13/89 | 211 | Carmen Smith | 1:13.55 |
| 100 Breast | Women | 3/13/89 | 232 | Jan Polanski | 1:14.67 |

**Figure 4.66.** Data Produced by the Record Selection of Step 6.

7. Construct a selection criterion to list records for all women's breaststroke and backstroke data, sorted by increasing times within each event. Report breaststroke data first. Note that the order in which the two sorts are done is important. Try both orders and observe the results. The correct data are shown in Figure 4.67.

| event | type | date | swimmer # | name | time |
|---|---|---|---|---|---|
| 100 Breast | Women | 3/13/89 | 211 | Carmen Smith | 1:13.55 |
| 100 Breast | Women | 6/17/89 | 211 | Carmen Smith | 1:14.04 |
| 100 Breast | Women | 6/17/89 | 254 | Mary Thomas | 1:14.19 |
| 100 Breast | Women | 3/13/89 | 232 | Jan Polanski | 1:14.67 |
| 100 Backstroke | Women | 5/23/89 | 211 | Carmen Smith | 1:07.23 |
| 100 Backstroke | Women | 6/17/89 | 232 | Jan Polanski | 1:07.88 |
| 100 Backstroke | Women | 6/17/89 | 267 | Gwen Holden | 1:08.01 |

Figure 4.67. Data Produced by the Record Selection of Step 7.

8. Create and print a report to display *type, date, name,* and *time* for all freestyle data, sorted by type and by increasing times within type. Report women's results first. The data your report should contain are shown in Figure 4.68.

9. Name your report *Freestyle.*

10. Save your database.

| type | date | name | time |
|---|---|---|---|
| Women | 2/10/89 | Jan Polanski | 0:58.12 |
| Women | 5/23/89 | Jan Polanski | 0:58.71 |
| Women | 2/10/89 | Carmen Smith | 0:59.11 |
| Men | 5/23/89 | Bill Jones | 0:52.11 |
| Men | 5/23/89 | Ramon Ryser | 0:53.12 |
| Men | 2/10/89 | Adam Wilmer | 0:53.44 |
| Men | 2/10/89 | Bill Jones | 0:54.62 |

Figure 4.68. Data for the Report of Step 8.

11. Create and print a report to display *event, date, name,* and *time* for all women's data, sorted by event and by increasing times within event. The data your report should contain are shown in Figure 4.69.

12. Name your report *WomenEvents.*

13. Save your database.

| event | date | name | time |
|---|---|---|---|
| 100 Backstroke | 5/23/89 | Carmen Smith | 1:07.23 |
| 100 Backstroke | 6/17/89 | Jan Polanski | 1:07.88 |
| 100 Backstroke | 6/17/89 | Gwen Holden | 1:08.01 |
| 100 Breast | 3/13/89 | Carmen Smith | 1:13.55 |
| 100 Breast | 6/17/89 | Carmen Smith | 1:14.04 |
| 100 Breast | 6/17/89 | Mary Thomas | 1:14.19 |
| 100 Breast | 3/13/89 | Jan Polanski | 1:14.67 |
| 100 Butterfly | 6/17/89 | Jan Polanski | 1:03.92 |
| 100 Butterfly | 6/17/89 | Mary Thomas | 1:04.07 |
| 100 Freestyle | 2/10/89 | Jan Polanski | 0:58.12 |
| 100 Freestyle | 5/23/89 | Jan Polanski | 0:58.71 |
| 100 Freestyle | 2/10/89 | Carmen Smith | 0:59.11 |

**Figure 4.69.** Data for the Report of Step 11.

## PROJECT 2

In this project you will construct a customer product registration custom form. An example of the form to be produced is shown in Figure 4.70. The customer's name and address will be supplied and merged from a database.

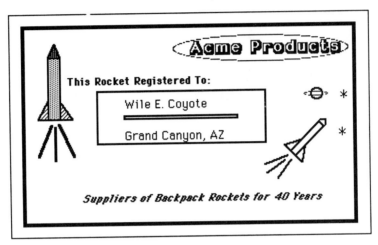

**Figure 4.70.** Customer Registration Form to Be Produced.

1. Create a folder on your disk and name it *DBProject2*.

2. Begin by creating a database with two text fields called *Name* and *Address*. Insert a few rows of fictitious data into your database.

3. Save the database by the name *Customer<your initials>* in your folder *DBProject2*.

4. Next create a merged word processing document with the data fields from the database *Customer* positioned as shown in Figure 4.71.

5. Save the document as *CustomerReg<your initials>* in your folder *DBProject2*.

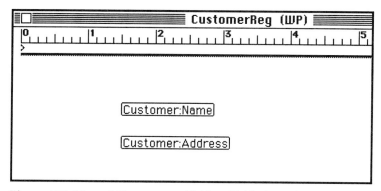

**Figure 4.71.** Merged Document with Data Fields from the *Customer* Database.

6. Select the *Draw On* command from the **Edit** menu and create the two rectangles as illustrated in Figure 4.72.

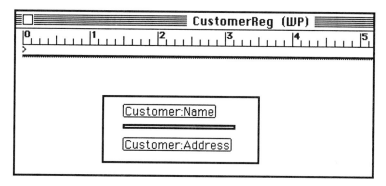

**Figure 4.72.** Rectangles Added to Document.

7. Next add the drawings of the rockets, stellar objects, and large rectangle as shown in Figure 4.73.

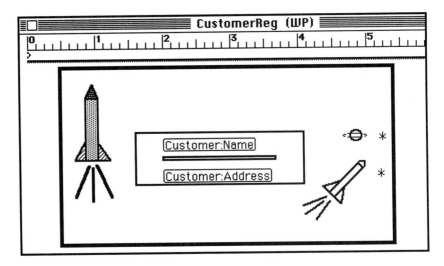

**Figure 4.73.** Form with Additional Graphics Objects.

8. To complete the form, select the *Draw Off* command from the **Edit** menu to return to the text mode. Type the remaining text in the form as shown in Figure 4.70.. Select the *Draw On* command once again and create the oval to go around the text *Acme Products* in the upper right corner of the form. Move the oval into place. You might need to create several ovals until you get one the right size. Your form should now look like the one shown in Figure 4.70.

9. Return to text mode by selecting the *Draw Off* command again.

10. Save vour document.

11. Merge and print the document.

# 5

# USING WORKS SS

When you have completed the Works SS tutorial you will be able to:

❏ Create, print, and save a worksheet.

❏ Enter data and formulas in a worksheet.

❏ Construct worksheet formulas.

❏ Replicate formulas with the Fill commands.

❏ Use absolute and relative references in formulas.

❏ Modify the appearance of a worksheet.

❏ Create charts.

❏ Understand built-in functions.

❏ Use the statistical built-in functions.

❏ Use the built-in IF function.

## TUTORIAL OUTLINE

## WHAT IS WORKS SS?

Works SS is the spreadsheet module of Works. Spreadsheets were based originally on the idea of automating the computations on the ruled worksheets used by accountants. The general applicability of the approach was quickly realized. Almost any computation involving data arranged in a table can be performed with a spreadsheet. This includes a very wide range of problems involving numerical calculations. In fact, modern spreadsheets are so powerful they can be used to solve problems that only a few years ago would have required the writing of complex computer programs. With Works SS we can do the following.

Create spreadsheet documents.

Save, retrieve, and print created documents.

Describe complex computations that will be made automatically on the spreadsheet documents.

Use the built-in functions provided in the Works spreadsheet module to solve problems of higher complexity.

Chart the results of spreadsheet calculations.

## BASIC SPREADSHEET CONCEPTS

Spreadsheets packages (or just "spreadsheets" for short) provide a framework within which many kinds of calculations can be performed with relative ease. These calculations can be "programmed" using the spreadsheet in a way that does not require the user to write computer programs. The purpose of a spreadsheet is to provide the same ease of performing, altering, and graphically displaying mathematical calculations as the word processor provides for manipulating text in reports or documents, or as a database management system provides for storing and retrieving information.

Calculations that would be tedious and time consuming when performed using a calculator can be quickly carried out, structured in an easy to read tabular form, and charted using a spreadsheet. Thus, someone needing to perform mathematical calculations would find the spreadsheet as useful and necessary to them as the writer of a report would find the use of a word processor.

Some applications of spreadsheets are accounts receivable, accounts payable, balance sheets, payroll, and profit and loss statements. Other miscellaneous examples are inventory, grade calculations, budget modeling, simple statistics, and some scientific calculations.

The variety of calculations that can be performed using a spreadsheet is very impressive. Most spreadsheets have built-in capabilities for calcu-

lating certain financial functions, standard statistical functions, trigonometric functions, logarithmic functions, and others.

**Worksheet Structure.** The spreadsheet worksheet (equivalent to the blank
starting page of a word processor) is a rectangular table of cells as shown
in Figure 5.1. Each cell is identified by giving the column and row in
which the cell is located. For example, cell E5 is located at the intersection
of column E and row 5.

Worksheets can be quite large. For example, the Works SS worksheet
can contain as many as 16,382 rows and 256 columns.

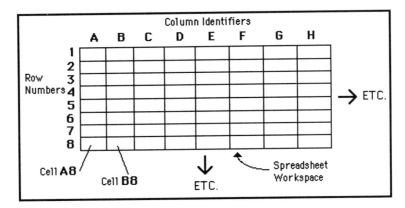

Figure 5.1. A Typical Spreadsheet Program Worksheet.

**Formulas.** Spreadsheet calculations are performed by entering formulas
into some of these cells. For example, in Works SS a formula is an object
that starts with an equals sign, "=". These formulas will usually reference
the contents of other cells as variables. As an example, in Figure 5.2, a
formula is used to add the values in cells A3, A4, and A5. Part (a) of the
figure shows the formula that is typed into cell A6, and part (b) shows the
value computed by the formula. The formula is typed into the cell, but the
value computed by the formula is displayed in the cell.

**What If Analysis.** Even with such a simple example as shown above, we
can illustrate some of the power of the spreadsheet as a computational
tool. By changing values in cells that are referenced in a formula, we can
automatically initiate the recomputation of the value corresponding to the
formula. For example, if we were to change the value in cell A3 of Figure
5.2(b) to 100, then the value in cell A6 would be automatically adjusted to
150 by the spreadsheet.

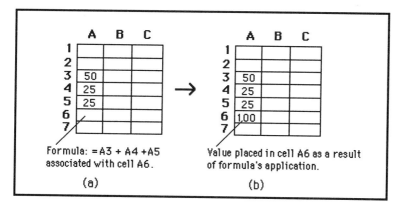

**Figure 5.2.** A Spreadsheet Calculation Using a Formula.

The ability to change values and have the spreadsheet automatically recalculate all its formulas allows us to perform quite easily what is often called **"what if" analysis**. For example, we might produce an amortization table that calculates our monthly principal and interest payments on a loan. We can then vary the interest rate used in our calculations by simply changing the value in one cell (the cell holding the interest rate). In this way, we can easily observe how our principal and interest payments change with the interest rate and thus answer questions of the form "What if the interest rate changes to ... ?"

**Spreadsheet Language.** The language that you will learn in this chapter for entering spreadsheet formulas is intuitive and easy to learn. The language you will use is patterned after that of a formula in algebra. In fact, many beginners feel that using a spreadsheet is a natural extension of doing tabular calculations by hand or with a calculator. In the small sample spreadsheet of Figure 5.3 the values in the *Gross Pay* column were all computed by entering a single formula that described the calculation and **replicating** (copying) the formula into other cells. Hence the table can be produced very quickly. In addition, any changes made to the *Rate* column or *Hours* column are automatically reflected in the values displayed in the *Gross Pay* column.

|   | A | B | C | D | E | F | G |
|---|---|---|---|---|---|---|---|
| 1 | Last Name | First Name | Initial | Title | Rate | Hours | Gross Pay |
| 2 | Ableston | David | G | Inspector | $9.00 | 45 | $405.00 |
| 3 | Highmaster | Jonathon | A | Salesman | $7.50 | 55 | $412.50 |
| 4 | Jasper | Thomas | I | Salesman | $12.00 | 48 | $576.00 |
| 5 | Siththe | Bernard | R | Gardener | $6.25 | 40 | $250.00 |
| 6 | Zebbley | Arthur | P | Clerk | $7.30 | 42 | $306.60 |
| 7 |   |   |   |   |   |   |   |

**Figure 5.3.** A Sample Worksheet.

**Graphic Display.** An important feature of a spreadsheet is the ability to present the worksheet data in a visual or graphical form, such as is shown in Figure 5.4. Data tables and graphs produced from worksheets can also be easily transferred to word processing documents.

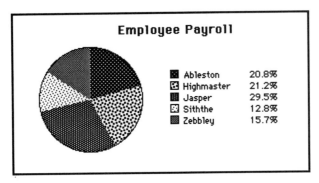

Figure 5.4. A Pie Chart of Gross Pay from the Sample Spreadsheet.

**Cells.** The objects that make up a worksheet are called *cells*. Cells are the objects through which calculations are carried out and the results of computations are displayed. It is necessary for a cell to have a name so we can specify which *unique* cell is being selected or referenced out of all the cells that make up a worksheet. *Default names* for cells are provided by the *coordinates* of a cell in the table.

As illustrated in Figure 5.1 above, the coordinates of a cell are the column label of a cell followed by the row label of a cell. To find the location of a cell whose name is specified, find the position where the column and row coordinates of the cell intersect. For example, to find the location of cell C2, draw an imaginary line down the middle of the column named C and draw another imaginary line across the middle of the row named 2. The place where these two imaginary lines cross is the location of the cell C2.

Note that the name of a cell is distinct from its contents. Think of the name of a cell as being like the address of a mail box. The address (name of the cell) tells us which mailbox (cell of the worksheet) is being referenced, but to determine its contents we must go to the mailbox in question and open it up. Cells are *structured objects*. This means that a cell can contain more than one kind of object at the same time. A formula object and/or a data object will be contained in a cell into which information has been entered. In addition, some spreadsheet environments allow us to attach notes to a cell; these notes can be very useful for documenting the purpose of formulas, referencing sources of data, or associating with a particular cell any other source of relevant information.

**Data Objects.** We think of the data object of a cell as holding the data/information that is displayed by the cell. Data in a spreadsheet are similar to the kind of information that can be entered into a field of a database record. In the case of the worksheet it is information that often will be used in a computation. Recall from the database discussion in the previous chapter that we must distinguish between textual and numeric kinds of information. This is because the computer stores each of these kinds of information differently and must choose to operate on the information consistent with how it is stored. In a spreadsheet there also are different kinds of internal representations of information, called **data types**. Principal spreadsheet data types include:

Text data—any string of characters typed in from the keyboard.

Numeric data—items that are in the form of numbers, i.e., a list of numerical digits that may include a dollar sign, unary minus sign, decimal point.

Date and time data—these can be displayed in a variety of formats, and arithmetic can be performed on them.

Logical data—the values of *True* or *False* only; these are represented in Works SS as any non zero value for *True* and 0 for *False*.

For most spreadsheets the data type of a data object is not specified at the time information is entered into a cell. Instead, the spreadsheet interprets a cell's data type depending upon the way a cell is used in a calculation. Thus, a worksheet cell is said to be *implicitly* typed in contrast to the *explicit* typing that is used in the Works database. Cell A2 in Figure 5.3 contains the text data *Ableston*. This information could never be interpreted as a numerical value. In contrast, cell F2 contains 45. This latter value can be interpreted as either a text or a numeric data type depending upon the context in which it is used.

**Formula Objects.** A formula object contains an algebraic formula entered using a syntax specific to a given spreadsheet package. To distinguish between entering a data object value and a formula object value an equal sign "=" is used as the first symbol typed whenever a formula object is to be entered. In other spreadsheet environments a different symbol may be used to distinguish a formula object from a data object. The formula entered describes in spreadsheet language how to compute the value of the data object in that same cell. Consequently, if a formula object is entered in a cell, the data object value is obtained by evaluating the formula of the cell.

Formula objects are constructed by using arithmetic operations such as addition, subtraction, multiplication, and special functions that are built into the spreadsheet program along with the names of other cells in a worksheet. As a result, an extremely wide range of computations can be carried out by properly constructing a formula object. In the example of Figure 5.3, the formula object for cell G2 has the form $=E2*F2$. Thus the data object for cell G2 will be obtained by multiplying the data object of cell E2 times the data object of cell F2.

The **syntax** for entering a formula is specific to each spreadsheet package and is checked as you enter the formula into a cell's formula object. If an entered formula has incorrect syntax, an error message will be displayed. As an example, the formula =E2F2 is not valid syntactically because no operation such as addition or multiplication separates the two cell values. Typically, the spreadsheet will not assign the formula to the formula object until the formula syntax has been corrected.

A formula may be entered as a syntactically correct formula—one that obeys the rules of the spreadsheet language—but not produce the desired result. As one example, while we may have wanted the formula object for G2 to be of the form =E2*F2, if we had typed =E2+F2 instead, the spreadsheet would not find the syntax of this formula in error even though the result computed would be wrong. As another example, we might attempt to insert the formula =D2+F2 into the worksheet of Figure 5.3. In this case an error in evaluation arises because cell D2 has a text type data object, and hence should not be involved in an addition operation. Unfortunately, Works SS will simply evaluate this expression assuming that cell D2 has the value zero. No error message is displayed! Clearly, we must check our formula computations carefully to avoid errors of this kind. The latter kinds of errors associated with the meaning of a formula rather than its syntax are termed **semantic** errors.

**Entering Objects Into Cells.** A cell selected for object entry or editing is called the **active cell**. Only the contents inside the active cell may be altered directly by an editing operation. The active cell on a Works worksheet is highlighted to distinguish it from other cells. In Figure 5.5 cell C4 is the active cell. When a cell becomes the active cell, its coordinates are displayed in the left area of the formula bar. If the cell contains a formula object, the active cell's formula is displayed in the right area of the formula bar. If the active cell contains no formula object, then the data object of the selected cell is displayed in the right area of the formula bar. Before a formula or value has been entered into the active cell, its data object and formula object are empty and the formula bar display will be blank.

Once a cell is selected as the active cell, data can be entered into its data object from the keyboard. Thus, for example, if B3 is the active cell, and 200 is typed, 200 becomes the value of the data object of this cell and will be displayed both in the formula bar and in the cell's location. Keyboard input is assigned by default to the data object of a cell.

Recall that the = symbol is used in Works SS to signal the entry of a formula object into a cell. Hence entering the characters, =C3+C2, into cell C4 would be interpreted as assigning a formula to the formula object of cell C4. Note in Figure 5.5 that the formula object value =C3+C2 is displayed in the formula bar, and the data object value that results from evaluating the formula (i.e., adding the value of cell C3 to the value of cell C2) is displayed in cell C4. This is a general feature of most spreadsheets and allows both the data object value and the formula object value of the selected cell to be displayed simultaneously.

The $ appearing in cell C4 is present because the cell has been *formatted*—given a form with which to display the data object value. The $ was not typed at the keyboard. We will discuss formatting in a later section.

**Figure 5.5.** Works SS Starting Worksheet with Key Components Identified.

There are several ways to indicate to Works SS that the entry of a data or formula object into a cell has been completed.

Press the *Tab* key.

Press the *Return* key or *Enter* key.

Click the *Enter* box (see Figure 5.5) that appears in the space just left of the formula bar when the object is entered.

The choice of which of the above methods to use will depend on which is the most natural action to set up the next activity you want to perform. If you decide that the object you entered is *not* what you intended, you can restore a cell to its original state by selecting the *Undo* command from the **Edit** pull-down menu or clicking the *Cancel* box (see Figure 5.5) that appears in the area just left of the formula bar when a cell is active and an object is being entered.

Another way to terminate the entry of a data object in a cell is to move the cell-selection pointer over another cell and click. If a data object value is being entered, moving the cell-selection pointer to a new cell and clicking will terminate the entry of the information shown in the formula bar for the first cell and then make the newly selected cell the active cell.

Note that the operation of the cell-selection pointer is quite different when a formula object is being entered into the active cell. In this case, moving the cell-selection pointer to a new cell and clicking will cause the coordinates of that new cell to be entered into the formula in the first cell and the first cell *will remain* the active cell. This feature allows you to enter formulas conveniently by clicking on the cells whose values you wish to

287

reference. The spreadsheet then enters those cell references automatically into the formulas for you. To complete the entry of the formula you must then use one of the other methods mentioned above. Cell references may be directly typed instead of using the cell-selection pointing method. The advantage of letting the spreadsheet do it for you is that you are less likely to make an error in entering the cell location. Consequently, your formulas are more likely to compute the correct values.

**Range Selection.** The process of entering information, selecting a different cell, entering information into that cell, selecting a new cell, and so on, can be awkward if a large number of cells is involved. Spreadsheets provide a very convenient way to mark a rectangular group of cells that are each to be used successively to receive information. This process of marking contiguous (adjacent) groups of cells is called *range selection*.

A range of cells is selected by moving the cell-selection pointer to a corner of the rectangle of cells we wish to select. We drag the mouse and a rectangular area becomes highlighted. The proportions of this highlighted area can be controlled by positioning the mouse. When this highlighted area is satisfactory for our purposes, we release the button. The area remains highlighted and the first cell selected is the initial active cell.

We describe a range by listing the first and last cells in the selected area, separated by a colon. For example, the range A1:C3 consists of the nine cells that start at A1 and end at C3. Figure 5.6 shows a worksheet having a selected range of A2:D4.

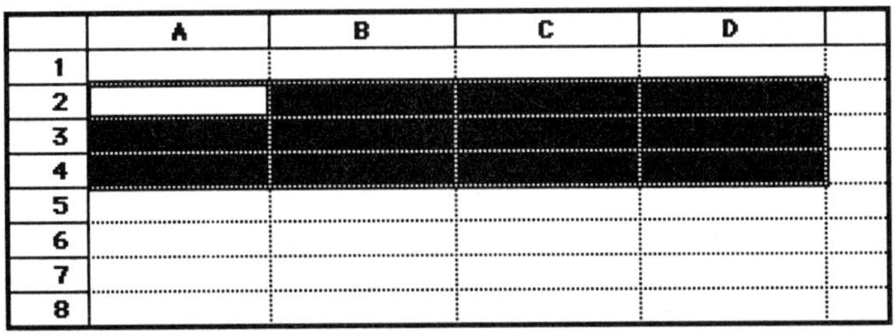

**Figure 5.6.** A Worksheet Having the Range A2:D4 Selected.

Once a range of cells is selected, typing will cause information to appear in the initial active cell's formula bar. Pressing the *Tab* key or *Return* key will insert the information into the cell and automatically cause the cell in the next position of the darkened area to become the active cell. The desired information may then be typed in for this new cell. Pressing the *Tab* key or *Return* key for this cell enters the information, and another position in the darkened area becomes active, and so on. The difference between pressing the *Tab* and *Return* key for entering the data is that *Tab* moves across a row before starting the next lower row while *Return* moves down a column before moving to the next column to the right in the highlighted area.

If the cell-selection pointer is used at any time to select a new cell while a range is active (indicated by a darkened rectangular area) and a data object is being assigned to the active cell, then the range of cells is deactivated and the cell selected becomes the active cell. If a formula object is being assigned to the active cell, then the coordinates of that selected cell are entered into the current active cell as discussed above. In this latter case, the cell remains the active cell open for additional data entry, and the range selection is still valid.

**Editing Cell Contents.** As noted above, each keystroke entered is displayed in the formula bar. You may think of the formula bar as being like a one-line document in the Works WP component. The editing commands you learned for word processing are available to operate on the information in the formula bar. Recall in this connection the function of the insertion pointer and the I-beam pointer. As information is typed into the formula bar, the position at which characters are inserted is indicated by the insertion pointer. The position of the insertion pointer can be controlled by moving the I-beam pointer to the position desired in the formula bar and clicking, just as was done in Works WP.

Moving the cell selection pointer into the formula bar after a cell has been selected will cause the pointer to become an I-beam pointer. All the word processing actions such as cut, paste, click and drag to select, and so on are now available *within* the formula bar. Both data objects (except those that are produced as the action of a formula) and formula objects can be edited using standard word procession actions. *Note:* Data objects that result from evaluation of their associated formula cannot be changed directly. Instead, only the form of the associated formula objects can be edited.

**Setting Column Widths.** In many instances it will be desirable to set the widths of columns in a worksheet. When the pointer is positioned inside the column label area and intersects one of the lines demarking the edge of

a column, the pointer will change into a double-headed arrow, ✛. We can use drag operations to increase or decrease the width of the column whose right boundary is delimited by this line. The widths of other columns are not affected by this operation. Hence, using this method we can easily set each column to the width we desire for display purposes. Usually, there is no option to alter the height of a row of cells in the worksheet. This process is demonstrated in Figure 5.7.

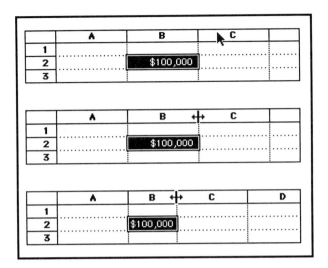

Figure 5.7. Reducing the Width of Column B.

Changing the width of a column can effect the value displayed in a cell. As long as there is sufficient room to display the numerical value in a cell, the spreadsheet will not complain; it will simply display the value. If, however, the width of a cell becomes too small for a numerical value to be displayed properly, the spreadsheet displays a string of display error symbols such as #### across a cell. Figure 5.8 shows this effect as the width of cell B is further reduced.

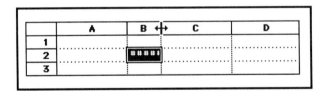

Figure 5.8. Error Symbols Indicating the Width Is Too Small.

This form of error display is chosen to protect us from inadvertently misinterpreting the numerical value in the cell. The spreadsheet still retains the correct numerical value of this cell, and the correct value will be used in any formula that references this cell. Note, however, that if the spreadsheet were to display only a few of the digits of the number in a cell instead of the symbols above, *we* would not know that only part of the number was displayed. We would naturally assume that the digits displayed represented the *entire* number and would interpret the value displayed incorrectly. To see the correct value, we simply increase the column width sufficiently and the number will reappear.

# OVERVIEW OF WORKS SS

After completing this lesson, you will be able to:

❑ Create a new Works SS worksheet.

❑ Enter data into a worksheet.

❑ Enter a formula into a worksheet.

❑ Attach a note to a cell.

❑ Print a worksheet.

❑ Create a pie chart for a worksheet.

## CREATING A WORKSHEET IN WORKS SS

To create a new spreadsheet document, perform the following.

- Start Works SS.

- Create an empty Works SS worksheet by double clicking the spreadsheet icon, which is highlighted in Figure 5.9. Alternately, you could click the spreadsheet icon to select it and then either click the *New* button on the dialog box or select the *New* command from the **File** menu.

- Save your document with the name *ProjectedSalaries1<your initials>* in the folder *Lesson1* in the folder *Works SS* on your disk.

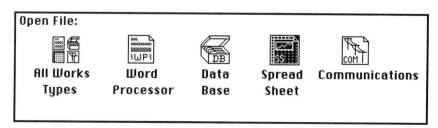

**Open File:**

| All Works Types | Word Processor | Data Base | Spread Sheet | Communications |

**Figure 5.9.** Module Icons Displayed after Works Is Opened.

- Examine the initial Works SS window, a portion of which is shown in Figure 5.10. Notice that the form of the mouse pointer in Works SS is an arrow. Use the pointer to drag the vertical scroll box to the bottom of the vertical scroll area and notice that the last row is numbered 16,382. Repeat this process with the horizontal scroll arrow and scroll box. Notice that as you scroll horizontally, the column names proceed through the letters A to Z and then continue with AA, AB, . . . , AZ, BA, BB, . . . , BZ, and so on. Observe that the rightmost column of the worksheet has the name IV. If you were to count the number of columns you would find that there are 256 columns. (You can easily compute this number by noting that there are 9 groups of 26 columns each = 234 columns from A through HZ. The first group is A-Z, the second is AA-AZ, the third BA-BZ, and so on to HA-HZ. There are an additional 22 columns from IA to IV, thus giving a total of 256 columns.) The width of the columns is preset to 12 characters per column.

| ⌘ File Edit Window Select Format Options Chart Macro |
|---|

Untitled (SS)

| | A | B | C | D | E | |
|---|---|---|---|---|---|---|
| 1 | | | | | | |
| 2 | | | | | | |
| 3 | | | | | | |
| 4 | | | | | | |
| 5 | | | | | | |
| 6 | | | | | | |
| 7 | | | | | | |
| 8 | | | | | | |
| 9 | | | | | | |

Figure 5.10. A Portion of the Works SS Starting Window.

## ENTERING DATA

In this part of the lesson you will enter the data shown on the worksheet of Figure 5.11.

Perform the following.

Enter the textual data objects of column A:

- Point to cell A1 and click to make it the active cell. Notice that the cell becomes surrounded by a heavy line.

- Type the column heading *Salaries by Department*. If you make an error in this or subsequent data entry, correct it by backspacing or by using editing techniques in the formula bar. Notice that even though the text is too long to be displayed in the cell, the text is accepted and is displayed in both columns A and B. If data were to be entered in cell B1, the new text would be displayed in cell B1's area instead of the text from cell A1. Note that no text from A1 would be lost—only that text fitting in cell A1's area would be displayed. (Recall that the width of a column can be altered by dragging.)

| | A | B | C |
|---|---|---|---|
| | Projected Salaries 1 (SS) | | |
| 1 | Salaries by Department | | 1990 |
| 2 | Lingerie | | 200000 |
| 3 | Hardware | | 300000 |
| 4 | Automotive | | 700000 |
| 5 | Electronics | | 250000 |
| 6 | Sports | | 275000 |
| 7 | | | |
| 8 | Total Salaries | | |
| 9 | | | |

Figure 5.11. The Data to Be Entered in Your Worksheet.

- Press the *Return* key. The data are entered into cell A1, and cell A2 becomes highlighted.

- Type the entry *Lingerie*. Press the *Return* key to enter the data and select cell A3.

- Type the entry *Hardware*. Press the *Return* key to enter the data and select cell A4.

- Type the entry *Automotive*. Press the *Return* key to enter the data and select cell A5.

- Type the entry *Electronics*. Press the *Return* key to enter the data and select cell A6.

- Type the entry *Sports*. Press the *Return* key twice to enter the data and to select cell A8.

- Type the summary line title *Total Salaries*.

Enter the data objects in column C:

- Click cell C1 to make it the active cell.

- Type *1990* into cell C1. Press the *Return* key to select cell C2.

- Type *200000* into cell C2. Press the *Return* key to select cell C3.

- Type *300000* into cell C3. Press the *Return* key to select cell C4.

293

- Type *700000* into cell C4. Press the *Return* key to select cell C5.

- Type *250000* into cell C5. Press the *Return* key to select cell C6.

- Type *275000* into cell C6. The worksheet should now look like Figure 5.11. Check your entries carefully and make corrections as necessary.

## ENTERING A FORMULA

Next you will compute the total of the salaries found in cells C2 through C6 of the worksheet. To accomplish this, you will enter a formula object into a cell.

Perform the following.

- Click cell C8 to make it the active cell.

- Type the equal symbol, = . Recall that if the equal symbol is entered as the first symbol in a cell, it is interpreted as the signal that a formula object is being entered. The contents of the formula bar should change immediately to display the = and the *Cancel* and *Enter* boxes. If you do not see these changes, you have made a mistake, and you should pause and discover the error before proceeding.

Method 1, typing in a formula:

- Type *C2+C3+C4+C5+C6* as the remaining part of the formula. If you make a mistake, edit it before proceeding. The formula bar of your worksheet should look exactly like that shown in Figure 5.12, except that you may have extra blank spaces between the cell names and the plus signs.

- Click the *Enter* box. The worksheet should immediately look like the worksheet shown in Figure 5.13. Notice that the sum of the salaries is now displayed in cell C8. Also, the formula is still displayed in the formula bar, but the *Cancel* and *Enter* boxes are absent.

Method 2, cell clicking method:

- Delete the formula in cell C8 by selecting the *Clear* command from the **Edit** menu.

- Type the equal symbol.

- Point to cell C2 and click. This places the cell name, C2, in the formula.

- Click cell C3.

- Click cell C4.

- Click cell C5.

- Click cell C6. The correct formula should now be in the formula bar. If this is not the case, edit the formula.

- Click the *Enter* box. The correct total should now appear in cell C8.

Method 2 demonstrates that Works SS allows you to click on a cell to enter its name into a formula. If no operation is specified, then Works SS assumes that an addition operation is to be used and will automatically insert it for you as well as the name of the cell. Alternatively, if you needed a different operation than addition, you may type the operation symbol and then click on the cell to have its name entered in the formula.

Yet another method exists for constructing the formula for this worksheet. However, because the method involves using a built-in function, the discussion of the method is delayed until a later lesson.

| | File | Edit | Window | Select | Format | Options |
|---|---|---|---|---|---|---|

| C8 | ☒☑ =C2+C3+C4+C5+C6 |
|---|---|

Projected Salaries 1 (SS)

| | A | B | C |
|---|---|---|---|
| 1 | Salaries by Department | | 1990 |
| 2 | Lingerie | | 200000 |
| 3 | Hardware | | 300000 |
| 4 | Automotive | | 700000 |
| 5 | Electronics | | 250000 |
| 6 | Sports | | 275000 |
| 7 | | | |
| 8 | Total Salaries | | |
| 9 | | | |

**Figure 5.12.** Formula Bar with Correct Formula for Cell C8.

|  File  Edit  Window  Select  Format  Options |
|---|

| C8 | | =C2+C3+C4+C5+C6 |
|---|---|---|

**Projected Salaries 1 (SS)**

| | A | B | C |
|---|---|---|---|
| 1 | Salaries by Department | | 1990 |
| 2 | Lingerie | | 200000 |
| 3 | Hardware | | 300000 |
| 4 | Automotive | | 700000 |
| 5 | Electronics | | 250000 |
| 6 | Sports | | 275000 |
| 7 | | | |
| 8 | Total Salaries | | 1725000 |
| 9 | | | |

**Figure 5.13.** The Worksheet after Clicking the *Enter* Box.

## ATTACHING A CELL NOTE

A cell note may be attached to any cell to provide explanations, reminders, or any other information that may be of future value.  Each cell note has its own window in which text can be entered and edited like any word processing document.  A small black rectangle in the upper right-hand corner of a cell indicates that the cell has an associated cell note.  In this part of the lesson you will enter the cell note for cell C1 that is shown in Figure 5.14.

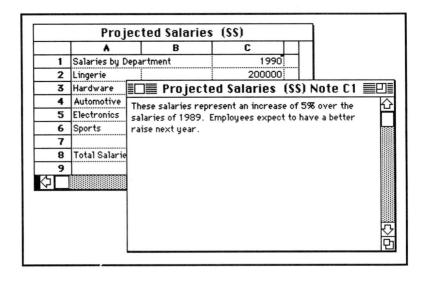

**Figure 5.14.** Example Cell Note for Cell C1.

Perform the following.

- Click cell C1 to make it the active cell.

- Select the *Open Cell Note* command from the **Edit** menu. An empty window will be displayed.

- Type the text shown in Figure 5.14 into the cell note window.

- Click the *Close* box on the cell window.

- Examine the worksheet. Notice the small black rectangle in the upper right-hand corner of cell C1.

- Select the *Save* command from the **File** menu.

You could examine the cell note at any time by selecting the *Open Cell Note* command.

## PRINTING A WORKSHEET

Printing a worksheet is similar to printing a word processing document. A large worksheet may have to be divided into pages in order to be printed. Pagination is done automatically both vertically and horizontally. If you do not like the location of the automatic page breaks, you can create manual page breaks just as you did for word processing documents. A worksheet may also have headers or footers just like a word processing document.

Perform the following.

- Select a printer using the *Chooser* command from the **Apple** menu. Review Lesson 4 of Chapter 1 as necessary for the printer selection process.

- Select the *Page Setup* command from the **File** menu, and verify that an appropriate printer has been selected.

- Click the *Print Row and Column Numbers* box on the *Page Setup* dialog box, if it does not contain an x.

- Select the *Print* command from the **File** menu.

- Click the *Print Preview* button and preview the worksheet before printing it.

- In the Print Preview screen click the *Print* (or *OK*) button. The worksheet will now be displayed. Click *Cancel* to return to the worksheet.

## CREATING A PIE CHART FOR A WORKSHEET

If the results of a worksheet computation are contained in a single column and you would like to visualize how each value compares with the whole, a pie chart is very useful. In this situation Works SS makes it easy to produce a pie chart. As an illustration you will generate a pie chart for the *ProjectedSalaries1* worksheet.

Perform the following.

- Select the *New Pie Chart* command from the **Chart** menu. A chart definition window will be displayed.

- Type *Salaries By Department* into the *Chart Title* box of the chart definition window.

- Type *C* into the *Plot Values in Column* box.

- Type *2* into the *From Row* box.

- Type *6* into the *Through Row* box.

- Type *A* into the *Column of Value Titles* box of the chart definition window. The chart window should now contain the entries shown in Figure 5.15. Compare your entries to those shown in the figure and edit entries as necessary to obtain the correct values.

- Change the name of the chart worksheet by selecting the *Change Chart Name* command of the **Edit** menu and typing *Salaries Chart* into the resulting dialog box.

- Click the *Plot It* button on the chart definition window. A pie chart will be displayed similar to that shown in Figure 5.16. You can change the size of the chart by dragging the size box in the lower right-hand corner of the window. Close the chart window.

- Select the *Save* command of the **File** menu to save the document and the chart. Close your document.

You have completed this lesson. If you do not wish to proceed directly to the next lesson, quit Works, clean up the desktop and shut down your computer.

**Salaries Chart**

**Pie Chart Definition:**

Chart Title: | Salaries By Department

Plot Values in Column: | C

From Row: | 2

Through Row: | 6

Column of Value Titles: | A

[ Cancel ]   [ Plot It! ]

**Figure 5.15.** Pie Chart Definition Window for Worksheet *ProjectedSalaries1*.

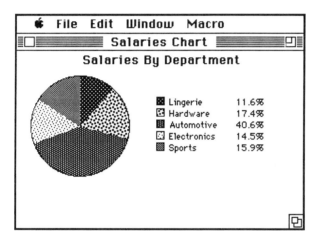

**File   Edit   Window   Macro**

**Salaries Chart**

**Salaries By Department**

| Lingerie | 11.6% |
| Hardware | 17.4% |
| Automotive | 40.6% |
| Electronics | 14.5% |
| Sports | 15.9% |

**Figure 5.16.** Pie Chart for Worksheet *ProjectedSalaries1*.

# CONSTRUCTING FORMULAS

After completing this lesson you will be able to:

❑ Use arithmetic operators in creating formulas.

❑ Use comparison operators in creating formulas.

❑ Apply the precedence rules in creating formulas.

❑ Translate algebraic formulas into worksheet formulas.


## OPERATORS IN SPREADSHEETS

Often in implementing specific worksheets it is necessary to construct complex formulas containing some combination of arithmetic, comparison, and logical operators. This section presents the fundamental information you need to produce correct formulas.

**Arithmetic Operators.** The most common kind of formula is one that performs arithmetic operations. The standard arithmetic operators and the symbols used by Works SS to represent them are shown in Figure 5.17.

| Operator | Symbol |
|----------|--------|
| addition | + |
| subtraction | − |
| multiplication | * |
| division | / |
| exponentiation | ^ |

**Figure 5.17.** The Works SS Arithmetic Operators.

The order in which calculations involving several arithmetic operators are made is very important. For example, if $x$ is computed by the formula $x = 3+4*6$, different answers are obtained depending on whether the addition or the multiplication is done first (we get 42 in the former case and 27 in the latter). To avoid such ambiguities, a convention or rule known as **precedence of operators** has been adopted. The precedence rule for the arithmetic operators is shown in Figure 5.18. Note that this rule implies that the correct answer for our example above is 27.

| Operator | Meaning | Precedence |
|----------|---------|------------|
| ^ | exponentiation | highest |
| +, − | unary plus, unary minus | ↕ |
| *, / | multiplication, division | |
| +, − | addition, subtraction | lowest |

**Figure 5.18.** Works SS Arithmetic Operator Precedence.

The precedence rule is not adequate for all circumstances. For example, what is the correct order of evaluation of the operators in the following expression in which both operators have the same precedence level?

$$x = a / b * c$$

Note that two different answers can be obtained from this expression. One answer is divide $a$ by $b$ and then multiply by $c$. That is, work left to right. A different answer would be multiply $c$ times $b$ and divide the result into $a$. That is, work right to left. This ambiguity is resolved by the **left-to-right rule**, which states that if no other rule determines the precedence of operators, the operators should be applied in left to right order. Alas, as with all rules, there is an exception to this rule: *exponentiation is performed right-to-left*.

Parentheses can be used to change the order of operator evaluation. In general, operators within parentheses are evaluated first, starting with the innermost parentheses and working outward. You have probably learned all these rules before when you first learned to evaluate arithmetic expressions.

To illustrate the precedence and left-to-right rules, consider the evaluation of the following expression:

$$14 - 2 * 3 \wedge 2 / 2 + 3 * 4.$$

Using the precedence rule, first evaluate $3 \wedge 2 = 9$, leaving

$$14 - 2 * 9 / 2 + 3 * 4.$$

Next do all multiplication and division from left to right. The sequence is

$$= 14 - 18 / 2 + 3 * 4$$

$$= 14 - 9 + 3 * 4$$

$$= 14 - 9 + 12.$$

Finally, do all addition and subtraction from left to right, yielding:

$$= 5 + 12$$

$$= 17.$$

You can make the order of evaluation explicit by using parentheses and writing this expression as

$$(14 - ((2 * (3 \wedge 2)) / 2)) + (3 * 4).$$

Where possible ambiguities can occur it is often wise to use parentheses to ensure that order of evaluation you intend is followed by the spreadsheet rather than have it decide the order using implicit rules..

**Translating Algebraic Formulas into Worksheet Formulas.** Before you can develop a worksheet, you should write out the algebraic formulas corresponding to the computations you want to perform. Examine the formulas, revising them as necessary, so that they make the correct computations when all the precedence rules are applied. Then as the worksheet is developed, translate the algebraic formulas into worksheet formulas.

As a simple example, suppose that you decide to create a worksheet to compute the formula, $z=x+y$, for various values of $x$ and $y$. Recall from algebra that the variables $x$, $y$, and $z$ are just names. Also recall that before you can compute a value for $z$, you must first substitute actual numerical values for $x$ and $y$. For this simple example, the natural language statement of the problem is *add values of* x *and* y *to obtain the value of* z. This statement needs no further subdivision because it is already sufficiently precise to allow you to solve the problem.

Next you layout the worksheet. Any formula, such as the one above, can be directly translated into a worksheet computation by applying the following interpretation. First, you may think of a cell name in a worksheet as being like the variable name in a formula. Second, you may think of the data object value in a cell as being like the value assigned to a variable in a formula. Thus, you may always pair a spreadsheet cell with a variable name appearing in an algebraic formula. Any desired pairing of cells and variable names can be chosen. Thus, we may arbitrarily choose a layout of cells in the spreadsheet to hold the actual values for $x$, $y$, and $z$. It is advantageous to label cells to remind yourself what the numbers in the cells represent.

Suppose, for example, that cell C2 is paired with $x$, cell C3 with $y$, and cell C4 with $z$. To make the data object value of cell C4 always equal to the value of $z$ in the algebraic formula, you would enter the formula =C3+C2 into cell C4. Here + is an arithmetic operator whose semantic meaning is to add the values of the data objects of cells whose names are C3 and C2. That is, this operator operates on the data object values in spreadsheet cells just like the algebraic operator + operates on algebraic variables. In fact, each of the operators listed in the table above operates on spreadsheet cells analogous to its algebraic equivalent and with the same syntax for its use. Note that the symbols C3 and C2 are not valid numeric data but are instead the names of two cells that have values associated with them—just as $x$ and $y$ are names and not the actual data values to be used.

To remind you what you are computing, you would enter the symbols $x$, $y$, and $z$ into cells B2, B3, and B4, respectively. See Figure 5.19. Note that these labels have nothing to do with the spreadsheet computation. The spreadsheet would compute results whether or not these labels are entered. The labels serve only as documentation for you. This completes the design of the simple worksheet.

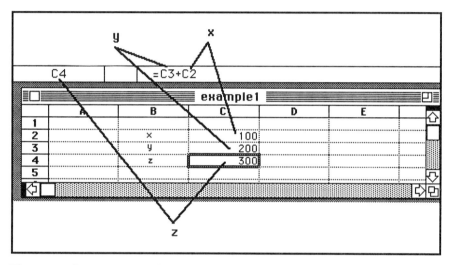

**Figure 5.19.** Interpretation of a Worksheet Formula as an Algebraic Formula.

# LOGICAL OPERATORS

To perform certain computations in a spreadsheet it is necessary to use logical operators. These operators are already familiar to you from the discussion in the database lessons. They are the operators AND, OR, and NOT. Recall that logical operators have logical values (*True* or *False* only) as input and they return a logical value as their result.

Logical operators are often used to incorporate a set of conditions into a spreadsheet computation. Suppose, for example, that a bonus should be awarded to a salesman only if his total sales were greater that $100,000 *and* his current salary was less than or equal to $50,000. That is, both these conditions must be *True* before a bonus is given. On the other hand, if either or both conditions are *False*, then no bonus is given. In English usage we may think of the term *and* as coupling two conditions together to produce a new condition that itself is either *True* or *False*. The new condition produced is the answer to the question whether or not to grant a bonus. Thus, the use of the AND operator allows us to combine two independent conditions (each of which is either *True* or *False*) into the result as to whether to grant a bonus-itself a *True* or *False* value.

You will find that building logical decisions based on the use of a hierarchy of these logical operators in spreadsheet formulas is an essential part of designing a spreadsheet to solve most useful problems.

Logical operators in the Works SS are defined as functions rather than operators. Thus, when a generic operator of the form $x$ AND $y$ is used above, it would be translated into Works SS as AND(x, y). The value of this function is the same as would be obtained if the operator AND had been applied to the values of $x$ and $y$. Similarly, the OR function of Works SS has the form OR(x, y), and evaluates exactly the same as the OR operator shown in Figure 4.36. Finally, the NOT function of Works is defined to be of the form NOT(x), and evaluates to *False* if its argument is *True* and *True* if its argument is *False*. We note here that arguments for the logical functions in Works SS are 0 to represent *False* and any other number to represent *True*. The functions AND, OR, NOT each return a value of either 0 (*False*) or 1 (*True*) only.

One reason that AND and OR are often defined as functions in spreadsheets is that they can be easily generalized to have more than two arguments. For example, the function AND(V1, V2, . . . , VN), where there are now $N$ arguments each taking on a value of *True* or *False* can be naturally defined as an extension of the two-argument AND function such that the $N$-argument AND function evaluates to *True* only if *each* of its arguments V1, ..., VN is *True*. If one or more of the arguments V1, ..., VN is *False* then the $N$-argument AND function evaluates to *False*. For two arguments this generalization reproduces the standard truth table for the AND operator.

A natural generalization also exists for the $N$-argument OR function. Here the function OR(V1, V2, . . . , VN) evaluates to *False* only if all of its $N$ arguments are *False*. If one or more of the $N$ arguments is *True* then the $N$-argument OR function evaluates to *True*. This generalization reproduces the truth table for the two-argument OR operator.

The NOT function cannot have more than one argument. When computations depend on various conditions to decide which of several formulas need to be used to compute the final results, it is very desirable to have access to AND and OR functions with more than two arguments.

## COMPARISON OPERATORS

Comparison operators produce conditions that evaluate to either *True* or *False*. Just as the arithmetic operators take two numerical values and produce a single numerical value as a result, the comparison operators take two values (not necessarily numerical) and produce a logical result of

*True* or *False*. The commonly used comparison operators and the symbols that are used to represent them are shown in Figure 5.20. *Comparison operators in Works SS are defined only for numerical values.*

```
Operator                      Symbol

equal                           =
greater than                    >
less than                       <
greater than or equal           >=
less than or equal              <=
not equal                       <>
```

**Figure 5.20.** Works SS Comparison Operators.

In conditions, the comparison operators can be thought of as asking a question. For example, the condition $x>y$ asks the question: *Is the current value of the variable x greater than the current value of the variable y?* The value of the condition is then *True* or *False* depending on whether the answer to the question is *True* or *False*.

## OPERATOR PRECEDENCE

Conditions can contain both arithmetic operators and comparison operators. In such cases the arithmetic operators take precedence and are always performed before the comparison operators are evaluated, as summarized in Figure 5.21. For example, the following are all valid conditions:

$x + y >= x * y$

$x * (y - z) <= (x - y)$

$(x + y) * (x + 10) < ((a + b) / (x + b)).$

If $x=2$, $y=4$, $a=5$, and $b=1$, the third condition would be evaluated as follows:

$(2 + 4) * (2 + 10) < ((5 + 1) / (2 + 1)).$

$6 * 12 < (6 / 3)$

$72 < 2$

*False*

| Operator | Meaning | Precedence |
|----------|---------|------------|
| ^ | exponentiation | highest |
| +,- | unary plus, minus | |
| *,/ | multiplication/ division | |
| +,- | addition/subtraction | |
| =,<>,<,>,<=,>= | comparison operators | lowest |

Figure 5.21. Summary of Works SS Operator Precedence.

## PRACTICING ENTERING FORMULAS

In this part of the lesson you will enter a number of formulas into a worksheet to obtain experience with the operators and their precedence rules. In the process you will also practice translating algebraic formulas into worksheet formulas. In this practice there is no attempt to design a meaningful worksheet.

Perform the following.

- Open Works.

- Double click the *Spreadsheet* button to create a new worksheet.

- Save your worksheet with the name *PracticeFormulas<your initials>* in the *Lesson2* folder in the *Works SS* folder on your disk.

Create the data:

- Point to cell A2 and click to make it the active cell.

- Type the label *A* into cell A2.

- Press the *Tab* key. Cell B2 becomes the active cell.

- Type the label *B* into cell B2.

- Press the *Tab* key. Cell C2 becomes the active cell.

- Type the label *C* into cell C2.

- Point to cell A3 and click to make it the active cell.

- Type 2, the value for A, into cell A3.

- Press the *Tab* key. Cell B3 becomes the active cell.

- Type 5, the value for B, into cell B3.

- Press the *Tab* key. Cell C3 becomes the active cell.

- Type 12, the value for C, into cell C3.

Create labels for formulas with arithmetic operators:

- Point to cell A5 and drag to cell A13. Release the mouse button. The area into which the labels will be typed should now be highlighted.

- Type the phrase: *Formulas with arithmetic operators.*

- Press the *Return* key. Cell A6 becomes the active cell and the original highlighted area remains highlighted.

- Type the following labels. After each label press the *Return* key to select the cell for the next label.

| Cell | Label |
|------|-------|
| A6 | A*B+C |
| A7 | A+B*C |
| A8 | (A+B)*C |
| A9 | A^2 |
| A10 | A^B |
| A11 | A+B^A |
| A12 | A/B |
| A13 | B/A |

Enter the formulas corresponding to the labels:

- Click cell B6 to make it the active cell.

- Type the formula =*A3\*B3+C3* into the cell and press the *Return* key. The computed value of the formula, 22, should appear in cell B6. Cell B7 becomes the active cell.

- Type a formula in the appropriate cell corresponding to each of the remaining labels under the heading *Formulas with arithmetic operators.* If you make a syntax error when entering a formula, a dialog box will be displayed containing a message intended to describe the error. You should correct the mistake and click the *OK* button.

Notice that the computations for cells A7, and A8 involve the same variables and the same operators, but different values are computed. This is the result of the precedence rules. Be sure you understand the differences.

- Compare your answers to those shown in Figure 5.22. If any of your answers are different, find out why and make corrections.

- Verify that the actual formulas in your cells are the same as those shown in Figure 5.23 by selecting the *Show Formulas* command of the **Options** menu.

- Return the cell display to show data objects by selecting the *Show Values* command of the **Options** menu.

Create labels for formulas with comparison operators:

- Point to cell A14, press the mouse button, and drag to cell A18. The area into which the labels will be typed should now be highlighted.

- Type the phrase: *Formulas with comparison operators.*

- Press the *Return* key. Cell A15 becomes the active cell and the original highlighted area remains highlighted.

- Type the following labels. After each label press the *Return* key to select the cell for the next label.

| Cell | Label |
|------|-------|
| A15 | A=A |
| A16 | A>A |
| A17 | A<B |
| A18 | 4*A+1 > B+C |

Enter the formulas having comparison operators corresponding to the labels:

- Click cell B15 to make it the active cell.

- Type the formula =A3=A3 and press the *Return* key. This formula looks strange because it contains two equal symbols. The first equal indicates that a formula is being defined. The second equal symbol is the comparison operator equals. Also, notice that both values being compared are numeric, and thus, the operation is defined for Works SS.

| | A | B | C | |
|---|---|---|---|---|
| 1 | | | | |
| 2 | A | B | C | |
| 3 | 2 | 5 | 12 | |
| 4 | | | | |
| 5 | Formulas with arithmetic operators | | | |
| 6 | A*B+C | | 22 | |
| 7 | A+B*C | *5x12+2* | 62 | |
| 8 | (A+B)*C | | 84 | |
| 9 | A^2 | | 4 | |
| 10 | A^B | | 32 | |
| 11 | A+B^A | *5² + 2* | 27 | |
| 12 | A/B | | 0.4 | |
| 13 | B/A | | 2.5 | |
| 14 | Formulas with comparison operators | | | |
| 15 | A=A | *⊤* | 1 | |
| 16 | A>A | *F* | 0 | |
| 17 | A<B | *⊤* | 1 | |
| 18 | 4*A+1 > B+C | *False* | 0 | |
| 19 | Formulas with built-in functions | | | |
| 20 | SQRT(A) | 1.4142135624 | | |
| 21 | B+SQRT(A) | 6.4142135624 | | |
| 22 | SUM(A:C) | 19 | | |
| 23 | | | | |
| 24 | | | | |

*Formula Practice (SS)*

**Figure 5.22.** Formula Practice Worksheet with Values Displayed.

- Type a formula in the appropriate cell for each of the remaining labels for formulas with comparison operators. During the typing if you make a syntax error, a dialog box will be displayed containing a message intended to describe the error. You should correct the mistake and click the *OK* button.

- Compare your answers to those shown in Figure 5.22. If any of your answers are different, find out why and make corrections. If you cannot find your error, look at the correct formula as it is displayed in Figure 5.23.

- Verify that the actual formulas in your cells are the same as those shown in Figure 5.23 by selecting the *Show Formulas* command of the **Options** menu.

- Return the cell display to show data objects by selecting the *Show Values* command of the **Options** menu.

Create labels for formulas with built-in functions:

- Click cell A19, and drag to cell A22. The area into which the labels will be typed should now be highlighted.

- Type the phrase: *Formulas with built-in functions.*

- Press the *Return* key. Cell A20 becomes the active cell and the original highlighted area remains highlighted.

- Type the following labels. After each label press the *Return* key to select the cell for the next label.

| Cell | Label |
|------|-------|
| A20 | SQRT(A) |
| A21 | B+SQRT(A) |
| A22 | SUM(A:C) |

Enter the formulas containing built-in functions.

- Click cell B20 to make it the active cell.

- Select *Paste Function* from the **Edit** menu.

- Scroll in the dialog box presented until the function Sqrt() is displayed and double click this name. The formula =*SQRT( )* will be pasted into the formula bar. Note that the insertion pointer is positioned between the parenthesis.

- Click cell A3 and the formula becomes =*SQRT(A3).*

- Click the *Accept* box. The square root of A, *1.414...,* is computed and displayed as cell B20's data object.

- Click cell B21 to make it the active cell.

- Type = to indicate a formula object entry.

- Click cell B3

- Type +.

- Select *Paste Function* from the **Edit** menu.

- Scroll in the dialog box presented until the function Sqrt() is displayed and double click this name. *SQRT( )* will be pasted into the formula bar following the + symbol.

- Click cell A3 and the formula becomes =*B3 + SQRT(A3)*.

- Click the *Accept* box. The value of cell B21 displayed in Figure 5.22 should be obtained.

- Click cell B22 to make it the active cell.

- Select *Paste Function* from the **Edit** menu.

- Scroll in the dialog box presented until the function Sum() is displayed and double click this name; the formula =*SUM( I )* will be pasted into the formula bar. Note the position of the insertion pointer.

- Click cell A3 and drag to cell C3. The formula becomes =*SUM(A3:C3)*.

- Click the *Accept* box. The value of cell B22 displayed in Figure 5.22 should be obtained.

- Verify that the actual formulas in your cells are the same as those shown in Figure 5.23 by selecting the *Show Formulas* command of the **Options** menu.

- Return the cell display to show data objects by selecting the *Show Values* command of the **Options** menu.

- Select *Save* from the **File** menu. Close your document.

You have completed this lesson. If you do not wish to proceed directly to the next lesson, quit Works, clean up the desktop, and shut down your computer.

| | A | B | C | |
|---|---|---|---|---|
| | **Formula Practice  (SS)** | | | |
| **1** | | | | |
| **2** | A | B | C | |
| **3** | 2 | 5 | 12 | |
| **4** | | | | |
| **5** | Formulas with arithmetic operators | | | |
| **6** | A*B+C | =A3*B3+C3 | | |
| **7** | A+B*C | =A3+B3*C3 | | |
| **8** | (A+B)*C | =(A3+B3)*C3 | | |
| **9** | A^2 | =A3^2 | | |
| **10** | A^B | =A3^B3 | | |
| **11** | A+B^A | =A3+B3^A3 | | |
| **12** | A/B | =A3/B3 | | |
| **13** | B/A | =B3/A3 | | |
| **14** | Formulas with comparison operators | | | |
| **15** | A=A | =A3=A3 | | |
| **16** | A>A | =A3>A3 | | |
| **17** | A<B | =A3<B3 | | |
| **18** | 4*A+1 > B+C | =4*A3+1>B3+C | | |
| **19** | Formulas with built-in functions | | | |
| **20** | SQRT(A) | =Sqrt(A3) | | |
| **21** | B+SQRT(A) | =B3+Sqrt(A3) | | |
| **22** | SUM(A:C) | =Sum(A3:C3) | | |
| **23** | | | | |
| **24** | | | | |

**Figure 5.23.**  *Formula Practice* Worksheet with Formulas Displayed.

# REPLICATING FORMULAS WITH THE FILL COMMANDS

After completing this lesson, you will be able to:

❑ Predict the effect of replicating a formula in which all cell references are relative references.

❑ Use the *Fill Down* command.

❑ Use the *Fill Right* command.

❑ Use the *Set Cell Attributes* command to make a worksheet more readable.

## LESSON BACKGROUND

The fundamental activity in creating worksheets is entering formulas to make the computations of interest. In many instances the same kind of computation is made repeatedly, and the formulas for these similar computations differ only in their references to variables. To assist in generating these related formulas, Works SS provides two commands, *Fill Down* and *Fill Right*, that replicate a formula and simultaneously change the references to the variables. An understanding of how these commands function is essential to using a spreadsheet.

Understanding the fill commands requires us to understand the methods used for referencing worksheet cells. There are three kinds of referencing: relative, absolute, and mixed. For this lesson we will restrict the discussion to relative referencing. The other referencing types are discussed in a later lesson.

## RELATIVE CELL REFERENCING AND THE FILL COMMANDS

**Relative Reference.** Relative reference means that the cell in which a formula is contained becomes the *origin* from which the cell locations referenced in its formula are determined. Thus, for example, the formula =C3+B2 entered into cell A4 as a *relative* reference might be thought of as being in the form =r2u1+r1u2, where r2u1 describes how to reach cell C3 from A4's position and r1u2 describes how to reach cell B2 from A4's position. Specifically, r2 means move right two columns from cell A4's column, and u1 means move up one row from cell A4's row position, and so on.

These relative reference descriptions may be thought of as forming a **formula template** that can be placed over a new cell and will describe which cell locations are to be used to compute the new cell's data object value. This relationship is depicted graphically in Figure 5.24a. If this same formula template is applied to another cell, say A5, then the first cell used in the new formula must be located r2u1 from A5, which is C4. The second cell used in the formula would then be located r1u2 from A5, which is B3. The equivalent formula would then have the form =C4+B3. This relationship is also shown in Figure 5.24b.

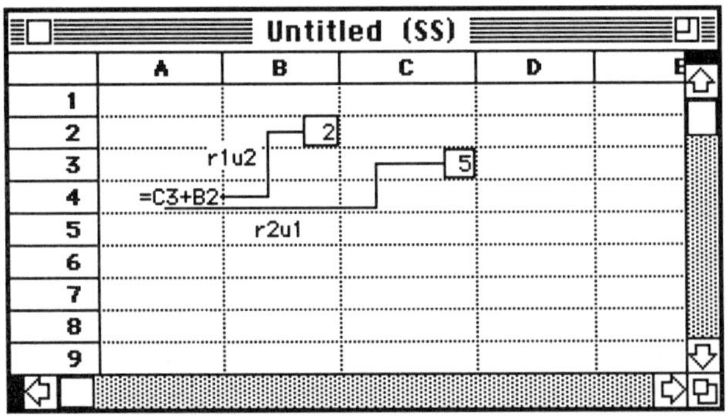

**Figure 5.24a.** Illustration of Formula Template Construction.

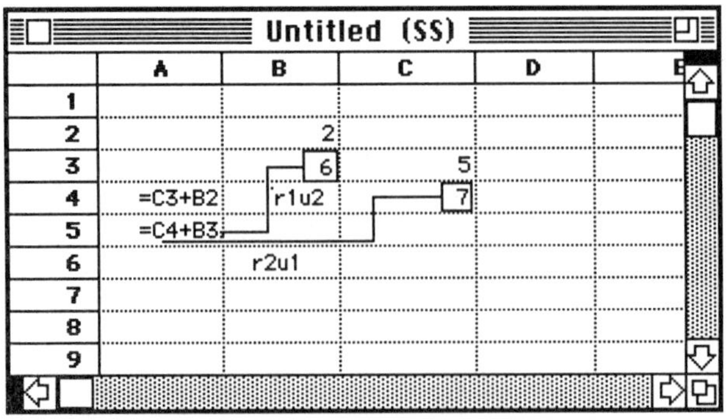

**Figure 5.24b.** Illustration of Formula Replication Using Relative Addressing and a Template.

**Fill Commands.** When the *Fill Down* and *Fill Right* commands from the **Edit** menu are used to replicate formulas, relative references are updated using the formula template so that the cell names used in the new formulas preserve the same relative positions as for the original formula. Thus, this template is applied to the cell into which the formula is to be copied and determines where the copied formula references are located—using the new cell as the origin.

Consider again the formula =C3+B2 in cell A4 where the C3 is *r2u1* from A4, and the B2 is *r1u2* from A4. If the formula is replicated into cell A5 using *Fill Down*, the first member of the new formula must be *r2u1* from A5, which is C4. The second member must be *r1u2* from A5, which is B3. The final formula in A5 is then =C4+B3. This is shown in Figure 5.24b.

Again consider the formula =C3+B2 in cell A4. If the formula is replicated into cell B4 using *Fill Right*, the first member of the new formula must be *r2u1* from B4, which is D3. The second member must be *r1u2* from B4, which is C2. The formula in B4 is then =D3+C2.

**Copy and Paste.** When the *Copy* and *Paste* command sequence is chosen from the **Edit** menu to replicate a formula, relative references are updated using a formula template just as when using *Fill Down* or *Fill Right*. Thus, for example, if the formula =C3+B2 in cell A4 is copied to the Clipboard and then pasted into cell B7, the first member is *r2u1* from B7, which is D6. The second member is *r1u2* from B7, which is C5. Thus, the formula in B7 is then =D6+C5.

# USING THE FILL DOWN AND FILL RIGHT COMMANDS

You will now use the *Fill Down* and *Fill Right* commands to create a more useful version of the *ProjectedSalaries* spreadsheet of Figure 5.13. You have entered the current year's total salaries for several departments. Also in cell C10 you have computed the total salaries for all departments using the formula =C4+C5+C6+C7+C8. Suppose that you wish to project salaries for various departments for years 1991 and 1992 using the formula:

next year's salary = current salary * 1.06.

Perform the following.

- Open Works SS, if it is not already open.

- Open the document *ProjectedSalaries1* in the *Lesson1* folder in the *Works SS* folder on your disk.

- Save your worksheet with the name *ProjectedSalaries2<your initials>* in the *Lesson3* folder in the *Works SS* folder on your disk.

- Point to cell D1 and click to make it the active cell.

- Type 1991 and press the *Tab* key to enter the value. Cell E1 becomes the active cell.

- Type 1992 in cell E1 and click the *Enter* box to enter the value.

Use Fill Down to replicate formulas:

- Select cell D2 and type the formula =C2*1.06. Click the *Enter* box and the value 212000 will be displayed in cell D2.

- Point to cell D2 and drag to cell E6 to select the range D2:E6. At this time your document should look like Figure 5.25.

- Select the *Fill Down* command from the **Edit** menu. This causes the formula in D2 to be replicated into all the selected cells below it, as shown in Figure 5.26.

| ⌘ File | Edit | Window | Select | Format | Options | Chart | Macro |
|---|---|---|---|---|---|---|---|

| D2 | | =C2*1.06 |
|---|---|---|

**Projected Salaries 2 (SS)**

| | A | B | C | D | E |
|---|---|---|---|---|---|
| 1 | Salaries by Department | | 1990 | 1991 | 1992 |
| 2 | Lingerie | | 200000 | 212000 | |
| 3 | Hardware | | 300000 | | |
| 4 | Automotive | | 700000 | | |
| 5 | Electronics | | 250000 | | |
| 6 | Sports | | 275000 | | |
| 7 | | | | | |
| 8 | Total Salaries | | 1725000 | | |
| 9 | | | | | |

**Figure 5.25.** Selection of Cells for Formula Replication Using *Fill Down* Operation.

| ⌘ File | Edit | Window | Select | Format | Options | Chart | Macro |
|---|---|---|---|---|---|---|---|

| D2 | | =C2*1.06 |
|---|---|---|

**Projected Salaries 2 (SS)**

| | A | B | C | D | E |
|---|---|---|---|---|---|
| 1 | Salaries by Department | | 1990 | 1991 | 1992 |
| 2 | Lingerie | | 200000 | 212000 | |
| 3 | Hardware | | 300000 | 318000 | |
| 4 | Automotive | | 700000 | 742000 | |
| 5 | Electronics | | 250000 | 265000 | |
| 6 | Sports | | 275000 | 291500 | |
| 7 | | | | | |
| 8 | Total Salaries | | 1725000 | | |
| 9 | | | | | |

**Figure 5.26.** Use of *Fill Down* for Formula Replication.

Use the Fill Right command to replicate formulas:

- Select the *Fill Right* command from the **Edit** menu to replicate the formulas into the selected cells to the right. The result is shown in Figure 5.27.

Notice that you obtained the entire table with only two fill operations. In a later lesson you will see that you could have produced this table using *Copy* and *Paste*, but it would have been more time consuming.

- Complete the *Total Salaries* line by selecting the range C8:E8 and then selecting the *Fill Right* command from the **Edit** menu. The result is shown in Figure 5.28.

| ⌘ File Edit Window Select Format Options Chart Macro |
|---|
| D2 · · · · · =C2*1.06 |

| Projected Salaries 2 (SS) | | | | |
|---|---|---|---|---|
|  | A | B | C | D | E |
| 1 | Salaries by Department | | 1990 | 1991 | 1992 |
| 2 | Lingerie | | 200000 | 212000 | 224720 |
| 3 | Hardware | | 300000 | 318000 | 337080 |
| 4 | Automotive | | 700000 | 742000 | 786520 |
| 5 | Electronics | | 250000 | 265000 | 280900 |
| 6 | Sports | | 275000 | 291500 | 308990 |
| 7 | | | | | |
| 8 | Total Salaries | | 1725000 | | |
| 9 | | | | | |

*(handwritten note: fill right from D2 NOT C2)*

**Figure 5.27.** Use of *Fill Right* for Replication of Remaining Formulas.

| ⌘ File Edit Window Select Format Options Chart Macro |
|---|
| C8 · · · · · =C2+C3+C4+C5+C6 |

| Projected Salaries 2 (SS) | | | | |
|---|---|---|---|---|
|  | A | B | C | D | E |
| 1 | Salaries by Department | | 1990 | 1991 | 1992 |
| 2 | Lingerie | | 200000 | 212000 | 224720 |
| 3 | Hardware | | 300000 | 318000 | 337080 |
| 4 | Automotive | | 700000 | 742000 | 786520 |
| 5 | Electronics | | 250000 | 265000 | 280900 |
| 6 | Sports | | 275000 | 291500 | 308990 |
| 7 | | | | | |
| 8 | Total Salaries | | 1725000 | 1828500 | 1938210 |
| 9 | | | | | |

**Figure 5.28.** Using *Fill Right* for the *Total Salaries*.

Examine the formulas produced by replication:

- Select *Show Formulas* from the **Options** menu. This will produce a display of all the formulas in the worksheet as shown in Figure

5.29. In the figure only a portion of each formula is showing for row 8. If any of these cells is selected, the complete formula will be shown in the formula bar. Alternately, the column widths could be changed by dragging if it were necessary to examine these formulas.

- Examine the display of formulas carefully to make sure that you understand the effects of using the *Fill Down* and the *Fill Right* commands. Notice, for example, that the effect of using *Fill Down* in column D was to change the cell references to column C so that the computations are made on the relevant data. The *Fill Right* command changed column references so that the computations were made on the relevant data.

- Select *Show Values* from the **Options** menu. Your display should again appear as that in Figure 5.28.

| | A | B | C | D | E |
|---|---|---|---|---|---|
| | Projected Salaries 2 (SS) | | | | |
| 1 | Salaries by Department | | 1990 | 1991 | 1992 |
| 2 | Lingerie | | 200000 | =C2*1.06 | =D2*1.06 |
| 3 | Hardware | | 300000 | =C3*1.06 | =D3*1.06 |
| 4 | Automotive | | 700000 | =C4*1.06 | =D4*1.06 |
| 5 | Electronics | | 250000 | =C5*1.06 | =D5*1.06 |
| 6 | Sports | | 275000 | =C6*1.06 | =D6*1.06 |
| 7 | | | | | |
| 8 | Total Salaries | | =C2+C3+C4+C5 | =D2+D3+D4+D5 | =E2+E3+E4+E5+ |
| 9 | | | | | |

**Figure 5.29.** Display of Formulas for Worksheet *Projected Salaries 1*.

Format the cells:

The goal of this part of the lesson is to make the table easier to read.

- Select the range C2:E8.

- Select the *Set Attributes* command from the **Format** menu. A dialog box will be displayed.

- On the dialog box click the *Comma* and *Dollar* options and type 0 (i.e., zero) into the *Decimal Places* box. Click the *OK* button. This sequence produces the display of Figure 5.30.

- Select the *Save* command of the **File** menu to save the document. Close the document.

You have completed this lesson. If you do not wish to proceed directly to the next lesson, quit Works, clean up the desktop, and shut down your computer.

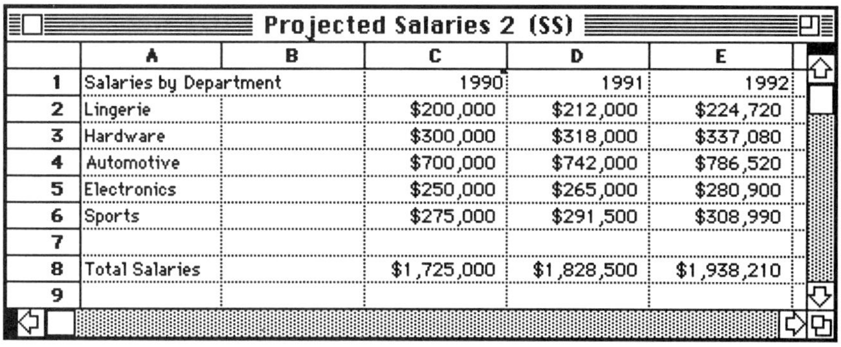

| | A | B | C | D | E |
|---|---|---|---|---|---|
| | | | Projected Salaries 2 (SS) | | |
| | **A** | **B** | **C** | **D** | **E** |
| 1 | Salaries by Department | | 1990 | 1991 | 1992 |
| 2 | Lingerie | | $200,000 | $212,000 | $224,720 |
| 3 | Hardware | | $300,000 | $318,000 | $337,080 |
| 4 | Automotive | | $700,000 | $742,000 | $786,520 |
| 5 | Electronics | | $250,000 | $265,000 | $280,900 |
| 6 | Sports | | $275,000 | $291,500 | $308,990 |
| 7 | | | | | |
| 8 | Total Salaries | | $1,725,000 | $1,828,500 | $1,938,210 |
| 9 | | | | | |

**Figure 5.30.** Using the **Format** Menu for Style.

319

# USING ABSOLUTE AND RELATIVE REFERENCE

After completing this lesson, you will be able to:

❏ Create absolute or relative references as needed.

❏ Use explicit parameters in a worksheet.

❏ Insert rows into a worksheet using the *Insert* command.

❏ Predict the effect of the *Insert* command on cell references in formulas.

❏ Turn off the grid to obtain a more finished-looking worksheet.

❏ Make *what if* calculations using a worksheet.

## LESSON BACKGROUND

In Lesson 3 you created a worksheet containing projected salaries. The design of that worksheet is deficient in at least two ways. First, the percentage increase in the salaries is not obvious. It can be deduced from the data in the worksheet, but some effort is required. Second, to change the percentage increase in the salaries, it is necessary to clear formulas from columns, create new formulas, and replicate the new formulas into the appropriate columns. It would be far better to change the contents of a single cell and have automatic recomputation of the projected salaries. Then it would be easy to investigate the impact of various percentage increases, that is, make *what if* analyses. Your ability to design such worksheets depends critically on an understanding of absolute and relative reference.

## CELL REFERENCE

Recall from the last lesson that when relative reference is used in a formula, any replication of that formula constructs a template that is used to determine which new cell locations are to be used. If only relative reference were available in formulas, it would not be possible to reference the same cell in a series of formula replications. From the above discussion, it is clear that having a number of formulas reference the same cell is desirable for *what if* analyses. Also, if rows or columns are added to or deleted from a worksheet, it is essential that formulas in all cells be updated to take these changes into account and that the spreadsheet continue to compute correct values for all formulas. Clearly, there are limits to the corrections that the spreadsheet can make. For example, if a cell is deleted from a worksheet and its value is used in a formula in one or more other cells, there is nothing the spreadsheet can do to correct the problem.

Spreadsheet designers have anticipated these kinds of problems and have provided worksheet editing commands that not only move cells on the worksheet while preserving formula values but also allow replication of cell formulas in two different ways. Consequently, the result of replicating a formula depends on whether *absolute reference* or *relative reference* has been used in the formula definition.

**Relative Reference.** Recall that relative reference means that the cell in which a formula is contained becomes the *origin* from which the cell locations referenced in its formula are determined. For example, the references in the formula =A1+B1 in cell A2 are relative references. If the formula is replicated in cell B2, the replicated formula would become =B1+C1.

**Absolute Reference.** In Works all cell references are assumed to be relative unless a special syntax is used when specifying the cell addresses. A $ sign in front of a column or row label indicates when a reference is absolute. Thus, the formula =$A$2 entered, say, into cell D10 of a Works SS worksheet indicates an absolute reference to the cell A2. It is important to remember that absolute references in formulas are *unchanged* during replication. Hence, if the formula of cell D10 is replicated into cell H21, the formula in H21 is also =$A$2. As a result, both cell D10's and H21's formulas reference the same cell A2.

**Mixed Reference.** Combinations of absolute and relative references are allowed in defining formulas. For example, the formula =$A1 entered in cell D3, means that the column label is absolute, but the row label is relative. Alternatively, the formula =A$1 would mean that the column label is relative but the row label is absolute. Mixed references are useful in creating two-dimensional tables of values.

# REVISING THE WORKSHEET

You will create another version of the worksheet *ProjectedSalaries2* that makes the percentage increase in salary explicit. Then you will perform *what if* analysis with the worksheet. To reduce the typing, you will revise the existing worksheet.

Perform the following.

- Open Works SS, if it is not already open.

- Open the document *ProjectedSalaries2* in the *Lesson3* folder in the *Works SS* folder on your disk.

- Save your worksheet with the name *ProjectedSalaries3<your initials>* in the *Lesson 4* folder in the *Works SS* folder on your disk.

Insert new rows at the beginning of the worksheet:

- Select the row label for row 1 by pointing at it and clicking.

- Select the *Insert* command from the **Edit** menu twice. Each time a new empty row will be inserted.

- Observe that the effect of the *Insert* command is to preserve the values in all computations.

- Click cell D4. Note that the formula has become =C4*1.06 in response to the insertion of the two new rows and thus continues to reference the correct cell in the altered spreadsheet. As mentioned above, the general rule when insertions or deletions of rows and columns are performed is that formula values will be preserved where possible no matter whether relative or absolute reference is used.

Clear the current formulas:

- Select the range D4:E8 by pointing to cell D4 and dragging to cell E8.

- Select the *Clear* command from the **Edit** menu. The formulas in the highlighted area will be removed, and each of these cells will be empty. If you make a mistake using *Clear*, you can undo it with the *Undo* command of the **Edit** menu.

Cells D10 and E10 will now contain $0 because their formulas refer to empty cells. When formulas are reentered for the area just cleared, the totals will be correctly recomputed.

Enter the percentage information:

- Click cell B1 to make it the active cell.

- Type *Percentage increase in salaries.*

- Press the *Tab* key twice to enter the text and to make D1 the active cell.

- Type *0.06* in cell D1 and press the *Tab* key to enter the number. E1 becomes the active cell.

- Type *0.06* in cell E1. Click the *Enter* box to enter the number.

- Select the range D1:E1 by pointing at D1 and dragging to E1.

- Select the *Set Cell Attributes* command from the **Format** menu.

- Click the *Percent* button in the leftmost column of the resulting dialog box.

- Click the *OK* button.

Each of the percentage values in cells D1 and E1 is called a **parameter**. Because of the way the worksheet will be set up, a change in either of these values will cause a change in the values computed by many formulas. Parameters such as these are essential for *what if* analysis.

Enter the formulas:

- Click cell D4 to make it the active cell.

- Type =*C4\*(1+$D$1)* into the cell and press the *Tab* key to make E4 the active cell. The value in cell D1 is the percentage increase in salaries for the year 1991.

In the formula =*C4\*(1+$D$1)* the C4 is a relative reference because you want it to change when the *Fill Down* command is executed. The $D$1 is an absolute reference to cell D1 because you do not want it to change when the formula is replicated.

- Type =*D4\*(1+$E$1)* into cell E4. The value in cell E1 is the percentage increase in salaries for the year 1992.

- Select the range D4:E8 by clicking cell D4 and dragging to cell E8.

- Select the *Fill Down* command from the **Edit** menu. Formulas will be filled into the cells and values computed. Your worksheet should now look like Figure 5.31.

The critical feature that you must understand is how the cell references are affected by the *Fill* commands.

- Select the *Show Formulas* command from the **Options** menu. Your worksheet should look like Figure 5.32. Notice that the absolute cell references $D$1 and $E$1 did not change as formulas were replicated. The relative cell references all changed as desired as formulas were replicated. Try to decide what would have happened if you had not used the absolute cell reference $D$1.

| | A | B | C | D | E |
|---|---|---|---|---|---|
| | | **Projected Salaries 3 (SS)** | | | |
| 1 | | Percentage increase in salaries | | 6.00% | 6.00% |
| 2 | | | | | |
| 3 | Salaries by Department | | 1990 | 1991 | 1992 |
| 4 | Lingerie | | $200,000 | $212,000 | $224,720 |
| 5 | Hardware | | $300,000 | $318,000 | $337,080 |
| 6 | Automotive | | $700,000 | $742,000 | $786,520 |
| 7 | Electronics | | $250,000 | $265,000 | $280,900 |
| 8 | Sports | | $275,000 | $291,500 | $308,990 |
| 9 | | | | | |
| 10 | Total Salaries | | $1,725,000 | $1,828,500 | $1,938,210 |
| 11 | | | | | |

**Figure 5.31.** *ProjectedSalaries* with Explicit Parameters for Percentages.

| | A | B | C | D | E |
|---|---|---|---|---|---|
| | | **Projected Salaries 3 (SS)** | | | |
| 1 | | Percentage increase in salaries | | 6.00% | 6.00% |
| 2 | | | | | |
| 3 | Salaries by Department | | 1990 | 1991 | 1992 |
| 4 | Lingerie | | 200000 | =C4*(1+$D$1) | =D4*(1+$E$1) |
| 5 | Hardware | | 300000 | =C5*(1+$D$1) | =D5*(1+$E$1) |
| 6 | Automotive | | 700000 | =C6*(1+$D$1) | =D6*(1+$E$1) |
| 7 | Electronics | | 250000 | =C7*(1+$D$1) | =D7*(1+$E$1) |
| 8 | Sports | | 275000 | =C8*(1+$D$1) | =D8*(1+$E$1) |
| 9 | | | | | |
| 10 | Total Salaries | | =C4+C5+C6+C7 | =D4+D5+D6+D7 | =E4+E5+E6+E7+ |
| 11 | | | | | |

**Figure 5.32.** *ProjectedSalaries* with Explicit Parameters and Formulas Displayed.

- Return to the display of values by selecting the *Show Values* command of the **Options** menu.

Add an overall totals line:

- Select cell A12 and type *Salaries for three years*.

- Select Cell C12 and type the formula =C10+D10+E10. Click the *Enter* box. Format cell C12 as you did the other cells holding dollar amounts. The resulting worksheet is shown in Figure 5.33.

| | A | B | C | D | E |
|---|---|---|---|---|---|
| 1 | | Percentage increase in salaries | | 6.00% | 6.00% |
| 2 | | | | | |
| 3 | Salaries by Department | | 1990 | 1991 | 1992 |
| 4 | Lingerie | | $200,000 | $212,000 | $224,720 |
| 5 | Hardware | | $300,000 | $318,000 | $337,080 |
| 6 | Automotive | | $700,000 | $742,000 | $786,520 |
| 7 | Electronics | | $250,000 | $265,000 | $280,900 |
| 8 | Sports | | $275,000 | $291,500 | $308,990 |
| 9 | | | | | |
| 10 | Total Salaries | | $1,725,000 | $1,828,500 | $1,938,210 |
| 11 | | | | | |
| 12 | Salaries for three years | | $5,491,710 | | |
| 13 | | | | | |

**Figure 5.33.** *ProjectedSalaries* with Explicit Parameters and a Grand Total.

- Save the worksheet.

Turn off the grid lines:

- Select the *Show Grid* command of the **Options** menu. This command when checked shows the grid lines and when not checked removes the grid lines. Your selection should remove the check mark. Your worksheet should now be identical to Figure 5.34.

| | A | B | C | D | E |
|---|---|---|---|---|---|
| 1 | | Percentage increase in salaries | | 6.00% | 6.00% |
| 2 | | | | | |
| 3 | Salaries by Department | | 1990 | 1991 | 1992 |
| 4 | Lingerie | | $200,000 | $212,000 | $224,720 |
| 5 | Hardware | | $300,000 | $318,000 | $337,080 |
| 6 | Automotive | | $700,000 | $742,000 | $786,520 |
| 7 | Electronics | | $250,000 | $265,000 | $280,900 |
| 8 | Sports | | $275,000 | $291,500 | $308,990 |
| 9 | | | | | |
| 10 | Total Salaries | | $1,725,000 | $1,828,500 | $1,938,210 |
| 11 | | | | | |
| 12 | Salaries for three years | | $5,491,710 | | |

**Figure 5.34.** *ProjectedSalaries* with Grid Lines Turned Off.

- Select the *Show Grid* command of the **Options** menu again to restore the grid lines to the worksheet.

Do what if analysis:

- Experiment with different percentage increases by setting the values in cells D1 and E1 to 8% and 7%, respectively. A sample worksheet is shown in Figure 5.35.

How much additional money would it cost the company to give a 9 % raise in 1991? (Don't forget that the raise in salary in 1991 affects the dollar amount of raise in 1992.)

How much more will 10% raises in 1991 and 1992 cost than 6% raises in both of these years?

| | A | B | C | D | E |
|---|---|---|---|---|---|
| | | **Projected Salaries 3 (SS)** | | | |
| 1 | | Percentage increase in salaries | | 8.00% | 7.00% |
| 2 | | | | | |
| 3 | Salaries by Department | | 1990 | 1991 | 1992 |
| 4 | Lingerie | | $200,000 | $216,000 | $231,120 |
| 5 | Hardware | | $300,000 | $324,000 | $346,680 |
| 6 | Automotive | | $700,000 | $756,000 | $808,920 |
| 7 | Electronics | | $250,000 | $270,000 | $288,900 |
| 8 | Sports | | $275,000 | $297,000 | $317,790 |
| 9 | | | | | |
| 10 | Total Salaries | | $1,725,000 | $1,863,000 | $1,993,410 |
| 11 | | | | | |
| 12 | Salaries for three years | | $5,581,410 | | |
| 13 | | | | | |

**Figure 5.35.** *ProjectedSalaries* Worksheet with Different Values for the Parameters.

- Close your worksheet.

You have completed this lesson. If you do not wish to proceed directly to the next lesson, quit Works, clean up the desktop, and shut down your computer.

# CREATING CHARTS

After completing this lesson, you will be able to:

❑ Set up a worksheet for creating a series chart.

❑ Create a series chart based on the worksheet.

## LESSON BACKGROUND

It is easy to generate large amounts of computational data in a short time using a spreadsheet. However, it can be very difficult to make sense of a table of hundreds or even thousands of numbers. Graphical display of data is often essential to understand or interpret results of computations. In Lesson 1 you created a pie chart for a worksheet. In this lesson you will create a worksheet and make a series and a bar chart for it.

Let us assume that we wish to graph the function:

$$y = x^2$$

To graph this function you will require a series of values for $x$, the independent variable, that are evenly spaced; that is, the difference between any adjacent values of $x$ is the same. For our example, we use the series 1, 5, 9, 13, and 17 for $x$. The tables of data for which line or bar charts can be created must be *row organized* in Works SS. This means that the independent and corresponding dependent variables each must be arranged across a row of the table.

## CREATING THE WORKSHEET

In this part of the lesson you will create the worksheet on which the graphs will be based.

Perform the following.

• If not already open, open Works.

- Create a new worksheet and save it as *Xsquared<your initials>* in the folder *Lesson5* in the folder *Works SS* on your disk.

Enter the labels:

- Click cell A1 to make it the active cell.

- Type the label *x* in cell A1.  You are entering *x* to remind *yourself* when you see this table what values appear in this row.

- Press the *Return* key to make A2 become the active cell.

- Type the label *f(x)=x^2* in cell A2.  Click the *Enter* box.  This label will remind you that the function being computed is $f(x)=x^2$.  Here ^ is the symbol for exponentiation in Works SS formula syntax.

Enter the values for the independent variable:

- Select cell B1 and type *1* into it.  Press the *Tab* key to enter the data and to make C1 the active cell.

- Type *5* into cell C1.  Press the *Tab* key to enter the data and to make D1 the active cell.

- Type *9* into cell D1.  Press the *Tab* key to enter the data and to make E1 the active cell.

- Type *13* into cell E1.  Press the *Tab* key to enter the data and to make F1 the active cell.

- Type *17* into cell F1.  Click the *Enter* box in the formula bar to enter the value.

Enter formulas to compute the values of $x^2$:

- Select cell B2 and type the formula =B1^2 into it.  Click the Enter box to enter the formula.  Because cell B1 contains the value 1, and 1*1 is 1, the value 1 will be displayed in cell B1.

- Point to cell B2 and drag to cell F2 to select the range B2:F2.

- Select the *Fill Right* command from the **Edit** menu.  The formula in cell B2 will be replicated into the selected cells to the right of B2.  The value computed by each formula will be displayed in the appropriate cell.  The worksheet should now look like that shown in Figure 5.36.

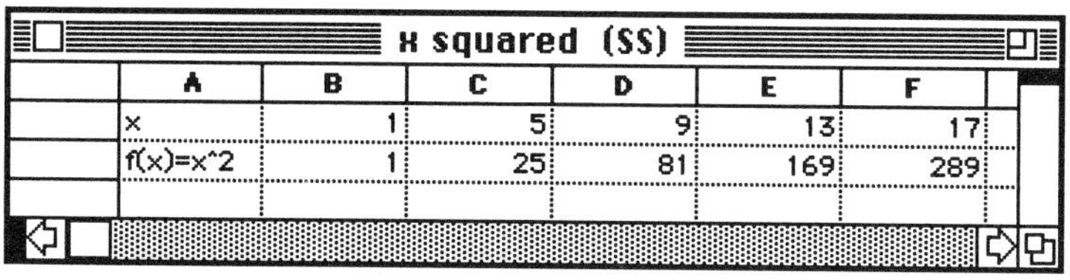

| | A | B | C | D | E | F |
|---|---|---|---|---|---|---|
| | x | 1 | 5 | 9 | 13 | 17 |
| | f(x)=x^2 | 1 | 25 | 81 | 169 | 289 |



**Figure 5.36.** Results after Computing Function Values.

## CREATING THE CHARTS

Next you will create a chart of the function values.

Perform the following.

- Select the *New Series Chart* command from the **Chart** menu. The dialog box of Figure 5.37 will be displayed. Through this dialog box you will specify the location of the data to be charted, the kind of chart to be drawn, the kind of vertical scale to use, and so on.

Create a line chart:

- Click the *Line* button in the upper left-hand corner of the dialog box under the title *Type of Chart*.

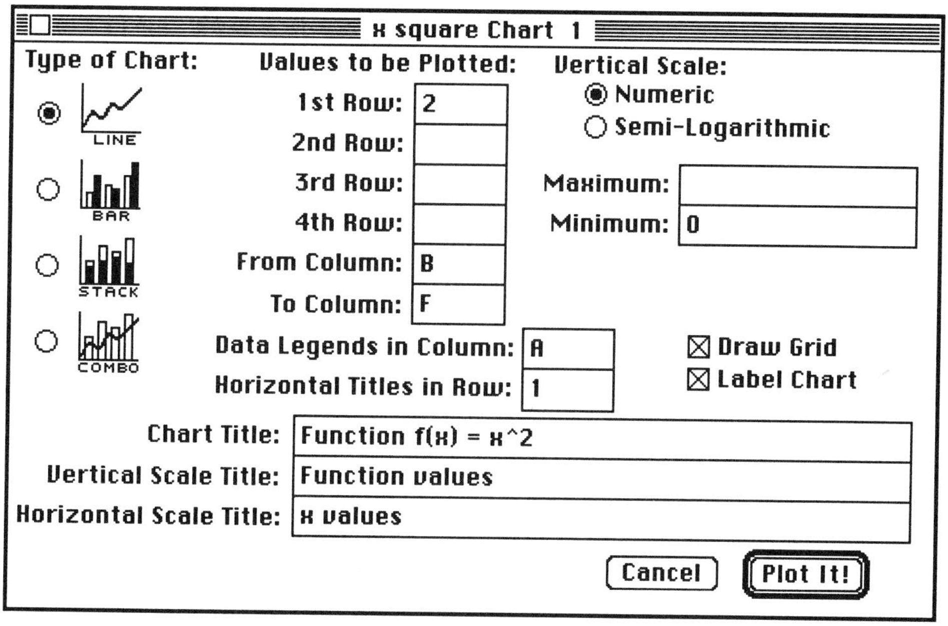



**Figure 5.37.** Selecting Location of Data to Be Charted.

Enter information into the column titled *Values to be Plotted*.

- Type 2 in the box titled *1st Row* because the function values to be plotted are in row 2 of the worksheet. Note that for this example, there is only one function to plot so that all other *Row* box values should be made blank. Do this by selecting and dragging across each one that is not empty and pressing the *Backspace* or *Delete* key. If more than one function were computed, it would be possible to chart each one (up to a total of four) on the same chart by entering the row location for each function's values.

- Type *B* in the box titled *From Column* because the first value to be plotted is in column B.

- Type *F* in the box titled *To Column* because the last value to be plotted is in column F.

Specify the locations of the data legends:

- Type A into the box titled Data Legends in Column because the label $f(x)=x^2$ is located in column A.

- Type *1* into the box titled *Horizontal Titles in Row* because the independent variable values, $x$, called horizontal titles in Works line charts, are in row 1.

  Note that in a strict sense Works SS charts are not really graphs since the independent variable values are just labels that are attached at equal distances on the horizontal axis. In other words, even if your $x$ values were not at equal distances apart, Works SS would place them on the graph as if they were. There is no method available to you to circumvent this restriction. For function computation this is rarely a problem because you may choose which $x$ values you wish to use. For data obtained from other sources, however, you must use the data that are available to you, and so this restriction becomes important.

Enter title information:

- Type *Function f(x) = x^2* in the box titled *Chart Title*.

- Type *Function values* in the box titled *Vertical Scale Title*.

- Type *x values* in the box titled *Horizontal Scale Title*.

Enter the remaining information for the chart.

- Click the *Numeric* button under the title *Vertical Scale*. (Selecting the *Semi-Logarithmic* button would cause the logarithm of the function values to be taken and the chart would be drawn using a logarithmic scale for the vertical axis.)

- Make the *Maximum* box empty and enter 0 for the *Minimum* box. In certain cases the range of values to be graphed may be so large that you cannot see details of the graph. By changing the maximum and minimum values you would be able to observe the values of interest. If you enter nothing here, Works SS will compute these values for you according to the range of values present in the data to be graphed.

- Click the boxes *Draw Grid* and *Label Chart*.

- Change the name of the chart by selecting the *Change Chart Name* command from the **Edit** menu. Type the name *X Sq. Graph* into the resulting dialog box and click the *OK* box.

- When you are returned to the dialog box shown in Figure 5.37, make sure you have selected all the entries shown there, then click the *Plot It!* button. A chart identical to that shown in Figure 5.38 should then appear. Close the chart window.

- Save your document.

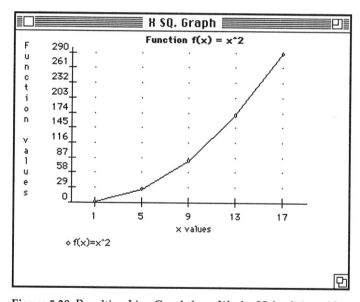

**Figure 5.38.** Resulting Line Graph from Works SS for f(x) = x^2.

Create a bar chart:

- Select the *New Series Chart* command from the **Chart** menu. The dialog box of Figure 5.37 will be displayed. Modify the entries as necessary to obtain the values shown there.

- Click the *Bar* button in the first column under the title *Type of Chart*.

- Change the name of the chart by selecting the *Change Chart Name* command from the **Edit** menu. Type the name *X Sq. Bar Graph* into the resulting dialog box and click the *OK* box.

- When you are returned to the dialog box shown in Figure 5.37, make sure you have correct values for all the entries shown there, and then click the *Plot It!* button. A chart identical to that shown in Figure 5.39 should then appear.

- Close your chart and then save your worksheet. Close your worksheet.

You have completed this lesson. If you do not wish to proceed directly to the next lesson, quit Works, clean up the desktop, and shut down your computer.

## ADDITIONAL CHARTING INFORMATION

Once a chart has been created, you may gain access to the *Chart Definition* dialog box by choosing *Select Definition* from the **Chart** menu. Alternately, you may double click in the chart display area. When the *Chart Definition* dialog box appears, you may alter the choice of items you used in creating the first chart.

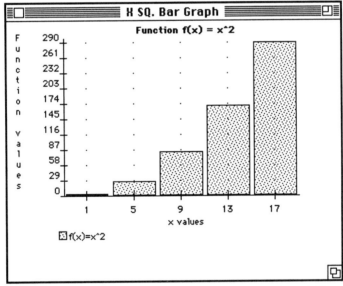

Figure 5.39. Resulting Bar Graph from Works SS for f(x) = x^2.

In addition to line charts and bar charts that can be drawn within the *New Series Chart* command, Works SS also allows you to construct pie charts such as the one displayed in Figure 5.4. Pie charts are a very effective means to display data that consists of parts of a whole. Pie charts in Works SS are *column organized* as opposed to row organized.

A maximum of eight chart definitions may be active at one time during a Works SS session. If you exceed this number of chart definitions, you must erase some of these definitions before any additional charts can be constructed. This is accomplished by selecting *Erase Chart* command from the **Chart** menu. A dialog box will appear that will allow you to select the name of the chart you wish to erase. Active charts are saved automatically with the worksheet.

The command *Draw Chart* in the **Chart** menu is used to draw a previously defined chart. Selection of this command will cause a dialog box to be displayed in which the name of a given chart can be selected and subsequently drawn.

By properly sizing and positioning your worksheet and charts, you can alter the worksheet and simultaneously observe the effect on the charts produced from the worksheet. For example, assume you had constructed a worksheet for a budget and a corresponding pie chart. The window sizes for the worksheet and the pie chart could be reduced so they could be placed alongside each other. By clicking in the worksheet to make it the active window and changing entries, you would observe that the pie chart is automatically updated to reflect the worksheet changes.

# UNDERSTANDING BUILT-IN FUNCTIONS

After completing this lesson, you will be able to:

❏ Enter a built-in function into a formula.

❏ Use arguments to pass values to a built-in function.

❏ Create a worksheet using the built-in function, FV, for computing future value.

## LESSON BACKGROUND

In a previous section, you constructed formulas using the data object operators that are provided in a typical spreadsheet package. Spreadsheets also normally provide a group of functions that are more complex than those that you would wish to construct directly as spreadsheet formulas. These functions allow the spreadsheet user to develop solutions to a broader range of problems than would be possible without them. Some of the functions provided are similar in purpose to those found on an advanced scientific or financial calculator. While it is possible for spreadsheet users to create formulas of their own to compute such function values, it is often true that the typical spreadsheet user possesses neither the knowledge, the desire, nor the time to develop such formulas. Hence, the availability of these built-in functions represents a great enhancement in your ability to solve worthwhile problems.

Typical spreadsheets provide built-in functions to perform operations such as sum a set of values, average a set of values, find the minimum of a set of values, find the maximum of a set of values, find the mean and standard deviation of a set of values, find the future value of an investment, take the logarithm of a value, take the exponential function of a value, find the positive square root of a value, and find the sine, cosine, or tangent of a value. An annotated list of many of the built-in functions provided in Works SS is presented later in this section.

## BUILT-IN FUNCTION CONCEPTS

To use a built-in function in a spreadsheet it is necessary to know both the name of the function and the information the function requires to compute its value. The syntax required to specify the information to the function is particular to each spreadsheet. However, some general comments will help to illustrate the underlying concepts.

**Black Box Model.** As a model of a function for a computation, it is convenient to think of a black box into which we place elements of information and receive in return a data object value. The function is called a black box because we care nothing about how the function computes its value—only that it returns the correct value to us. This concept is illustrated in Figure 5.40. Different elements of information that are required by a function to compute a value are called *arguments*. Arguments are used to pass values into the function, where they can be acted on to produce the resulting value.

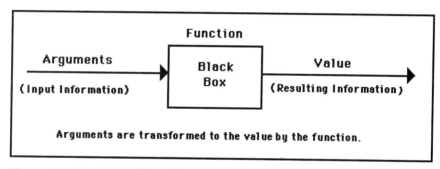

Figure 5.40. Conceptual View of a Function as a Black Box.

For example, if a function is used to compute the area of a rectangle, then the function must have two arguments: the *length* and the *width* of the rectangle. These two elements of information are always necessary to compute the area. Thus, if a rectangle has a *length* of 10 units and a width of 20 units, then the rectangle area function would return the value 200, that is, the *length* times the *width*. Each time you wish to invoke a built-in function, you need only specify its name and give values for the arguments it will use to compute the data object value.

**Syntax.** The basic syntax required to invoke a built-in function in Works SS is carried over from algebra and includes:

The name of the function.

A left parenthesis.

A list of the arguments separated from each other by commas.

A right parenthesis.

Thus, the invocation of a built-in function has the appearance:

name( argument 1, argument 2, . . . )

In a built-in function, an argument may be provided as an expression, another built-in function, a cell name, or the actual numerical value that is to be used in the computation.

**Semantics.** To use a built-in function correctly we must know the following:

The name of the function that performs the desired operation.

The meaning of each argument.

The data type of each argument.

The order of the arguments in the call on the built-in function.

**An Example Function.** To illustrate these ideas more fully, let us suppose that we wish to compute the formula

$$z = \text{the square root of } (b^2 - 4ac).$$

That is, we wish to compute the square root of $b$ squared minus four times $a$ times $c$.

In Works SS, the built-in function to compute the square root is named SQRT, and it has one argument, a numerical value. To translate the algebraic formula into a worksheet formula, we must identify a cell to represent each variable in the formula. Assume then that variables and cells are paired as

| Variable | Cell |
|----------|------|
| a | A1 |
| b | B1 |
| c | C1 |
| z | D1 |

Because $z$ is to receive the resultant data object value, we enter into cell D1 the formula

=SQRT(B1*B1-4*A1*C1).

Notice in this case that the argument to the built-in function SQRT is an expression that must evaluate to a numerical value. The value of the expression, $b^2-4ac$, is passed to the square root function, just as in the original algebraic formula. Cell D1 will display the value that is be computed for $z$.

In most cases where functions are used, numerical values will be passed as arguments and a numerical value will be returned for the answer, just as for the SQRT function above. However, functions need not operate only on numerical values or return only numerical values. Furthermore, the data type of the arguments of a function need not match the data type that the function returns.

# SUMMARY OF WORKS BUILT-IN FUNCTIONS

Works SS version 2.0 provides 64 different functions for problem solving. These functions are too numerous to list completely here. However, you may examine the name of each of the Works SS functions by selecting the *Paste Function* command of the **Edit** menu. As we have previously discussed, you must also know the arguments that are required to use a function in addition to its name. You may determine the arguments required by looking up the function definition in the Works manual or using the restricted list provided below. We describe many of the Works SS functions in detail here. In this and remaining lessons, you will be given an opportunity to work with several of the functions in Works SS.

Selected Mathematical Built-in Functions.

| | |
|---|---|
| EXP(*number*) | Computes e to the power *number*. |
| LN(*number*) | Computes logarithm, base e, of *number*. |
| LOG10(*number*) | Computes logarithm, base 10, of *number*. |
| MOD(*number, divisor*) | Computes remainder of *number*, after being divided by the *divisor*. |
| RAND() | Computes a random number between 0 and 1; note that this function has no arguments. |
| ROUND(*number, # of digits*) | Computes *number* rounded to the number of digits, *# of digits*. |

SIGN(*number*)            +1 or -1 dependent on the sign of the *number:* +1 if *number* >=0, -1 if *number* < 0.

SQRT(*number*)            Computes the square root of *number*.

**Selected Trigonometric Functions.** Arguments to the sine, cosine and tangent functions are assumed by Works SS to be expressed in radians. Values returned by the arcsine, arccosine, and arctangent are also expressed in radians. The function DEGREES will return the number of degrees, given a value in radians. The function RADIANS will return the number of radians, given a value in degrees.

ACOS(*number*)            Computes arccosine of *number*.

ASIN(*number*)            Computes arcsine of *number*.

ATAN(*number*)            Computes arctangent of *number*.

COS(*number*)            Computes cosine of *number*, where *number* is in radians.

DEGREES(*number*)            Converts *number* in radians to degrees.

RADIANS(*number*)            Converts *number* in degrees to radians.

SIN(*number*)            Computes sine of *number*, where *number* is in radians.

TAN(*number*)            Computes tangent of *number*, where *number* is in radians.

Logical Functions.

AND(V1, V2,...,VN)            1(True) if all V1, . . . , VN are not zero; 0 (False) otherwise.

OR(V1, V2,...,VN)            1(True) if any of V1, . . . , VN is not zero; 0 (False) otherwise.

IF(value, # if true, # if false)            *# if true*, if value is not zero; *# if false,* if value is zero.

NOT(V1)            1(True) if V1 is zero; 0 (False) otherwise.

**Financial Functions.** In the following, *rate* is expressed as a decimal value and is the interest rate for the number of periods, *nper*. *PV* is the present value, *FV* is the future value, and *PMT* is the periodic constant payment amount. *Type* contains a value of 1 or 0 to select, respectively, between payments at the beginning of the payment period or at the end of the payment period. If *type* is not included as an argument, then its value is assumed to be 0. The arguments PV, FV, and PMT use the following cash flow convention: cash received is considered positive, while cash paid out is considered negative.

| | |
|---|---|
| FV(*rate,nper,pmt,pv,type*) | Computes the future value at a compounded interest rate, *rate,* of *nper* payment periods, *pmt,* payment amount, and *pv* present value. *Type* is 0 or 1 as discussed above. |
| PV(*rate,nper,pmt,fv,type*) | Computes the present value needed to reach a given future value *fv,* with compounded interest rate, *rate,* in *nper* payment periods, with *pmt* payment amount. *Type* is 0 or 1 as discussed above. |
| NPER(*rate,pmt,pv,fv,type*) | Computes the number of payments necessary to reach a given future value *fv,* given the present value *pv,* with periodic payment amount *pmt,* at a compounded interest rate, *rate,* per period. *Type* is 0 or 1 as discussed above. |
| PMT(*rate,nper,pv,fv,type*) | Computes the periodic payment amount required to reach the future value *fv* from the present value *pv* in the number of payments *nper,* with a compounded interest rate, *rate.* *Type* is 0 or 1 as discussed above. |
| RATE(*nper,pmt,pv,fv,type,g*) | Computes the interest rate per period that is required to reach the future value *fv* from the present value *pv,* in the number of payments, *nper,* with periodic payments *pmt.* *Type* is 0 or 1 as discussed above. The argument, *g,* is an initial guess at the expected value for this |

interest rate. RATE uses an iterative process involving subsequent guesses to arrive at its results. This process may not always converge to a correct value. If not, the function reports an error and you may need to try a different value for $g$.

**Statistical Functions.** For the following functions, there may be any number of arguments V1, . . . , VN. Often it is desirable to select a range of values for the arguments by clicking on the first member of the range, dragging to the last member, and then releasing the mouse button. Entries entered in this way show in a *range form*. For example, if cells A1 to A10 were selected by dragging, then the argument would appear as A1:A10 and would contain 10 cell references. Arguments that contain text or blank values are ignored for each function listed below. Hence, for example, if the arguments for the AVERAGE function include one or more blank cells or cells containing textual data as arguments, these cells are not included in the computation of the average; this means that each such cell contributes neither to the count of the number of cells used for the average nor to the total value for summing all the cells.

| | |
|---|---|
| AVERAGE($V1, V2, \ldots ,VN$) | Computes the average value of the list of arguments $V1, \ldots, VN$ by summing each value and dividing by the total number of values. |
| COUNT($V1, V2, \ldots, VN$) | Counts the number of arguments that contain nonblank, nontext values. |
| MAX($V1, V2, \ldots, VN$) | Finds the largest value in the list of arguments $V1, \ldots, VN$. |
| MIN($V1, V2, \ldots, VN$) | Finds the smallest value in the list of arguments $V1, \ldots, VN$. |
| SUM($V1, V2, \ldots, VN$) | Sums the values of the arguments $V1, \ldots, VN$. |
| STDEV($V1, V2, \ldots, VN$) | Computes the standard deviation of the arguments $V1, \ldots, VN$. |
| VAR($V1, V2, \ldots, VN$) | Computes the variance of the arguments $V1, \ldots, VN$. |

## COMPUTING THE FUTURE VALUE OF A BANK ACCOUNT

As example of the use of a built-in function, you will compute the future value of a bank account that you start with a given initial value and into which you make equal monthly payments. Assume that you start with an initial deposit of $1,000 (called the present value) and that you make monthly payments of $100. Finally, assume that the interest rate paid is 6% per year, and that the interest is compounded monthly.

Note that the values of $1,000, $100, and 6% are representative values that you might wish to change for *what if* considerations. These values are then properly termed parameters of this problem.  Hence, we should reserve places on the spreadsheet where we may place these numbers, labeling them clearly.  In the sample spreadsheet of Figure 5.41, we have placed the labels for these values in column B. We next entered the actual numerical values in column C.  Note that 6% has been entered as the decimal value 0.06.

Perform the following.

- Open Works, if it is not already open.

- Create a new Works SS worksheet.

- Save your worksheet with the name *Savings<your initials>* in the *Lesson6* folder in the *Works SS* folder on your disk.

- Look up the future value built-in function in the previous section. You will find that it has following description.

FV(*rate,nper,pmt,pv,type*)  where the arguments have the meanings:
| | |
|---|---|
| rate | compound interest rate |
| nper | number of payment periods |
| pmt | payment amount |
| pv | present value |
| type | 1 for payments at the beginning of the period |
| | 0 for payments at the end of the period |

- Select cell B1 and type the phrase *Future Value of Savings*.

Enter the labels:

- Select cell B3 and type the word *Principal*. Press the *Return* key to enter the word and make cell B4 active.

- In cell B4 type the phrase *Monthly Payment*. Press the *Return* key. Cell B5 becomes active.

- In cell B5 type the phrase *Yearly Interest Rate*. Press the *Return* key. Cell B6 becomes the active cell.

- In cell B6 type the phrase *Interest Rate per Month* and press the *Return* key twice. Cell B8 becomes the active cell.

- In cell B8 type the phrase *Number of Years* and press the *Return* key. Cell B9 becomes the active cell.

- In cell B9 type the phrase *Accumulated Savings* and click the *Enter* box.

Enter the data values:

- Point to cell C3 and click to make it the active cell. In cell C3 type 1000, the value of the present value. Press the *Return* key to make C4 the active cell.

- In cell C4 type the monthly payment $100. Press the *Return* key to make C5 the active cell.

- In cell C5 type 0.06, the value of the monthly interest rate. Press the *Return* key to make C6 the active cell.

- In cell C6 enter the formula =C5/12 to compute the monthly interest rate in cell C5. Press the *Return* key twice to make C8 the active cell.

- In cell C8 type *10*, the value of the number of years. Press the *Return* key to make C9 the active cell.

Enter the built-in formula, FV:

- With cell C9 the active cell, choose *Paste Function* from the **Edit** menu, and scroll down to find the function *FV()*. Double click on *FV()*. The function name *FV()* will be inserted into cell C9 preceded by an equal sign, and the insertion pointer will be positioned between the parentheses. That is, the formula bar will contain *=FV( I )*.

Insert the arguments:

- Argument 1—Interest rate *per payment period*. Type C6 because it contains the interest rate per period. Type a comma.

- Argument 2—*Number of payment/compounding periods*. With the insertion pointer positioned just after the comma as above, type

C8*12, followed by a comma. Because the second argument of FV *must* contain the total number of monthly periods in the number of years specified, it is necessary to multiply C8 times 12.

- Argument 3—*Periodic payment amount.* Type -C4 followed by a comma. Each month you will make a payment of C4 dollars to the savings account. To maintain agreement with the cash flow convention discussed in the financial function section of this chapter, you must enter -C4. (Recall the negative sign indicates this is a payment.)

- Argument 4—*Present value of savings.* Type -C3 followed by a comma. Again because this is money paid *into* the savings account, it must be negative.

- Argument 5—*Type.* Enter a 0 (zero) assuming that the first interest will be paid at the end of the first month.

- Click the *Entry* box to enter the formula.

- Select the *Set Cell Attributes* command from the **Format** menu. Click the *Dollar* option and enter 2 for the number of digits to the right of the decimal. Your worksheet should now be identical to Figure 5.41.

- Save the document. Close the document.

You have completed this lesson. If you do not wish to proceed directly to the next lesson, quit Works, clean up the desktop, and shut down your computer.

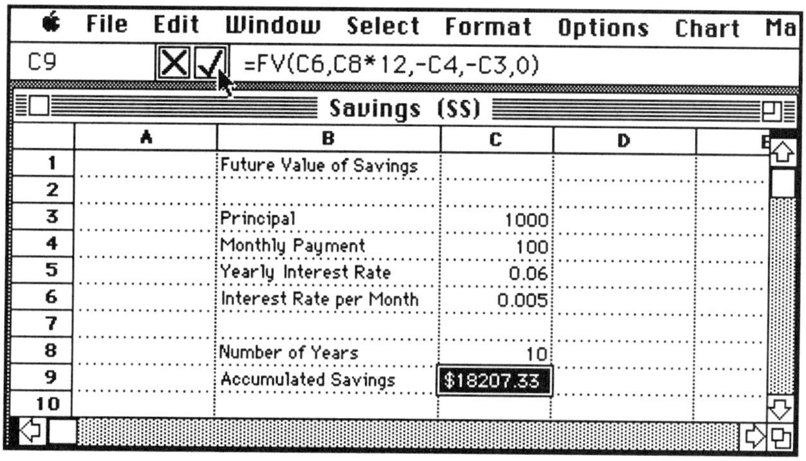

**Figure 5.41.** Example Worksheet Using Built-in Function FV.

# USING THE STATISTICAL BUILT-IN FUNCTIONS

After completing this lesson, you will be able to:

❏ Set up a worksheet that uses several different built-in functions.

❏ Use the built-in functions for average, maximum, and minimum.

❏ Appreciate the power of worksheets for *what if* analysis.


## LESSON BACKGROUND

The built-in functions are an invaluable addition to a spreadsheet environment. The example that will be studied in this lesson is the computation of grade averages for a hypothetical class. The number of students has intentionally been made quite small to reduce the typing necessary to enter the data. The important aspect of this lesson is how the built-in functions and the techniques for using them simplify solving worksheet problems. As you do this lesson try to visualize how you can use the techniques with problems of interest to you.


## THE BUILT-IN FUNCTIONS AVERAGE, MAX, AND MIN

The built-in functions AVERAGE, MAX, and *MIN* were briefly described in the previous lesson. That description is repeated below for your convenience.

| | |
|---|---|
| AVERAGE(V1, V2, . . . ,VN) | Computes the average value of the list of arguments V1, . . . , VN by summing each value and dividing by the total number ofvalues. |
| MAX(V1, V2, . . . , VN) | Finds the largest value in the list of arguments V1, . . . , VN. |

MIN(V1, V2, . . . , VN)  Finds the smallest value in the list of arguments V1, . . . , VN.

Notice that for each of these functions the arguments are a list of numbers separated by commas. In general, if the arguments are of the same data type and are in adjacent cells on the worksheet, a range description can be used instead of the list of arguments. For example, the following formulas are equivalent:

=AVERAGE(B7, B8, B9, B10, B11, B12, B13, B14, B15, B16, B17)

=AVERAGE(B7:B17)

The range representation is easier to read, less likely to contain an error, and easily entered into a formula by pointing to the first cell and dragging to the last cell in the range.

Generally, an empty cell is treated by a built-in function as containing a 0 (zero). The statistical built-in functions, however, ignore empty cells. If one or more of the cells is empty in the formula =AVERAGE(B7:B17), the correct answer will still be computed because empty cells are ignored.

## MAKING THE COMPUTATIONS

Take a look at the incomplete worksheet in Figure 5.42. You are going to enter the data so that you have a worksheet identical to that shown. Then you are going to make the following calculations. (Don't make the calculations yet, they are just being described.)

For each student (each row for rows 7 through 17) calculate the exam average of the three exams in columns B, C, and D. The result is to be placed in column E.

For each student calculate the overall average that goes in column H by applying the following:

exam average * 0.55 + lab average * 0.15 + final exam * 0.30

The weights 0.55, 0.15, and 0.30 are given as percentages in E3 through G3. Because it may be necessary to change these weights, they should not be made part of the formulas as numeric values. Instead, they should be treated as parameters.

For each column of data in rows 7 through 17, you will compute the average, maximum, and minimum values.

Finally, you will make various *what if* investigations of the results.

345

The computations are not difficult, but they would be time consuming if there were more students and thus, more data. The time required to make the calculations by hand for more students would preclude doing much what if analysis. You will observe, however, that with the use of the built-in functions nearly all the work is entering the data. Making the calculations will be very easy.

Perform the following.

- Obtain a new Works SS worksheet.

- Save your worksheet with the name *Grades<your initials>* in the *Lesson7* folder in the *Works SS* folder on your disk.

- Enter all the data shown in Figure 5.42 using the techniques you have learned in previous lessons.

The percentage values shown in cells E3, F3, and G3 should be entered as 0.55, 0.15, and 0.30.

- Select the reange E3:G3. Select the *Set Cell Attributes* command of the **Format** menu and click the *Percent* button.

- Click the *OK* button.

When you finish the data entry, your worksheet should look exactly like Figure 5.42.

Calculate the *Exam Average* for the first student:
- Select cell E7 by clicking.
- Select the *Paste Function* command from the **Edit** menu.

- Enter the incomplete formula =AVERAGE( I ) in cell E7 by double clicking AVERAGE on the resulting dialog box.

- Enter the range of the values to be averaged by pointing to cell B7 and dragging to cell D7. The formula should now have the appearance =AVERAGE(B7:D7).

- Click the *Enter* box. The value 77.3 should be displayed in cell E7. Use the *Set Cell Attributes* command to set the format to *fixed* and one digit to the right of the decimal. This completes the calculation of the exam average for the first student. Now you will obtain this average for the remaining students.

| | A | B | C | D | E | F | G | H | |
|---|---|---|---|---|---|---|---|---|---|
| 1 | | | | Grade Summary | | | | | |
| 2 | | | | | | | | | |
| 3 | | | weights: | | 55% | 15% | 30% | | |
| 4 | | | ------Hour Exams----- | | Exam | Laboratory | Final | Overall | |
| 5 | Name | Exam 1 | Exam 2 | Exam 3 | Average | Average | Exam | Average | |
| 6 | | | | | | | | | |
| 7 | Abler, JN | 76 | 72 | 84 | | 95 | 83 | | |
| 8 | Bakker, JK | 68 | 42 | 76 | | 98 | 65 | | |
| 9 | Beastly, ML | 98 | 91 | 82 | | 100 | 90 | | |
| 10 | Ervins, QT | 83 | 88 | 94 | | 100 | 88 | | |
| 11 | Hardy, RA | 68 | 72 | 72 | | 99 | 70 | | |
| 12 | Ingersal, YS | 45 | 63 | 79 | | 100 | 60 | | |
| 13 | Kissten, RX | 78 | 76 | 76 | | 100 | 75 | | |
| 14 | Mastson, PF | 82 | 86 | 87 | | 100 | 80 | | |
| 15 | Ryyir, KK | 56 | 57 | 64 | | 90 | 60 | | |
| 16 | Smitye, AY | 84 | 67 | 85 | | 100 | 71 | | |
| 17 | Verron, EH | 81 | 83 | 80 | | 97 | 85 | | |
| 18 | | | | | | | | | |
| 19 | Average | | | | | | | | |
| 20 | Maximum | | | | | | | | |
| 21 | Minimum | | | | | | | | |
| 22 | | | | | | | | | |

**Figure 5.42.** The Data to Be Entered for the *Grades* Worksheet.

Calculate the *Exam Average* for the remaining students:

- Point to cell E7 and drag to cell E17.

- Select the *Fill Down* command from the **Edit** menu. The formula in cell E7 will be replicated into the selected cells.

- Your partially completed worksheet should look like Figure 5.43. Check the exam averages to see if they are correct. If you find an incorrect average, you probably have an incorrectly entered grade. Make changes as necessary to obtain the correct averages.

Compute the *Overall Average* for the first student:

- Select cell H7 by clicking. The formula for the Overall Average is to be entered into this cell by performing the following steps. (Recall that the parameters in cells E3, F3, and G3 are to be used.)

- Type the equal sign.

- Type the following formula:

=E7*$E$3+F7*$F$3+G7*$G$3

Instead of typing the cell references, you can use the point and click method to enter them. Be sure you enter the dollar signs to make the parameter references absolute cell references.

- Click the *Enter* box.

- Format the entry to have one digit to the right of the decimal. At this stage your worksheet should look like Figure 5.44.

Compute the *Overall Average* for the remaining students:

- Point to cell H7 and drag to cell H17.

- Select the *Fill Down* command from the **Edit** menu. The formula in cell H7 will be replicated into the selected cells.

| | Grades (SS) | | | | | | |
|---|---|---|---|---|---|---|---|
| | **A** | **B** | **C** | **D** | **E** | **F** | **G** | **H** |
| **1** | | | | Grade Summary | | | | |
| **2** | | | | | | | | |
| **3** | | | weights: | | 55% | 15% | 30% | |
| **4** | | | ------Hour Exams------ | | Exam | Laboratory | Final | Overall |
| **5** | Name | Exam 1 | Exam 2 | Exam 3 | Average | Average | Exam | Average |
| **6** | | | | | | | | |
| **7** | Abler, JN | 76 | 72 | 84 | 77.3 | 95 | 83 | |
| **8** | Bakker, JK | 68 | 42 | 76 | 62.0 | 98 | 65 | |
| **9** | Beastly, ML | 98 | 91 | 82 | 90.3 | 100 | 90 | |
| **10** | Ervins, QT | 83 | 88 | 94 | 88.3 | 100 | 88 | |
| **11** | Hardy, RA | 68 | 72 | 72 | 70.7 | 99 | 70 | |
| **12** | Ingersal, YS | 45 | 63 | 79 | 62.3 | 100 | 60 | |
| **13** | Kissten, RX | 78 | 76 | 76 | 76.7 | 100 | 75 | |
| **14** | Mastson, PF | 82 | 86 | 87 | 85.0 | 100 | 80 | |
| **15** | Ryyir, KK | 56 | 57 | 64 | 59.0 | 90 | 60 | |
| **16** | Smitye, AY | 84 | 67 | 85 | 78.7 | 100 | 71 | |
| **17** | Verron, EH | 81 | 83 | 80 | 81.3 | 97 | 85 | |
| **18** | | | | | | | | |
| **19** | Average | | | | | | | |
| **20** | Maximum | | | | | | | |
| **21** | Minimum | | | | | | | |
| **22** | | | | | | | | |

**Figure 5.43.** *Grades* Worksheet with *Exam Average* Computed for Each Student.

- Your partially completed worksheet should look like the top part of the completed worksheet shown in Figure 5.45. Check the overall averages to see if they are correct. If you find an incorrect overall average, you probably have an incorrect *Laboratory Average* or an incorrect *Final Exam* grade. Make changes as necessary to obtain the correct overall averages.

Compute the average, maximum, and minimum for *Exam 1*:

- Select cell B19 by pointing and clicking.

- Enter the formula =AVERAGE(*B7:B17*). Click the *Enter* button.

- Format the entry to have one digit to the right of the decimal.

- Select cell B20 by pointing and clicking.

- Enter the formula =MAX(*B7:B17*). Click the *Enter* button.

- Select cell B21 by pointing and clicking.

- Enter the formula =MIN(*B7:B17*). Click the *Enter* button.

| File | Edit | Window | Select | Format | Options | Chart | Macro |
|------|------|--------|--------|--------|---------|-------|-------|

| H7 | | =E7*$E$3+F7*$F$3+G7*$G$3 | | | | | |

Grades (SS)

| | A | B | C | D | E | F | G | H |
|---|---|---|---|---|---|---|---|---|
| 1 | | | | Grade Summary | | | | |
| 2 | | | | | | | | |
| 3 | | | weights: | | 55% | 15% | 30% | |
| 4 | | | ------Hour Exams------ | | Exam | Laboratory | Final | Overall |
| 5 | Name | | Exam 1 | Exam 2 | Exam 3 | Average | Average | Exam | Average |
| 6 | | | | | | | | |
| 7 | Abler, JN | 76 | 72 | 84 | 77.3 | 95 | 83 | 81.7 |
| 8 | Bakker, JK | 68 | 42 | 76 | 62.0 | 98 | 65 | |
| 9 | Beastly, ML | 98 | 91 | 82 | 90.3 | 100 | 90 | |
| 10 | Ervins, QT | 83 | 88 | 94 | 88.3 | 100 | 88 | |

**Figure 5.44.** The Top Part of the *Grades* Worksheet after Entering the Formula in Cell H7.

Compute the *Average, Maximum,* and *Minimum* for the remaining columns:

- Select the range B19:H21 by pointing to cell B19, clicking, and dragging to cell H21.

- Select the *Fill Right* command from the **Edit** menu. The formulas in cells B19, B20, and B21 will be replicated into the selected cells to their right. Your worksheet should now look like the completed worksheet of Figure 5.45.

- Save the worksheet.

Experiment with the worksheet:

- Cell C8 contains a grade of 42. Assume this student did not take the exam by deleting the value from cell C8. Notice that in column C, the average (C19) and the minimum (C21) both change values. All relevant formulas are recalculated.

If you were to compute this average by hand, you would find that the value in the worksheet is obtained by ignoring cell C8. Because of formula recalculations the values change in cells C19, C21, E8, E19, H8, and H19.

- Return the value of 42 to cell C8.

- Assume that the grade in cell C16 is incorrect because the digits were typed in the wrong order. The value 67 should be 76. Select cell C16 and change the value to 76. Cells C19, E16, E19, H16, and H19 change value as the formulas are recalculated.

- Assume that the instructor is so pleased with the laboratory grades that she decides to make them more important in computing the overall grade. Select cell E3 and change the value to 0.45.

- Select cell F3 and change the value to 0.25. Notice that for each change in a parameter all values in column H change. Even for this small worksheet, it would have been time consuming to make all the calculations again by hand.

- Save the modified worksheet with the name Grades2<your initials> in the Lesson7 folder in the Works SS folder on your disk.

You have completed this lesson. If you do not wish to proceed directly to the next lesson, quit Works, clean up the desktop, and shut down your computer.

|  | A | B | C | D | E | F | G | H |
|---|---|---|---|---|---|---|---|---|
| 1 | | | | Grade Summary | | | | |
| 2 | | | | | | | | |
| 3 | | | weights: | | 55% | 15% | 30% | |
| 4 | | | ------Hour Exams----- | | Exam | Laboratory | Final | Overall |
| 5 | Name | Exam 1 | Exam 2 | Exam 3 | Average | Average | Exam | Average |
| 6 | | | | | | | | |
| 7 | Abler, JN | 76 | 72 | 84 | 77.3 | 95 | 83 | 81.7 |
| 8 | Bakker, JK | 68 | 42 | 76 | 62.0 | 98 | 65 | 68.3 |
| 9 | Beastly, ML | 98 | 91 | 82 | 90.3 | 100 | 90 | 91.7 |
| 10 | Ervins, QT | 83 | 88 | 94 | 88.3 | 100 | 88 | 90.0 |
| 11 | Hardy, RA | 68 | 72 | 72 | 70.7 | 99 | 70 | 74.7 |
| 12 | Ingersal, YS | 45 | 63 | 79 | 62.3 | 100 | 60 | 67.3 |
| 13 | Kissten, RX | 78 | 76 | 76 | 76.7 | 100 | 75 | 79.7 |
| 14 | Mastson, PF | 82 | 86 | 87 | 85.0 | 100 | 80 | 85.8 |
| 15 | Ryyir, KK | 56 | 57 | 64 | 59.0 | 90 | 60 | 64.0 |
| 16 | Smitye, AY | 84 | 67 | 85 | 78.7 | 100 | 71 | 79.6 |
| 17 | Verron, EH | 81 | 83 | 80 | 81.3 | 97 | 85 | 84.8 |
| 18 | | | | | | | | |
| 19 | Average | 74.5 | 72.5 | 79.9 | 75.6 | 98.1 | 75.2 | 78.9 |
| 20 | Maximum | 98 | 91 | 94 | 90.3 | 100 | 90 | 91.7 |
| 21 | Minimum | 45 | 42 | 64 | 59 | 90 | 60 | 64.0 |
| 22 | | | | | | | | |

**Figure 5.45.** The Completed *Grades* Worksheet.

# USING THE BUILT-IN IF FUNCTION

After completing this lesson, you will be able to:

❏ Use the IF function to make a decision in a worksheet.

❏ Design a worksheet.

❏ Reason about absolute and relative references in formulas.

## LESSON BACKGROUND

Suppose that you are managing a small company. As the manager, you must compute the gross pay, net pay, and deductions for each employee. Some employees work overtime and any hours over 40 per week must be paid at some increased rate; let us assume double time (100% *increase* over normal hourly rate). We will also assume for simplicity that deductions for tax, and the like, are all computed at 40% of gross pay.

Notice that the problem requires a decision to be made for each employee, namely, does the employee receive overtime pay or not? This is typical of spreadsheets in that many problems require that a different sequence of computations be performed dependent on intermediate results obtained during the computations. To make a decision in a spreadsheet, we use the built-in IF function. In the next section we will discuss the IF function. Then we will return to the design of a worksheet to solve the problem.

## THE IF FUNCTION

One very important kind of function that spreadsheets invariably contain is the *conditional function*. In Works SS, this function is given the name *IF*, and it has three arguments:

A logical value (must be *True* or *False* ).

The value to be returned by the function if the first argument is *True*.

The value to be returned by the function if the first argument is *False*.

The first argument is called the *condition* of the IF function, and its value is often assigned by the use of one of the comparison operators. These operators are listed in Figure 5.20. In general, however, *any* expression that evaluates to a logical value can be used to assign the value to the first argument.

IF can be used to assign one of two different values to a data object dependent on whether the first argument is *True* or *False*. A graphical depiction of the operation of the IF function is shown Figure 5.46. Note that when the condition is *True*, the value of Expression1 is computed and returned as the data object value. If the condition is *False*, then the value of Expression2 is returned as the data object value. Only one path is followed (either the left side or right side) for a given condition.

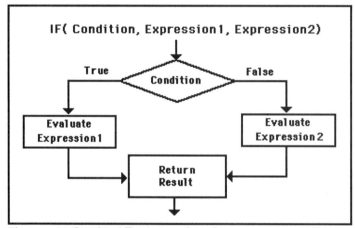

Figure 5.46. Graphical Depiction of the Operation of the IF Function.

As an example, suppose an employer wishes to give a 10% bonus to every salesperson whose total sales are greater than or equal to $100,000. An English-like statement of this decision process using the IF syntax above would be:

IF( sales >= 100,000, bonus is salary*0.10, bonus is 0 )

Let us see how to enter this formula in a worksheet. We assume that cell Q2 contains the total sales for a particular salesperson while cell G2 contains the salesperson's salary. The bonus using the spreadsheet formula is then:

=IF(Q2>=100000, G2*0.10, 0)

The first argument in the IF function is *Q2>=100000*. A comparison operator, such as >=, requires two arguments and produces a *True* or *False* result. Because Q2 is a cell name, the value of the data object of this cell is the first argument that will be used. The second argument is the number 100000. If the value of cell Q2 is greater than or equal to 100000, the result of the comparison is *True*; otherwise, the result is *False*. When the value of cell Q2 is greater than or equal to 100000, then the value the IF function returns is 10% of the value contained in cell G2 (10% of a salesperson's salary). Otherwise, the IF function returns a bonus of 0.

Let us consider a slightly more complex example. Suppose we wish to compute a salesperson's bonus using the following rule: a bonus should be awarded to a salesperson only if the person's total sales are greater than $100,000 *and* the person's current salary is less than or equal to $50,000. Because the result of the computation will be different, depending on a condition, we must again employ an IF function.

The condition itself requires that two subconditions, *(Q2>=100000)* and *(G2<=50000)*, and both subconditions must be *True* to receive a bonus. If either or both of the subconditions is *False* then no bonus is to be awarded. The built-in AND function describes exactly the way the two subconditions must be combined for this particular example. Consequently we use the formula:

$$=IF(AND((Q2>=100000),(G2<=50000)), G2*0.10, 0)$$

to describe the bonus computation.

Note in this example, that there is a hierarchy of evaluations of functions that must be performed to arrive at the IF function's value. Such a hierarchy of evaluations is called *nesting* of functions. Before the IF function can be evaluated, the condition of the IF must be determined. In this case, this requires that the AND function first be evaluated. The AND function returns a logical value, the data type required for the first argument of the IF function. The first input to the AND function is the comparison operator *Q2>=100000* that returns a logical value. The second input for the AND function is *G2<=50000* and is also a comparison operator that returns a logical value. When a *True* or *False* result has been returned by the AND function for the IF condition, a decision can then be made about whether the second or third argument of the IF function is to be evaluated and returned.

# DESIGNING THE WORKSHEET

Given the previous general description of the problem in the Lesson Background section, we can now choose the *form* of the worksheet. It would be desirable to have a table organization in which we list *employee name, hourly pay rate, total number of hours worked, gross pay, deductions,* and *net pay*. Thus, six columns having titles similar to the items listed above will be required.

Also there are certain parameters that we are using in the problem that are subject to change. These include the *overtime hourly rate increase percentage* and the *percentage to be used for deductions*. It is good worksheet design to reserve cells to hold each parameter value. If changes in these parameter values occur, these changes will automatically propagate to the final answers computed in the worksheet. To complete the form of the worksheet we also add the *date* to allow us to determine to which pay period the worksheet refers. The sample worksheet design we produce then is shown in Figure 5.47.

*Note that it is a dangerous practice to bury parameter values in formulas!* It is all too easy to forget which formulas need to be modified to reflect the new assumed values when you haven't used a worksheet for a while. Missing only one formula when you change the assumptions is all it takes to have disaster strike! Important decisions are sometimes based on the results of worksheet computations. *It cannot be overemphasized that care and extreme caution must be exercised in the developing and checking of spreadsheet computations.*

| File | Edit | Window | Select | Format | Options | Chart | Macro |
|------|------|--------|--------|--------|---------|-------|-------|

G11

**Net Pay Example (SS)**

|  | A | B | C | D | E | F |
|---|---|---|---|---|---|---|
| 1 |  |  |  |  |  |  |
| 2 | Sheet Inputs: | Overtime Rate | Deductions/Tax | Date |  |  |
| 3 |  | 1.00 | 0.40 | Aug 29, 1988 |  |  |
| 4 |  |  |  |  |  |  |
| 5 | Name | Hourly Rate | Hours Worked | Gross Pay | Deductions | Net Pay |
| 6 | Doe, John | $10.00 | 45 |  |  |  |
| 7 | Adams, Bill | $12.00 | 35 |  |  |  |
| 8 | Mack, Steve | $5.00 | 60 |  |  |  |
| 9 | Fuller, Jill | $7.50 | 40 |  |  |  |
| 10 | Mack, Pat | $3.50 | 40 |  |  |  |
| 11 | Woods, Evelyn | $7.00 | 48 |  |  |  |

**Figure 5.47.** Setup for the *Net Pay* Worksheet.

# COMPLETING THE WORKSHEET

Perform the following.

- Obtain a new worksheet

- Save your worksheet with the name *NetPayExample<your initials>* in the folder *Lesson8* in the folder *Works SS* on your disk.

Enter the worksheet data:

- In rows 2, 3 and 5 point to each cell that contains a label or data, click, and type the information. Note that we have entered the overtime percentage increase and percentage deductions using a decimal value in cells B3 and C3. Thus 100% and 40% translate to 1.0 and 0.40, respectively, as decimals. Format cell D3 to *Date Medium*.

- Select the range A6:C11 by pointing to cell A6 and dragging to cell C11. For each row:

  - Type the *Name*.

  - Press the *Tab* key.

  - Type the value for the *Hourly Rate*.

  - Press the *Tab* key.

  - Type the value of the *Hours Worked*.

  To move to the next row press the *Tab* key. Remember that the active cell will wrap around within the selected area automatically when the *Tab* key is used.

- Format the values in the cells below the *Hourly Rate* heading by doing the following. Select the range B6:B11. Select the *Set Cell Attributes* command of the **Format** menu. On the resulting dialog box click the *Dollar* button and set the number of decimal digits to two.

Compute the *Gross Pay* for the first employee:

- There are two cases, each requiring a formula:

  If the number of hours worked is 40 or less then

  gross pay = (hours*pay rate)

  If the number of hours worked is not 40 or less (i.e., number of hours must be greater than 40) then

  gross pay = (40*pay rate)+(1+overtime rate)*(pay rate)*(hours-40)

  From the formulas, you can see that the formula to use is determined by the value of the condition: number of hours worked <= 40.

- Type into D6 the following worksheet formula that is a translation of the above algebraic formulas.

$$=IF((C6<=40), B6*C6, 40*B6+(1+B3)*B6*(C6-40))$$

- Click the *Enter* box. The result is shown in Figure 5.48.

Because the *Overtime Rate*, B3, is a parameter, you should suspect that it should be an absolute reference. For the moment, however, assume the formula is valid.

| ● File | Edit | Window | Select | Format | Options | Chart | Macro |
|---|---|---|---|---|---|---|---|

D6 ☒☑ =If((C6<=40),B6*C6,40*B6+(1+B3)*B6*(C6-40))

Net Pay Example (SS)

|  | A | B | C | D | E | F |
|---|---|---|---|---|---|---|
| 1 |  |  |  |  |  |  |
| 2 | Sheet Inputs: | Overtime Rate | Deductions/Tax | Date |  |  |
| 3 |  | 1.00 | 0.40 | Aug 29, 1988 |  |  |
| 4 |  |  |  |  |  |  |
| 5 | Name | Hourly Rate | Hours Worked | Gross Pay | Deductions | Net Pay |
| 6 | Doe, John | $10.00 | 45 | 500 |  |  |
| 7 | Adams, Bill | $12.00 | 35 |  |  |  |
| 8 | Mack, Steve | $5.00 | 60 |  |  |  |
| 9 | Fuller, Jill | $7.50 | 40 |  |  |  |
| 10 | Mack, Pat | $3.50 | 40 |  |  |  |
| 11 | Woods, Evelyn | $7.00 | 48 |  |  |  |

**Figure 5.48.** Entry of Formula to Compute *Gross Pay* for John Doe.

Compute the *Gross Pay* for the remaining employees:

- Select the range D6:D11 by pointing at D6, clicking, and dragging to D11.

- Select the *Fill Down* command from the **Edit** menu. The formula will be replicated into the selected cells. The result is shown in Figure 5.49.

- Examine the results carefully. There is an error in the value in cell D8. If you compute the values that should be obtained for the *Gross Pay*, you will find that with the exception of the first cell, anyone working more than 40 hours does not get paid enough.

*To find errors you must critically evaluate all of the results your worksheet produces.* You should never trust spreadsheet formulas until you have verified them yourself by many simple test computations. The larger the worksheet, the more difficult it is to determine if its formulas are correct. Validating any computer solution to a problem can be a time-consuming process, but it is essential if you are to have confidence in those solutions

The error in this problem comes from the fact that we used relative reference for *all* cells in the formula. If you check the formula for cell D8 as it is displayed in the formula bar, you will see that because relative reference was employed in the original formula for the *Overtime Rate*, B3, the formula template has shifted the cell reference from B3 to B5. The formula in cell D8 is:

$$=IF((C8<=40), B8*C8, 40*B8+(1+B5)*B8*(C8-40)).$$

| <br>&#9786; File Edit Window Select Format Options Chart Macro | | | | | |
|---|---|---|---|---|---|
| D8 | | =If((C8<=40),B8*C8,40*B8+(1+B5)*B8*(C8-40)) | | | |

**Net Pay Example (SS)**

|  | A | B | C | D | E | F |
|---|---|---|---|---|---|---|
| 1 | | | | | | |
| 2 | Sheet Inputs: | Overtime Rate | Deductions/Tax | Date | | |
| 3 | | 1.00 | 0.40 | Aug 29, 1988 | | |
| 4 | | | | | | |
| 5 | Name | Hourly Rate | Hours Worked | Gross Pay | Deductions | Net Pay |
| 6 | Doe, John | $10.00 | 45 | 500 | | |
| 7 | Adams, Bill | $12.00 | 35 | 420 | | |
| 8 | Mack, Steve | $5.00 | 60 | 300 | | |
| 9 | Fuller, Jill | $7.50 | 40 | 300 | | |
| 10 | Mack, Pat | $3.50 | 40 | 140 | | |
| 11 | Woods, Evelyn | $7.00 | 48 | 616 | | |

**Figure 5.49.** Results Obtained after Replicating Cell D6.

Cell B5 contains the textual value *Hourly Rate* instead of the value of the *Overtime Rate*. This text is treated as the value of zero by Works SS—subsequently giving you a wrong answer. The choice of cell reference is critical for correct computation by the worksheet.

Correct the error.

- Select the range D7:D11.

- Select the *Clear* command of the **Edit** menu. This will clear the formulas from the selected cells.

- Select cell D6. Make the reference to the value of the *Overtime Rate*, B3, an absolute reference, $B$3, and then click the *Enter* box.

- Select the range D6:D11.

- Select the *Fill Down* command from the **Edit** menu. The new version of the formula is replicated into the highlighted cells.

- The resulting correct version of the partially complete worksheet is shown in Figure 5.50.

Compute the *Deductions* for the first employee:

- The formula for payroll deductions is given by

  payroll deduction = (gross salary)*(percent deduction)

You will next translate this into a spreadsheet formula.

- Select cell E6. Type the formula =D6*$C$3. Here, you need to use absolute reference for the *Deductions/Tax* percentage to avoid generating a template that will cause an incorrect value to be used.

- Click the *Enter* box.

| &#xF8FF; File | Edit | Window | Select | Format | Options | Chart | Macro |
|---|---|---|---|---|---|---|---|

| D6 | | =If((C6<=40),B6*C6,40*B6+(1+$B$3)*B6*(C6-40)) |
|---|---|---|

**Net Pay Example (SS)**

| | A | B | C | D | E | F |
|---|---|---|---|---|---|---|
| 1 | | | | | | |
| 2 | Sheet Inputs: | Overtime Rate | Deductions/Tax | Date | | |
| 3 | | 1.00 | 0.40 | Aug 29, 1988 | | |
| 4 | | | | | | |
| 5 | Name | Hourly Rate | Hours Worked | Gross Pay | Deductions | Net Pay |
| 6 | Doe, John | $10.00 | 45 | 500 | | |
| 7 | Adams, Bill | $12.00 | 35 | 420 | | |
| 8 | Mack, Steve | $5.00 | 60 | 400 | | |
| 9 | Fuller, Jill | $7.50 | 40 | 300 | | |
| 10 | Mack, Pat | $3.50 | 40 | 140 | | |
| 11 | Woods, Evelyn | $7.00 | 48 | 392 | | |

**Figure 5.50.** Corrected Absolute Reference to Cell B3 and Replication.

Compute the *Deductions* for the remaining employees:

- Select the range E6:E11 and replicate the formula downward. The result is shown in Figure 5.51.

| &#xF8FF; File | Edit | Window | Select | Format | Options | Chart | Macro |
|---|---|---|---|---|---|---|---|

| E6 | | =D6*$C$3 |
|---|---|---|

**Net Pay Example (SS)**

| | A | B | C | D | E | F |
|---|---|---|---|---|---|---|
| 1 | | | | | | |
| 2 | Sheet Inputs: | Overtime Rate | Deductions/Tax | Date | | |
| 3 | | 1.00 | 0.40 | Aug 29, 1988 | | |
| 4 | | | | | | |
| 5 | Name | Hourly Rate | Hours Worked | Gross Pay | Deductions | Net Pay |
| 6 | Doe, John | $10.00 | 45 | 500 | 200 | |
| 7 | Adams, Bill | $12.00 | 35 | 420 | 168 | |
| 8 | Mack, Steve | $5.00 | 60 | 400 | 160 | |
| 9 | Fuller, Jill | $7.50 | 40 | 300 | 120 | |
| 10 | Mack, Pat | $3.50 | 40 | 140 | 56 | |
| 11 | Woods, Evelyn | $7.00 | 48 | 392 | 156.8 | |

**Figure 5.51.** Computation of the Payroll *Deductions*.

Compute the *Net Pay* for the first employee:

- The formula relating net pay, gross pay, and deductions is given by:

net pay = (gross pay) - (deductions)

Translating this formula into a worksheet formula for computing John Doe's net pay gives =D6-E6.

- Select cell F6 and type the formula =D6-E6, and then click the *Enter* box.

Compute the *Net Pay* for the remaining employees:

- Select the range F6:F11 and replicate the formula downward. The result is shown in Figure 5.52. The basic computations for the worksheet are now complete. You should now make the worksheet more readable.

Alphabetize the worksheet by employee name:

- The worksheet would be more readable if it were arranged alphabetically by employee. Sorting can be done in Works SS.

- Select the range A6:F11 by pointing at cell A6 and dragging to cell F11. The selection must be done carefully because only the selected items will be rearranged as a result of the sort. For example, if only the column of names in Figure 5.52 (column A) were selected and then sorted, none of the other columns of the table would be altered as a result of the sort. This would mean that the name Bill Adams (the first name alphabetically) would be moved to the top of the list of names in column A. His name would then appear on the same row with John Doe's *Gross Pay*, *Deductions*, and *Net Pay*.

| | A | B | C | D | E | F |
|---|---|---|---|---|---|---|
| 1 | | | | | | |
| 2 | Sheet Inputs: | Overtime Rate | Deductions/Tax | Date | | |
| 3 | | 1.00 | | 0.40 | Aug 29, 1988 | |
| 4 | | | | | | |
| 5 | Name | Hourly Rate | Hours Worked | Gross Pay | Deductions | Net Pay |
| 6 | Doe, John | $10.00 | 45 | 500 | 200 | 300 |
| 7 | Adams, Bill | $12.00 | 35 | 420 | 168 | 252 |
| 8 | Mack, Steve | $5.00 | 60 | 400 | 160 | 240 |
| 9 | Fuller, Jill | $7.50 | 40 | 300 | 120 | 180 |
| 10 | Mack, Pat | $3.50 | 40 | 140 | 56 | 84 |
| 11 | Woods, Evelyn | $7.00 | 48 | 392 | 156.8 | 235.2 |

F6 = =D6-E6 — Net Pay Example (SS)

Figure 5.52. Computing the *Net Pay* for Each Employee.

- Select the *Sort* command from the **Edit** menu.

- On the resulting dialog box type *A* into the *1st Key Column* and click the *Ascending* button. All other boxes should be blank, and no other button should be highlighted.

- Click the *OK* button. The result of sorting the highlighted area of the worksheet by employee name is shown in Figure 5.53.

Format the cells for the *Gross Pay, Net Pay,* and *Deductions*:

- Notice that in the worksheet some values have decimals and some do not. You will now make the display of the values uniform in the employee area.

- Select the range D6:F11.

- Select the *Set Cell Attributes* from the **Format** menu.

- On the resulting dialog box, click the *Fixed* button and type 2 into the *Decimal Places* box.

- Click the *OK* button.

Compute the sum of the columns for *Gross Pay, Deductions,* and *Net Pay*:

- Select cell D13.

- Select the *Paste Function* from the **Edit** menu.

- Scroll until you find the function SUM().

- Double click the function, SUM, to place =SUM(I) into cell D13.

- Select the range D6:D11. This will cause the formula to have the form =SUM(*D6:D11*).

- Click the *Enter* box. The result is shown in Figure 5.55.

- Replicate the formula into cells E13 and F13 by selecting the range D13:F13, and then selecting the *Fill Right* command from the **Edit** menu.

- Format the highlighted cells by selecting the *Set Cell Attributes* command from the **Format** menu.

- Click the *Dollar* button.

- Click the *OK* button. The result is shown in Figure 5.56.

| | A | B | C | D | E | F |
|---|---|---|---|---|---|---|
| | File | Edit | Window Select | Format Options | Chart Macro | |
| A6 | | | Adams, Bill | | | |

Net Pay Example (SS)

| | A | B | C | D | E | F |
|---|---|---|---|---|---|---|
| 1 | | | | | | |
| 2 | Sheet Inputs: | Overtime Rate | Deductions/Tax | Date | | |
| 3 | | 1.00 | 0.40 | Aug 29, 1988 | | |
| 4 | | | | | | |
| 5 | Name | Hourly Rate | Hours Worked | Gross Pay | Deductions | Net Pay |
| 6 | Adams, Bill | $12.00 | 35 | 420 | 168 | 252 |
| 7 | Doe, John | $10.00 | 45 | 500 | 200 | 300 |
| 8 | Fuller, Jill | $7.50 | 40 | 300 | 120 | 180 |
| 9 | Mack, Pat | $3.50 | 40 | 140 | 56 | 84 |
| 10 | Mack, Steve | $5.00 | 60 | 400 | 160 | 240 |
| 11 | Woods, Evelyn | $7.00 | 48 | 392 | 156.8 | 235.2 |

**Figure 5.53.** Result of Performing the Sort.

| | File | Edit | Window Select | Format Options | Chart Macro | |
|---|---|---|---|---|---|---|
| | | | | | | |

Net Pay Example (SS)

| | A | B | C | D | E | F |
|---|---|---|---|---|---|---|
| 1 | | | | | | |
| 2 | Sheet Inputs: | Overtime Rate | Deductions/Tax | Date | | |
| 3 | | 1.00 | 0.40 | Aug 29, 1988 | | |
| 4 | | | | | | |
| 5 | Name | Hourly Rate | Hours Worked | Gross Pay | Deductions | Net Pay |
| 6 | Adams, Bill | $12.00 | 35 | 420.00 | 168.00 | 252.00 |
| 7 | Doe, John | $10.00 | 45 | 500.00 | 200.00 | 300.00 |
| 8 | Fuller, Jill | $7.50 | 40 | 300.00 | 120.00 | 180.00 |
| 9 | Mack, Pat | $3.50 | 40 | 140.00 | 56.00 | 84.00 |
| 10 | Mack, Steve | $5.00 | 60 | 400.00 | 160.00 | 240.00 |
| 11 | Woods, Evelyn | $7.00 | 48 | 392.00 | 156.80 | 235.20 |

**Figure 5.54.** Results of Formatting the Display of Data Object Values.

Create a cell note to explain the calculation of *Gross Pay*:

- Click cell D5 to make it active.

- Select the *Open Cell Note* command from the **Edit** menu. A blank cell note window will be displayed.

- Type the information shown in Figure 5.57 into the cell note window.

- Click the *Close* box on the cell note window.

- Save the worksheet.

- Click cell B3 to make it active.

- Enter the value 1.5 in cell B3.

- Click the *Enter* box and observe the changes that are made throughout the worksheet.

- Close the document.

| | File | Edit | Window | Select | Format | Options | Chart | Macro |
|---|---|---|---|---|---|---|---|---|

D13 ☒✓ =Sum(D6:D11)

**Net Pay Example (SS)**

| | A | B | C | D | E | F |
|---|---|---|---|---|---|---|
| 1 | | | | | | |
| 2 | Sheet Inputs: | Overtime Rate | Deductions/Tax | Date | | |
| 3 | | 1.00 | 0.40 | Aug 29, 1988 | | |
| 4 | | | | | | |
| 5 | Name | Hourly Rate | Hours Worked | Gross Pay | Deductions | Net Pay |
| 6 | Adams, Bill | $12.00 | 35 | 420.00 | 168.00 | 252.00 |
| 7 | Doe, John | $10.00 | 45 | 500.00 | 200.00 | 300.00 |
| 8 | Fuller, Jill | $7.50 | 40 | 300.00 | 120.00 | 180.00 |
| 9 | Mack, Pat | $3.50 | 40 | 140.00 | 56.00 | 84.00 |
| 10 | Mack, Steve | $5.00 | 60 | 400.00 | 160.00 | 240.00 |
| 11 | Woods, Evelyn | $7.00 | 48 | 392.00 | 156.80 | 235.20 |
| 12 | | | | | | |
| 13 | | | | 2152.00 | | |

**Figure 5.55.** Defining the Sum Function for a Range of Cells.

| | File | Edit | Window | Select | Format | Options | Chart | Macro |
|---|---|---|---|---|---|---|---|---|

D13 =Sum(D6:D11)

**Net Pay Example (SS)**

| | A | B | C | D | E | F |
|---|---|---|---|---|---|---|
| 1 | | | | | | |
| 2 | Sheet Inputs: | Overtime Rate | Deductions/Tax | Date | | |
| 3 | | 1.00 | 0.40 | Aug 29, 1988 | | |
| 4 | | | | | | |
| 5 | Name | Hourly Rate | Hours Worked | Gross Pay | Deductions | Net Pay |
| 6 | Adams, Bill | $12.00 | 35 | 420.00 | 168.00 | 252.00 |
| 7 | Doe, John | $10.00 | 45 | 500.00 | 200.00 | 300.00 |
| 8 | Fuller, Jill | $7.50 | 40 | 300.00 | 120.00 | 180.00 |
| 9 | Mack, Pat | $3.50 | 40 | 140.00 | 56.00 | 84.00 |
| 10 | Mack, Steve | $5.00 | 60 | 400.00 | 160.00 | 240.00 |
| 11 | Woods, Evelyn | $7.00 | 48 | 392.00 | 156.80 | 235.20 |
| 12 | | | | | | |
| 13 | | | | $2152.00 | $860.80 | $1291.20 |

**Figure 5.56.** Final Worksheet Showing Totals for Each Column.

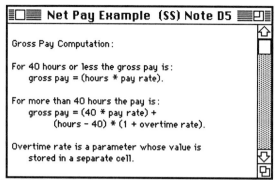

**Figure 5.57.** *Cell Note* Window for Cell D5 of the *Net Pay Example* Worksheet.

You have completed this lesson. If you do not wish to proceed directly to the next lesson, quit Works, clean up the desktop, and shut down your computer.

# REMOVING AND INSERTING COMPLETE ROWS AND COLUMNS

After completing this lesson, you will be able to:

❏ Use the *Insert* command to create new rows and columns in a worksheet.

❏ Use the *Cut* command to remove a row or column of a worksheet.

❏ Create a new worksheet from an existing worksheet.

## LESSON BACKGROUND

Suppose that you have created a large worksheet that is important to your organization. After the worksheet has been completed, you are told to redo the worksheet using a slightly different design. Because so much data would have to be entered, recreating the worksheet is not practical. Instead, you will have to revise the existing worksheet. In the redesign process the *Insert* and *Cut* commands will be used for inserting complete rows (or columns) and removing complete rows (or columns).

In this lesson you will revise the *NetPayExample* worksheet that was prepared in Lesson 8. This worksheet is so small that it could be reentered quickly using the new design, but instead you will change it using the *Insert* and *Cut* commands. This will allow you to learn how to use these commands without having to retype the data. These techniques can be used with any size worksheet.

## INSERTING/ DELETING ROWS AND COLUMNS OF CELLS

The operations of *Insert* and *Cut* allow, respectively, a row or column of cells to be added or deleted from the worksheet. Clearly, to *Insert* or *Cut* it is necessary to indicate where a row or column of cells is to be added or deleted. To select a column (row), move the cell-selection pointer into the column (row) label area, point to the column (row) of interest, and click.

The entire column (row) will become highlighted. By pulling down the Edit menu and selecting *Insert*, an entire new column (row) will be inserted in the worksheet *before* the column (row) selected. When cell positions are altered as the result of adding the new column (row), *both* absolute and relative addresses of cells referenced in formulas will be automatically updated. To use *Insert* on a row, it is not necessary to highlight the entire row. In fact, if only one cell is highlighted and *Insert* is selected, then an entire row is automatically added to the worksheet *before* the selected row.

When an entire column (row) is selected, *Cut* will cause the highlighted column (row) to be removed from the worksheet. That is, *Cut* works similarly to *Insert* above in that the entire column (row) is altered. When cell positions are altered as the result of cutting a column (row), *both* absolute and relative addresses of cells referenced in formulas will be automatically updated provided the referenced cells aren't removed. When cells that are referenced by formulas in other cells are removed, an *OffSheet* error condition will be reported in those formulas.

If one cell or a group of cells (but not a row or column) is highlighted, then *Cut* will only remove the contents of the cell and place it on the Clipboard. When a formula is cut and pasted, relative addresses in the formula are updated, but absolute addresses are not, just as with a *Copy/Paste* operation. However, when a cell that is referenced by formulas in other cells is cut and pasted, *neither* absolute nor relative references to the cell are updated in those other cell formulas.

The *Clear* operation removes any information in a cell without deleting the actual cell from the worksheet. Thus, if the contents of a cell or group of cells is not what you desire, you may select the range desired and select the *Clear* operation from the **Edit** pull-down menu. *Clear* functions identically to *Cut* except that nothing is placed on the Clipboard.

## USING THE INSERT AND CUT COMMANDS

You are to revise the final worksheet of Lesson 8, Figure 5.56, to divide the contents of column E, *Deductions*, into two columns: *Tax Deductions* and *Other Deductions*. Also, you are to remove the row containing data for John Doe, who is no longer employed. You are also to revise the format of the worksheet. The desired final result is shown in Figure 5.58. You should compare this worksheet with its original version before proceeding.

Before beginning, we preview the actions that will be required to produce the revised worksheet:

Insert a new row at the top of the worksheet.

Insert a new row just above the row containing the column headings (old row 5).

Insert a column before the old column E to hold the values for the *Tax Deductions*.

Cut the row containing the data for John Doe.

Enter formulas for the new columns, *Tax Deductions* and *Other Deductions*.

Revise the formulas for computing the *Net Pay*.

Change the format (set cell attributes) for various parts of the worksheet.

| | A | B | C | D | E | F | G |
|---|---|---|---|---|---|---|---|
| 1 | | | | | | | |
| 2 | | Overtime | | | | | |
| 3 | Sheet Inputs | Rate | Deductions | Date | Tax | | |
| 4 | | 1.00 | 0.15 | Aug 29, 1989 | 0.25 | | |
| 5 | | | | | | | |
| 6 | | Hourly | Hours | | Tax | Other | |
| 7 | Name | Rate | Worked | Gross Pay | Deduction | Deductions | Net Pay |
| 8 | Adams, Bill | $12.00 | 35 | 420.00 | 105.00 | 63.00 | 252.00 |
| 9 | Fuller, Jill | $7.50 | 40 | 300.00 | 75.00 | 45.00 | 180.00 |
| 10 | Mack, Pat | $3.50 | 40 | 140.00 | 35.00 | 21.00 | 84.00 |
| 11 | Mack, Steve | $5.00 | 60 | 400.00 | 100.00 | 60.00 | 240.00 |
| 12 | Woods, Evelyn | $7.00 | 48 | 392.00 | 98.00 | 58.80 | 235.20 |
| 13 | | | | | | | |
| 14 | | | | $1652.00 | $413.00 | $247.80 | $991.20 |

Title bar: **Net Pay Revised (SS)**

**Figure 5.58.** Revised *NetPay* Worksheet to be Created.

Perform the following:

- Open the *NetPayExample<your initials>* worksheet in the *Lesson8* folder in the Works SS folder on your disk.

- Save the worksheet with the name *NetPayRevised<your initials>* in the *Lesson9* folder in the *Works SS* folder.

Insert the new rows and columns:

- Select the row label for row 1 by pointing to the label and clicking. The entire row will become highlighted.

- Insert a row by selecting the *Insert* command under the **Edit** menu. A new row will be inserted above the current row 1. It should appear to you as if the original worksheet has been moved down one row.

- Select the row label for row 5 by pointing to the label and clicking. Again, the entire row will become highlighted.

- Insert a new row 5 by selecting the *Insert* command under the **Edit** menu. It should appear to you as if the worksheet below row 5 has been moved down one row.

- Select column label for column E by pointing at it and clicking. The entire column should become highlighted as shown in Figure 5.59.

- Insert a column by selecting the *Insert* command under the **Edit** menu. A new column will be inserted before column E. It should appear to you that columns E and F have been moved to the right one column.

| | A | B | C | D | E | F |
|---|---|---|---|---|---|---|
| | | | | Net Pay Revised (SS) | | |
| 1 | | | | | | |
| 2 | | | | | | |
| 3 | Sheet Inputs | Overtime Rate | Deductions/tax | Date | | |
| 4 | | 1.00 | | 0.40 | Aug 29, 1989 | |
| 5 | | | | | | |
| 6 | | | | | | |
| 7 | Name | Hourly Rate | Hours Worked | Gross Pay | Deductions | Net Pay |
| 8 | Adams, Bill | $12.00 | 35 | 420.00 | 168.00 | 252.00 |
| 9 | Doe, John | $10.00 | 45 | 500.00 | 200.00 | 300.00 |
| 10 | Fuller, Jill | $7.50 | 40 | 300.00 | 120.00 | 180.00 |
| 11 | Mack, Pat | $3.50 | 40 | 140.00 | 56.00 | 84.00 |
| 12 | Mack, Steve | $5.00 | 60 | 400.00 | 160.00 | 240.00 |
| 13 | Woods, Evelyn | $7.00 | 48 | 392.00 | 156.80 | 235.20 |
| 14 | | | | | | |
| 15 | | | | $2152.00 | $860.80 | $1291.20 |

Figure 5.59. Revised Worksheet with Column E Selected.

Delete the row containing data for John Doe:

- Select row 9 (row containing John Doe) by pointing at row label 9 and clicking.

- Delete row 9 by selecting the *Cut* command under the **Edit** menu. The rows below row 9 will appear to move up a row in the worksheet. The worksheet should now have the appearance shown in Figure 5.60.

Change the column headings:

- Select cell B2 by pointing and clicking and type the word *Overtime.*

- Select cell B3 and remove the word *Overtime* by editing the display in the formula bar.

- Select cell B6 and type the word *Hourly*.

- Select cell B7 and remove the word *Hourly* by editing the display in the formula bar.

- Select cell C6 and type the word *Hours*.

- Select cell C7 and remove the word *Hours* by editing the display in the formula bar.

- Select cell E6 and type the word *Tax*.

- Select cell F6 and type the word *Other*.

- Select cell E7 and type the word *Deductions*.

| | A | B | C | D | E | F | G |
|---|---|---|---|---|---|---|---|
| 1 | | | | | | | |
| 2 | | | | | | | |
| 3 | Sheet Inputs | Overtime Rate | Deductions/tax | Date | | | |
| 4 | | 1.00 | 0.40 | Aug 29, 1989 | | | |
| 5 | | | | | | | |
| 6 | | | | | | | |
| 7 | Name | Hourly Rate | Hours Worked | Gross Pay | | Deductions | Net Pay |
| 8 | Adams, Bill | $12.00 | 35 | 420.00 | | 168.00 | 252.00 |
| 9 | Fuller, Jill | $7.50 | 40 | 300.00 | | 120.00 | 180.00 |
| 10 | Mack, Pat | $3.50 | 40 | 140.00 | | 56.00 | 84.00 |
| 11 | Mack, Steve | $5.00 | 60 | 400.00 | | 160.00 | 240.00 |
| 12 | Woods, Evelyn | $7.00 | 48 | 392.00 | | 156.80 | 235.20 |
| 13 | | | | | | | |
| 14 | | | | $1652.00 | | $660.80 | $991.20 |

Title bar: Net Pay Revised (SS)

Figure 5.60. Revised Worksheet after Inserting/Deleting Rows and Columns.

Change the parameter values for *Deductions* and *Tax*:

- Select cell C4 and change the displayed value to *0.15*.

- Select C3 and remove the */tax* from the label.

- Select cell E4 and type the value *0.25*. If the value displayed in cell E4 is not *0.25*, select the *Set Cell Attributes* command under the **Format** menu; in the resulting dialog box, click the *Fixed* button, enter 2 as the number of decimal digits, and click the *OK* button.

- Label the new parameter by selecting cell E3 and typing the word *Tax*. The revised worksheet should now have the appearance shown in Figure 5.61. Notice that the values for *Other Deductions* in cells F8:F12 were automatically recomputed because the value of the parameter in cell C4 was changed.

| | A | B | C | D | E | F | G |
|---|---|---|---|---|---|---|---|
| | | | | Net Pay Revised (SS) | | | |
| 1 | | | | | | | |
| 2 | | Overtime | | | | | |
| 3 | Sheet Inputs | Rate | Deductions | Date | Tax | | |
| 4 | | 1.00 | 0.15 | Aug 29, 1989 | 0.25 | | |
| 5 | | | | | | | |
| 6 | | Hourly | Hours | | Tax | Other | |
| 7 | Name | Rate | Worked | Gross Pay | Deductions | Deductions | Net Pay |
| 8 | Adams, Bill | $12.00 | 35 | 420.00 | | 63.00 | 357.00 |
| 9 | Fuller, Jill | $7.50 | 40 | 300.00 | | 45.00 | 255.00 |
| 10 | Mack, Pat | $3.50 | 40 | 140.00 | | 21.00 | 119.00 |
| 11 | Mack, Steve | $5.00 | 60 | 400.00 | | 60.00 | 340.00 |
| 12 | Woods, Evelyn | $7.00 | 48 | 392.00 | | 58.80 | 333.20 |
| 13 | | | | | | | |
| 14 | | | | $1652.00 | | $247.80 | $1404.20 |

**Figure 5.61.** Revised Worksheet after Changing Column Headings and Typing New Values.

Compute the values for *Tax Deductions*:

- Select cell E8 by pointing and clicking.

- Type the formula =D8*$E$4 and click the *Enter* box. Be sure that you include the dollar signs to make the reference to cell E4 an absolute reference. The value *105.00* should appear in cell E8.

- Select the cell range E8:E12 by clicking and dragging.

- Compute values for the range by reproducing the formula in cell E8 with the *Fill Down* command of the **Edit** menu. The values shown in Figure 5.62 should be displayed.

Recompute values for *Net Pay*:

- Select cell G8 by pointing and clicking.

- Edit the formula shown in the formula bar to change it from =D8-F8 to =D8-E8-F8.

- Click the *Enter* box. The value *252.00* should appear in cell G8.

- Select the cell range G8:G12 by clicking cell G8 and dragging to cell G12.

369

- Compute values for the range by reproducing the formula of cell G8 with the *Fill Down* command of the **Edit** menu. The values shown in Figure 5.63 should be displayed.

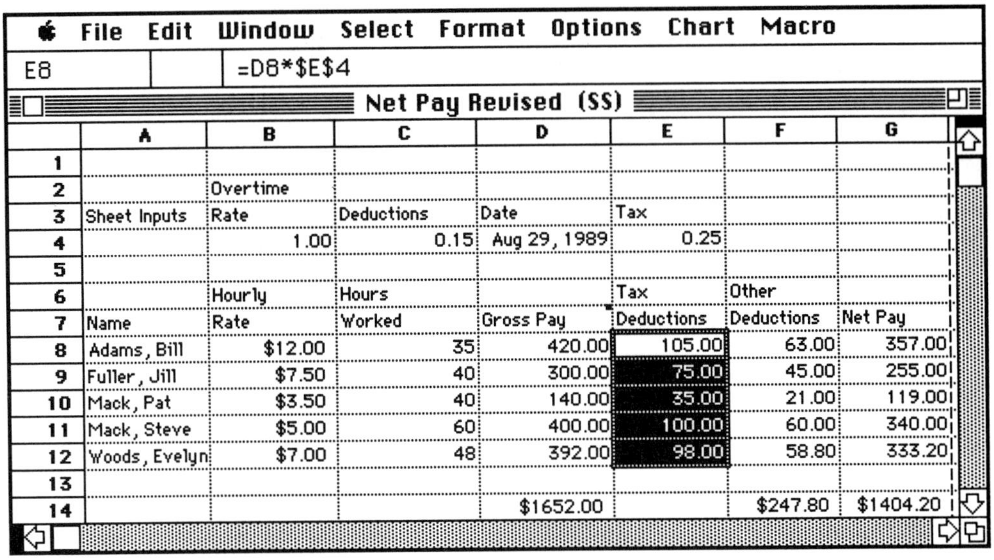

**Figure 5.62.** Revised Worksheet after Entering the Formula in E8 and Using *Fill Down*.

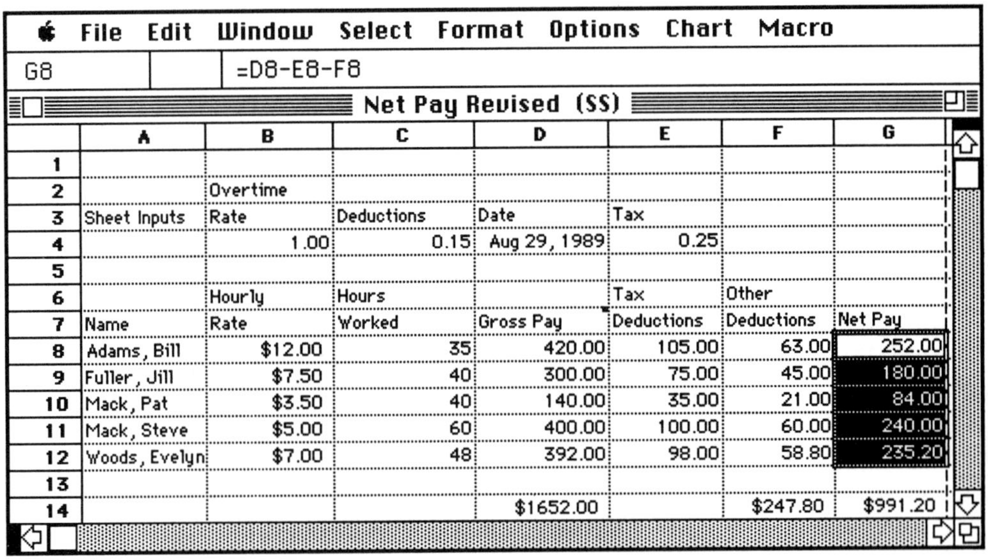

**Figure 5.63.** Revised Worksheet after Entering the Formula in G8 and Using *Fill Down*.

Compute the sum of the *Tax Deductions*:

- Select the cell range D14:E14 by pointing at cell D14 and dragging to cell E14.

- Insert a formula in cell E14 by selecting the *Fill Right* command under the **Edit** menu. The result should be that shown in Figure 5:64.

| | File | Edit | Window | Select | Format | Options | Chart | Macro | | |
|---|---|---|---|---|---|---|---|---|---|---|

**D14** | =Sum(D8:D12)

Net Pay Revised (SS)

| | A | B | C | D | E | F | G |
|---|---|---|---|---|---|---|---|
| 1 | | | | | | | |
| 2 | | Overtime | | | | | |
| 3 | Sheet Inputs | Rate | Deductions | Date | Tax | | |
| 4 | | 1.00 | 0.15 | Aug 29, 1989 | 0.25 | | |
| 5 | | | | | | | |
| 6 | | Hourly | Hours | | Tax | Other | |
| 7 | Name | Rate | Worked | Gross Pay | Deductions | Deductions | Net Pay |
| 8 | Adams, Bill | $12.00 | 35 | 420.00 | 105.00 | 63.00 | 252.00 |
| 9 | Fuller, Jill | $7.50 | 40 | 300.00 | 75.00 | 45.00 | 180.00 |
| 10 | Mack, Pat | $3.50 | 40 | 140.00 | 35.00 | 21.00 | 84.00 |
| 11 | Mack, Steve | $5.00 | 60 | 400.00 | 100.00 | 60.00 | 240.00 |
| 12 | Woods, Evelyn | $7.00 | 48 | 392.00 | 98.00 | 58.80 | 235.20 |
| 13 | | | | | | | |
| 14 | | | | $1652.00 | $413.00 | $247.80 | $991.20 |

**Figure 5.64.** Revised Worksheet after Entering the Formula in D14 and Using *Fill Right*.

Center the column headings:

- Select the cell range B6:G7 by pointing to cell B6 and dragging to cell G7 as shown in Figure 5.65.

- Center the words in their respective columns by selecting the *Set Cell Attributes* command under the **Format** menu, and then clicking the *Center* button on the resulting dialog box.

Center the employee data in columns B through G:

- Select the cell range B8:B12 by pointing at cell B8 and dragging to cell B12 as shown in Figure 5.66.

- Center the selected data by selecting the *Set Attributes Command* under the **Format** menu, and then clicking the *Center* button on the resulting dialog box.

- Select the cell range C8:C12 by pointing at cell C8 and dragging to cell C12.

| | A | B | C | D | E | F | G |
|---|---|---|---|---|---|---|---|
| 1 | | | | | | | |
| 2 | | Overtime | | | | | |
| 3 | Sheet Inputs | Rate | Deductions | Date | Tax | | |
| 4 | | 1.00 | 0.15 | Aug 29, 1989 | 0.25 | | |
| 5 | | | | | | | |
| 6 | | Hourly | Hours | | Tax | Other | |
| 7 | Name | Rate | Worked | Gross Pay | Deductions | Deductions | Net Pay |
| 8 | Adams, Bill | $12.00 | 35 | 420.00 | 105.00 | 63.00 | 252.00 |
| 9 | Fuller, Jill | $7.50 | 40 | 300.00 | 75.00 | 45.00 | 180.00 |
| 10 | Mack, Pat | $3.50 | 40 | 140.00 | 35.00 | 21.00 | 84.00 |
| 11 | Mack, Steve | $5.00 | 60 | 400.00 | 100.00 | 60.00 | 240.00 |
| 12 | Woods, Evelyn | $7.00 | 48 | 392.00 | 98.00 | 58.80 | 235.20 |
| 13 | | | | | | | |
| 14 | | | | $1652.00 | $413.00 | $247.80 | $991.20 |

Figure 5.65. Preparing to Center the Column Headings.

- Center the selected data by selecting the *Set Attributes Command* under the **Format** menu, and then clicking the *Center* button on the resulting dialog box.

- Select the cell range D8:G12 by pointing at cell D8 and dragging to cell G12.

- Center the selected data by selecting the *Set Attributes Command* under the **Format** menu, and then clicking the *Center* button on the resulting dialog box.

The data in the range B8:G12 should now be like that shown in Figure 5.67.

| | A | B | C | D | E | F | G |
|---|---|---|---|---|---|---|---|
| 1 | | | | | | | |
| 2 | | Overtime | | | | | |
| 3 | Sheet Inputs | Rate | Deductions | Date | Tax | | |
| 4 | | 1.00 | 0.15 | Aug 29, 1989 | 0.25 | | |
| 5 | | | | | | | |
| 6 | | Hourly | Hours | | Tax | Other | |
| 7 | Name | Rate | Worked | Gross Pay | Deductions | Deductions | Net Pay |
| 8 | Adams, Bill | $12.00 | 35 | 420.00 | 105.00 | 63.00 | 252.00 |
| 9 | Fuller, Jill | $7.50 | 40 | 300.00 | 75.00 | 45.00 | 180.00 |
| 10 | Mack, Pat | $3.50 | 40 | 140.00 | 35.00 | 21.00 | 84.00 |
| 11 | Mack, Steve | $5.00 | 60 | 400.00 | 100.00 | 60.00 | 240.00 |
| 12 | Woods, Evelyn | $7.00 | 48 | 392.00 | 98.00 | 58.80 | 235.20 |
| 13 | | | | | | | |
| 14 | | | | $1652.00 | $413.00 | $247.80 | $991.20 |

Figure 5.66. Preparing to Center the Data in Cells B8:B12.

Center the parameters and their identifying labels:

- Select the cell range B2:E4 by pointing at cell B2 and dragging to cell E4 as shown in Figure 5.67.

- Center the selected data by selecting the *Set Attributes Command* under the **Format** menu, and then clicking the *Center* button on the resulting dialog box. This step produces the desired revised worksheet of net pay.

- Save the modified worksheet.

You have completed this chapter. Quit Works, clean up the desktop, and shut down your computer.

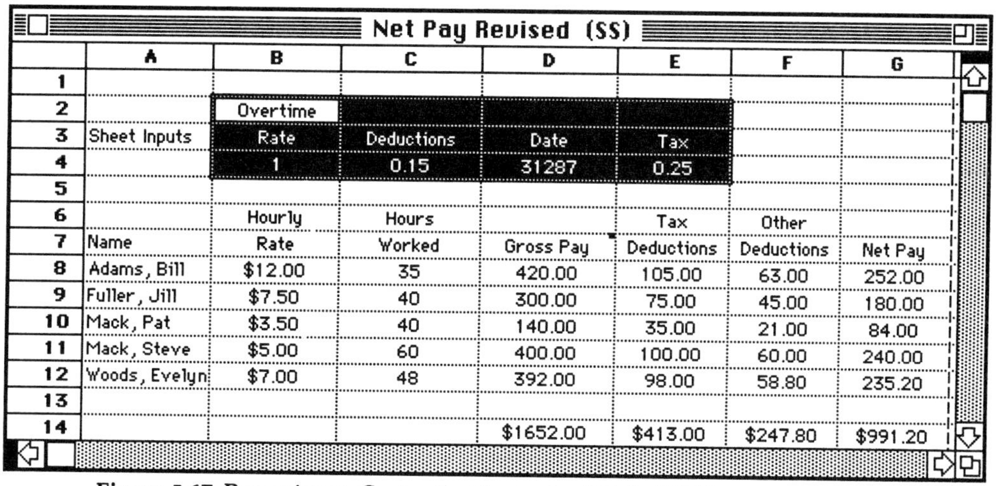

## Net Pay Revised (SS)

|   | A | B | C | D | E | F | G |
|---|---|---|---|---|---|---|---|
| 1 | | | | | | | |
| 2 | | Overtime | | | | | |
| 3 | Sheet Inputs | Rate | Deductions | Date | Tax | | |
| 4 | | 1 | 0.15 | 31287 | 0.25 | | |
| 5 | | | | | | | |
| 6 | | Hourly | Hours | | Tax | Other | |
| 7 | Name | Rate | Worked | Gross Pay | Deductions | Deductions | Net Pay |
| 8 | Adams, Bill | $12.00 | 35 | 420.00 | 105.00 | 63.00 | 252.00 |
| 9 | Fuller, Jill | $7.50 | 40 | 300.00 | 75.00 | 45.00 | 180.00 |
| 10 | Mack, Pat | $3.50 | 40 | 140.00 | 35.00 | 21.00 | 84.00 |
| 11 | Mack, Steve | $5.00 | 60 | 400.00 | 100.00 | 60.00 | 240.00 |
| 12 | Woods, Evelyn | $7.00 | 48 | 392.00 | 98.00 | 58.80 | 235.20 |
| 13 | | | | | | | |
| 14 | | | | $1652.00 | $413.00 | $247.80 | $991.20 |

**Figure 5.67.** Preparing to Center the Contents of Cells B2:E4.

# PRACTICE PROJECTS

## PROJECT 1

In this project you will open Works SS, create and manipulate a worksheet, save it to your disk, and create a chart using the data in the worksheet. Step by step instructions will be given, but they will not be as detailed as the tutorial material.

1. Create a folder on your disk and name it *SSProject1*.

2. Open Works SS to get a new untitled document. Save the document inside the folder *SSProject1* under the name *GradeCalc<your initials>*.

Set up the spreadsheet shown in Figure 5.68:

3. First click on cell B2. Enter the text *My Course 101 Grade Components*.

4. Click on cell A4 and drag down to cell A10. The range A4:A10 should now be highlighted. You next will enter values into this range.

    Enter *Component*, press *Return*.

    Enter *Two Tests*, press *Return*.

    Enter *Final Exam*, press *Return*.

    Enter *Labs/Homework*, press *Return*.

    Enter *My Project*, press *Return*.

    Press *Return*, (This produces the blank line)

    Enter *Total*, and press *Return*.

| | A | B | C | D | E |
|---|---|---|---|---|---|
| 1 | | | | | |
| 2 | | MyCourse 101 Grade Components | | | |
| 3 | | | | | |
| 4 | Component | | Point Values | Percentages | |
| 5 | Two Tests | | 250 | 37.04% | |
| 6 | Final Exam | | 175 | 25.93% | |
| 7 | Labs/Homework | | 150 | 22.22% | |
| 8 | My Project | | 100 | 14.81% | |
| 9 | | | | | |
| 10 | Total | | 675 | 100.00% | |
| 11 | | | | | |

**Figure 5.68.** Grade Calculation Worksheet.

5. Your worksheet should now have the title and entries in column A as shown in Figure 5.68. If you find mistakes iń a cell's value, click in that cell to make it the active cell and then edit the cell's contents. When you have completed editing any errors in a cell, click on the *Check* box just to the left of the formula bar. Once your worksheet has the title and entries in column A as shown in Figure 5.68, save your document.

Enter the information in column C:

6. Click in cell C4 and drag down to cell C8. This entire range of cells should now be highlighted.

   Enter *Point Values*, press *Return*.

   Enter *250*, press *Return*.

   Enter *175*, press *Return*.

   Enter *150*, press *Return*.

   Enter *100*, press *Return*.

7. Next you will enter a function into cell C10 to total the number of points.

   Click on cell C10 to make it the active cell.

   Select *Paste Function* from the **Edit** menu.

   Scroll in the dialog box presented until you see the function SUM() listed. Double click on this function. The dialog box will disappear and the formula =SUM(1) will appear in the formula bar.

   You must now enter the arguments for the SUM function. Click on cell C5 and drag down to cell C8  This causes the range C5:C8 to be inserted between the parentheses of the SUM function. You

375

are specifying that Works SS should sum the values in these four cells. Now click on the *Check* box to enter the formula.

The value 675 should now appear in cell C10 as shown in Figure 5.69. If this does not happen, click on cell C10 to make it the active cell and carefully repeat this step. Once you have column C entered correctly, save your document.

|   | A | B | C | D | E |
|---|---|---|---|---|---|
| 1 | | | | | |
| 2 | | | MyCourse 101 Grade Components | | |
| 3 | | | | | |
| 4 | Component | | Point Values | | |
| 5 | Two Tests | | 250 | | |
| 6 | Final Exam | | 175 | | |
| 7 | Labs/Homework | | 150 | | |
| 8 | My Project | | 100 | | |
| 9 | | | | | |
| 10 | Total | | 675 | | |
| 11 | | | | | |

Figure 5.69. Grade Calculation Worksheet Partially Completed.

Create a pie chart:

8. You will now create a pie chart to display the percentage that each of the grade components contributes to your total grade. Select *New Pie Chart* from the **Chart** menu. A dialog box similar to that shown in Figure 5.70 will be displayed.

9. Click on the box titled *Plot Values in Column* and enter C. In the remaining boxes enter the values shown in Figure 5.70. [Column C is the location of the data to be plotted in the pie chart. The range of rows that hold the data to be plotted begins with 5 and terminates with 8. Finally, the grade component categories to use for the legend of the pie chart are found in column A].

**Untitled Chart 1**

**Pie Chart Definition:**

**Chart Title:** Untitled

**Plot Values in Column:** c

**From Row:** 5

**Through Row:** 8

**Column of Value Titles:** A

Cancel   Plot It!

Figure 5.70. Example Database Data Displayed in List Mode.

10. Next, give your chart a title by entering the title *Grade Components* into the box named *Chart Title* in Figure 5.70. Now click the *Plot It* button to display your chart as illustrated in Figure 5.71.

11. Notice in Figure 5.71 that the chart itself has been named *Pie Chart #1*. To do this for your chart, double click in your chart window to access the chart definition dialog box (shown in Figure 5.70). When this box appears, select the *Change Chart Name* command from the **Edit** menu. Type the name *Pie Chart #1* into the resulting dialog box, then click *OK*. When you are returned to the chart definition dialog box, click the *Plot It* button once again to display the chart of Figure 5.71, complete with its new name.

12. Save your spreadsheet document — remember that any chart definitions are saved automatically with your worksheet whenever you save a spreadsheet document.

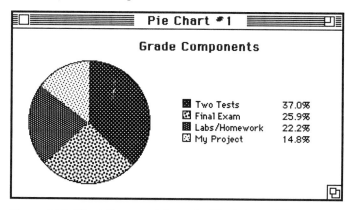

**Figure 5.71.** Chart Generated from the Worksheet of Figure 5.70.

13. Alter the chart size by placing the mouse pointer in the size box at the lower right-hand corner of the screen and dragging. Practice changing the chart size until you feel comfortable with this operation. Click the close box on the *Chart* window to return to the worksheet.

Enter formulas to compute percentage grade factors:

14. The formula to compute grade component percentages requires as a first step dividing the points in a given grade component by the total number of points awarded.

    Click on cell D4. Enter *Percentages* and press *Return*.

    Click on cell D5. Enter =, then move the mouse pointer to cell C5 and click. The value C5 will be entered automatically for you.

    Type / *$C$10* and click on the *Check* box.

377

Your worksheet should now appear as shown in Figure 5.72. Note the formula in the formula bar.

| D5 | | =(C5/$C$10) | | |
|---|---|---|---|---|

**GradeCalc (SS)**

| | A | B | C | D |
|---|---|---|---|---|
| 1 | | | | |
| 2 | | MyCourse 101 Grade Components | | |
| 3 | | | | |
| 4 | Component | | Point Values | Percentages |
| 5 | Two Tests | | 250 | 0.3703703703 |
| 6 | Final Exam | | 175 | |
| 7 | Labs/Homework | | 150 | |
| 8 | My Project | | 100 | |
| 9 | | | | |
| 10 | Total | | 675 | |
| 11 | | | | |

**Figure 5.72.** Inserting the Formula to Calculate Percentages.

15. Next you will format the appearance of the data so that the fraction appears as a percentage. With cell D5 still the active cell, choose option *Set Cell Attributes* from the **Format** menu. The dialog box shown in Figure 5.73 will then appear. Respond as shown there and then click *OK*.

**Set Cell Attributes:**

**Display:**
- ○ General
- ○ Fixed
- ○ Dollar
- ◉ Percent
- ○ Scientific

- ○ Date Short
- ○ Date Medium
- ○ Date Long
- ○ Time
- ☐ Show Day

**Align:**
- ○ Left
- ○ Center
- ○ Right

**Style:**
- ☐ Bold
- ☐ Underline
- ☐ Commas

[2] **Decimal Places**

[ Cancel ] [ OK ]

**Figure 5.73.** Formatting Percentage Values.

16. Now you will replicate the formula in cell D5 to compute the percentages for the other grade components.

Click on cell D5 and drag down to cell D8.

Choose *Fill Down* from the **Edit** menu.

You should now see the values shown in Figure 5.68 produced in column D of your worksheet. Click on cell D6. Note that it contains the formula =C6/$C$10. This is the correct formula for computing the percent that the *Final Exam* row contributes to the grade. Note that the replication of the relative reference C5 in the original formula was changed to C6 by replication. Note also that the absolute reference $C$10 was unchanged by the replication.

17. Next, to enter the formula in cell D10 to sum the percentage components, first click on cell C10. Note that the formula in this cell sums the values in cells C5 through C8 using relative reference. Thus, if you simply replicate this cell's formula to cell D10 it will sum the percentage values in cells D5 through D8. Drag across to cell D10, highlighting both cells. Choose *Fill Right* from the **Edit** menu.

18. Now, format cell D10 so that it displays entries in the same format as cells D5 through D8 (see step 15 if you need to review this process). Your worksheet should now appear just like the one in Figure 5.68. Save your document.

Observe the link between chart and worksheet:

19. You will now make changes on the worksheet and see that any associated charts are automatically updated. Using the size box on the worksheet, resize the worksheet so that only columns A to C are visible.

20. Next, reduce the width of column B until it nearly disappears. The worksheet will then look somewhat like that shown on the left of Figure 5.74.

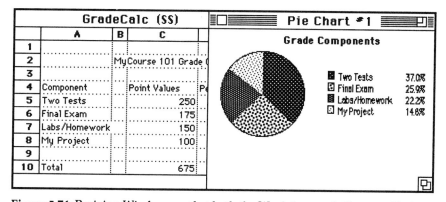

**Figure 5.74:** Resizing Windows so that both the Worksheet and Chart are Visible.

21. Now, from the **Chart** menu select *Draw Chart*. You will see listed in the dialog box, the name of the chart, *Pie Chart #1*, that you created earlier. Double click on this name. The chart will appear.

22. Resize the chart and reposition it so that it appears next to the worksheet as shown in Figure 5.74.

23. Experiment with changing various of the values in cells C5 to C8 and notice that each change is immediately reflected in the chart's display.

24. This completes Project 1. Save your spreadsheet, then quit Works.

## PROJECT 2

In this project you will learn to set up *what if* tables that allow you to investigate how different parameter values influence the results computed. In particular, you will study how the amount of a monthly house payment depends upon the interest rate and the number of years of a loan. For this solution we stress the importance of first setting up a sample calculation that has all of the elements of the *what if* calculation. This sample calculation can then be used to help construct the solution to the more complex problem. Once again, step by step instructions will be given, but they will not be as detailed as for Project 1.

1. Create a folder on your disk and name it *SSProject2*.

2. Open Works SS to get a new untitled document. Save the document inside the folder *SSProject2* under the name *PaymentCalc<your initials>*.

Construct a sample mortgage payment calculation:

You will begin by constructing the sample calculation shown in Figure 5.75. Notice in that figure, that formulas are displayed instead of data for the cells that contain formulas. Displaying formulas allows you to check formula definitions easily. You may tell Works SS to display formula object values instead of data objects values by selecting *Show Formulas* in the **Options** menu. You may reset to data object values by selecting *Show Values* in the same menu.

3. Select *Show Formulas* in the **Options** menu. Now construct the worksheet of Figure 5.75. Note that you will use the Works SS built-in function PMT. Recall that the form for the PMT function is:

=PMT(*rate, nper, pv, fv, type*)

where

   *rate* = interest rate per payment;

   *nper* = number of payment periods;

   *pv* = present value (loan amount);

   *fv* = future value of loan (0.0 if paid off);

   *type* = 0 if payments are due at end of period;

   1 if payments are due at beginning of period.

Make sure that you understand why each formula entry appears as shown in Figure 5.75. Note that given this set up of the sample calculation, changing the *Yearly Interest Rate*, the *Number of Years*, and/or the *Loan Amount* will produce the correct answer for the *Monthly Mortgage Payment*.

|    | A | B |
|----|---|---|
| 1  | | |
| 2  | Sample Calculation of House Payment | |
| 3  | | |
| 4  | Loan Amount | 80,000 |
| 5  | Number of Years | 20 |
| 6  | Number of Payments | =B5*12 |
| 7  | Yearly Interest Rate | .11 |
| 8  | Interest Rate per Payment | =B7/12 |
| 9  | | |
| 10 | Mortgage Payment | =Pmt(B8,B6,B4,0,1) |
| 11 | | |

**Figure 5.75.** Worksheet for Sample Calculation with Formulas Displayed.

4. Select *Show Values* in the **Options** menu. The results you should now see are shown in Figure 5.76. [Recall that the Works SS built-in financial function cash flow conventions state that money you pay out is negative, while money you receive is positive. Because you receive 80,000 as a loan amount the number is positive. Because you pay out the *Monthly Mortgage Payment* it is computed as a negative value by Works SS.

5. Notice that none of the values displayed in Figure 5.76 have been formatted. This is useful for some calculations so that you can check the full accuracy of your results. In this case, format all the cells so that the appearance is more aesthetically pleasing (see rows 2 through 10 in Figure 5.77). Save your document.

|    | A | B |
|----|---|---|
| 1  | | |
| 2  | Sample Calculation of House Payment | |
| 3  | | |
| 4  | Loan Amount | 80000 |
| 5  | Number of Years | 20 |
| 6  | Number of Payments | 240 |
| 7  | Yearly Interest Rate | .11 |
| 8  | Interest Rate per Payment | 0.0091666666 |
| 9  | | |
| 10 | Mortgage Payment | -818.2500881 |
| 11 | | |

**Figure 5.76.** Worksheet for Sample Calculation with Data Displayed.

Compute a *what if* table of values to study the effects of varying parameters:

6.. You will now compute a table of values to study the variation of the mortgage payment with different interest rates and numbers of years for payment. We will choose interest rates of 8, 10, 12 and 14 percent, and the values 10, 20, and 30 for the number of years. Set up the borders of the table as illustrated in row 14 and cells A15 through A17 in Figure 5.77. Type in the table title as shown in cell B12.

7. Enter into cell B15 the formula shown in the formula bar of Figure 5.77.

Note that the form of this formula is chosen to allow replication using *Fill Down* to form column B of the table and *Fill Right* using the column B entries to complete the table. For example, the third parameter of PMT references (with an absolute reference) the *Loan Amount* of the sample calculation. Thus, by changing the *Loan Amount* in cell B4 the entire table will be recomputed automatically.

Carefully reflect on each parameter entry for PMT to understand why a particular choice of relative and/or absolute reference is being made. Note in particular the use of mixed absolute/relative references in the references to cells B14 AND A15. Why are these necessary?

8. Format cell B15 so that it appears as shown in Figure 5.77.

9. Select cell B15 and drag to cell B17. Select the *Fill Down* command from the **Edit** menu to replicate the formula in cell B15 to the cells B16 and B17.

10. Select cell B15 and drag to cell E17. Now, choose the *Fill Right* command from the **Edit** menu to replicate the formulas in cells B15 through B17 to columns C, D, and E.

11. Click in cell D20 and examine the formula in the formula bar closely. Pay particular attention to the way relative and absolute references produced the correct formula for this cell through replication. Save your document.

Extend the *what if* analysis to investigate the total payout for a given loan:

We will now extend the calculations made previously to investigate how the total payout (the sum of all payments made over the lifetime of a loan) varies as we change the interest and year parameters. The bottom of the worksheet in Figure 5.78 illustrates the table you are going to construct.

| B15 | | =Pmt(B$14/12,$A15*12,$B$4,0,1) | | | |
|---|---|---|---|---|---|

**PaymentCalc (SS)**

| | A | B | C | D | E |
|---|---|---|---|---|---|
| 2 | Sample Calculation of House Payment | | | | |
| 3 | | | | | |
| 4 | Loan Amount | $80,000 | | | |
| 5 | Number of Years | 20 | | | |
| 6 | Number of Payments | 240 | | | |
| 7 | Yearly Interest Rate | 11.00% | | | |
| 8 | Interest Rate per Payment | 0.00917 | | | |
| 9 | | | | | |
| 10 | Mortgage Payment | -$818.25 | | | |
| 11 | | | | | |
| 12 | | What if" Table for Mortage Payments | | | |
| 13 | | | | | |
| 14 | | 8.00% | 10.00% | 12.00% | 14.00% |
| 15 | 10 | -964.19 | -1048.47 | -1136.40 | -1227.81 |
| 16 | 20 | -664.72 | -765.64 | -872.15 | -983.34 |
| 17 | 30 | -583.12 | -696.26 | -814.74 | -936.97 |
| 18 | | | | | |

**Figure 5.77.** Constructing a What If Analysis for Mortgage Payments.

12. Set up the new table's borders as shown in row 22 and cells A23 through A25 in Figure 5.78. Because we would like the new table to correspond to the previously entered *Mortgage Payment* table, you will enter the table border values by formula instead of as simple values. Then if we change the border values in the first table, these changes will be made automatically in the second table as well.

Enter =*B14* into cell B22.

Enter =*C14* into cell C22.

Enter =*D14* into cell D22.

Enter =*E14* into cell E22.

Similarly for the columnar border:

Enter =*A15* into cell A23.

Enter =*A16* into cell A24.

Enter =*A17* into cell A25.

13. Type in the table title as shown in cell B20.

14. Enter the formula shown displayed for cell B23 in Figure 5.78. Format the entry in cell B23 as shown in that figure. The ABS

function has been used in the table computation to simplify the charting of the results that we will perform shortly.

15. Replicate the formula in B23 to the range B23:E25 using the *Fill Down* and *Fill Right* commands (see steps 9 and 10 if you need to review this procedure). Your worksheet should now have the data shown in Figure 5.78. Save your document.

16. Try changing the loan amount in cell B4 and observe how the two *what if* tables change values. Can you find a loan amount for which you can afford the payments?

17. Change the interest rate in cell E14 to 15% and observe that the corresponding entry for the second table (in cell E22) changes as well.

18. Change the loan amount in cell B4 back to 80,000 and change the interest rate in cell E14 back to 14%.

| B23 | | =Abs(B15*$A15*12) | | |
|---|---|---|---|---|
| | | PaymentCalc (SS) | | |
| | A | B | C | D | E |

| | A | B | C | D | E |
|---|---|---|---|---|---|
| 11 | | | | | |
| 12 | | What if" Table for Mortage Payments | | | |
| 13 | | | | | |
| 14 | | 8.00% | 10.00% | 12.00% | 14.00% |
| 15 | 10 | -964.19 | -1048.47 | -1136.40 | -1227.81 |
| 16 | 20 | -664.72 | -765.64 | -872.15 | -983.34 |
| 17 | 30 | -583.12 | -696.26 | -814.74 | -936.97 |
| 18 | | | | | |
| 19 | | | | | |
| 20 | | What if" Table for the Total Loan Cost | | | |
| 21 | | | | | |
| 22 | | 8.00% | 10.00% | 12.00% | 14.00% |
| 23 | 10 | 115,703.14 | 125,816.24 | 136,368.43 | 147,336.85 |
| 24 | 20 | 159,532.94 | 183,752.88 | 209,315.38 | 236,002.63 |
| 25 | 30 | 209,924.70 | 250,651.85 | 293,307.35 | 337,307.81 |
| 26 | | | | | |

**Figure 5.78.** Extending Analysis to Include Total Loan Cost.

Produce a chart of the total cost to buy a house:

19. You are going to create the chart shown in Figure 5.79. Select *New Series Chart* from the **Chart** menu. Set up the chart by using the responses of Figure 5.80 in the chart definition dialog box. When you have completed all the entries in the chart definition dialog box, select the *Change Chart Name* command from the **Edit** menu. Type the name *Payout Chart #1* into the resulting dialog box, then click *OK*. When you are returned to the chart definition

dialog box, click the *Plot It!* button to see the chart displayed. Save your document.

20. Close the chart window and return to the worksheet. Change the loan amount in cell B4 to some value of your choice. Observe in your *Total Loan Cost* table the largest payout amount (in cell E25). Remember this number for the next step.

21. Select the *Chart Definition* command from the **Chart** menu, and then double click on your chart's name to open the chart definition dialog box again. Change the value in the *Maximum* box to be the next largest number measured in hundreds of thousands from the maximum payout amount you observed in step 19. For example, if you observed a maximum payout of $478,233.99, then put the value 500000 in the *Maximum* box. This will create a more readable set of vertical values on your chart than if you let Works choose its own maximum value. Click *Plot It!* to see the new chart.

22. This completes Project 2. Save your document and quit Works.

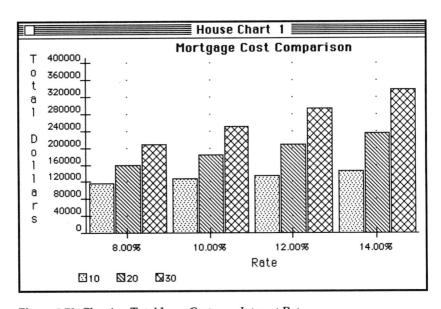

**Figure 5.79.** Charting Total Loan Costs vs. Interest Rate.

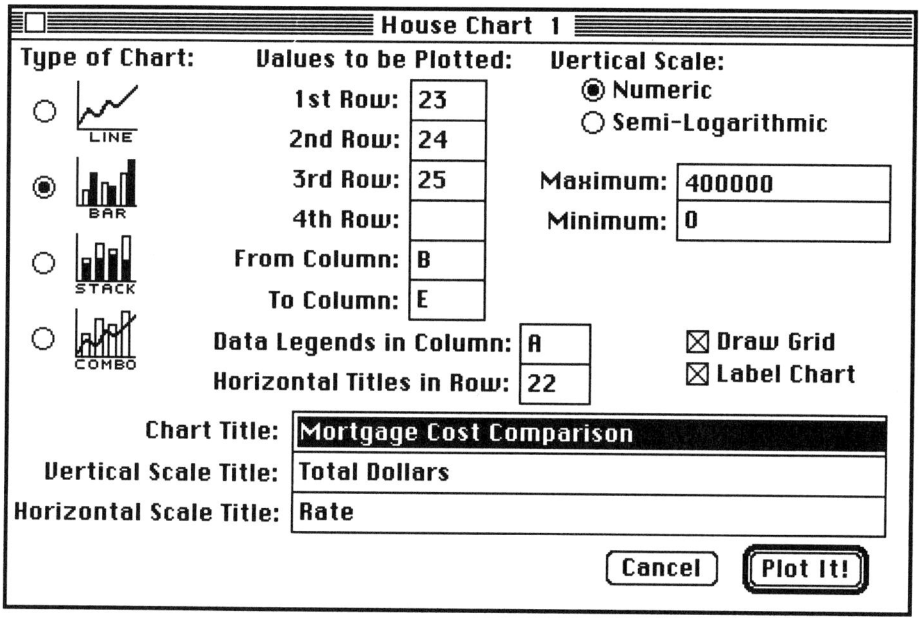

**Figure 5.80.** Setting Up the Total Loan Costs vs. Interest Rate Chart.

# 6

# A PROJECT INTEGRATING THE WORKS MODULES

When you have completed this Works integrated project, you will have:

❑ Produced graphics enhanced documents for a survey packet.

❑ Created two databases for storing survey information.

❑ Merged database information with word processing documents to create individualized forms and letters.

❑ Moved database data to a spreadsheet to perform calculations.

❑ Created charts to illustrate the results of the spreadsheet calculations.

❑ Copied spreadsheet-generated charts and calculations into a word processing report.

## TUTORIAL OUTLINE

# DESCRIPTION OF THE PROJECT

The project in this chapter shows how Works WP, Works DB, and Works SS modules can be used jointly to solve a significant information management problem that could not be done without integrating the use of such programs.  A solution is constructed to a realistic example problem which involves:

> The production of graphics enhanced documents.
>
> Storing and retrieving database information.
>
> Merging database information with word processing documents to create individualized forms and letters.
>
> Moving database data to a spreadsheet to perform calculations and create charts.
>
> Copying spreadsheet-generated charts and calculations into a word processing report.

Although the chapter is written in a tutorial style, not as many detailed steps will be provided as was the case in earlier tutorials in the text. Hence, this example will provide you an opportunity to test what you have previously learned. However, if you do need to refresh your memory on some activity or technique, refer to the earlier more detailed tutorial lessons.

We begin with a high-level description of the problem to be solved. Details will be discussed as we progress through the problem solution. Ace Consultants, Inc. has been hired to investigate the relationships between various lifestyle factors and the values of certain health parameters for males between the ages of 40 and 50. The major steps needed to solve this problem are:

Select at random from census data, names and addresses for males between the ages of 40 and 50. Store this information in a database.

Create a survey packet and send a copy to each chosen participant.

Save the survey results in a database.

Select information from the database and transfer it to a spreadsheet.

Make calculations in the spreadsheet to produce a chart of a lifestyle factor versus a health factor.

Repeat the previous two steps as many times as is necessary to complete the analysis.

Summarize the results in a final report.

# CREATING THE DATABASE OF NAMES AND ADDRESSES

For our survey, assume that names and addresses for males between the ages of 40 and 50 have been selected at random from census-type data. This information is to be stored in a database. Figure 6.1 shows the form for records of the database, and Figure 6.2 shows the nine records of our example database in list format.

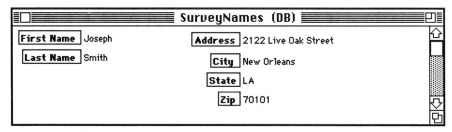

**Figure 6.1.** Database Design for Names and Addresses.

| First Name | Last Name | Address | City | State | Zip |
|------------|-----------|---------|------|-------|-----|
| Joseph | Smith | 2122 Live Oak Street | New Orleans | LA | 70101 |
| Thomas | Dedmond | 1212 Palm Lane | Santa Clara | CA | 95050 |
| William | White | 1020 Lakeview Way | Jonesville | OH | 44444 |
| Paul | Wrangler | 1122 Hillside Dr. | Hyatt | NY | 10800 |
| George | Belton | 1011 Maple Leaf St. | Hazel Green | AL | 35820 |
| Clancy | Duggan | 105 Park Ave. | New York | NY | 10045 |
| Harrison | Matthews | 220 Quincy St. | Roaring Spring | PA | 16673 |
| Joel | Harmon | 102 E. Main | Taylors | SC | 29687 |
| Frank | Walker | 339 Wellington St. | New York | NY | 10034 |

**Figure 6.2.** The Example Database.

**Lesson 1. CREATING THE DATABASE OF NAMES AND ADDRESSES**

Create a Works database to hold the names and addresses for our project by performing the following.

- Create a new folder on your disk and name it *Works Project*.

- Create the database and construct the form of Figure 6.1 using Works DB.

- Enter the records shown in Figure 6.2 into the database. You may use either the above form display or a list display mode for data entry.

- Save the database in the folder *Works Project* with the name *SurveyNames<your initials>*.

# CREATING THE SURVEY PACKET

## DESCRIPTION OF THE SURVEY PACKET

We will mail a packet to all chosen participants and encourage them to participate by offering them a gift. Each of the documents in the packet is to be created using Works WP and is to contain graphics to make them more interesting. Appealing, easy-to-read, easy-to-complete documents are essential to obtain a high response rate from the chosen participants. The merge feature of Works is to be used with the WP documents and the *SurveyNames* database to create an inside address and salutation on each copy of the documents. The packet will consist of:

A form letter briefly describing the survey and asking for participation. See Figures 6.3 and 6.4.

A gift sheet describing (and showing diagrams of) the gifts offered. The participant is to return this sheet, with his choice of gift marked, along with his portion of the survey. See Figure 6.5.

Part A of the survey to be filled out by the participant. See Figure 6.6.

Part B of the survey to be filled out by a physician. See Figure 6.7. Included at the bottom of this sheet will be the physician's reimbursement form.

**Ace Consultants, Inc.**
**103 South Elm Street**
**Nashua, NH 03061**

March 12, 1989

Mr. SurveyNames: First Name  SurveyNames: Last Name
SurveyNames: Address
SurveyNames: City , SurveyNames: State  SurveyNames: Zip

Dear Mr. SurveyNames: Last Name

    Your name has been selected at random by our computer as a participant in a nationwide survey to assess the effects of certain lifestyle factors on important health parameters.  As a token of our appreciation for your participation in this survey, we would like to send you one of the gifts shown on the enclosed gift sheet.  Just check the gift you would prefer and return the gift sheet with your survey.

    It will take you less than 15 minutes to complete Part A of the survey and place it in the postage-paid return envelope.  The completion of Part B of the survey will require you to make a brief visit, at our expense, to your family doctor.

                          Sincerely,

                          John H. Watkins
                          Chief, Survey Division

**Figure 6.3.** Form Letter in Merged Form.

**Ace Consultants, Inc.**
**103 South Elm Street**
**Nashua, NH 03061**

March 12, 1989

Mr. Joseph Smith
2122 Live Oak Street
New Orleans, LA 70101

Dear Mr. Smith:

Your name has been selected at random by our computer as a participant in a nationwide survey to assess the effects of certain lifestyle factors on important health parameters.  As a token of our appreciation for your participation in this survey, we would like to send you one of the gifts shown on the enclosed gift sheet.  Just check the gift you would prefer and return the gift sheet with your survey.

It will take you less than 15 minutes to complete Part A of the survey and place it in the postage-paid return envelope.  The completion of Part B of the survey will require you to make a brief visit, at our expense, to your family doctor.

Sincerely,

John H. Watkins
Chief, Survey Division

**Figure 6.4.** Form Letter in Regular Form.

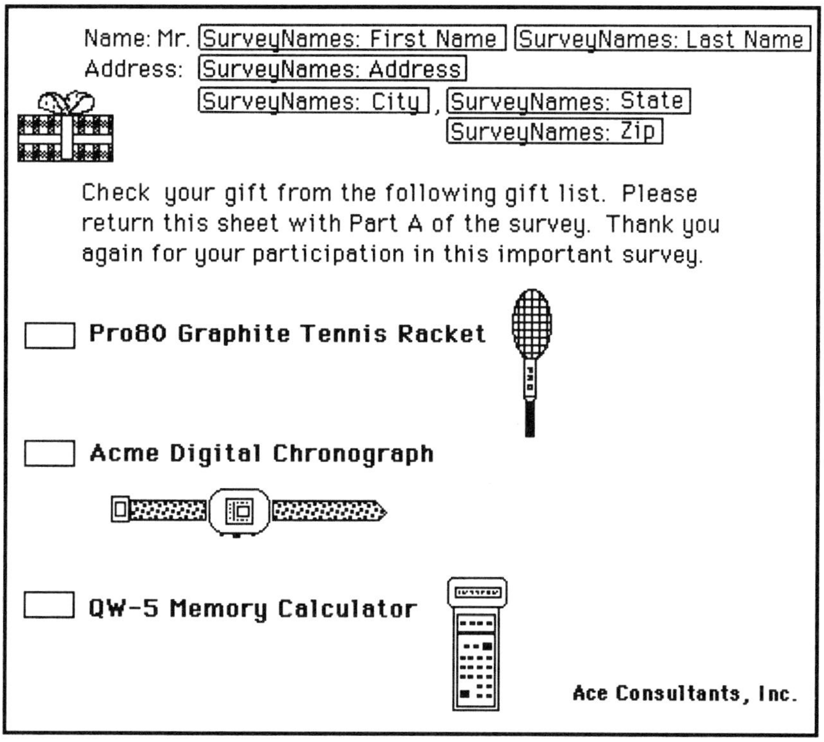

Name: Mr. [SurveyNames: First Name] [SurveyNames: Last Name]
Address: [SurveyNames: Address]
[SurveyNames: City] , [SurveyNames: State]
[SurveyNames: Zip]

Check your gift from the following gift list. Please
return this sheet with Part A of the survey. Thank you
again for your participation in this important survey.

Pro80 Graphite Tennis Racket

Acme Digital Chronograph

QW-5 Memory Calculator

Ace Consultants, Inc.

**Figure 6.5.** The Gift Sheet.

397

```
┌────────────────────────────────────────────────────────┐
│              Ace  Consultants, Inc.                      │
│         Lifestyle and Health Parameter                   │
│                   Survey                                 │
│                                                          │
│  ┌────────┐                                              │
│  │ Part A │                                              │
│  └────────┘                                              │
│                                                          │
│  Name: Mr. [SurveyNames: First Name] [SurveyNames: Last Name] │
│  Address: [SurveyNames: Address]                         │
│             [SurveyNames: City] , [SurveyNames: State]   │
│  Age [   ]                         [SurveyNames: Zip]    │
│                                                          │
│  Occupation Code         1 = Executive/Professional      │
│        [ ]               2 = Manager                     │
│                          3 = Clerical Worker             │
│                          4 = Laborer                     │
│                          5 = Other (specify) _____   │
│                                                          │
│  Exercise Pattern        1 = Frequent (6 or more times per week) │
│        [ ]               2 = Regular  (3-5 times per week) │
│                          3 = Infrequent (1-2 times per week) │
│                          4 = No regular exercise pattern │
│                                                          │
│  How often do you eat:                                   │
│        [ ] Beef?         1 = More than 5 times per week   │
│        [ ] Poultry?      2 = 3 or 4 times per week        │
│        [ ] Fish?         3 = 1 or 2 times per week        │
│        [ ] Dairy Products? 4 = Less than once per week    │
│                                                          │
│  How would you rate      1 = Highly stressful            │
│  the stress level of     2 = Moderately stressful        │
│  your job?               3 = Somewhat stressful          │
│        [ ]               4 = Not stressful at all        │
│                                                          │
│  Cigarette Smoking       1 =  2 or more packs per day    │
│  Habits                  2 =  Between 1/2 and 2 packs per day │
│        [ ]               3 =  10 or fewer cigarettes per day │
│                          4 =  Do not smoke at all        │
└────────────────────────────────────────────────────────┘
```

**Figure 6.6.** Survey Part A, Recipients Form.

```
┌─────────────────────────────────────────────────────────┐
│              Ace   Consultants, Inc.          ╱◇╲╔═╗      │
│          Lifestyle and Health Parameter       ╲ A█████ I  │
│                     Survey                     ╱◇╲╚═╝      │
│                                                ▬▬▬▬▬       │
│   ┌──────────┐                                            │
│   │ Part B   │                                            │
│   └──────────┘                                            │
│                                                           │
│   Name: Mr. [SurveyNames: First Name] [SurveyNames: Last Name] │
│   Address:  [SurveyNames: Address]                        │
│             [SurveyNames: City] , [SurveyNames: State]    │
│                                   [SurveyNames: Zip]      │
│                                                           │
│  ┌──────────────────────────────────────────────────┐   │
│  │ To the doctor:                                     │   │
│  │      After completing this portion of the survey, please mail │
│  │ this sheet using the prepaid envelope. Be sure to fill in the │
│  │ bottom portion completely, so that we can compensate you │
│  │ promptly. Thank you very much for assisting in this important │
│  │ project.                                           │   │
│  └──────────────────────────────────────────────────┘   │
│                                                           │
│   Height [    ]    Weight [    ]    Pulse Rate [    ]     │
│                                                           │
│   Respiration Rate [    ]   Blood Pressure [    ] / [    ]│
│                                                           │
│   Blood Hemoglobin Level [    ]                           │
│                                                           │
│   Serum Cholesterol Level [    ]                          │
│                                                           │
│  ─ ─ ─ ─ ─ ─ ─ ─ ─ ─ ─ ─ ─ ─ ─ ─ ─ ─ ─ ─ ─ ─ ─ ─ ─ ─    │
│                      (Please Type or Print)               │
│                                                           │
│   Doctor's Name:  _____    │
│   Mailing Address: _____    │
│                    _____    │
│                    _____    │
│                                                           │
└─────────────────────────────────────────────────────────┘
```

**Figure 6.7.** Survey Part B, Doctors Form.

## THE FORM LETTER

The goal of this activity is to produce the form letter that appears in Figures 6.3 and 6.4. The method suggested is only one of many possibilities. You could do the steps in a different order.

- Open Works WP and create a new word processing document.

- Type the Ace letterhead in bold at the top right-hand side of the document in size 10 font. Set a left tab to align the separate lines.

- Put in a blank line and then type the date in normal text, size 12 font. See Figure 6.3 for an illustration.

- Type *Mr.* after spacing down about 6 lines. Type *Dear Mr.* after spacing down several more lines. Type the remainder of the letter (except for the merged database fields) as it appears in Figure 6.3.

- Open the *SurveyNames* database, and then make the form letter the active window by selecting it using the **Window** menu.

- Enter the database field names into the form letter in the positions illustrated in Figure 6.3. Recall that this requires using the *Prepare to Merge* command in the **Edit** menu. The dialog box is shown in Figure 6.8.

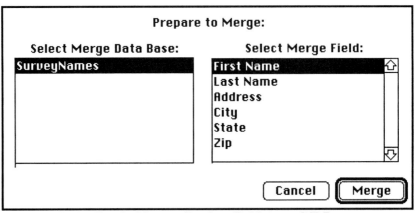

**Figure 6.8.** Dialog Box for Merging Database Fields into a WP Document.

- Choose the *Draw On* command from the **Edit** menu to move to graphics mode. Create the logo for Ace Consultants, as shown in Figure 6.9, at the top of the document.

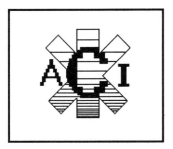

**Figure 6.9.** Ace Logo to Be Created in Works WP Drawing Mode.

- Save the final version of the form letter in the folder *Works Project* with the name *FormLetter<your initials>*.

## THE GIFT SHEET

The gift sheet portion of the mailing packet is shown in Figure 6.5. Notice that it also uses the merge feature and that it contains several figures. The goal of this activity is to produce the gift sheet.

- Open a new empty word processing window.

- Type *Name: Mr.* after spacing down a few lines.

- Type *Address* after spacing down several more lines.

- Type the remainder of the gift sheet as it appears in Figure 6.5. Do not concern yourself too much with the line spacing—you can edit the gift sheet to obtain proper spacing after you have added the graphics.

- Open the *SurveyNames* database, and then make the gift sheet the active window by selecting it using the **Window** menu.

- Enter the database field names into the gift sheet in the positions shown in Figure 6.5. Recall that this requires using the *Prepare to Merge* command in the **Edit** menu. The dialog box was shown in the description of the previous project activity.

- Draw the boxes for selecting a gift using the Works draw feature. It is suggested that you draw one box (e.g., the box before Pro80 Graphite Tennis Racket). Then that box can be copied and pasted in other locations. You may need to move the boxes to align them.

401

- Create the figures for the gift box, tennis racket, chronograph, and calculator, which are illustrated in Figure 6.10, and place them in the appropriate places within the document.

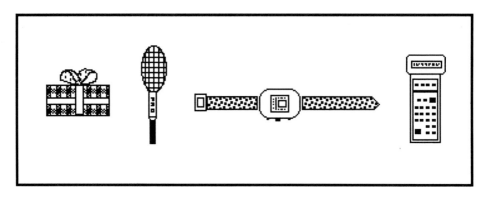

**Figure 6.10.** Graphics Objects for the Gift Sheet.

- Save the final version of the gift sheet in the folder *Works Project* with the name *GiftSheet<your initials>*.

## THE SURVEY FORMS

In this activity you are to create the survey forms that are shown in Figures 6.6 and 6.7. There are no new concepts required to prepare these forms, so the details on how to proceed are being omitted. Note that you need not create new Ace logos, because you can easily copy your logo from the *FormLetter* document saved previously, by opening that document at the same time you have your survey forms documents open. Save the documents as *SurveyPartA* and *SurveyPartB*, respectively.

# CREATING THE SURVEY DATABASE

In this lesson you will create a database to hold the results of the survey. The advantage of using a database in this instance is that the selection features of Works DB can be used to isolate particular sets of records for later analysis.

We can create the new database (see Figure 6.11) and import the name and address data from the old database *SurveyNames* at the same time by opening the *SurveyNames* database, adding the new fields, and then saving the database under a new name.

Notice in Figure 6.11 that the field names are displayed in a manner to mimic the layout of the survey forms. This will minimize errors in the process of transferring the survey data from the returned forms to the database. Using the *Tab* key will access the fields in exactly the same order as they appear in the survey forms.

## THE NEW DATABASE

To create the new database, follow these steps.

- Open Works and open the *SurveyNames* database.

- Add the following new fields to the database. The data type for each new field is given. For those fields that are not of type text, you will need to use the *Set Field Attributes* command in the **Format** menu to define the appropriate data type.

| Field | Data Type |
|---|---|
| *Survey Returned?* | Text |
| *Age* | Numeric, 0 decimals |
| *Occupation* | Text (we won't do arithmetic on the categories) |
| *Exercise* | Text |

| | |
|---|---|
| *Beef* | Text |
| *Poultry* | Text |
| *Fish* | Text |
| *Dairy* | Text |
| *JobStress* | Text |
| *Smoking* | Text |
| *Height* | Numeric, 0 decimals |
| *Weight* | Numeric, 0 decimals |
| *Pulse* | Numeric, 0 decimals |
| *Respiration* | Numeric, 0 decimals |
| *Blood Pressure 1* | Numeric, 0 decimals |
| *Blood Pressure 2* | Numeric, 0 decimals |
| *Hemoglobin* | Numeric, 2 decimals |
| *Cholesterol* | Numeric, 2 decimals |

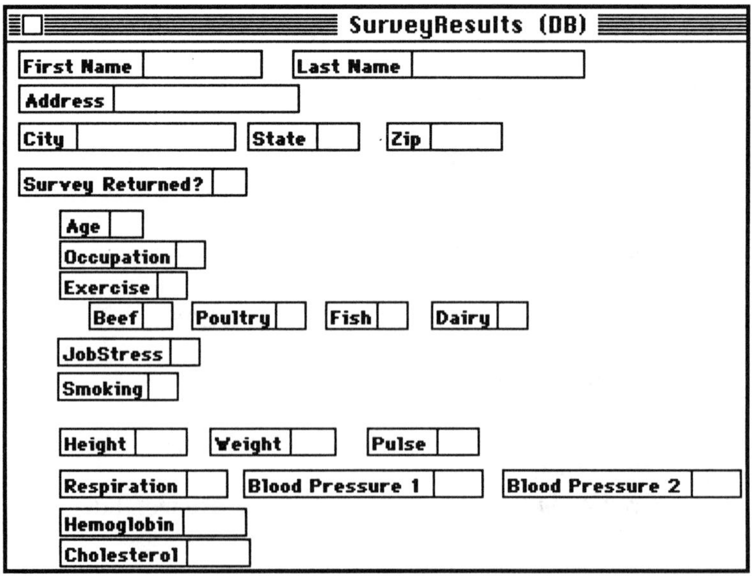

**Figure 6.11.** Design of the *SurveyResults* Database.

- Move the fields on the database form to obtain a design that is similar that shown in Figure 6.11.

- Enter the data shown in Figure 6.28 into the database. You may find the list dipslay mode more convenient for this purpose.

- Save the database in the folder *Works Project* with the name *SurveyResults<your initials>*.

## ADDING A COMPUTED FIELD

In our analysis of the collected data, we will be interested in the weight to height ratio (rather than the individual weight and height values). To facilitate this analysis, we will add a new field to the database called *HW Ratio*. This will be a computed field. Proceed as follows.

- Open the *SurveyResults* database, and display the database in list mode (it isn't necessary to use list mode, but you will be able to see more clearly the effect of creating the computed field in this mode).

- Select the *Add New Field* command from the **Edit** menu.

- Type the new field name, *HW Ratio*, when the box shown in Figure 6.12 is displayed:

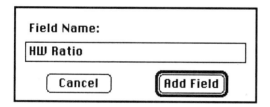

**Figure 6.12.** Dialog Box for Adding a New Database Field.

- Once you have added the *HW Ratio* field to the database, select it by pointing at the name of the field and clicking.

- Select the *Set Field Attributes* command from the **Format** menu. The dialog box of Figure 6.13 will be displayed. Make the entries shown in the figure (don't forget to click the *Computed* box) and click the *OK* button. The dialog box will disappear, the *HW Ratio* field will be filled with zeros, and an equal mark will be entered in the formula bar.

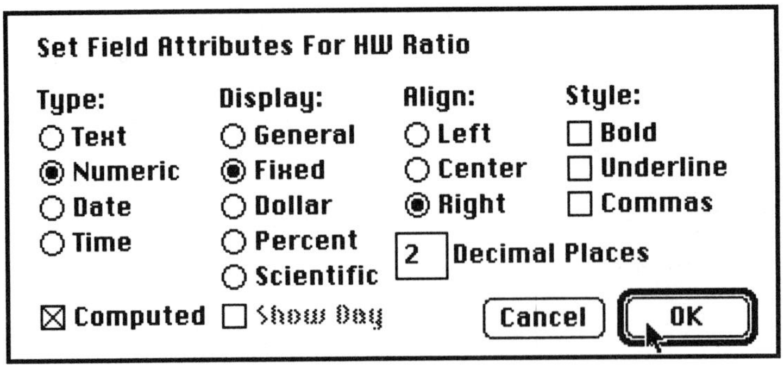

```
Set Field Attributes For HW Ratio

Type:          Display:        Align:        Style:
○ Text        ○ General       ○ Left        ☐ Bold
◉ Numeric     ◉ Fixed         ○ Center      ☐ Underline
○ Date        ○ Dollar        ◉ Right       ☐ Commas
○ Time        ○ Percent       ┌─┐
              ○ Scientific    │2│ Decimal Places
                              └─┘
☒ Computed  ☐ Show Day        ┌────────┐ ┌──────────┐
                              │ Cancel │ │    OK    │
                              └────────┘ └──────────┘
```

**Figure 6.13.** Setting Parameters for a Calculated Field.


- To make the computation, select the cell of the first record under the heading *HW Ratio*. Type the following formula into the formula bar:

  Weight/Height

  When the *Accept* box in the formula bar is clicked, the computed values shown in Figure 6.14 will be shown.

- Save the database.

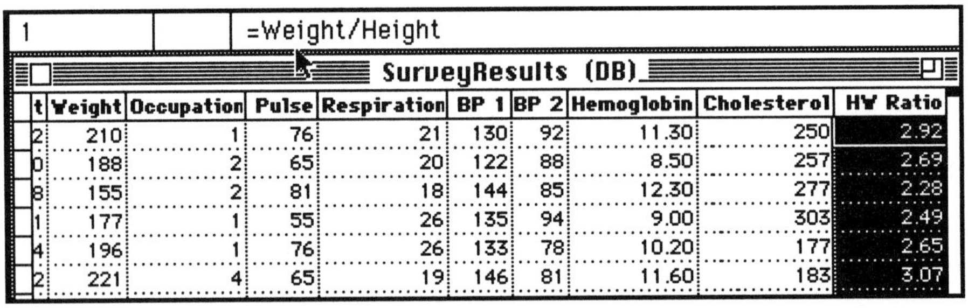

| 1 | | =Weight/Height | | | | | | | |
|---|---|---|---|---|---|---|---|---|---|

SurveyResults (DB)

| t | Weight | Occupation | Pulse | Respiration | BP 1 | BP 2 | Hemoglobin | Cholesterol | HW Ratio |
|---|---|---|---|---|---|---|---|---|---|
| 2 | 210 | 1 | 76 | 21 | 130 | 92 | 11.30 | 250 | 2.92 |
| 0 | 188 | 2 | 65 | 20 | 122 | 88 | 8.50 | 257 | 2.69 |
| 8 | 155 | 2 | 81 | 18 | 144 | 85 | 12.30 | 277 | 2.28 |
| 1 | 177 | 1 | 55 | 26 | 135 | 94 | 9.00 | 303 | 2.49 |
| 4 | 196 | 1 | 76 | 26 | 133 | 78 | 10.20 | 177 | 2.65 |
| 2 | 221 | 4 | 65 | 19 | 146 | 81 | 11.60 | 183 | 3.07 |

**Figure 6.14.** Part of the Database after Computing HW Ratio.

# ANALYSIS OF THE DATA

Many analyses can be performed with our data. We make a single analysis to illustrate the approach. We will prepare a spreadsheet to allow us to explore the relationships between occupation categories and the various health parameters: *Pulse, Respiration, BP1, BP2, Hemoglobin, Cholesterol,* and *HW Ratio*. In particular, we will graphically display the relationship between occupations and average pulse rates. (*Note:* These data are not based on actual survey results and any results derived from them have no scientific validity.)

## SELECTING DATA FOR ANALYSIS

Because we first wish to collect information for each occupation separately, we set a record selection rule in the database to choose only those records with *Occupation* = 1. (Later this process will be repeated for other occupation categories.) The screen in Figure 6.15 shows the fields of interest after the selection. The records are selected and can be copied to the Clipboard and then transferred to a spreadsheet. Note that we have moved the *Occupation* field to the right of its original position (by the way, this won't affect our form display — only the list display) so it will be next to the health parameters.

Selecting the set of records having *Occupation* = 1 is accomplished as follows.

- Open the *SurveyResults* database.

- Move the *Occupation* field to the right of the *Weight* field, as shown in Figure 6.15.

- Select the *Record Selection* command from the **Organize** menu. The *Record Selection* dialog box will be displayed.

- In the *Record Selection* boxes select the *Occupation* field in the left box and the *equals* operator in the right box.

- Type *1* into the box titled *Record Comparison Information*.

- Click the *Install Rule* button.

- Click the *Select* button. A screen will be displayed that is similar to Figure 6.15 except that the records are not selected.

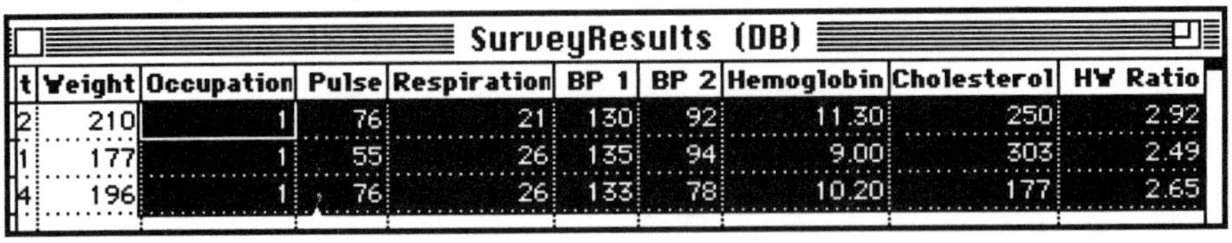

| t | Weight | Occupation | Pulse | Respiration | BP 1 | BP 2 | Hemoglobin | Cholesterol | HW Ratio |
|---|--------|------------|-------|-------------|------|------|------------|-------------|----------|
| 2 | 210 | 1 | 76 | 21 | 130 | 92 | 11.30 | 250 | 2.92 |
| 1 | 177 | 1 | 55 | 26 | 135 | 94 | 9.00 | 303 | 2.49 |
| 4 | 196 | 1 | 76 | 26 | 133 | 78 | 10.20 | 177 | 2.65 |

SurveyResults (DB)

**Figure 6.15.** Selection of Fields of Interest in Records with *Occupation* Equal to 1.

- Select the cells by dragging diagonally from the first cell of the *Occupation* column to the last filled cell of the *HW Ratio* column. The screen should now look like Figure 6.15.

## TRANSFERRING DATABASE DATA TO A SPREADSHEET

Transfer the selected Works DB data to a new Works SS worksheet by performing the following.

- Select the *Copy* command from the **Edit** menu. This will place a copy of the data (and the column titles) on the Clipboard.

- Create a worksheet to receive the information by selecting the *New* command from the **File** menu, and then double clicking the spreadsheet icon in the resulting dialog box.

- Save the new worksheet in your folder *Works Project* with the name *OccupationAnalysis<your initials>*.

- Select cells A1 through H4 on the *OccupationAnalysis* worksheet. Note that the size of this rectangular area corresponds to the number of data cells (plus one row for the column titles) selected earlier and stored on the Clipboard. This is illustrated in Figure 6.16.

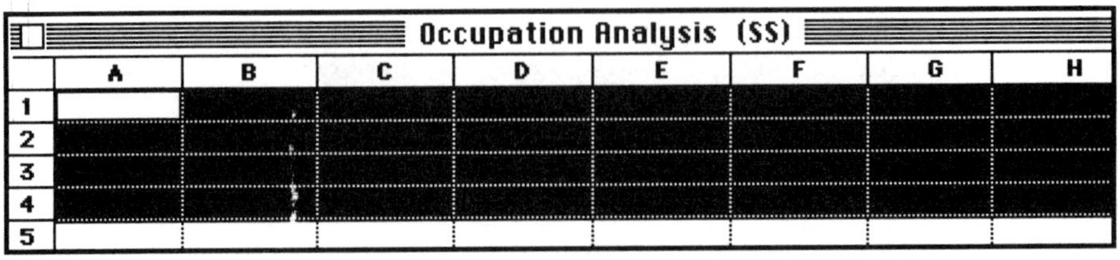

Occupation Analysis (SS)

| | A | B | C | D | E | F | G | H |
|---|---|---|---|---|---|---|---|---|
| 1 | | | | | | | | |
| 2 | | | | | | | | |
| 3 | | | | | | | | |
| 4 | | | | | | | | |
| 5 | | | | | | | | |

**Figure 6.16.** Spreadsheet with Area Selected for Pasting.

- Select the *Paste* command from the **Edit** menu.

- Resize your columns to get a result similar to that shown in Figure 6.17.

- Save the spreadsheet.

| | A | B | C | D | E | F | G | H |
|---|---|---|---|---|---|---|---|---|
| | Occupation | Pulse | Respiration | BP 1 | BP 2 | Hemoglobin | Cholesterol | HW Ratio |
| 2 | 1 | 76 | 21 | 130 | 92 | 11.30 | 250 | 2.92 |
| 3 | 1 | 55 | 26 | 135 | 94 | 9.00 | 303 | 2.49 |
| 4 | 1 | 76 | 26 | 133 | 78 | 10.20 | 177 | 2.65 |

**Occupation Analysis (SS)**

**Figure 6.17.** The Spreadsheet after Pasting *Occupation* Data and Resizing Columns.

## MAKING COMPUTATIONS

Make computations for the average and standard deviation on the *OccupationAnalysis* worksheet by proceeding as follows:

- Type *Average* in cell A6, and type *Std. Deviation* in cell A7.

- To compute the value of the average for *Pulse*:

  - Select cell B6.

  - Select the *Paste Function* command from the **Edit** menu. Find the *AVERAGE* function in the scroll box, click it, and click the *OK* button. The partial formula, =*AVERAGE(I)*, will appear in the formula bar with the insertion bar positioned between the parentheses.

  - Select the range for the computation by pointing to cell B2 and dragging to cell B4. This is illustrated in Figure 6.18.

  - Click the check box in the formula bar, and the computed average will appear in cell B6.

| B6 | ☒☑ | =AVERAGE(B2:B4) | | | | | | |
|----|----|----|----|----|----|----|----|----|

**Occupation Analysis (SS)**

| | A | B | C | D | E | F | G | H |
|---|---|---|---|---|---|---|---|---|
| 1 | Occupation | Pulse | Respiration | BP 1 | BP 2 | Hemoglobin | Chloresterol | HV Ratio |
| 2 | 1 | 76 | 21 | 130 | 92 | 11.30 | 250 | 2.92 |
| 3 | 1 | 55 | 26 | 135 | 94 | 9.00 | 303 | 2.49 |
| 4 | 1 | 76 | 26 | 133 | 78 | 10.20 | 177 | 2.65 |
| 5 | | | | | | | | |
| 6 | Average | | | | | | | |
| 7 | Std. Deviation | | | | | | | |

Figure 6.18. Entering the Formula into Cell A6.

- Compute the value of the standard deviation for *Pulse* by performing steps similar to those just completed for the computation of the average.

  - Select cell B7.

  - Find the *STDEV* function in the *Paste Function* submenu under the **Edit** menu.

  - Paste the formula =*STDEV()* in cell B7.

  - Select the range B2 through B4. This is illustrated in Figure 6.19.

  - Click the check box, and the computed standard deviation will appear in cell B7.

- Format your entries for the average and standard deviation so that two digits appear to the right of the decimal.

- Save the spreadsheet.

| B7 | ☒☑ | =STDEV(B2:B4) | | | | | | |
|----|----|----|----|----|----|----|----|----|

**Occupation Analysis (SS)**

| | A | B | C | D | E | F | G | H |
|---|---|---|---|---|---|---|---|---|
| 1 | Occupation | Pulse | Respiration | BP 1 | BP 2 | Hemoglobin | Chloresterol | HV Ratio |
| 2 | 1 | 76 | 21 | 130 | 92 | 11.30 | 250 | 2.92 |
| 3 | 1 | 55 | 26 | 135 | 94 | 9.00 | 303 | 2.49 |
| 4 | 1 | 76 | 26 | 133 | 78 | 10.20 | 177 | 2.65 |
| 5 | | | | | | | | |
| 6 | Average | 69 | | | | | | |
| 7 | Std. Deviation | | | | | | | |

Figure 6.19. Entering the Formula into Cell A7.

- Make the computations for the other health categories by selecting cells B6 through H7 and choosing the *Fill Right* command of the **Edit** menu. The resulting spreadsheet is shown in Figure 6.20.

**Occupation Analysis (SS)**

| | A | B | C | D | E | F | G | H |
|---|---|---|---|---|---|---|---|---|
| 1 | Occupation | Pulse | Respiration | BP 1 | BP 2 | Hemoglobin | Chloresterol | HW Ratio |
| 2 | 1 | 76 | 21 | 130 | 92 | 11.30 | 250 | 2.92 |
| 3 | 1 | 55 | 26 | 135 | 94 | 9.00 | 303 | 2.49 |
| 4 | 1 | 76 | 26 | 133 | 78 | 10.20 | 177 | 2.65 |
| 5 | | | | | | | | |
| 6 | Average | 69.00 | 24.33 | 132.67 | 88.00 | 10.17 | 243.33 | 2.69 |
| 7 | Std. Deviation | 12.12 | 2.89 | 2.52 | 8.72 | 1.15 | 63.26 | 0.21 |
| 8 | | | | | | | | |

**Figure 6.20.** The Worksheet after the Formulas Are Filled Right.

Because the goal is to produce an analysis of occupations versus pulse health parameters, information for the second and remaining occupations must be selected from the database and copied to the spreadsheet. Corresponding calculations can then made for these data.

- Create entries on the *Occupation Analysis* worksheet for *Occupation* = 2 by repeating the above steps with appropriate changes in the locations of the cells used. The resulting spreadsheet is shown in Figure 6.21.

- Complete the computations for the remaining occupations.

- Save the spreadsheet.

**Occupation Analysis (SS)**

| | A | B | C | D | E | F | G | H |
|---|---|---|---|---|---|---|---|---|
| 1 | Occupation | Pulse | Respiration | BP 1 | BP 2 | Hemoglobin | Chloresterol | HW Ratio |
| 2 | 1 | 76 | 21 | 130 | 92 | 11.30 | 250 | 2.92 |
| 3 | 1 | 55 | 26 | 135 | 94 | 9.00 | 303 | 2.49 |
| 4 | 1 | 76 | 26 | 133 | 78 | 10.20 | 177 | 2.65 |
| 5 | | | | | | | | |
| 6 | Average | 69.00 | 24.33 | 132.67 | 88.00 | 10.17 | 243.33 | 2.69 |
| 7 | Std. Deviation | 12.12 | 2.89 | 2.52 | 8.72 | 1.15 | 63.26 | 0.21 |
| 8 | | | | | | | | |
| 9 | | | | | | | | |
| 10 | | | | | | | | |
| 11 | Occupation | Pulse | Respiration | BP 1 | BP 2 | Hemoglobin | Chloresterol | HW Ratio |
| 12 | 2 | 65 | 20 | 122 | 88 | 8.50 | 257 | 2.69 |
| 13 | 2 | 81 | 18 | 144 | 85 | 12.30 | 277 | 2.28 |
| 14 | | | | | | | | |
| 15 | Average | 73.00 | 19.00 | 133.00 | 86.50 | 10.40 | 267.00 | 2.48 |
| 16 | Std. Deviation | 11.31 | 1.41 | 15.56 | 2.12 | 2.69 | 14.14 | 0.29 |
| 17 | | | | | | | | |

**Figure 6.21.** The Worksheet after Calculations for *Occupation 2*.

## CHARTING RESULTS OF THE CALCULATIONS

Next you will produce the screen of Figure 6.22 in preparation for charting *Pulse Rate* versus *Occupation*. To make a series chart, information must be copied from other parts of the spreadsheet to put it in the necessary row form .

- Copy *Occupation* and average *Pulse* data to rows 26 and 27 of the *Occupation Analysis* worksheet. The simplest method is to type the labels and values for the occupation categories. The values in row 27 can be generated as follows:

- Select cell B27 and type =B6 into the formula bar. Click the *Accept Box*. The advantage of this method over simply entering the value 69.00 in cell B27 is that if the calculations that produce the average pulse rate for occupation category 1 change later, this change will be automatically updated in cell B27.

- Type in similar formulas for cells C27, D27, and E27. (Note that the *Fill Right* command does us no good in this situation because the relationships between the cells being referenced and the cells into which we are putting the formulas do not form a consistent template.)

- You should have the data shown in Figure 6.22 when you finish the above steps.

| | A | B | C | D | E | F | G |
|---|---|---|---|---|---|---|---|
| 25 | | | | | | | |
| 26 | Occupation | 1 | 2 | 3 | 4 | | |
| 27 | Avg Pulse | 69.00 | 73.00 | 74.50 | 65.50 | | |
| 28 | | | | | | | |
| 29 | | | | | | | |

Occupation Analysis (SS)

Figure 6.22. Data in Row Form for Series Chart Creation.

Create the *Pulse Rates* chart by performing the following:

- Select the *New Series Chart* command from the **Chart** menu. The dialog box of Figure 6.23 will be displayed.

- Make the entries in the dialog box that are shown in Figure 6.23.

- Select the *Change Chart Name* command from the **Edit** menu, and name your chart *Pulse Rates Chart*.

- Click the *Plot It!* button. The chart of Figure 6.24 will be displayed.

- Save your spreadsheet.

**Pulse Rates Chart**

Type of Chart: Values to be Plotted: Vertical Scale:

⊙ LINE

1st Row: 27

○ Numeric
○ Semi-Logarithmic

2nd Row:

○ BAR

3rd Row:

Maximum:

4th Row:

Minimum: 0

○ STACK

From Column: B

To Column: E

○ COMBO

Data Legends in Column: A

Horizontal Titles in Row: 26

☒ Draw Grid
☒ Label Chart

Chart Title: Average Pulse Rates

Vertical Scale Title: Averages

Horizontal Scale Title: Occupations

Cancel     Plot It!

Figure 6.23. Dialog Box for Creating the Series Chart.

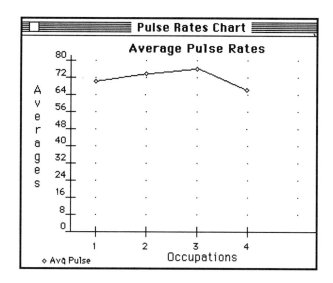

Figure 6.24. Series Chart for OccupationsVersus Pulse Averages.

413

# PREPARING A FINAL REPORT

When the report detailing the results of the study is prepared for the agency that requested the study, charts and computations will be included. It is easy to copy any Works SS charts or computations and paste them into a Works WP report.

- Open a new Works WP document and save it in your folder *Works Project* as *SurveyReport<your initials>*.

- Open your Works SS document *OccupationAnalysis*, and choose the *Draw Chart* command from the **Chart** menu.

- Plot the chart *Pulse Rates Chart* by double clicking on its name in the resulting dialog box.

- Resize the displayed chart to a smaller size, similar to that illustrated in Figure 6.25, by using the grow box in its lower right corner.

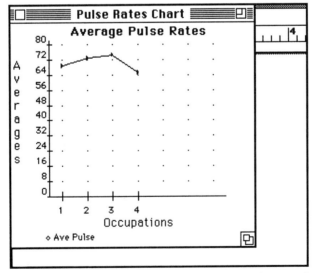

**Figure 6.25.** Resizing a Chart in Preparation for Copying It.

- Select *Copy* from the **Edit** menu to copy the chart to the Clipboard.

- Select the document *SurveyReport* from the **Window** menu, and then paste the chart into the WP document.

- Select the *OccupationAnalysis* worksheet from the **Window** menu.

- Select the *No Grid* option from the SS **Options** menu.

- Select the data from which the *Pulse Rate Chart* was created. The situation is illustrated in Figure 6.26.

| | A | B | C | D | E | F | G |
|---|---|---|---|---|---|---|---|
| **17** | Occupation | Ave | Ave | | Ave | Ave | Ave | Ave |
| **18** | | Pulse | Respiration | BP 1 | BP 2 | Hemoglobin | Chloresterol |
| **19** | 1 | 69.00 | | 24.33 | 132.67 | 88.00 | 10.17 | 7.30 |
| **20** | 2 | 73.00 | | 19.00 | 133.00 | 86.50 | 10.40 | 8.00 |
| **21** | 3 | 74.50 | | 17.60 | 145.00 | 92.00 | 11.20 | 7.30 |
| **22** | 4 | 65.50 | | 21.30 | 133.00 | 88.00 | 9.80 | 8.20 |
| **23** | | | | | | | |
| **24** | | | | | | | |
| **25** | Occupation | 1 | | 2 | 3 | 4 | |
| **26** | Ave Pulse | 69.00 | | 73.00 | 74.50 | 65.50 | |

**Occupation Analysis (SS)**

**Figure 6.26.** Preparing to Copy Works SS Data to the Report.

- Copy the selected SS data to the Clipboard, return to the *SurveyReport* WP document, and paste the data into the report. Note that you may have to move your chart to get an orderly display.

- Use the Works WP *Draw On* command in the **Edit** menu to place a border around the chart, as illustrated in Figure 6.27.

You can also add your own descriptive text if you like. With a little effort, you should be able to produce a document with an appearance similar to that shown in Figure 6.27.

- Save the document.

By proceeding as described above, you can put as many charts and as much spreadsheet data into your report as you like. In fact, in a quite similar way, you could also place information from the database into your report as well. If you desire, the graphics material can be modified or enhanced using the Works drawing capabilities. As you can see, it is quite easy to generate an interesting and informative Works WP report.

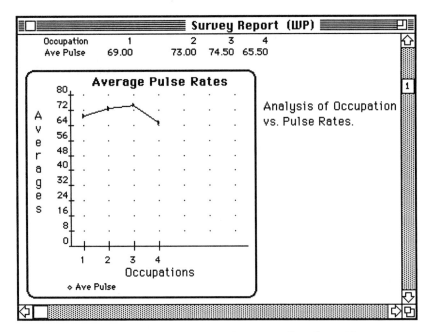

**Figure 6.27.** A Portion of the Report with Chart and Data Pasted In.

This concludes our discussion of the project problem. There are, of course, many more comparisons that could be made based on the data. You are invited to explore this example project further in the Practice Projects that follow.

This completes the activity of Lesson 5 and this chapter. If you are not proceeding directly to the Practice Projects, quit Works, clean up the desktop, and shut down your Macintosh.

## SurveyResults (DB)

| First Name | Last Name | Address | City | State | Zip | Age | Exercise | Beef |
|---|---|---|---|---|---|---|---|---|
| Joseph | Smith | 2122 Live Oak Street | New Orleans | LA | 70101 | 42 | 1 | 1 |
| Thomas | Dedmond | 1212 Palm Lane | Santa Clara | CA | 95050 | 45 | 2 | 3 |
| William | White | 1020 Lakeview Way | Jonesville | OH | 44444 | 48 | 1 | 2 |
| Paul | Wrangler | 1122 Hillside Dr. | Hyatt | NY | 10800 | 43 | 3 | 3 |
| George | Belton | 1011 Maple Leaf St. | Hazel Green | AL | 35820 | 44 | 3 | 4 |
| Clancy | Duggan | 105 Park Ave. | New York | NY | 10045 | 44 | 4 | 3 |
| Harrison | Matthews | 220 Quincy St. | Roaring Spring | PA | 16673 | 42 | 1 | 2 |
| Joel | Harmon | 102 E. Main | Taylors | SC | 29687 | 43 | 2 | 4 |
| Frank | Walker | 339 Wellington St. | New York | NY | 10034 | 47 | 4 | 1 |

## SurveyResults (DB)

| Beef | Poultry | Fish | Dairy | JobStress | Smoking | Survey Returned? | Height | Weight | Occupa |
|---|---|---|---|---|---|---|---|---|---|
| 1 | 4 | 4 | 4 | 1 | 4 | YES | 72 | 210 | |
| 3 | 2 | 2 | 3 | 2 | 3 | YES | 70 | 188 | |
| 2 | 2 | 1 | 3 | 3 | 4 | YES | 68 | 155 | |
| 3 | 1 | 2 | 4 | 2 | 1 | YES | 71 | 177 | |
| 4 | 4 | 3 | 2 | 2 | 3 | YES | 74 | 196 | |
| 3 | 1 | 1 | 3 | 4 | 1 | YES | 72 | 221 | |
| 2 | 2 | 2 | 2 | 3 | 4 | YES | 65 | 144 | |
| 4 | 3 | 3 | 1 | 4 | 2 | YES | 73 | 188 | |
| 1 | 3 | 4 | 1 | 1 | 2 | YES | 66 | 143 | |

## SurveyResults (DB)

| Occupation | Pulse | Respiration | BP 1 | BP 2 | Hemoglobin | Chloresterol | HW Ratio |
|---|---|---|---|---|---|---|---|
| 1 | 76 | 21 | 130 | 92 | 11.30 | 250 | 2.92 |
| 2 | 65 | 20 | 122 | 88 | 8.50 | 257 | 2.69 |
| 2 | 81 | 18 | 144 | 85 | 12.30 | 277 | 2.28 |
| 1 | 55 | 26 | 135 | 94 | 9.00 | 303 | 2.49 |
| 1 | 76 | 26 | 133 | 78 | 10.20 | 177 | 2.65 |
| 4 | 65 | 19 | 146 | 81 | 11.60 | 183 | 3.07 |
| 3 | 71 | 20 | 131 | 92 | 9.50 | 153 | 2.22 |
| 3 | 78 | 23 | 134 | 89 | 9.00 | 166 | 2.58 |
| 4 | 66 | 17 | 113 | 76 | 11.00 | 177 | 2.17 |

**Figure 6.28.** Sample Database Used in the Examples.

# PRACTICE PROJECTS

## PROJECT 1

1. Repeat the analysis described in Lesson 4 of this chapter, but for *Occupation* versus *Cholesterol*. Save your modified spreadsheet in your folder *Works Project* under the name *OccupationAnalysisA<your initials>*.

2. Add a chart summarizing the above analysis along with relevant data to the *SurveyReport* document created in Lesson 5. Save the modified report in your folder *Works Project* under the name *SurveyReportA<your initials>*.

# PROJECT 2

1. Create a new spreadsheet and save it in your folder *Works Project* under the name *SmokingAnalysis<your initials>*. Make an analysis of *Smoking* (habits) versus *Pulse Rate* in this spreadsheet, using the analysis in Lesson 4 as a model. Save your spreadsheet.

2. Add a chart summarizing the above analysis along with relevant data to the *SurveyReport* document created in Lesson 5 (or you could use the version modified in step 2 of Practice Project 1). Save the modified report in your folder *Works Project* under the name *SurveyReportB<your initials>*.

## PROJECT 3

1. Using the spreadsheet *SmokingAnalysis* created in step 1 of Practice Project 2, repeat the analysis described in Lesson 4 of this chapter, but for *Smoking* versus *Cholesterol*. Save your modified spreadsheet in your folder *Works Project* under the name *SmokingAnalysisA<your initials>*.

2. Add a <u>bar chart</u> summarizing the above analysis along with relevant data to the *SurveyReportB* document created in step 2 of Practice Project 2. Save the modified report in your folder *Works Project* under the name *SurveyReportC<your initials>*.

# 7

# USING WORKS CM

When you have completed the Works CM tutorial you will be able to:

❏ Create a communications document.

❏ Save a communications document.

❏ Dial another computer.

❏ Capture the text transmitted during the communications process.

❏ Enter and save telephone information in the phone list.

❏ Select appropriate settings for a communications document.

❏ Send text files.

❏ Send binary files.

❏ Receive files.

## TUTORIAL OUTLINE

# WHAT IS WORKS CM?

The main purpose of a communications package such as Works CM is to allow a user to "exchange" information with other computers. There are, of course, many different reasons for using computer communications.

The information services such as CompuServe, The Source, and Dow Jones provide a vast array of different kinds of information for a fee. News, weather, business, entertainment, travel, and many other kinds of information are available. This information is the latest available, and therefore, exceedingly valuable for some purposes.

Some information services provide electronic mail services that allow users to communicate with each other. In addition many of these services provide bulletin boards that contain information of special interest for some users. For example, CompuServe has bulletin boards for users of different computers and even particular software packages. If you are a user of a given software package, you can exchange ideas with other users of the package, keep up with the latest developments with the package, and even transfer software to your computer to improve or enhance the performance of the software package.

To use an information service, you must pay an initial subscription fee at which time you would be given a password and directions for connecting to the service. Thereafter, the charges are based on how much you use the system.

There are also hundreds of free (or minimal-fee) bulletin board services run by hobbyists. These allow you to communicate with individuals having similar interests. A sample of the kinds of different subjects covered includes: real estate, genealogy, religion, sports, medicine, humor, games, law, graphics, food, and music. As a user of a bulletin board, in addition to having discussions with other users, you may want to transfer files from the bulletin board to your computer or send one of your files to the bulletin board. Public domain software, which you can copy to your computer, is available from some services and many bulletin boards. With this free software you may be able to use your computer more effectively or to have fun with an interesting game.

You may also use a Macintosh as a terminal to a large mainframe computer. This could, for example, allow you to do some work at home instead of at the office; or if you are a student, you could use your computer as a terminal for working with the college's main computer. These kinds of usage can improve your efficiency.

Information can also be transferred between different kinds of microcomputers. For example, files can be moved between the Macintosh and IBM PC compatible personal computers. Because computers of different manufacturers use different formats for writing to disks, direct connection between two computers may be the only convenient way to transfer information from one computer to another.

The list of possible uses of computer communications given above is only indicative of the kinds of things that you might do. The possibilities are vast, and you will have to become involved to learn how best to use computer communications for your own purposes.

# BASIC COMMUNICATIONS CONCEPTS

The required components of a communications system that uses Works is shown in Figure 7.1. The block called "other computer" can be, for example, another Macintosh, a microcomputer of another manufacturer, a mainframe computer, or the computer of an information service. The other computer can be located anywhere that can be reached using the phone system. The line labeled "phone line" represents a connection through the phone system, and it does not imply that there must be a direct line between the computers.

**Modems.** Let us assume that you are in the process of sending information to the other computer. The modem attached to your computer takes digital signals received from your computer and converts them into a form--often tones of different frequencies--suitable for transmission through the telephone system. At the receiving modem the information is converted back into digital signals that can be used by a computer. These processes are called **modulation** and **demodulation**, respectively. This is the origin of the term modem: **mo**dulation and **dem**odulation.

Modems for the Macintosh are available with a wide range of features at discount prices ranging from approximately $100 to $450. Less expensive modems tend to operate at slower transmission rates and to have fewer features. A full featured modem, known as a **smart modem**, has its own microprocessor and can help with the communications process. Desirable features include:

> The ability to communicate at a variety of speeds. Speed is particularly important for interactions with information services that charge for the time they are used.

> The ability to operate in a mode corresponding to the **Hayes AT** standard, a popular modem control language used by many microcomputers. This control language is supported by Works.

> The ability to dial automatically the modem number of another computer.

The ability to answer an incoming call automatically. This allows you to perform other work with your computer while you are waiting for the initiation of communications.

The ability to support different communications protocols.

You may encounter modems with few of these features or with all. The steps required in Works to connect your computer to another will depend on whether or not your modem has the automatic dialing feature. Without automatic dialing, it will be necessary for you to manually dial the number to establish a link with the other computer. You should determine what features are on any modem available to you.

The modems at the two ends of the data transmission link can be of different design, but it must be possible to set various parameters in the modems so that they behave in the same way. In a later section you will examine the settings allowed by Works. The operation of a modem is controlled by the computer to which it is attached.

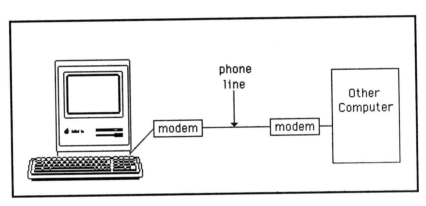

**Figure 7.1.** Configuration for Computer Communications.

The Works communications module, in turn, controls the computer and its communication with the modem. A similar situation exists at the other computer. Hence, to the users of the computers it appears as though the computers are communicating directly with each other. A hypothetical conversation between the computers using English to represent the control signals might be the following:

| Macintosh | Other Computer |
|---|---|
| I am ready to send a file. Are you ready to receive? | |
| | I am ready.  Send the file. |
| Here is the file. (Data are relayed.) | |
| | There was an error in the last block of data.  Send it  again. |
| OK.  Sending it again. (Data are relayed again.) | |
| | Entire file received without error. |
| I am finished.  Signing off. | |
| | OK.  So long. |

**Protocols.** As the information is being transmitted between the computers, the machines must agree that an action is allowable.  For example, one of the computers may not be able to process the incoming information fast enough and may need to request the other computer to pause temporarily in the communications process to allow it to catch up.  Before each significant communications action, the computers signal agreement that the action is permitted.  This process is called a **handshake** between the computers.  For example, the slower machine, which needs extra time for the processing of the incoming data, does not complete the handshake until it is ready.

The details of how the transmission process will be managed is called a **protocol.** Although you do not need to know any of the technical details of any protocol, you need to know they exist and when to use a particular protocol.  For example: if the communication is between two Macintoshes, a particular protocol is used; if only one of the computers is a Macintosh, a different protocol is used.  The number of different protocols supported depends on the communications software.  Works supports three protocols: MacBinary, Xmodem text, and Xmodem data.  These will be discussed later.

The rate of information transfer over a telephone or telegraph line is called a **baud** in honor of Baudot, a pioneer in telegraph communications. For the purposes of our discussion, you may think of a baud as being equivalent to one bit per second.  A text character is represented by seven or eight bits depending on the system being used.  A start bit, one or two stop bits, and sometimes a parity bit are also added for the transmission process. Hence a total of between 9 and 12 bits are required per character transmitted. Baud rates above 110 usually use 10 bits for each character. Thus, dividing the baud rate by 10 gives a reasonable estimate of the number of characters transmitted per second. High baud rates are desirable to reduce transmission times and thus the cost of sending information. A common problem in communications is the failure to set the two modems to the same baud rate, which produces garbled transmissions.

The communications system may be either **half-duplex** or **full-duplex**. In a half-duplex system information may be transmitted in either direction, but in only one direction at a time. This is analogous to a one-lane bridge on which cars cross in either direction, but in only one direction at a time. A full-duplex system allows simultaneous transmission in both directions, analogous to traffic on a multilane bridge. The system used in a particular situation depends upon both the communications software and the modems. Works supports full-duplex communications.

**Echo mode** refers to the immediate retransmission of every character by the receiving computer. This has the advantage of allowing the user to verify that the information is being transmitted as planned. If the system is set for echo mode, every character will be doubled on the screen of the sending computer. This situation is demonstrated in Figure 7.2 for transmission between two Macintoshes. Works provides an option to accept or reject the echo.

```
JJooee, II aamm rreeaaddyy ttoo ttrraannssffeerr
tthhee ffiillee yyoouu wwaannttteedd. AArree
yyoouu rreeaaddyy??
```

**Figure 7.2.** Data Transmission with Echo.

From the user's perspective the communications process can be divided into the following major steps.

Set the modem parameters for the particular communication.

Establish a link between the two computers.

Transfer information in either or both directions. This may involve creating new disk files for received information.

Break the link between the two computers.

These steps will be discussed in detail for Works in the following lessons.

# OVERVIEW OF WORKS CM

After completing this lesson you will be able to:

❏ Create a communications document.

❏ Dial another computer.

❏ Save a communications document.

## LESSON BACKGROUND

In this lesson you will look at Works CM at an overview level by simulating the communication process. This will allow you to observe the components of a Works communication document and to obtain a feeling for the actions that are required in the communication process.

**Creating a Communications Document.** A Works communication document consists of:

A document for viewing communications as they occur.

A group of stored settings necessary for the communications process.

A list (which may be empty) of telephone numbers that can be dialed automatically.

An optional document, the captured text document, in which all communications will be saved automatically.

The technique for creating a document is similar to that for creating other Works documents. For example, the *Communications* icon can be double clicked. The stored settings are then displayed automatically, so they can be modified as needed. The other document components—the phone list and the captured text—can be accessed by commands found in the **Communications** menu.

**Communicating.** Assuming that you have a Hayes-compatible smart modem, you can have Works dial the telephone number to initiate the communications between the computers. This process is called establishing the physical link between the computers. Also, as you will see later, you can create a communications document and set the modem to answer when it is contacted.

After the physical link has been established, you may have to perform other actions to ensure that the computers are using the same protocol for the communication process, that they are both using the same baud rate, and so on.

During the communications session you may type messages, and you may receive or transmit any number of files. You may use the other Works modules during communications, letting the communications occur in the background.

**Saving a Communications Document.** The technique for saving a communications document is similar to that for saving other types of documents. Select the *Save* or *Save As* command from the **File** menu. If the *Save As* command is being used, enter a meaningful name in the *Save* dialog box and click the *Save* button.

When a communications document is saved, the settings and telephone numbers are automatically saved. If an optional document has been created to capture the communications text, it will also be saved. The contents of the window for viewing the exchange of information during the communications are not saved.

**Logging Off.** Finally, when you are finished you may have to log off the system (break the communications link) and then hang up the telephone. The term *log off* means to complete a sequence of steps that tell the other computer that you have finished the communication. It is important to log off information services that are charging for the time you are connected to them because hanging up the phone may not disconnect you from the service. The log off procedure is different for the various information services, so you will need to learn the log off procedure for each of the services you are using. In the case of direct communication between Macintoshes or other microcomputers, there will normally be no log off procedure—hanging up the phone is sufficient.

**Ending a Communications Session.** To end a communications session, you would perform the following steps.

Log off the system if you are using an information service or other system that required you to log on. The phone connection between the computers may still exist after you have logged off.

Hang up your telephone by selecting the *Hang Up* command of the **Communications** menu. Works directs your modem to hang up.

Save the communications document if appropriate. It should be saved if the communications settings and telephone numbers will be used again. Let us assume that the communications settings are the standard ones for future work. Then we suggest saving the document with the name *Standard Communications*. Later when the document is opened, the blank window with the title *Standard Communications (CM)* will be displayed; and the communications settings and the telephone number saved with the document are available.

Quit the Works Communications module by selecting the *Quit* command in the **File** menu.

If you conduct different kinds of communications such as using an information service, participating in a round table discussion with other computer users, or calling non-Macintosh computers, you should create a different communications document for each category of use. Then the communications settings and telephone numbers will be immediately available when you need them. Without these documents, you are likely to forget some important setting and to spend unnecessary time trying to start a session.

## SIMULATING A COMMUNICATIONS SESSION

Here you will simulate a communications session. You should pay particular attention to identify the components of a Works CM document and to recognize the sequence in which actions must be performed. Subsequent lessons will fill in many details that are omitted here.
Perform the following.

- Create a folder *Works CM* on your disk.

- Create within *Works CM* the folders *Lesson1*, *Lesson2*, and *Lesson3*.

- Find the Works icon and double click to start Works.

Create a Works CM document:

- Create an empty Works CM document by double clicking the *Communications* icon, which is highlighted in Figure 7.3. Alternately, you could click the *Communications* icon to select it, and then either click the *New* button on the dialog box or select the *New* command from the **File** menu.

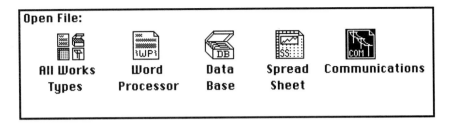

**Figure 7.3.** Module Icons Displayed after Works Is Opened.

- Look at the *Communications Settings* dialog box, which is displayed automatically whenever a new CM document is created. (See Figure 7.9). In the next-to-last line, if the *Capture Text When Document Opens* box does not contain an x, click the box to obtain an x. Do not change any other settings. The settings are the subject of the next lesson.

- Click the *OK* button on the *Communications Settings* dialog box.

Because the *Capture Text* box was selected in the last step, the dialog box shown in Figure 7.4 is displayed. The highlighted box contains the name of the document in which all the text you type or receive in the communications session will be saved. The default name for the document is *Captured Text*.

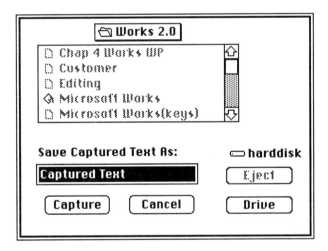

**Figure 7.4.** The *Capture Text* Dialog Box.

- Navigate to the *Lesson1* folder in the *Works CM* folder on your disk. Click the *Capture* button to save a copy of the information you will type later in the lesson. The dialog box will disappear, and an empty communications document named *Untitled (CM)* will be displayed.

Prepare for dialing a modem:

- Select the *Dial* command from the **Communications** menu. The **Communications** menu is shown in Figure 7.5. An empty phone list will be displayed. (See Figure 7.6.)

- Type the name *John Doe* into the *Name* box. Press the *Tab* key and type the phone number 1-803-284-2334 into the *Phone Number* box. The *Phone List* dialog box should now look like that shown in Figure 7.6.

Dial the modem at John Doe's computer:

- Click the *Dial* button beside *John Doe's* name. The message *Dialing. . .* will be displayed in the communications window.

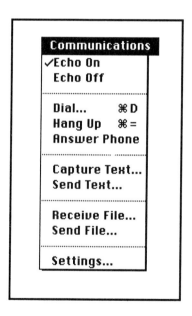

Figure 7.5. The **Communications** Menu.

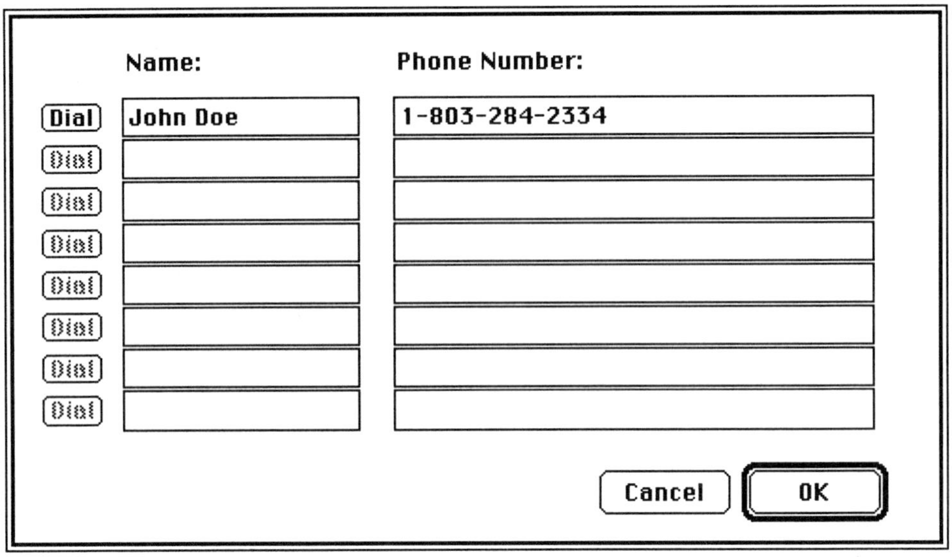

```
    Name:               Phone Number:

[Dial]  John Doe          1-803-284-2334

[Dial]

[Dial]

[Dial]

[Dial]

[Dial]

[Dial]

[Dial]

                            [ Cancel ]  [ OK ]
```

**Figure 7.6.** The *Phone List* Dialog Box.

Send a message to John Doe:

- Press the *Return* key to obtain a blank line.

- Type the message shown in Figure 7.7. Make each line a paragraph by pressing the *Return* key.

- Press the *Return* key to obtain a blank line.

```
John:

Please send me a copy of the document called Works Summary.
I need it as soon as possible.

Thanks,
Sam Jones
```

**Figure 7.7.** Message to Be Typed.

Break the phone connection:

- Select the *Hang Up* command from the **Communications** menu. A message will be displayed. This will break the phone connection.

Prepare to receive a document:

- Select the *Answer Phone* command from the **Communications** menu. A message will be displayed. At this stage you will wait to receive a message from John Doe. This requires that the communications document remain open. You can use the other components of Works, allowing the communications to occur in the background. If you are using MultiFinder, you can use other applications while you are waiting.

Save the communications document:

- Assume that the document has been sent to you by John Doe.

- Select the *Save As* command from the **File** menu. Enter the name *PracticeComm<your initials>* and click the *Save* button. Place the document in the folder *Lesson1* within the folder *WorksCM* on your disk. This document will be used in the practice at the end of the next section.

- Click the *Close* box.

Examine the captured text:

- Open the document *Captured Text*. It should have the appearance shown in Figure 7.8. The file sent by John Doe would appear immediately after the *Setting modem* message. Close the document.

If you have made typing errors during the simulated sending of the message, the errors will show in the captured text.

- This completes Lesson 1. If you do not wish to continue directly to the next lesson, quit Works, clean up the desktop, and shut down your computer.

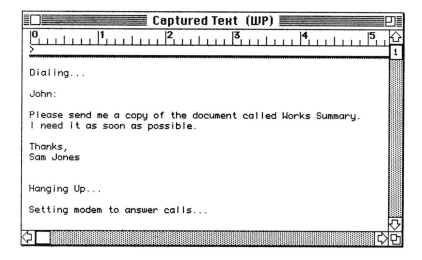

Figure 7.8. An Example of Captured Text.

# THE COMMUNICATIONS SETTINGS DIALOG BOX

After completing this lesson you will be able to:

❏ Select appropriate settings for a communications document.

## LESSON BACKGROUND

As soon as a new communications document is created, the communications dialog box of Figure 7.9 is displayed. Also, the dialog box can be displayed at any time during a session by selecting the *Settings* command from the **Communications** menu. The appropriate buttons should be clicked to correspond to the particular communications session. To make the correct settings, you will have to know what the receiving modem and/or computer requires. Information services will supply the required settings when you subscribe to them. For other situations ask about the settings if that is possible. Otherwise, you will have to experiment by trying the possible choices to find the correct settings.

## MAKING THE COMMUNICATION SETTINGS

Perform the following.

• Open the document *PracticeComm* in the *Lesson1* folder inside the folder *Works CM* on your disk.

An empty communications window will opened, and the *Capture Text* dialog box will be displayed with the default name *Captured Text*. (See Figure 7.4.)

• Click the *Cancel* box because you are not interested in capturing text in this lesson.

If you click the *Capture* button, a dialog box will be displayed that asks whether or not you wish to replace the existing capture text document.

- Select the *Settings* command from the **Communications** menu. The *Communications Settings* dialog box of Figure 7.9 will be displayed.

- Make the following settings by clicking the appropriate buttons. In some instances the default value of a parameter is the same as the requested setting.

Set the type:

- Click the *TTY* button.

   **Type.** The type refers to the kind of terminal that Works is emulating in this session. The default type is TTY, which corresponds to a teletype or dumb terminal. Works can also emulate two other terminals, the Digital Equipment Company terminals VT-100 and VT-52.

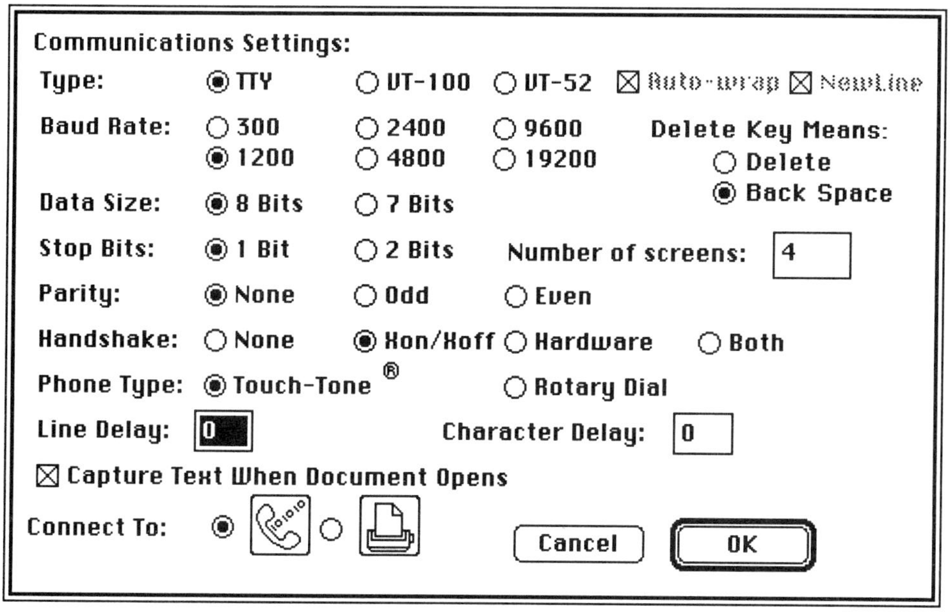

Figure 7.9. The *Settings* Dialog Box.

Set the baud rate

- Set the baud rate to 2400 by clicking that button.

   **Baud Rate.** The baud rate should correspond to that used by the modem of the other computer. This will likely be a value of 300, 1200, or 2400 baud. The higher settings, above 2400, are normally used when the Macintosh is emulating a terminal and is connected directly to a computer without the need for a modem. Note, however, that modems for personal computers that operate at 9600 baud are now available. Remember that failure to select the same rate as that used by the receiving modem will result in garbled transmission.

Set the data size:

- Click the *8 Bits* button.

    **Data Size.** Characters are represented within the Macintosh using 8 bits per character. However, Works can transmit the characters using either 7 or 8 bits per character. The choice of data size will depend upon the requirements of the receiving computer. Data size will also be affected by whether or not a parity bit (discussed below) is used.

Set the stop bits:

- Click the *1 Bit* button.

    **Stop Bits.** An extra bit, called a stop bit, is attached to the end of each transmitted character. Some computers require two stop bits per character.

Set the number of screens:

- Type 4 into the *Number of screens* box. This box is on the same line as the *Stop Bits* parameter.

    **Number of Screens.** The *Number of Screens* feature allows a user to save some number of the most recent screens in RAM. The value of 4 means that the contents of the four most recent screens are saved in RAM and can be examined by scrolling with the scroll arrows or box. As new information is received during a communications session, it is placed at the bottom. A corresponding amount of the oldest information is displaced from the top and is no longer available for viewing. If zero is selected as the number of screens, you will still be able to see information being transferred on the screen, but you will not be able to scroll to see information that has passed off the screen. If you attempt to specify more screens than can be saved in RAM, a warning message will be displayed and Works will use the maximum number of screens that it can save.

Set the parity:

- Click the *None* button.

**Parity.** A parity bit is an extra bit attached to the binary representation of a character for error checking purposes. For odd parity, the parity bit is set to 0 or 1 to make the total number (including the parity bit) of "1" bits be odd. For even parity, the parity bit is set to make the total number of "1" bits even. The types of parity are illustrated in Figure 7.10 for the character *A*. Information services tend not to use a parity bit.

For transmissions that use parity, a 0 or 1 is added at the source computer to produce a grouping of bits having, for example, even parity. At the receiving computer each grouping of bits is checked to see if it has the expected parity, in this case even parity. If the parity is wrong, an error has occurred during the transmission that changed one or more bits in the group. The receiving computer can then request that the data be sent again.

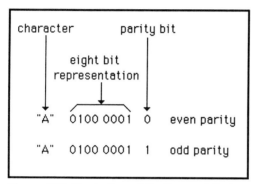

**Figure 7.10.** Illustration of the Types of Parity.

Set the handshake:

• Click the *Xon/Xoff* button.

**Handshake.** Recall that handshaking refers to the way communicating computers synchronize the transmission of data. Again, you will need to know what the other computer is expecting. The handshaking may be done by the software, the hardware, or both. If high data transmission rates, 2400 baud or greater, are to be used, handshaking will be required. The Xon/Xoff handshaking is used by most information services.

Set the phone type:

• Click the *Touch-Tone* button.

Set the line delay/character delay:

- Type the value 0 (zero) in the *Line Delay* box and the *Character Delay* box if it does not already appear in these boxes.

  **Line Delay/Character Delay.** In some cases it is very difficult to send and receive data without errors occurring; for example, one computer may be sending information when the other computer is not looking for it. It may help to introduce a time delay between each line sent and/or each character sent. The line delay and character delay options are used to introduce these time delays. Integers entered in these blocks correspond to delays in units of 1/60 of a second. For example, entering a 5 in the character delay box produces a delay of 5/60 seconds between each character.

Set the Capture Text parameter:

- Click the *Capture Text When Document Opens* box as necessary to obtain an empty box.

  **Capture Text When Document Opens.** In some sessions, it is desirable to save in a disk file a copy of all the text displayed during the communications. Clicking the *Capture Text When Document Opens* box causes Works to enter a capture text mode immediately when a session is started. The name of a file is requested for saving the text. If the box is not checked, no text capture occurs unless the *Capture Text* command is selected under the **Communications** menu.

Set the Connect To parameter:

- Click the *Phone* button.

  **Connect To.** Ordinarily the modem should be attached by a cable to a modem port. In some circumstances, the modem port may be used already for attaching some other device. In this case, the printer port can be used for attaching the modem. Select the proper port in the *Setting* dialog box by clicking the appropriate button.

Save the document:

- Click the *OK* button on the *Communications Settings* box. The dialog box will disappear, and the document *PracticeComm* will be displayed.

- Use the *Save As* command to save the communications document as *PracticeComm2<your initials>* in folder *Lesson2* in the folder *Works CM* on your disk. Close the document.

- This completes Lesson 2. If you do not wish to continue directly to the next lesson, quit Works, clean up the desktop, and shut down your computer.

# MORE ABOUT THE CAPTURE TEXT AND DIAL COMMANDS

After completing this lesson, you will be able to:

❏ Use the *Capture Text* command.

❏ Use the *Dial* command.

❏ Use the *End Capture Text* command.

In this computer practice session you will gain experience with the *Capture Text/End Capture Text* commands and with the *Dial* command. You will *simulate* signing on to the Universal On-line News and Services information service. (Of course, this is not as informative as actually signing on to an information service, but it is less expensive.)

## CAPTURE TEXT COMMAND

The *Capture Text* command, which switches with the *End Text Capture* command, can be given at any time during a communications session. For example, *Capture Text* could be used to capture text early in the session, and then the *End Text Capture* command could be given to stop the capture of text. These commands can be used repeatedly during the session.
   Perform the following.

• Open the communications document *PracticeComm2*, which was saved in the folder *Lesson2* inside the *Works CM* folder on your disk.

• Click *Cancel* on the dialog box that is presented. The empty communications window *PracticeComm2 (CM)* will appear.

Prepare to capture text:

- Select the *Capture Text* command from the **Communications** menu. This will cause the dialog box of Figure 7.11 to be displayed.

- Type *Universal On-line News* in the box titled *Save Captured Text As*. All communications that appear in the communications window will be saved in this file. (Of course, the file will be empty because we are only simulating the communications session.)

- Click the *Capture* button on the dialog box to complete the command to capture text.

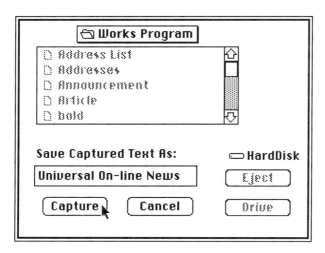

**Figure 7.11.** The *Capture Text* Dialog Box.

# DIALING

If the modem is a Hayes compatible smart-modem, clicking the *Dial* button causes the telephone number to be dialed. If the modem also has a speaker, you will be able to hear the number being dialed. If the modem is not Hayes compatible, the *Dial* command cannot be used. It will be necessary for you to consult the reference manual for your modem to obtain directions about making a connection with another computer.

Prepare to dial the other computer:

- Select the *Dial* command from the **Communications** menu. The telephone list box (see Figure 7.6.) will appear.

- Type the name of the information service, Universal On-line, in the second box under the heading *Name*.

- Type the phone number, 1-212-555-0001, in the second box under the heading *Phone Number*. The *Phone List* box should now have the appearance shown in Figure 7.12.

  **Entering Phone Numbers.** A telephone number can consist of 50 or fewer characters, which is long enough for even an international number and a password. Hyphens, spaces, slashes, and parentheses are ignored by Works (if a Hayes compatible modem is used) and can be used to make the numbers more readable. The following are all equivalent:

  12125550001

  1 212 555 0001

  1 (212) 555-0001

  1-(212)-555-0001

  1-212-5550001

  1-212-555-0001

  Commas can be used to introduce delays of approximately 2 seconds per comma. This is useful, for example, when it is necessary to dial 9 to get an outside line. For example, the entry 9,,1-212-555-0001 could be used to dial an outside line, wait 4 seconds for getting the outside line, and then dial the number of the information service. Any name or phone number in the phone list can be edited using normal word processing editing techniques.

Connecting to the other computer:

- Click the *Dial* button that is to the left of the name of the information service. At this time the dialing would occur if the modem were turned on. In our case, the telephone list box disappears, just as it would when the dialing was complete.

During the time the dialing is in progress, the message *Dialing* will appear on the screen. When the connection is made between the modems, the message *CONNECT* will appear on the screen. You are then ready to communicate with the other computer.

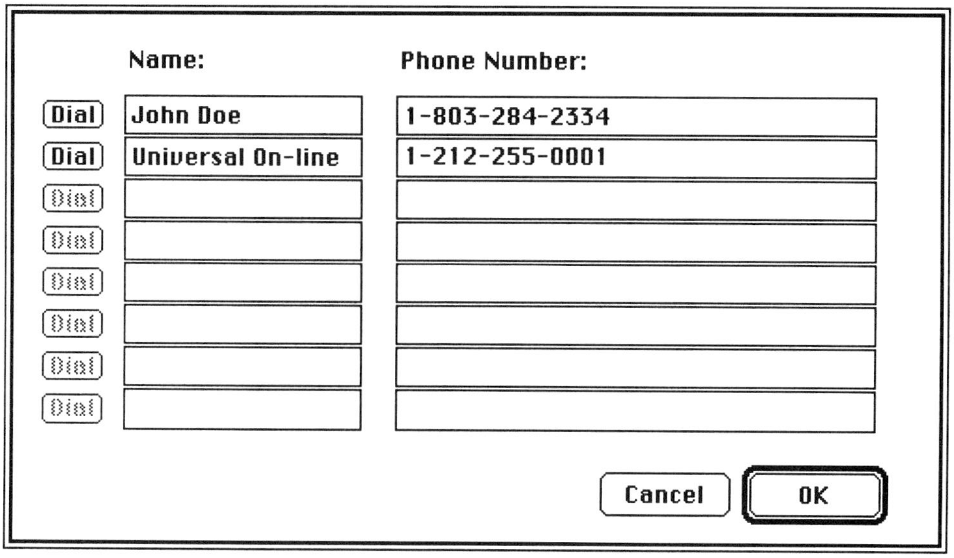

| | Name: | Phone Number: |
|---|---|---|
| Dial | John Doe | 1-803-284-2334 |
| Dial | Universal On-line | 1-212-255-0001 |
| Dial | | |
| Dial | | |
| Dial | | |
| Dial | | |
| Dial | | |
| Dial | | |

Cancel    OK

**Figure 7.12.** Phone List after Adding a Telephone Number.

End the capturing of text:

- Select the *End Capture Text* command from the **Communications** menu. In our case, no text was captured because this is only a simulation. Recall that you can use the commands *Capture Text/End Capture Text* repeatedly to collect just those parts of the communications session of interest to you.

Disconnect the phone:

- Select the *Hang Up* command from the **Communications** menu. If this had been a real communications session, the phone would now be disconnected.

- Use the *Save As* command to save the document as *PracticeComm3<your initials>* in folder *Lesson3* in the folder *Works CM* on your disk. Close your document.

- This completes Lesson 3. If you do not wish to continue directly to the next lesson, quit Works, clean up the desktop, and shut down your computer.

LESSON 4 _____

# TECHNIQUES FOR SENDING AND RECEIVING INFORMATION

After completing this lesson, you will be able to:

❑ Understand how to send and receive text files.

❑ Know when to use the Xmodem protocol.

❑ Use the *Send Text* command.

❑ Use the *Send File* command.

❑ Use the *Receive File* command.

## BASIC FILE TYPES AND PROTOCOLS

One of the main reasons for communications between computers is to exchange disk files. Works CM makes a distinction between simple word processing files and files that contain graphs or pictures.

**Sending Using the Keyboard.** The simplest way to communicate with the other computer is to use your keyboard. Whatever you type will appear almost simultaneously on the screens of both computers. If you are involved in a conversation, you should pause to give the other person an opportunity to respond. This method is ideal for the round table discussions conducted by some users groups. Each person can type replies as needed.

*Send Text* **Command.** The *Send Text* command is used to send simple word processing files to another computer. This can sometimes be used to save money when communicating with an information service that charges for the connect time. For example, to use the electronic mail service of the information service, you could type the text in advance. Then use the *Send Text* command to send the mail file, which would take much less time than

444

typing the text while connected to the service and would, therefore, cost less.

When the *Send Text* command is used only the text is transmitted; any formatting information is deleted before transmission. Only Works files can be transmitted; any other type of file must be imported by Works before it can be transmitted. The procedure for sending text files follows.

- Select the *Send Text* command in the **Communications** menu. A dialog box of the form shown in Figure 7.13 will be displayed.

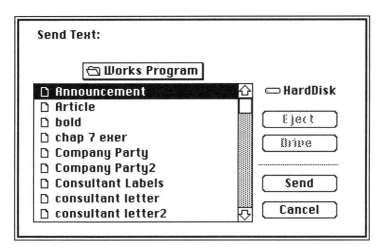

**Send Text:**

[🗂 **Works Program**]

| D **Announcement** |
| D **Article** |
| D **bold** |
| D **chap 7 exer** |
| D **Company Party** |
| D **Company Party2** |
| D **Consultant Labels** |
| D **consultant letter** |
| D **consultant letter2** |

⊂⊃ **HardDisk**

[ Eject ]

[ Drive ]

[ **Send** ]

[ **Cancel** ]

**Figure 7.13.** The *Send Text* Dialog Box.

- Select the document to be sent in the scroll box of the dialog box.

- Click the *Send* button on the dialog box to start the sending of the document to the other computer.

During the sending of the text you will not be able to use the communications module for other work. You can use the other Works modules if you wish. When the transmission of the text is complete, a message will be displayed. You may then perform other work with the communications module.

**Xmodem Protocol.** Works supports the Xmodem protocol for transfer of information between computers. Three variations of the Xmodem protocol are used by the Macintosh. You will have to select one of them in order to send a file to another computer. The variations are:

> **MacBinary.** The MacBinary version of Xmodem should be used if the information is being exchanged between two Macintoshes. MacBinary works for any kind of file.

**Xmodem Text.** The Xmodem Text version of Xmodem should be used for exchanging text files (no graphics or pictures) between a Macintosh and any other kind of computer.

**Xmodem Data.** The Xmodem Data version of Xmodem should be used for exchanging complex files (including graphics and pictures) between a Macintosh and any other kind of computer.

**Kermit** is another popular file transfer protocol. It is not available in Works, however. To use it, you would need a different communications package.

*Send File* **Command.** The *Send File* command of the **Communications** menu allows transmission of any Works files including those that contain graphs and/or pictures. The procedure for using this command is the same as that for the *Send Text* command except that a protocol must be specified.

As an example of *Send File* command usage, let us suppose we are to send the file *CompanyParty* (see Figure 3.1), which contains pictorial data, to another Macintosh. Because the file is to be sent to another Macintosh, the MacBinary protocol should be used. The steps follow.

- Select the *Send File* command in the **Communications** menu. A dialog box of the form shown in Figure 7.14 will be displayed.

- Click the *MacBinary* protocol button.

- Select the document to be sent, *CompanyParty*, in the scroll box of the dialog box.

- Click the *Send* button on the dialog box to start the sending of the document, *CompanyParty*, to the other Macintosh.

After the *Send* button is clicked, the message box of Figure 7.15 will be displayed. This box shows the status of the sending of the file to the other Macintosh. Because the transfer is just beginning, the *Blocks Completed* count is zero. As the transfer continues, this count will increase. Also note that a *Retransmissions* count greater than zero means that transmission errors occurred that required retransmitting one or more blocks of the file. If this count is high and more files are to be sent, you could try slowing the transmission by increasing the character and/or line delay in the communications settings window.

If the file *CompanyParty* is to be sent to a non-Macintosh computer, the protocol must be selected as Xmodem Data because the file contains pictorial data. (However, this does not mean that the pictorial data can be used in the new system.) The procedure for sending the file is the same as just considered except the *Xmodem Data* button must be clicked.

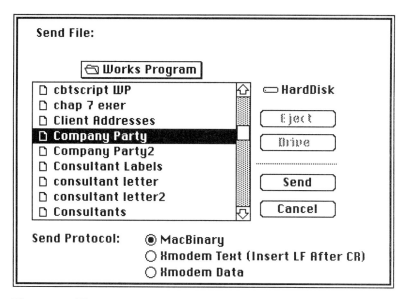

**Figure 7.14.** The *Send File* Dialog Box for Sending the *CompanyParty* File to Another Macintosh.

```
Transmitting Company Party with MacBinary Protocol

Press "⌘" plus "." to abort the transfer.

Total Blocks:        4
Blocks Completed:    0      Retransmissions:    0
```

**Figure 7.15.** *Transmission Information* Box for MacBinary.

*Receive File* **Command.**  Any kind of file can be received using the *Receive File* command.  The procedure for receiving a file is almost identical to that for sending a file.

- Select the *Receive File* command in the **Communications** menu.  A dialog box of the form shown in Figure 7.16 will be displayed.  Notice the default name for the received file is *Xmodem File.*  This default name is already selected, so a more meaningful name can be typed immediately if you wish.

- Click the appropriate protocol button.  You may know the correct protocol for some reason; for example, if the sending computer is a Macintosh choose MacBinary.  If you do not know, you can always select the *Xmodem Data* option, which assumes the file is as complex as possible.

447

- Click the *Receive* button on the dialog box to start receiving the document from the other computer.

After the *Receive* button is clicked, the transmission information box of Figure 7.17 is displayed. Notice that neither the name of the source file nor its size is known.

## USING TEXT AND BINARY FILES

In this part of the lesson you will *simulate* sending a text document and a document containing graphics to another Macintosh.

Perform the following.

- Open the *PracticeComm2* communications document stored in the folder *Lesson2* inside the *Works CM* folder on your disk.

- Click the *Capture* button on the *Text Capture* dialog box. (Use the *Capture Text* command in the **Communications** menu if the dialog box is not displayed automatically.)

- Select the *Settings* command from the **Communications** menu.

- Change the baud rate to 1200 by clicking that button. Click the *OK* button. The *Communications Setting* dialog box should disappear, and an empty communications window should be displayed.

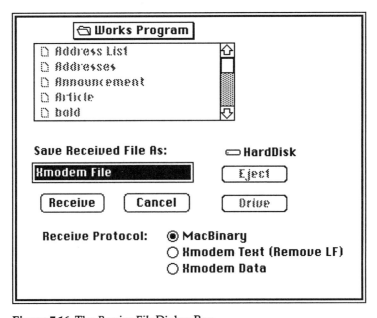

**Figure 7.16.** The *Receive File* Dialog Box.

```
┌─────────────────────────────────────────────────────────────┐
│ Receiving ???? with MacBinary Protocol                        │
│                                                               │
│ Press "⌘" plus "." to abort the transfer.                     │
│                                                               │
│ Total Blocks:          ????                                   │
│ Blocks Completed:        0      Retransmissions:      0        │
└─────────────────────────────────────────────────────────────┘
```

**Figure 7.17.** *Receive Information* Box for MacBinary Protocol.


Dial John Doe:

- Select the *Dial* command from the **Communications** menu.

- Click the *Dial* button beside John Doe's name. The *Dialing* message will be displayed.

Send a text document:

- Select the *Send Text* command from the **Communications** menu.

- Select a text document in the scroll box of the dialog box. (Any text document can be used. If it is available, *Practice1*, which was created in the WP tutorial, Lesson 1, would be ideal.)

- Click the *Send* button. The contents of the document will be displayed as it is being transmitted. Notice that all formatting information has been lost. Also, it is likely that your document will contain many extraneous characters because a simulation is being done.

Send a graphics document:

- Select the *Send File* command from the **Communications** menu. When the *Send File* dialog box is displayed, select a document containing graphics to be sent (it can be any document you choose) in the scroll box of the dialog box. The document *Table4*, which was created in the WP tutorial, Lesson 9, would be ideal.

- Click the *MacBinary* button because the document is to be sent to another Macintosh.

- Click the *Send* button to start the sending of the document. A transmission information box will be displayed.

- Read the transmission box which will not change because this is a simulation. Press simultaneously the *Clover* key and the *Period* key to end the simulated transmission.

Turn off text capture:

- Select the *End Text Capture* command from the **Communications** menu.

Examine the captured text:

- Open the document *Captured Text* by selecting the *Open* command from the **File** menu and double clicking the name of the document in the scroll box.

- Notice that the captured text is the same as that displayed in the communications window during the transmission of the text. No information is captured from the use of the *Send File* command.

You have now completed all the lessons in this chapter. Quit Works, clean up the desktop, and shut down your computer.

# GLOSSARY

**Note:**   Throughout the glossary the following abbreviations are used:

   CM:     communications module of Works.

   DB:     database module of Works.

   SS:     spreadsheet module of Works.

   WP:     word processing module of Works.

*About the Finder*:  A command under the **Apple** menu that gives information about the version of the Finder being used by the computer.

**Absolute reference, SS:**  A Works spreadsheet reference to a cell in which both the column and row designators are preceded by a $ as in $C$7. Such a reference is not changed by use of the *Fill Right* and/or *Fill Down* commands.

**Active cell, SS:** In a Works spreadsheet the currently selected cell in which you enter data or a formula.  The name of the cell (e.g., C6) appears in the upper left-hand side of the formula bar, and the cell is surrounded by a special rectangle.  The information to be entered into the cell is displayed first in the formula bar where it can be edited.  The information is actually entered into the cell when either the *Check* box is clicked, the *Return* key is pressed, the *Tab* key is pressed, or another cell is clicked to make it the active cell.

**Active window:** The window in which the next action will occur.  It is the front-most window and has a striped title bar.

*Alarm clock*:  A desk accessory that behaves like an alarm clock.

**Allocate a device:** The process of selecting a device on a network for your personal use such as allocating an ImageWriter printer on an AppleTalk network.

*AND* **operator:** The binary logical operator that has the value *true* only if both its arguments are *true*.

**Argument for a function:** A reference to a cell or a value that is entered into a call on a built-in Works function. You must understand the purpose of an argument and know its position in the list of arguments. For example, in the following spreadsheet formula to compute the average, =Average( C1, C2, D4), the arguments C1, C2, and D4 are cell references whose values are to be averaged.

**Arithmetic and logic unit:** The component of the central processing unit of a computer in which arithmetic and logical operations are performed.

**Arithmetic operators, SS:** Operators that can be used in performing arithmetic computations in spreadsheets. These operators are +, -, *, /, and ^ for performing addition, subtraction, multiplication, division, and exponentiation, respectively. Unary + and - are also available.

**Attribute:** 1) Another name for a field in a record. 2) Characterisitics of a database field or spreadsheet cell, as in *Set Field Attributes* and *Set Cell Attributes*.

**Backspace key:** The name for the *Delete* key on some keyboards. See *Delete key*.

**Baud:** A measure of the rate of transfer of information between communicating computers. The baud rate divided by 10 is approximately the number of characters transmitted per second. The name is in honor of Baudot, a pioneer in telegraph communications.

**Baud rate, CM:** The rate of transmission of characters during a Works communications session. The baud rate is set on the *Communications Settings* dialog box.

**Binary number system:** A number system using the digits 0 and 1. The system uses a positional notation based on powers of two. For example, the binary number 1001011 is equivalent to $2^6+2^3+2^1+2^0 = 64+8+2+1=75$. The state of a computer component can often be represented by sequences of low (0) or high (1) values; and consequently, binary numbers are often used for this representation.

**Binary:** A short term for the binary number system.

**Bit:** A binary digit, 0 or 1.

**Black box model:** A model in which a function is represented as a black box whose internal operation cannot be observed, and in which arguments are supplied as inputs, and a resulting computed value is returned as the value of the function.

**Booting:** The process of allowing the operating system to take control of the computer. This happens automatically when the computer is turned on if a system disk is available.

**Built-in functions, DB and SS:** A set of prewritten mathematical, statistical, trigonometric, logical, financial, date and time, and special-purpose functions in Works that can be used within formulas. The functions can be selected and pasted into formulas by selecting the *Paste Function* command of the **Edit** menu, or the function can be typed in.

**Bulletin board service:** A service accessed using a modem and microcomputer which individuals having similar interests use to exchange information. Some bulletin board services are free.

**Byte:** A sequence of eight consecutive bits used to hold a character of information (i.e., one symbol on the keyboard.). The byte is a standard unit for measuring the size of RAM or the amount of memory space on a disk.

*Calculator:* A desk accessory that allows calculations involving addition, subtraction, multiplication, and division. More complex calculators are available for use as a desk accessory.

**Cartridge tape drive:** A secondary memory storage device in which information is stored on magnetic tape that resembles an audio tape.

**Cell clicking method, SS:** A method for entering cell names into a formula. Point to a cell whose name is to be placed in a formula and click the cell. The name of the cell is entered automatically in the formula at the location of the insertion pointer. A range can be entered by clicking on the first cell in the range and dragging to the last cell in the range. The cell clicking method is usually more accurate than typing the name of a cell.

**Cell note, SS:** A note attached to a spreadsheet cell to provide additional information about the contents of the cell. A small black rectangle in the upper right hand corner of a cell indicates that it has a cell note. A cell note is created by using the *Open Cell Note* command of the **Edit** menu.

**Cells, SS:** The objects that make up a spreadsheet. They are the objects through which calculations are carried out and results are displayed. Each cell in a spreadsheet must have a name, which by default is the coordinates of the cell, that is, the column and row identifiers for the cell (e.g., C7). The name of a cell is distinct from the contents of the cell. Think of the name of the cell as the address on a mail box and the contents of the cell as what is stored in the mail box.

**Center tab, WP:** Tabs that cause text to be centered about the tab location. Clicking a decimal tab on the ruler changes it into a center tab.

**Central processing unit:** A microprocessor chip that contains the electronic circuitry for the control unit and the arithmetic and logic unit of a computer. This is an essential component of a computer. It is often abbreviated as the CPU.

**Character font:** See *Font.*

**Character formatting:** Changing the appearance of a sequence of characters. This includes changing the font, font size, and style of the characters.

**Character size:** See *Size.*

**Character style:** A variation in the form of a character font such as italic, bold, outlined, or underlined.

**Chart:** A pie, bar, or other graphical display of information created by a spreadsheet program or other program. In the Works spreadsheet module a chart is saved automatically when the spreadsheet is saved.

*Check* **box:** A box containing a check mark, √, in the formula bar of the Works spreadsheet module or the edit bar of the Works word processing module. When the check mark is clicked, changes that have been made to the text in the bar are placed in the document.

*Chooser* **command:** A desk accessory which allows you to select a printer, sign on to a network, and access other network resources.

**Clicking:** A rapid press and release of the mouse button usually while the mouse pointer is "touching" an object of interest. This is a fundamental operation with the mouse.

**Clipboard:** A system resource that holds the most recently copied or cut item. The contents of the Clipboard can be pasted repeatedly into documents. The contents of the Clipboard are lost when the computer is turned off.

*Close* **box:** A square box in the upper left-hand corner of a window, which if clicked will cause the window to close. An asterisk appears in the *Close* box if the mouse pointer is placed in it and the mouse button is pressed. Moving the pointer from the box without releasing the mouse button cancels the closing of the window.

*Close* **command:** A command in the **File** menu that can be selected to close an open document. In the context of an application program, the *Close* command closes a document without leaving the application context. In the desktop context, using the *Close* command is equivalent to clicking the *Close* box.

**Command:** A name for an action the computer is to perform. The name is usually found in a menu.

*Command* **key:** A keyboard key identified by an Apple, ⌘, and/or clover shaped symbol. The *Command* key is used in combination with other keys to execute keyboard commands and shortcuts for menu commands.

**Communicating:** The process of establishing a physical link between computers and transmitting information between the computers.

**Communications document, CM:** A Works communication document consists of a document for viewing communications as they occur, a group of stored settings for the communications process, and an optional document for storing the captured text.

*Communications Settings,* **CM:** A large dialog box displayed by the *Settings* command under the **Communications** menu for the Works communication module. Settings on this box are clicked to indicate the values for the communications process.

**Comparison operators, DB and SS:** The following operators: equals, not equal, greater than, greater than or equal, less than, less than or equal. Applying a comparison operator to a pair of objects produces *true* or *false* as the resulting answer. In a given application the comparison operators may be abbreviated as EQ, NE, GT, GE, LT, and LE, or they may be represented as their mathematical equivalents: $=$, $<>$, $>$, $>=$, $<$, and $<=$. You will need to know what form of the comparison operators your application uses.

**Computed field, DB:** A Works database field whose value is computed from the values of other database fields. Such a field must be identified in the *Set Field Attributes* dialog box by clicking the *Computed* box.

**Condition:** A general term for an expression that evaluates to *true* or *false*. One or more conditions are used for selection records in a database. The IF built-in function also uses a condition.

**Configuration:** A particular combination of memory, input devices, and output devices for a given computer.

**Context:** The computer environment in which you are currently working that determines the commands and operations you are allowed to use.

**Control character:** See *Invisible control character.*

*Control Panel:* A desk accessory for controlling various components of the computer system. Among the components controlled are the desktop pattern, the speaker volume, the rate of blinking of the insertion pointer, the rate of mouse tracking, the speed for double clicking, and many other features.

**Control Unit:** A component of the central processing unit of a computer that controls the operation of the various components of the computer.

*Copy:* A command in the **Edit** menu of Works. In the word processor it places a copy of the selected text on the Clipboard. In the spreadsheet it places the selected data or a selected formula, as appropriate, on the Clipboard. In the database it copies data from the database and places it on the Clipboard.

**Creating a folder:** The process of creating a new folder. Proceed as follows. Select the *New Folder* command of the **File** menu to create a new folder. While the folder is highlighted, type a name for the folder. A folder can be created whenever the *New Folder* command is not dimmed.

**Cut and paste technique:** A general technique for moving information to another location. The information to be moved is selected, and the *Cut* command found under the **Edit** menu is given. This removes the information from the document and places it on the Clipboard. The insertion pointer is moved to the new location for the information, and the *Paste* command found under the **Edit** menu is given. The information on the Clipboard is pasted in the new location.

*Cut:* A Works command found under the **Edit** menu. A copy of the deleted information is placed on the Clipboard. If an entire database record has been selected by clicking the record selection box, the entire record is removed from the database and placed on the Clipboard.

**Data object, SS:** The data displayed in a spreadsheet cell. A data object must have a data type. Data types available in the Works spreadsheet module are text, numeric, date, time, and logical.

**Data type, DB:** The kind of data associated with a given database field. The types available in Works are text, numeric, date, and time. Data types are set for a field by selecting the *Set Field Attributes* command in the **Format** menu, and then clicking the appropriate buttons on the resulting dialog box.

**Database:** One or more files containing related information managed by a database management system.

*Database Definition* **window, DB:** The Works database forms window displayed during the defining of a database table.

**Database file:** The name given to a collection of records in an electronic database.

**Database management system(DBMS):** A program that manages related information about persons, projects, or any other objects of interest.

**Database template, DB:** A Works database table or form ready for entering information.

**Date and time functions, DB and SS:** Built-in functions in Works for performing date and time calculations. The available functions are: Date, Day, Hour, Minute, Month, Now, Second, Time, Weekday, and Year.

**Decimal tab, WP:** A tab which causes decimals in numbers to be aligned at the location of the tab. Clicking a right tab on the ruler changes it into a decimal tab. Clicking a decimal tab changes it into a center tab.

**Default data type, DB:** The data type that is assumed for a field by Works if a data type is not entered using the *Set Field Attributes* command. The default data type is text.

**Default tabs, WP:** Works has default tabs located every half inch on the ruler. These default tabs are not visible. Inserting a tab by clicking on the ruler removes all default tabs to the left of the new tab.

*Delete* **key:** A key in the upper right-hand corner of the standard keyboard that when pressed deletes (i.e., erases) the character immediately to the left of the insertion pointer. The deleted character is not placed on the Clipboard. See *Backspace key.*

**Deleting text:** The process of removing text from a document. This may be accomplished by highlighting the text and using the *Delete* key or the *Cut* command from the **Edit** menu. In the latter case, a copy of the text is placed on the Clipboard.

**Demodulation:** The conversion of tones transmitted over telephone lines into digital signals that can be used by a computer.

**Desk accessory:** A program that can be accessed at almost any time by selecting the name of the desk accessory under the **Apple** menu. Popular desk accessories include the *Calculator, Note Pad, Alarm Clock, Chooser,* and *Control Panel.* Many desk accessories are available at no cost.

**Desktop:** The display screen of the Macintosh on which are placed icons representing documents, folders, and disks. These icons can be manipulated and thus perform actions on the objects they represent.

**Dimmed command:** A command that is not available in the current context.

**Dimmed icon:** An icon that is already open. Its window may be obscured by other windows.

**Directly connected printer:** A printer that is connected with a cable directly to the computer as opposed to a printer that is accessed through a network.

**Disk capacity:** The maximum number of bytes of memory on a disk, usually expressed in kilobytes for floppy disks or in megabytes for a hard disk. An example is a 40 Mbyte hard disk.

**Disk directory:** The top level of the hierarchical file system; it shows the files and folders available at that level. Also, the name given to the top level of the hierarchical file system of computers that use the Microsoft Disk Operating System.

**Disk drive:** A hardware device that holds a disk, reads information from the disk, and writes information on the disk.

**Disk drive port:** A connector on the back of a Macintosh into which a cable plug can be inserted to attach an external disk drive to the computer.

**Disk:** An information storage medium consisting of one or more flat, circular surfaces on which information is stored, usually in magnetic form.

**Document:** Any named output produced by an application program. For example, the word processing module of Works produces word processing documents.

**Double clicking:** The clicking of the mouse button twice in rapid succession. This both selects an object and opens it. The success of the double clicking operation depends upon its speed, which is set using the *Control Panel*. This is a fundamental operation with the mouse.

**Double-headed arrow pointer, DB, SS:** The appearance of the mouse pointer, **↔**, when changing column width in the database and spreadsheet environments. In the top line of a table containing either database column names or spreadsheet column labels, the pointer is placed on the vertical line that separates columns, the mouse button is pressed, and the column divider is dragged to a new location. This pointer also appears when changing field width in a database form.

**Dragging:** The process of pointing at an object, clicking and holding down the mouse button, and moving the mouse without releasing the mouse button. The process moves an object to another location on the desktop and selects text for further action. This is a fundamental operation with the mouse.

*Draw Off*, **SS and WP:** A command to turn off the drawing capabilities of Works. It is found under the **Edit** menu and is available in the spreadsheet and word processing modules.

*Draw On,* **SS and WP:** A command to turn on the drawing capabilities of Works. It is located under the **Edit** menu and is available in the both the spreadsheet and word processing modules.

**Echo mode, CM:** An option in the Works communication module to retransmit each character immediately to verify that information is being transmitted. This results in each transmitted character being displayed twice on the screen.

**Edit bar, DB:** In Works DB a strip just below the menu bar in which data appears as it is entered or edited. The edit bar contains the *Cancel* box and the *Accept* box, which can be clicked to revert to the previous data or accept the new data, respectively.

**Editing:** Changing the contents of a document by inserting text, deleting text, or moving text.

**Ending a communications session, CM:** A series of steps you must perform to end a communication session. The steps are 1) log off the system, 2) hang up your telephone, 3) save the communications document, and 4) quit the Works communication module.

*Enter* **key:** A key on the standard keyboard that is used to confirm certain commands or entries. The *Enter* key, which is not the same as the *Return* key, is located on the right-hand side of the keyboard as part of the number pad.

**Erasing a disk (or reinitializing a disk):** The process of removing all the information on a disk by giving the the *Erase Disk* command in the **Special** menu. To give this command, you must be in the desktop context.

**External hard drive:** A hard drive that is external to the computer enclosure as opposed to being within the enclosure.

**Field of a record:** A specific category of information in a record. Some examples are a social security number, a person's first name, last name, and street address. A record will contain as many fields as necessary to describe an entity such as a person.

**File:** A term with several meanings. It is a generic term meaning any information stored on a disk, a document, or a program. It may also mean a collection of related records for a database management system.

**File server:** A computer and associated software that allows users to share information in a network.

*Fill Down,* **SS:** A command in the Works spreadsheet module under the Edit menu that is used to replicate a formula down a column. The cell containing the formula to be replicated is selected and the mouse is dragged down the column to select the cells into which the formula is to be replicated. Choosing the *Fill Down* command then replicates the formula. Relative references to cells are changed automatically in the fill down process. Can also be used to replicate contiguous groups of cells in a row.

**Fill Right, SS:** A command in the Works spreadsheet module under the **Edit** menu that is used to replicate a formula across a row. The cell containing the formula to be replicated is selected, and the mouse is dragged across the row to select the cells into which the formula is to be replicated. Choosing the *Fill Right* command then replicates the formula. Relative references to cells are changed automatically in the fill right process. Can also be used to replicate contiguous groups of cells in a column.

**Financial functions, DB and SS:** Built-in functions in Works for performing financial calculations. The available functions are: FV, IRR, MIRR, NPer, NPV, Pmt, PV, and Rate.

**Find File:** A very useful desk accessory for finding misplaced or lost folders or files. Select the *Find File* command under the **Apple** menu. Type the name (or a portion of the name) into the *Search For* box and click the *Running Man* icon. If the file is found, the path to the file will be displayed.

**Finder:** An operating system program that manages the Desktop and handles the communication between users and the computer. Everything on the Desktop, including files, folders, menus, and windows, is managed by the Finder.

**First line indent marker:** See *Paragraph indents*.

**First page header/footer:** A header or footer for the first page of a document. Usually this header/footer is different from the header/footer that appears on all other pages.

**Floppy disk:** A small magnetic disk of 3.5 inches or 5.25 inches diameter. The larger sized disk tends to be limber or floppy which accounts for the name.

**Folder:** An electronic analog of a file folder that can contain documents and other folders. It is represented by an icon having the shape of a folder. See *Creating a folder*.

**Folder hierarchy:** The capability of creating folders within other folders to organize the storage of information. For example, a folder named *Courses* might contain folders for several courses. Each of these in turn might contain several folders.

**Font:** The overall design of a complete set of characters. A font is the name used in word processors for what the publishing industry calls a typeface. Geneva and New York are examples of fonts.

*Font/DA Mover:* A utility program, normally found in the *Utilities* folder of a System Disk, that allows you to transfer fonts and/or desk accessories into or out of a System File.

**Footer:** A special line of text that appears in the bottom margin of a printed page. Because of its location, a footer does not reduce the amount of text that can be entered on a page. In addition to information used to identify the document, the footer may include the page number, time, and date. The footer does not show unless the *Print Preview* is being used or the document is printed. In Works, footer information is entered in a box on the *Page Setup* dialog box.

**Form, DB:** A Works window that shows the fields for a single record in a database. The fields may be arranged to emphasize the structure of the record.

**Formatting:** 1) The process of changing the appearance of text in a document. It consists of several distinct kinds of operations including character formatting and paragraph formatting. See *Character formatting,* and *Paragraph formatting.* 2) Another name for initializing a disk. See *Initializing a disk.*

**Formatting cells, SS:** The process of changing the appearance of data displayed in spreadsheet cells. Select a cell or range of cells that are to have the same format. Then choose the *Set Cell Attributes* command under the **Format** menu in the Works spreadsheet module. On the resulting dialog box, indicate the desired format.

**Formula, SS:** A Works spreadsheet formula is an object that begins with an equals sign, =, and is followed by cell references and operators arranged according to the rules for algebra. A formula is typed into a cell, but the value computed by the formula is displayed in the cell.

**Formula object, SS:** Another name for a spreadsheet formula.

**Formula template, SS:** A template, or graphical representation, for a formula that gives the relative reference descriptions showing which cell locations are to be used to compute the value of the formula. If the template is moved from cell to cell, it shows the new locations (i.e., values) of the relative references.

**Full-duplex:** A communications connection between computers that allows data to be transmitted both ways simultaneously.

**Gigabyte:** A unit of measurement that refers to 1024 megabytes.

*Grow* **box:** See *Size* box.

**Half-duplex:** A communications connection between computers that allows data to be transmitted in only one direction at a time.

**Handshake:** A signal produced by a microcomputer during the communication process with another computer to indicate that it is ready to receive data or transmit data.

**Hard disk:** A nonremovable disk that usually contains 20 Mbytes or more of information. A hard disk drive, which contains the disk, may be mounted internally as part of a Macintosh, or it may be an external piece of equipment.

**Hardware:** The physical devices such as the mouse, microprocessor, RAM, ROM, keyboard, screen, disk drive, and printer that are the components of a computer.

**Hayes AT standard:** A popular modem control language used by many microcomputers.

**Header:** A special line of text that appears in the top margin of a printed page. Because of its location, a header does not reduce the amount of text that can be entered on a page. In addition to information used to identify the document, the header may include the page number, time, and date. The header does not show unless the *Print Preview* is being used or the document is printed. In Works, header information is entered in a box on the *Page Setup* dialog box.

**Header/footer special symbols:** In Works an ampersand character, &, followed by an upper case letter that is used to indicate header/footer printing information. For example, &L, &C, and &R are used to represent *align at the left margin, center between the margins,* and *align at the right margin,* respectively.

**Help pointer:** A pointer having the form of a question mark. In Works the help pointer is obtained by pressing *Command-?*. Selecting a command in a menu using the help pointer causes a *Help* window to be displayed containing information about the command.

*Help* **window:** A window containing information to help you use commands in an application. In Works the *Help* command under the **Window** menu causes the *Help* window to be displayed.

**HFS:** An acronym for the Hierarchical File System used by the Macintosh.

**Hierarchical file system:** The file system used by the Macintosh. It allows folders to be used to organize data and program files in a hierarchical structure that reflects your method of organizing the information.

**Highlight:** The inverse video format used for displaying selected text. Selected text is often referred to as highlighted text.

**I-beam pointer:** The shape of the mouse pointer when it is in a window or area of a window in which text can be entered and modified.

**Icon:** A symbolic representation of an object on the screen of the Macintosh. Normally, the appearance of an icon gives a hint as to its usage. For example, pages produced by a word processing document may be displayed as an icon of several typed pages.

**IF function, DB and SS:** A Works built-in function that makes different calculations depending upon the value of a condition. The IF function has three arguments in the following order: a condition, an expression to be evaluated if the condition is *true*, and an expression to be evaluated if the condition is *false*.

**Information service:** An organization such as CompuServe, The Source, or Dow Jones that provides a large number of different kinds of information for a fee.

**Initializing a disk:** A process that examines a disk to assure that it is suitable for use by a particular Macintosh computer and creates special areas on the disk that allow storage of data and programs. Whenever an uninitialized disk is inserted in a disk drive, the operating system asks whether it should be initialized.

**Input device:** Any hardware device that sends information into the computer. The keyboard and the mouse are examples of input devices.

**Inserting a record, DB:** The process of inserting a new record into a database file. Using the list display format, perform the following to insert a record at a particular location. Select any field in the record before which the record is to be inserted. Then select the *Insert Record* command from the **Edit** menu. A empty record is inserted into the database.

**Inserting a column, SS:** The process of inserting a column into a spreadsheet. This can be done at any time by performing the following. Select the column which should be to the right of the inserted column by clicking its name. The entire column will become highlighted. Select the *Insert* command under the **Edit** menu, and the new column will be inserted.

**Inserting a row, SS:** The process of inserting a row into a spreadsheet. This can be done at any time by performing the following. Select the row which is to be below the new inserted row by clicking its name. The entire row will become highlighted. Select the *Insert* command under the **Edit** menu, and the new row will be inserted.

**Inserting text:** The process of moving the insertion pointer to the desired location in a document and typing or pasting text.

**Insertion pointer:** A blinking pointer that marks the location in a document at which text would be entered if typing were done.

**Integrated software:** Application programs that typically provide modules for word processing, spreadsheets, database management, and communications. Such a program allows documents of several types to be open simultaneously, has a high degree of user interface consistency, and costs less than the several stand-alone packages required in its place.

**Invisible control character:** A character that normally is not visible on the screen and that is used in controlling the appearance of a document. For example, pressing the *Tab* key or the *Return* key causes an invisible control character to be placed in the document. Some word processors, but not the Works word processing module, have a command that causes the invisible characters to be displayed.

**Justification:** The smooth alignment of text along the left indent marker, the right marker, or both markers.

**Justification submenu:** A submenu in the **Format** menu. Commands in the submenu are *Left*, *Center*, *Right*, and *Justified*.

**K or Kilo:** A unit of measurement. One kilobyte, or 1K, $= 2^{10} = 1024$ or approximately 1,000 bytes.

**Kermit:** A popular file transfer protocol.

*Key Caps:* A desk accessory that displays a picture of the keyboard. When a key is clicked on the keyboard picture, the corresponding symbol is displayed. The accessory is very useful for locating foreign and mathematical symbols in special fonts. The font is changed by selecting the name of a font from the **Key Caps** menu which is shown whenever this desk accessory is active.

**Keyboard:** A standard input device that resembles the keyboard of a typewriter, but which may also have special purpose keys.

**Kilobyte:** See *K.*

**Left indent marker:** See *Paragraph indents.*

**Left justification:** The smooth alignment of text along the left indent marker.

**Left tab, WP:** A tab that causes the left edge of text to be aligned at the position of the tab and to extend to the right of the tab. Clicking at a location on the ruler inserts a left tab. All default tabs to the left of the inserted tab are automatically removed from the ruler. Clicking a left tab on the ruler changes it into a right tab.

**Left-to-right rule, SS:** A spreadsheet computational rule that states that if two operations have the same precedence, the left operation should be done before the right operation.

**Line spacing:** The distance between lines in a given paragraph. Single, 1-1/2, and double are typical spacings.

**List display, DB:** A Works tabular display of a database table in which many records are shown simultaneously.

**Local area network or LAN:** A group of computers located near one another that are connected in a network for the purpose of sharing resources.

**Logging off, CM:** The process of telling another computer that you have completed communication with it.

**Logical functions, DB and SS:** Built-in functions in Works for performing logical operations. The available functions are: And, Choose, False, If, IsBlank, IsError, IsNA, Not, Or, and True.

**Logical operators, DB:** The operators NOT, AND, and OR. These operators are defined elsewhere. (See the individual operator.) The logical operators in order of decreasing precedence are NOT, AND, and OR. This precedence is not used by all programs, so be sure you know the precedence for the program you are using.

**Logical operators, SS:** In the Works spreadsheet module, the logical operators are defined as built-in functions rather than as operators. An advantage of this approach is the operations can be generalized to have more than two arguments.

**M or Mega:** A unit of measurement. A megabyte, or 1M, = $2^{10} * 2^{10}$ = 1024 * 1024 = 1,048,576 or approximately 1,000,000 bytes.

**Macintosh operating system:** The combination of routines stored in ROM and on disk in the System Folder that together perform all the basic tasks such as booting the computer, shutting down the computer, managing windows and other objects, managing memory space, and transferring information to and from disks and input/output devices. The Macintosh operating system comes with the computer, and new versions are issued regularly. A new version of the operating system corrects problems in previous versions and adds new capabilities to the system.

**Macintosh user interface:** The use of a mouse, menus, menu commands, windows, and operations on windows and other objects that provides

Macintosh users with a consistent interface from one Macintosh model to another and from one application to another.

**Macro:** A recorded sequence of keystrokes that can be played back at a later time to automate frequently occurring tasks. In Works a macro can be recorded in any of the modules and played back later.

**Mail merge:** The creation of "personalized" letters or other documents by merging a word processing document and information from a database. See *Merging documents*.

**Main memory:** The part of computer memory that contains the programs being executed and the data being used by the programs themselves. It is composed of the random access memory, RAM, and the read only memory, ROM.

**Margins:** An area around the edge of a page in which text cannot be entered. There are four margins that may be set individually: left margin, right margin, top margin, and bottom margin. Margins are set on the dialog box displayed when the *Page Setup* command under the **File** menu is executed.

**Mathematical functions, DB and SS: Built-in functions in Works for performing mathematical calculations.** The available functions are: Abs, Exp, Int, Ln, Log10, Mod, Pi, Rand, Round, Sign, and Sqrt.

**Megabyte:** See *M*.

**Memory-mapped graphics screen:** A technique in which the value of each pixel on a Macintosh screen is associated with a specific area in ROM.

**Menu bar:** A thin bar at the top of the Macintosh screen that contains the names of the menus for the current context.

**Menu:** The name given to a group of commands that are shown under the title of a menu when it is pulled down.

**Merging documents, DB and WP:** The process of merging data from Works databases into Works word processing documents. To perform the merge, proceed as follows. Open the database and open a word processing document. From the word processing document choose the *Prepare to Merge* command under the **Edit** menu. A *Prepare to Merge* dialog box will be displayed. Database field names on the dialog box may then be merged into the word processing document.

**Microprocessor:** A chip that contains the central processing unit for a microcomputer.

**MiniFinder:** A smaller, less powerful version of the Finder. MiniFinder is valuable when RAM and disk space is limited.

**Mixed reference, SS:** A combination of absolute and relative reference to a cell. The absolute part of the reference is identified by its $ prefix. The relative part of the reference will be modified during replication of a formula containing a mixed reference.

**Modem:** A device for sending and receiving digital information over the telephone lines. To send digital data the modem converts data into different tones. Upon receiving tones the modem converts them into digital data. These processes are called modulation and demodulation.

**Modem port:** The point of connection between a computer and a modem.

**Modulation:** The conversion of digital data into tones suitable for transmission over telephone lines.

**Mouse:** A device whose motions on a desk top are translated into the movement of a pointer on the screen of the computer. Selection of commands and other actions can be accomplished by using the mouse to point at an object and clicking a button on the mouse.

**Mouse button:** A button on a mouse that is clicked for performing actions on the screen.

**Mouse pointer:** The pointer on the screen of the computer that corresponds to the location of the mouse on the desk top. The pointer is used to "touch" objects as the first step in performing an action with an object. The shape of the pointer, e.g., arrow head or I-beam, depends on the context in which the mouse is used.

**Moving the insertion pointer:** The process of moving the location at which text will be entered when typing is done. Move the mouse pointer, which has the form of an I-beam, to the desired location for the insertion pointer and click. The insertion pointer will appear in that location.

**Moving text, WP:** The process of relocating text within a document. See *Cut and paste technique.*

**Moving a window:** A given window may be moved any time it is visible. Point to any location on the title bar, press the mouse button, and drag the window to the desired location.

**MultiFinder:** A more powerful version of the Finder that allows, among other things, switching from application to application without closing applications. The MultiFinder uses more RAM and disk space than the Finder.

**Multiple condition record selections, DB:** The combining of two or more conditions with logical operators on the *Record Selection* dialog box. Each subcondition evaluates to *true* or *false,* and the overall condition evaluates to *true* or *false.*

**Nanosecond:** A time interval equal to one billionth of a second ($10^{-9}$ seconds). This is approximately the time required for light to travel one foot. It is also the lower limit of the time scale for retrieval of information from RAM and for operations within the computer.

**Navigating through the hierarchical file system:** The process of moving up or down through the Macintosh hierarchical file system to find an object of interest or to find the appropriate location for storing a document. Navigation can be done from the desktop context by opening a disk and successively opening folders. Navigation can be done from within an application by using the *Open* command (or *Save As* command) and using the resulting dialog box and its pull down menu over the file box to change contexts.

**Network:** An interconnection of groups of computers and devices to allow the sharing of information and equipment.

**Networked printer:** A printer that is accessed through a network. The printer must be allocated by the user before it can be utilized. The printer may use spooling.

*Not on Desktop* **error:** A Works error message that is displayed if a word processing document references database data, but the database is not open. The error message appears within the word processing document at the locations reserved for the database fields.

*NOT* **operator:** A unary logical operator that has a value that is the opposite of the value of its argument. For example, if $x$ has the value *true,* NOT$x$ has the value *false.*

*Note Pad*: A desk accessory that displays a note pad in which you may write notes.

**Object:** A generic name used to refer to anything that can be represented by an icon. Disks, windows, folders, applications, and documents are all objects. Objects share many kinds of operations. For example, the method for changing the location of an object on the desktop is similar for all objects.

*Open* **command:** A general Macintosh command used for accessing a disk, folder, or document, or starting a program.

**Operator precedence, SS:** See *Precedence rules.*

*Option* **key:**  A keyboard key marked *Option* that is used with other keys to form commands.  It is also known as the *Alt* key.

*OR* **operator:**  The binary logical operator that has the value *true* if either or both its arguments are *true*.  The operator has the value *false* only if both its arguments have the value *false*.

**Output device:**  A device that receives information from the CPU of the computer.  The screen (CRT), ImageWriter printer, and LaserWriter printer are examples of output devices.

**Page break, manual:**  In Works a page break that is inserted by selecting the *Insert Page Break* command of the **Format** menu.  In Works a manual page break is displayed as a horizontal dashed line across a page.  A manual page break is needed if you find the automatic division between pages to be unsatisfactory.

**Page break, automatic:**  In Works a page break that is inserted automatically if too much text has been entered to fit on the current page.  A Works automatic page break is displayed as a horizontal dotted line across a page.

**Page margins:**  See *Margins*.

**Page setup:**  A set of options regarding the format of pages that are to be printed.  The options available depend upon the output device selected by using the *Chooser* command under the **Apple** menu and upon the application being used.

*Page Setup* **command:**  A command under the **File** menu that causes a dialog box to be displayed for selecting options for printing pages.

**Paragraph:**  A sequence of typed words ended by pressing the *Return* key.  You should <u>not</u> press the *Return* key at the end of each line, but instead you should let the wordwrap feature move the next word to a new line.  Defining paragraphs in this way facilitates reformatting a document.

**Paragraph formatting:**  Formatting that is associated with the appearance of entire paragraphs.  For example, line spacing, indents, tabs, and justification are all paragraph formatting features.

**Paragraph indents:**  The indenting of a paragraph from the margins.  The left indent and right indent markers are displayed on the ruler as small triangles.  The left indent is dragged to the desired location to indent the paragraph on the left.  The right indent marker is dragged to the desired location to indent the paragraph on the left.  The first line indent is a small rectangle on the ruler.  It is often obscured by the left indent.  Drag the first line indent to the desired location to indent the first line.

**Parameter, SS:** A name given to a cell whose value is used in many calculations within a spreadsheet. To make the value obvious and to allow the value to be changed for what-if analysis, the value is not placed directly into formulas, but is placed in a cell with nearby identifying information. The cell containing the needed value is referenced in formulas. For example, the overtime rate on a payroll spreadsheet should be a parameter. Often references to parameters will need to be absolute.

**Parity, CM:** An extra bit attached to the binary representation of a character for error checking purposes. The parity bit makes the total number of 1's even (even parity) or odd (odd parity). In a given communications session all characters are expected to have a particular parity. The type of parity is set on the Works *Communications Settings* dialog box.

**Paste:** A generally available command with the Macintosh. Data on the Clipboard is pasted into the active window at the location of the insertion pointer. In Works, paste is available in all modules.

**Paste, SS:** A command in the Works spreadsheet module under the **Edit** menu that can be used to paste a copied formula into another spreadsheet cell. When a formula is pasted, all relative references are updated to reflect the location of the new cell.

**Path name:** A sequence of names that gives the path from the disk containing the file of interest to the file. For example, the path name for the Scrapbook file shown in Figure 1.17 is *MyDisk:MacDeskTop/Lesson4/ ScrapbookFile.*

**Pixel:** A picture element. On the Macintosh screen a pixel is a square of 1/72 inch per side. All text and graphic objects shown on the screen are groups of pixels.

**Pointing:** The process of moving the mouse on the desk top so that the pointer on the screen "touches" an object of interest. This is a fundamental operation with the mouse.

**Ports:** Connectors on the back of the Macintosh where you may plug in an external device, a network, or another computer.

**Precedence rules, arithmetic, SS:** In the Works spreadsheet module, and in spreadsheet programs in general, the arithmetic operations have a predefined precedence. The precedence of an operation determines when the operation will be done. Highest precedence is given to exponentiation ($^\wedge$), followed by unary plus and unary minus ( + and - ), followed by multiplication and division ( * and / ), with lowest precedence being given to addition and subtraction ( + and - ). For operations having the same precedence, the left operation is done first (left-to-right rule). Operations in parentheses are done before operations not in parentheses.

**Previewing a report, DB:** The process of reviewing a report on the screen before printing it. The report will be shown in reduced size exactly as it would be printed. The magnifying glass icon can be used for examining the details of a report. See *Print Preview option*.

***Print* command:** A Works command in the **File** menu that allows you to print a document or preview the document layout. If your computer is part of a network, use the *Chooser* command in the **Apple** menu to allocate a printer before you select the print command.

**Print parameters (page setup):** A series of options on the *Page Setup* dialog box. The particular options depend upon the printer to be used, but the options will include the printing orientation and the paper size.

***Print Preview* option:** A Works option to preview on the screen the layout of a document before printing it. The option becomes available when the *Print* command under the **File** menu is selected. Click the *Print Preview* box to preview the layout.

**Printer driver:** A small program used by the operating system that converts information from application format into printer format and manages the operation of a printer. A different printer driver is needed for each type of printer.

**Printer port:** A connector on the back of the Macintosh into which you can plug a cable from a printer.

**Protocol:** A set of rules for how the communication process between computers is to be handled. Protocols available in the Works communication module are MacBinary, Xmodem text, and Xmodem data.

**Pull-down menu:** A list of commands that appear when you point to the name of a menu and press the mouse button.

***Quit* command:** A command under the **File** menu that causes the termination of execution of an application program.

**RAM:** Random Access Memory.

**Random access memory:** A component of computer memory that holds the program being executed and data being used by the program. Information in RAM can be accessed in random order. Access times for RAM are measured in nanoseconds. The storage capacity of RAM is measured in Kilobytes and Megabytes. RAM is volatile, which means its contents are lost if power is lost.

**Range selection, SS:** The selection of a block of spreadsheet cells. The cells may be in a single column, in a single row, or be in several columns and rows. All cells in the range must form a contiguous highlighted block.

A colon separates the names of the first and last cells in the range. The range B1:C10 refers to the block of 20 cells starting in cell B1 and ending in cell C10. Cell ranges can be used as components of spreadsheet formulas.

**Read only memory:** A component of computer memory in which cell contents can be read but not changed. This type of memory is not volatile, that is, its contents are not lost when the power is turned off. Read only memory, ROM, contains that part of the Macintosh operating system which is accessed automatically when the Macintosh is turned on. Frequently used operating system routines are also stored in ROM.

*Record Selector* **box, DB:** In the list display format, a small rectangular box that is at the extreme left end of a record before the first field. Clicking this box selects the entire record which will become highlighted.

**Record selection, DB:** The process of selecting specific records for display in a database. Choose the *Record Selection* command found under the **Organize** menu. On the dialog box that is displayed as a result of giving the command, rules are entered for selecting rows from the database. See also *Multiple condition record selections.*

**Record, DB:** A complete set of information about one particular object in a database.

**Relative reference, SS:** Within a spreadsheet formula, a reference to a cell such that the cell address becomes the origin from which cell locations are referenced. Relative reference descriptions may be thought of as forming a template that is retained when a formula is duplicated into another location. A relative reference does not have a dollar sign ($) as a prefix for either its column name or its row name. (See *Absolute reference.*) For example, the formula =A1+B1 contained in cell C1 has two relative references A1 and B1.

**Removing a page break, WP:** This is accomplished using the *Remove a Page Break* command in the **Format** menu for removing a manual page break. Place the insertion pointer at the beginning of the line below the page break and give this command to remove the page break. This command will be available only when the insertion pointer is properly placed.

*Replace,* **WP:** A command in the **Search** menu that can be used to find and replace tabs, paragraph symbols, words, or phrases in a Works word processing document. An option replaces all occurrences of the found object. Alternately, you may examine each occurrence and make replacement decisions on an individual basis.

**Replication of formulas, SS:** The process of copying formulas into other spreadsheet cells. During the replication, relative cell references are updated to reflect the new locations of the formulas. See *Fill Down, Fill Right, Absolute reference,* and *Relative reference.*

*Report Definition* **screen, DB:** A report screen that is displayed as a result of giving the *New Report* command from the **Report** menu. The screen is used for eliminating unwanted fields, rearranging fields into a desired order, and specifying page totals.

**Report, DB:** A document that contains the results of a Works database retrieval. A report shows only fields of interest, and it may contain totals for numeric fields. A Works database may have a total of 8 reports. Reports are saved automatically when the database is saved.

**Retrieval:** A general term that refers to the obtaining of specific data from information stored in a data file. A major purpose of a database management system is to retrieve information from a database to produce reports.

*Return* **key:** A key on the standard keyboard used to confirm an entry or command. In word processing it is pressed to signal the end of a paragraph. The *Return* and *Enter* keys are different keys.

**Right justification:** The alignment of the right-hand edge of text at the location of the right indent marker.

**Right tab, WP:** A tab that causes the right edge of text to be aligned at the position of the tab and to extend to the left of the tab. Clicking a left tab changes it into a right tab. Clicking a right tab changes it into a center tab.

**ROM:** <u>R</u>ead <u>O</u>nly <u>M</u>emory.

**Ruler:** A diagram of a ruler at the top of a word processing screen that is used to set tabs and indents for a particular paragraph. The ruler can be displayed or hidden by selecting the *Show Ruler/Hide Ruler* command under the **Format** menu.

*Save As* **command:** A command under the **File** menu used for saving a document with a name supplied by the user. By using the *Save As* dialog box, you can navigate through the system to save a document in any desired location.

*Save As* **dialog box:** A dialog box displayed in response to the *Save As* command. The dialog box allows the document to be saved in any desired location. A button allows you to switch disk drives. A pull-down menu over the file box can be used to display the complete current path. You may move up or down in the hierarchy by selecting a different member of the path. At the current level in the hierarchical file system, you may enter a folder shown in the file box by opening it.

*Save* **command:** A command that saves a document immediately if it has been saved previously, and thus, has a name. If the document has not been saved previously, a dialog box is displayed for giving the document a name and indicating where it is to be saved. See *Save As*.

473

**Saving selected records, DB:** A method of saving rows selected from a database. Choose the *Save As* command under the **File** menu. On the resulting dialog box, click the *Save Selected Records Only* option and type the new name for the saved records. Be careful not to give the same name as your database because this causes the selected records to replace the database.

**Saving a communications document, CM:** A method for saving the communications document. Choose the *Save As* command of the **File** menu, type a name for the communications document, and save it in the proper context. When a communications document is saved, the settings and telephone numbers are automatically saved with it.

**Scanner:** An input device that scans graphical information and converts it into a digital form that can be manipulated by a computer.

**Scrapbook:** A system resource that can be used to save graphic information in permanent form. Information to be placed in the Scrapbook is first placed on the Clipboard. Then the Scrapbook is opened by selecting the *Scrapbook* command from the **Apple** menu. The *Paste* command under the **Edit** menu copies information from the Clipboard to the Scrapbook.

**Screen:** An output device on which most communication with the computer is displayed.

**Scroll arrows:** Arrows at the ends of the scroll bars that move the view into a document a small amount. For example, if an arrow on a vertical scroll bar in a WP document is clicked, it moves the window approximately one line. The window moves in the direction indicated by the arrow.

**Scroll bars:** Horizontal and vertical bars at the bottom and right-hand side of a window, respectively, that allow you to move through a large document horizontally and vertically from line to line and page to page.

**Scroll box:** A small white box in a scroll bar that shows the relative position of the current window in the document. The scroll box can be dragged to move quickly to new locations in the document.

**Scroll:** The process of moving through a document using the scroll box or scroll arrows.

**Search menu, WP:** A menu containing commands for finding and replacing words or phrases in a Works word processing document.

**Secondary memory:** Magnetic disks and other less expensive forms of memory for more permanent storage of programs and data.

**Select:** The general operation of selecting an object on which some operation is to be performed. This is a fundamental operation. On the

Macintosh, selected objects become highlighted. Many methods are available for selecting an object including pointing and clicking, dragging, and clicking in the blank area on the left-edge of a word processing document.

*Select All*: A command under the **Edit** menu that selects an entire Works document.

**Select and then do:** The process of defining an object to be operated on by selecting it, and then doing the operation on the selected object. This is a commonplace activity when using a word processor as well as other programs.

**Selecting a line, WP:** The process of selecting a line in a word processing document. Place the pointer in the blank left-edge of the document and click.

**Selecting a paragraph, WP:** The process of selecting a paragraph in a word processing document. Place the pointer in the blank left-edge of the document and double click.

**Selecting a word, WP:** The process of selecting a word in a word processing document. Double click the word.

**Selecting text:** The process of highlighting text to indicate that it is the object to which the next command should apply.

**Semantics:** The attaching of meaning to the symbols in a computer language.

**Serial ports:** Connectors on the back of the computer for devices such as a printer that transmit or receive information sequentially, that is, serially.

*Shift* key: A key on the keyboard labeled *Shift*. It is pressed to type upper case letters and to perform the shift click operation.

**Shift clicking:** The process of holding down the *Shift* key while the mouse pointer is touched repeatedly to different objects and clicked. This extends the selection operation to all these objects. This is a fundamental operation with the mouse.

*Shut Down*: A command in the **Special** menu in the desktop context that should always be executed to conclude working with the Macintosh. Information in RAM may be lost if the computer is turned off without using the *Shut Down* command.

**Size:** The size of the characters in a font. Size is usually measured in points where there are 72 points per inch. Thus, a character in 12 point type has a size of 12/72 inch (i.e., 1/6 inch)

*Size* **box:** A box in the lower right-hand corner of a window used to change the size of a window. Point to the box, press the mouse button, and drag to change the window to the desired size. An outline of the new window size is shown as the size box is moved. Also known as the *Grow* box.

**Smart modem:** A full featured modem which has its own microprocessor to help with the communication process between computers.

**Software:** Sets of instructions in the form of computer programs that make up the operating system of a computer and the application programs.

**Special-purpose functions, DB and SS:** Built-in functions in Works for special needs. The available functions are: Error, HLookup, Index, Lookup, Match, NA, Type, and VLookup.

**Split screens:** A Works feature available in the database and spreadsheet modules. The active window can be split horizontally, vertically, or both to view data that are too wide to fit on the screen or too far away in the document to view otherwise. The *Split* rectangles found near the top of the vertical scroll bar and near the left edge of the horizontal scroll bar are dragged into the window to split it. Each split window can be scrolled independently. You may perform work in any of the split windows.

**Spooling:** The creation of a temporary copy of a document for the purpose of printing or sending a document on a network. Control is returned to the application program after creation of the temporary copy. This allows, for example, printing to be done while further work is conducted using your computer.

**Spreadsheet:** A computational program based upon the metaphor of an accountant's ledger sheet. A spreadsheet is particularly valuable for exploring the consequences of various options. Graphical output is available to assist users to visualize their results.

**Spreadsheet structure:** A spreadsheet is composed of a large number of named rows and columns. For example, a Works spreadsheet contains 256 columns named "A" through "IV" and 16,382 rows. The intersection of a row and a column form a cell into which information can be entered, or a calculation can be made. A cell is identified by giving its column name followed by the row name. For example, E3 is the cell at the intersection of column E and row 3.

**Spreadsheet language:** All spreadsheet programs use a language for entering formulas that is based on algebra. Thus, the language is intuitive and easy to use. The syntax is very similar even for different spreadsheet programs.

**Startup disk:** A disk that contains the *System* folder and its files.

**Statistical functions, DB and SS:** Built-in functions in Works for performing statistical calculations. The available functions are: Average, Count, Max, min, SSum, Sum, StDev, and Var.

**Style:** See *Character style*.

**Submenu:** A menu that is displayed by selecting a command on a menu. In Works commands with a submenu are identified by a black, right-pointing triangle at the end of the command. These menus are accessed by moving the pointer through the arrow to the right, then moving down the exposed submenu to make a selection.

**Syntax:** Another word for the grammar of a computer language.

**System file:** The file the computer uses to start itself and to communicate with the computer user.

**System Folder:** A folder that contains the System file, Finder, and driver programs for devices attached to the computer.

**System disk:** A disk that contains a *System* folder and its required files.

**Tabs, WP:** Ruler settings used to align text at certain positions across a line of a document. Construction of tables and other tabular information should always be done using tabs. Tables constructed using spaces will not align correctly if the font is changed or if a new printer is selected that has a different resolution. Works has four types of tabs: left, right, decimal, and center tabs. The position of a tab on the ruler may be changed by dragging the tab to a new location. For additional information see the individual tab types. Also see *Default tabs*.

***Tab* key:** A key on the standard keyboard that advances the insertion pointer to the location of the next tab when it is pressed.

**Text:** Any sequence of characters entered into a document by means of typing at the keyboard.

**Title bar:** The top line of a window. It contains the *Close box*, the title of the window, and the *Zoom* box. A series of horizontal lines appears in the title bar of the active window.

**Tool palette, Drawing:** A palette of Works drawing tools that is displayed when the *Draw On* command of the **Edit** menu is selected.

**Trash Can:** An icon on the Macintosh desktop. Documents to be discarded are dragged into the trash can. A document can be removed from the trash can by double clicking the *Trash* icon, and then dragging the document from it. The *Empty Trash* command of the **Special** menu empties the trash can, that is permanently erases the documents in it.

**Trigonometric functions, DB and SS:** Built-in functions in Works for performing trigonometric calculations. The available functions are: ACos, ASin, ATan, ATan2, Cos, Degrees, Radians, Sin, and Tan.

**Truth table:** A table that shows the value of a condition for all the possible values of the constituent conditions.

**Upwardly compatible disk drive:** The property of disk drives that a disk initialized on a drive with a particular storage capacity, e.g., 400K, can be used by a drive that works with higher storage capacity disks, e.g., 1.4M.

**Utility program:** A special purpose program, such as the *Font/DA Mover*, that lets you perform some useful function on your files.

**Video port:** A port on the back of certain Macintoshes, e.g., the Macintosh IIci, that supports commonly used monitors.

***What if* analysis, SS:** The investigation of questions of the kind, "What if we change the rate to 8% and the term to 20 years." When the values in a spreadsheet are changed, new results are automatically calculated. This makes it very easy to examine many alternatives before deciding upon a course of action.

**Window:** A view into an object such as a document, folder, or disk. The window allows you to see the contents of the object. If the contents are too large to be seen in total through the window, the window can be moved by manipulating scroll bars.

**Windows, common operations:** Operations such as moving a window, changing the size of a window, and scrolling.

**Word processor:** A program for creating documents normally prepared using a typewriter. A word processor is more convenient and powerful than a typewriter.

**Wordwrap:** The automatic moving of a word at the end of the current line to the beginning of the next line when that word is too long to fit on the current line. Wordwrap is a very important property of word processing programs because it causes automatic rearrangement of the text when words are inserted or deleted.

**Works CM:** The communications module of Works.

**Works DB:** The database management module of Works.

***Works Desktop* icon:** An icon that, when activated, automatically opens the Works documents that were open at the time the *Quit* command was given. It is useful for restoring the environment that existed just before you quit.

**Works module:** A component of the Works integrated software package, either the word processor, spreadsheet, database management, or communications module.

**Works SS:** The spreadsheet module of Works.

**Works starting dialog box:** The dialog box that is displayed when Works is executed. It contains icons for All Works Types, Word Processor, Data Base, Spreadsheet, and Communications. Existing documents can be opened from this dialog box. New documents are created by double clicking the icon for the document type or by clicking document type and then clicking the *New* button.

**Works WP:** The word processing module of Works.

**Worksheet:** The spreadsheet of current interest.

**Worksheet structure, SS:** See *Spreadsheet structure.*

**Write-protect:** The prevention of a removable disk from being written on by pushing the sliding tab in the lower left-hand corner of the disk toward the bottom edge. This will allow you to see through the hole produced by moving the tab.

***Zoom* box:** A pair of nested squares in the upper right-hand corner of the title bar of a window. Clicking the box causes the window to switch a smaller or larger version of the window.

# MENUS

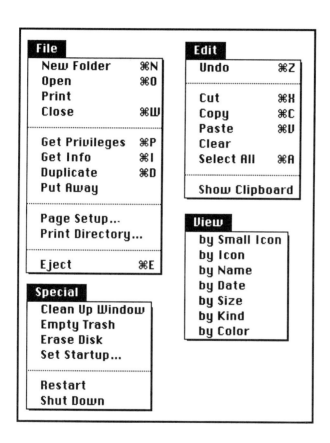

| File | | Edit | |
|---|---|---|---|
| New Folder | ⌘N | Undo | ⌘Z |
| Open | ⌘O | | |
| Print | | Cut | ⌘H |
| Close | ⌘W | Copy | ⌘C |
| | | Paste | ⌘U |
| Get Privileges | ⌘P | Clear | |
| Get Info | ⌘I | Select All | ⌘A |
| Duplicate | ⌘D | | |
| Put Away | | Show Clipboard | |
| | | | |
| Page Setup... | | View | |
| Print Directory... | | by Small Icon | |
| | | by Icon | |
| Eject | ⌘E | by Name | |
| | | by Date | |
| Special | | by Size | |
| Clean Up Window | | by Kind | |
| Empty Trash | | by Color | |
| Erase Disk | | | |
| Set Startup... | | | |
| | | | |
| Restart | | | |
| Shut Down | | | |

DESKTOP MENUS.

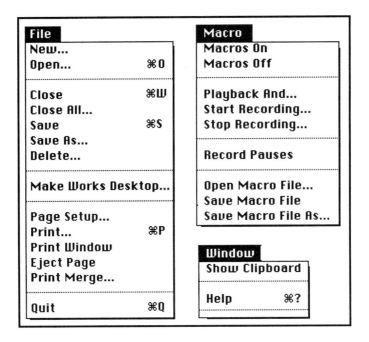

## WORKS COMMON MENUS.

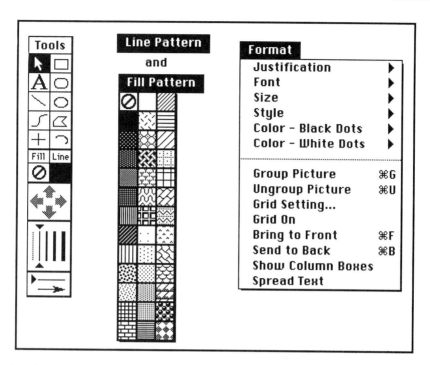

WORKS DRAWING MENUS.

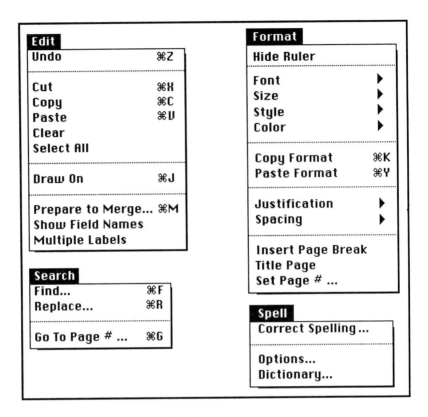

WORKS WP MENUS.

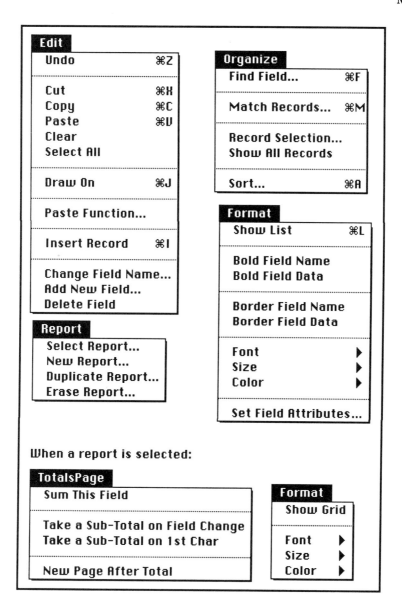

**WORKS DB MENUS.**

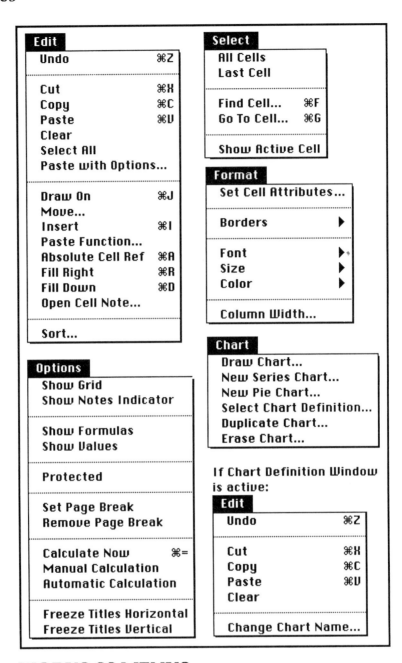

WORKS SS MENUS.

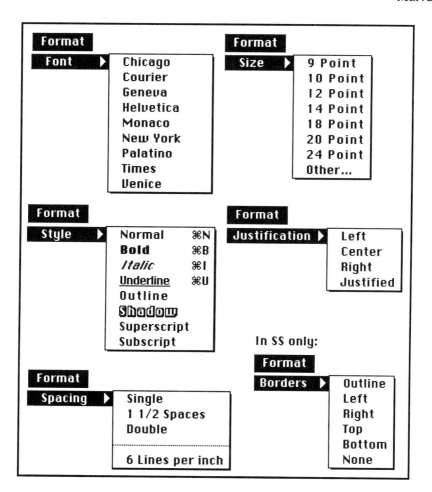

WORKS SUBMENUS UNDER FORMAT MENU.

| Communications | | Keypad | | | |
|---|---|---|---|---|---|
| Echo On | | | | | |
| Echo Off | | PF1 | PF2 | PF3 | PF4 |
| | | ← | → | ↑ | ↓ |
| Dial... | ⌘D | 7 | 8 | 9 | – |
| Hang Up | ⌘= | | | | |
| Answer Phone | | 4 | 5 | 6 | , |
| | | 1 | 2 | 3 | Enter |
| Capture Text... | | | | | |
| Send Text... | | 0 | | . | |
| Receive File... | | | | | |
| Send File... | | | | | |
| Settings... | | | | | |

## WORKS CM MENUS.

# INDEX

# INDEX

# NOTES

# NOTES

# NOTES

# NOTES

# NOTES